Boulder Hiking Trails

Boulder
Hiking Trails

The Best of the Plains, Foothills, and Mountains

Fourth Edition

Ruth Carol & Glenn Cushman

PRUETT PUBLISHING COMPANY
BOULDER, COLORADO

Fourth Edition 2006

09 08 07 06   5 4 3 2 1

Library of Congress Cataloging-in-Publication Data

Cushman, Ruth Carol, 1937—

  Boulder hiking trails : the best of the plains, foothills, and mountains / by Ruth Carol Cushman and Glenn Cushman ; photographs
by Glenn Cushman.— 4th ed.

     p. cm.

  Includes bibliographical references and index.

  ISBN 0-87108-940-8 (alk. paper)

  1. Hiking—Colorado—Boulder Region—Guidebooks. 2.
Trails—Colorado—Boulder Region—Guidebooks. 3. Boulder
Region (Colo.)—Guidebooks. I. Cushman, Glenn. II. Title.

  GV199.42.C62B6835 2006

  917.88'63—dc22

                              2005032664

Maps By Tony Moore
Design by MacWorks

To all who have walked and skied these trails with us and who share our love of open spaces and wild places, and to the memories of our parents, Florence and E. J. Scheerer and Eula and Ford Cushman.

We wish to add a special note of appreciation to the many people who work to preserve these wild places, not only for those of us who find recreation there, but also for the wildlife that cannot speak for itself and for future generations.

TABLE OF CONTENTS

PLAINS

FOOTHILLS

MOUNTAINS

NEARBY STATE AND COUNTY PARKS

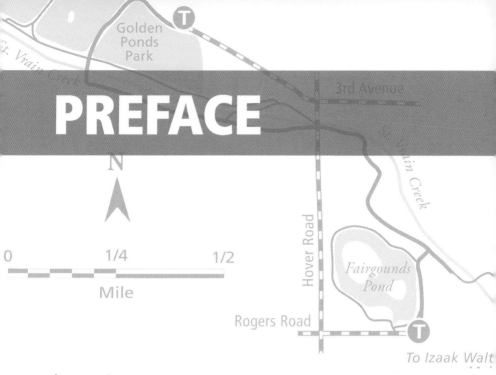

PREFACE

This book, intended chiefly for newcomers and visitors to the Boulder area, describes an array of our favorite trails, ranging from short strolls to strenuous hikes. We hope old-timers will also find it useful because of the historical tidbits and the section on connections, which allows hikers to plan permutations on old familiar routes. We've also included a few trails that are not well known.

Mileage is given from the most convenient parking area. When possible, we've taken mileages from signs and maps. When this information was not available, we used a "map wheel" and measured the distance on a map. However, trail measurement is not an exact science, so you may discover discrepancies. Elevations are from topographic maps. "Short distance" means too short to bother measuring and is usually the equivalent of a couple of city blocks.

Within each section of the book (Plains, Foothills, Mountains, and Nearby State and County Parks), the trails are arranged roughly from north to south. Although rating the difficulty of trails is subjective, we used the following guidelines: easy means three miles or less one way, with less than 1,000 feet of elevation gain and gentle gradients; moderate means between three and four miles one way and less than 1,500 feet elevation gain; strenuous means either more than four miles one way, more than a 1,500-foot elevation gain, or a gradient of more than 1,000 feet per mile.

A warning to the reader: Trails, like living organisms, tend to change—sometimes very quickly. New trails are constructed, old trails are rerouted or closed, trail names are changed, old bridges collapse, and (sometimes) new bridges are built. So, if you find outdated descriptions in our guide, please forgive us and realize that any outdoor adventure may involve coping with the unexpected.

ACKNOWLEDGMENTS

We would like to thank the following people for generously supplying information: Lois Anderton, Bev Baker, David Bell, Jim Benedict, Pat Butler, Terry Boone, Marta Bromschwig, Anne Dyni, Irby Downes, Topher Downing, Dennis Fisher, Paula Fitzgerald, Pascale Fried, Beverly Gholson, Ken Huson, Gary Lacy, Rich Lippincott, Dick Lyman, Steve Ransweiler, Joanna Sampson, Dock Teegarden (the first volunteer for City Open Space), Pam Tierney, and Jim Weibel. The resources of the Boulder Carnegie Branch Library and the University of Colorado Libraries were invaluable. Special thanks go to Steve Jones for past collaborations and for ongoing encouragement.

We are especially grateful to Peter Gleichman, Rich Koopmann, Mary McNellan, John Oppenlander, and Brent Wheeler, who not only provided essential information, but also critiqued large portions of the manuscript. Any errors that appear here, however, are ours.

We used the revised USGS topographic maps as our main source for the trail maps, and we freehanded minor trail revisions. We also relied on maps and brochures published by various public agencies and on maps created by the Colorado Mountain Club.

And finally, thanks to the people at Pruett Publishing Company who edited, proofed, and designed the book: Jim Pruett, Marykay Scott, Kim Adams, Dianne Nelson, and Merrill Gilfillan.

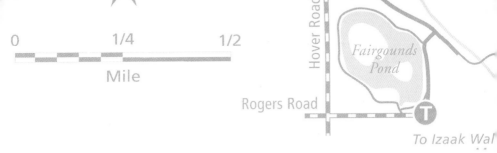

A BRIEF HISTORY
OF HIKING, PARKS, AND OPEN SPACE
IN THE BOULDER AREA

E ver since the first white settlement in 1858, hiking and
nature study have been popular activities in the Boulder
area. When the first gold seekers camped at Red Rocks
that year, some of them climbed the hill to observe the
last rays of the sun illuminate what they called "Sunset Rock," possibly the edge-on view of the first flatiron. In the late 1860s and
1870s, Martha Maxwell—one of the first women naturalists in the
country—explored the Boulder area on foot and horseback. It was
here that she gathered specimens for the collection she exhibited,
to worldwide acclaim, at the Philadelphia Centennial Exhibition in
1876.

Soon after Chautauqua was established in 1898, the Colorado
Chautauqua Climbers Club was formed and later incorporated
as the Rocky Mountain Climbers Club (RMCC). The articles of
incorporation listed various objectives, including, "to mark, build,
and establish and maintain trails to points of interest." Edwin
Chamberlain, a charter member, wrote: "We had no trail in those
days to Royal Arch, Green Mountain, nor Bear Peak. We just
clambered around like mountain goats." Another group, "The High
Hikers," also constructed trails throughout the county. This group

was organized in 1910 and later became the Boulder Chapter of the Colorado Mountain Club. A. T. Wheeler, who patrolled on horseback, was hired in 1911 as the first Boulder Mountain Parks ranger. In 1916, M. R. Parsons, who also patrolled on horseback, was hired. Parsons's extensive photo collection is an important historic source for Boulder.

Today, Boulder County is famous for its protected open spaces and trail systems. But when it was first settled, there was no need to set aside special parks—almost everything was "open space." Nevertheless, the original Boulder City town-site plan designated "The Public Square," the site of the present-day courthouse, as a park. In 1882, this park became the site for the courthouse, and Boulder had no municipal parks from 1882 to 1898. The Texas–Colorado Chautauqua popularized outdoor activities as well as cultural programs. Chautauqua was a "cultural retreat" with lectures, musical performances, and entertainment. The movement started in New York and spread to Boulder in 1898. Healthy living was emphasized, and, as Boulder Chautauquans did a lot of hiking, there was a growing demand for trails. In response, the Boulder City Council purchased eighty acres on the east slope of Flagstaff Mountain in 1898 and persuaded the U.S. government to grant the city additional land for a park.

Later, the city bought public lands extending from Sunshine Canyon to South Boulder Creek, and the park system was expanded by gifts from such individuals as Dr. and Mrs. William Baird, who donated 160 acres in Gregory Canyon in 1908, and Charles Buckingham, an early Boulder banker, who gave sites in Lefthand Canyon and at Boulder Falls.

Frederick Law Olmsted, Jr., a noted landscape architect, came out from Harvard University in 1908 to advise on the beautification of the city. He recommended burying all utility wires and that the city not be developed for the benefit of tourists, who, he said, "hastily pass through a place which attracts them ... taking not the slightest interest in the welfare ... of the permanent residents."

Olmsted urged the city to commit the Boulder Creek floodplain to playing fields and walkways: "If the matter is taken in hand now the city will spend less money on the hydraulic improvement and get a beautiful parkway to boot." Sixty-some years later, when the city finally acted on his advice and started developing the Boulder Creek Path, many buildings had already been built in the floodplain, and some officials favored channelizing the creek and lining it with concrete.

Boulder's Open Space Program, so popular today, began with the Blue Line Ordinance, passed by Boulder voters in 1959. The "Blue Line" is a boundary at an elevation of about 5,750 feet, above which the city will not provide water or sewer services. However, the ordinance did not protect the mountain backdrop sufficiently. This became evident in 1960, when a luxury hotel on Enchanted Mesa was proposed. "Save Enchanted Mesa" became the rallying cry for a successful campaign to purchase most of the mountain land, although some "unscenic" mansions are still being built on the mesa. In 1967, voters passed a small sales tax to be used for "greenbelt" acquisition.

In recent years, both Lafayette and Louisville have begun purchasing open space, and most communities in Boulder County are adding parks and building additional trails. In 1993, a county sales tax was passed by a majority of voters who hope to preserve what is left of our open spaces. Since then, Boulder County has made several large purchases, including the Heil Ranch north of Lefthand Canyon, the Hall Ranch near Lyons, and Caribou Ranch near Nederland.

In 2000, the City of Boulder Open Space and the Mountain Parks Departments merged, and their combined staffs continue to acquire and maintain land to preserve habitat and to provide recreation. However, new problems and conflicts arise with our soaring population growth. Today, we may be at the point of loving our trails and open space to death. Perhaps it is time to question whether every stream should have its trail and whether unlimited access to all areas is wise.

BEST OF THE BEST FOR ...

Aspen viewing: Caribou Ranch (page 171), Horseshoe Trail to Frazer Meadow or any Golden Gate Canyon State Park trail (page 209); lower portions of Hessie area trails (page 185); Switzerland Trail, west from the Sugarloaf parking area (page 56)

Sumac, autumnal shrubs, and fall flowers: Bluebell-Baird Trail (page 90); Mesa Trail, south end (page 96); South Boulder Creek Trail, upper end, from Mesa Trail to SR 93 (page 27); Towhee and Homested Loop (page 122); Rattlesnake Gulch (page 202)

Ski touring, foothills: Mesa Trail, north end (page 96); Mc-Clintock and Enchanted Mesa Loop (page 103); Meyers Homestead Trail (page 131)

Ski touring, plains (only when there's a good snowfall): East Boulder Trails (pages 23); Walden and Sawhill ponds (page 18); Coal Creek Trail (page 35)

Birdwatching: Golden Ponds section of St. Vrain Greenways Trail (page 2); Coot Lake and Boulder Reservoir (page 7); Sawhill and Walden Ponds (page 18); East Boulder Trail (page 23); Barr Lake State Park—usually a pair of bald eagles nest here (page 212) *(Helpful hint: you meet the nicest people when using binoculars!)*

People watching (and meeting people): Boulder Creek Path (page 23); Mesa Trail (page 96)

Early spring wildflowers: Rabbit Mountain (page 45); Gregory Canyon (page 82); Mesa Trail and any of its laterals (page 96); Doudy Draw (page 125); Hall Ranch (page 48)

Fairyslipper orchids: Ceran St. Vrain (page 154) and Calypso Cascade (page 134) in late May

Tundra and alpine wildflowers: Mount Audubon (page 158); Pawnee Pass (page 161); Arapaho Pass (page 178); South Arapaho Peak (page 178); Devils Thumb Pass (page 186); James Peak (page 198)

Waterfalls: Ouzel Lake via Calypso and Ouzel Falls (page 134); Devils Thumb Bypass Trail (page 186); Forsythe Canyon Creek (page 61)

Rock formations and interesting geology: Rabbit Mountain (page 45); Red Rocks (page 73); Hall Ranch (page 48); Heil Ranch (page 51); Mesa Trail and laterals (page 96); Rattlesnake Gulch (page 202)

Caves: Mallory Cave (page 107)

Natural stone arch: Royal Arch (page 93)

Glaciers: Gibraltar Lake, St. Vrain glaciers (page 142); Arapaho Pass Trail (page 178); Arapaho Glacier Trail (pages 176); Isabelle Glacier Trail (page 161)

Historical cabins and ranching artifacts: Betasso Preserve (page 68); Towhee and Homestead Loop (page 122); Meyers Homestead Trail (page 131); Hall Ranch (page 48); Heil Ranch (page 51); Caribou Ranch (page 171); Rawhide Loop (page 206)

Indian game-drive walls and blinds: Foothills Trail (page 64); Buchanan Pass (page 145); Arapahoe Pass (page 178); James Peak (page 198); Needles Eye Tunnel (page 196)

Weather interpretation: Walter Orr Roberts Nature Trail (page 105)

Fishing: Ceran St. Vrain Trail (page 154); Rainbow Lakes (page 174); Button Rock Preserve (page 42); South Boulder Creek Loop (page 127)

ABBREVIATIONS
AND MAP LEGEND

CR = County Road

SR = State Road

US = United States Highway

FS = Forest Service

NCAR = National Center for Atmospheric Research

RMNP = Rocky Mountain National Park

USGS = United States Geological Survey

Map Legend

73	Forest Service Road		———————	Featured Trail
73	County Road		———————	Other Trail
CO 128	State Highway		～～～～	River/Stream
36	U.S. Highway			Lake
NCAR	National Center for Atmospheric Research			Falls
				Glacier
■—·—·—·—·—■	Paved Road		▣	Point of Interest
═══════	Gravel Road		× (2,589)	Mountain Summit Elevation in feet
= = = = = =	Dirt Road			
┼┼┼┼┼┼┼┼┼┼	Railroad		Ⓣ	Trailhead
—·—·—·—·—	Continental Divide			

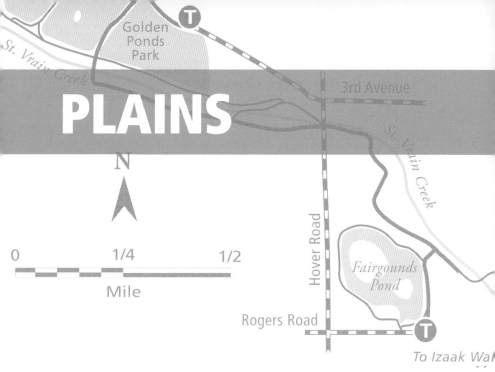

S ubdivisions and shopping centers cover much of what was
once prairie and, later, agricultural land in eastern Boulder County. Fortunately, some land is being preserved by
various city and county parks and open-space departments,
which have developed most of the trails described in this section.
Because many trails are relatively new, they may not be shown on
USGS topographic maps. Although we have listed the appropriate
topo maps, we recommend using the City of Boulder Open Space
and Mountain Parks Trail Map. All of these clearly marked trails are
easy, with little elevation change, and can be hiked at any time of
the year. However, in summer, they are more pleasant early or late
in the day. They are also good for ski touring immediately after a
heavy winter snowstorm.

St. Vrain Greenways Trail

Distance: 4.5 miles one way at present; 9 miles one way when completed

Elevation: 4,980 feet at Golden Ponds, with negligible elevation gain

Highlights: Ponds, birdwatching, fishing, mountain views, sculptures

Difficulty: Easy

Topo maps: Hygiene, Longmont

This paved trail along St. Vrain Creek in Longmont will eventually stretch from Golden Ponds, past the 313-acre Sandstone Ranch Park, to St. Vrain State Park near I-25. At present, the 4.5 completed miles stretch from Golden Ponds, under Main Street, to the confluence with Lefthand Creek. The trail crosses bridges over St. Vrain Creek several times and includes a spur around Fairgrounds Pond. Golden Ponds are restored gravel pits that attract a variety of birds

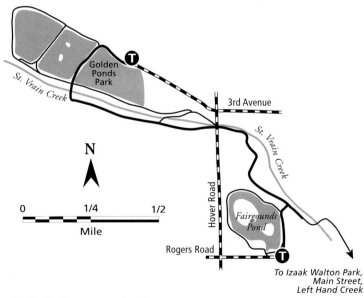

St. Vrain Greenways Trail

Golden Ponds along St. Vrain Greenways Trail

and offer superb views of Longs Peak and Mount Meeker. Along the trail and near Rogers Grove, look for the stone nature sculptures by artist Robert Tully. We especially love the one shaped like an ear, where you sit to hear the amplified roar of the creek. A short, paved spur trail follows Left Hand Creek from the confluence of the two creeks to the Longmont Museum and Cultural Center, where you can view exhibits on the history of the city.

Although St. Vrain Greenways Trail does not yet connect to Sandstone Ranch, it is worth driving to the park to explore the new 0.7-mile **Sandstone Loop Trail**. This trail, which consists of paved walkways and crusher fines, begins southeast of the sports fields. It climbs to an overlook of St. Vrain Creek and wetlands with distant mountain views, drops below a creamy sandstone bluff, and follows the creek past the historic home and outbuildings built by pioneer Morse Coffin in the early 1880s. Numerous prairie dogs and cottontails attract raptors, and white-tailed deer may bound away into the thickets. Another spur will eventually link with Union Reservoir.

History

A stone monument along the river west of Main Street marks the site of the original cabin of Alonzo Allen and his stepson, William Henry Dickens, the first farmers to arrive here in the 1860s. They founded the town of Burlington, a forerunner of Longmont. In the 1870s, a group of Chicago investors created a community here and built irrigation ditches to channel St. Vrain water to their farms.

Access

In Longmont, turn west off Hover Road where Hover and 3rd Street intersect, and park at Golden Ponds. Other trailheads begin at Fairgrounds Pond and Rogers Grove (east of Hover Road and 3rd Street) and at Izaak Walton Park (18 South Sunset Street). Sandstone Ranch is one mile east of the intersection of Weld CR 1 and SR 119. You can also park at the Longmont Museum, 400 Quail Road, and follow Left Hand Creek Trail to its junction with the Greenways Trail.

Pella Crossing: Braly and Marlatt Trails

Distance: 1.9-mile loop with spur to Webster Pond

Elevation: 5,097 feet with no elevation change

Highlights: Views of Longs Peak and Indian Peaks, waterbirds, fishing, picnicking

Difficulty: Easy

Topo map: Hygiene

The ponds at Pella Crossing attract a wealth of water-loving birds and are popular with fishermen. Braly Trails begin at the Pella Crossing Trailhead and loop around Sunset Pond and Heron Lake with a spur to Webster Pond. As you might guess from the names, great blue herons can be seen here, and the views at sunset or sunrise are spectacular. On a windless day at dawn, Longs Peak, bathed in alpenglow, is reflected in the lakes.

Marlatt Trail also begins at the Pella Crossing Trailhead and crosses 75th Street. It skirts the northwest shore of Dragonfly Pond and circles Poplar Pond, both of which are reclaimed gravel pits. St. Vrain Creek, lined with cottonwoods and willows, flows just to the

Heron Lake, Pella Crossing

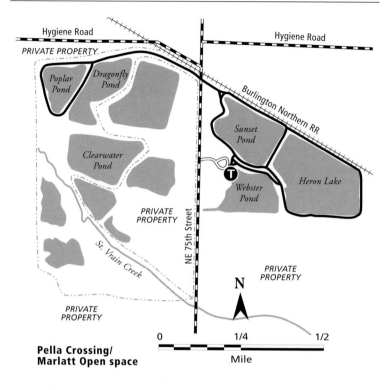

**Pella Crossing/
Marlatt Open space**

west of these ponds. Some additional trail construction is currently
underway, so watch for new trails to open.

History

The first settlers, George Webster (for whom the pond is named)
and Charles True, bought a 160-acre homestead claim here in
1859, and later, Webster planted plum, cherry, and apple orchards.
In the 1860s, the Overland Trail crossed the St. Vrain River at
"Upper Crossing" (original name for Pella Crossing) on the route
between Denver and Laramie. By 1861, Pella had become "one of
the busiest towns north of Denver," according to the sign at the
trailhead. The town even had a racetrack.

Access

One mile south of Hygiene, east of North 75th Street, or a half
mile north of the intersection of 75th Street and St. Vrain Road.

Coot Lake to Boulder Reservoir

Distance: 1.1 miles one way

Elevation: 5,173 feet with negligible elevation change

Highlights: Wetlands, waterbirds, wildflowers, prairie dogs, raptors, fishing, and mountain views

Difficulty: Easy

Topo map: Niwot

Skirt the south side of Coot Lake (turn left from the parking lot) and join an old road. For a longer but more scenic route, you can skirt the north and west sides of the lake by turning right from the parking lot. Walk along the dirt road to a bridge across an irrigation canal. Cross the canal on this bridge and don't even think of dropping down into the ditch—signs warn of "certain death" for anyone sucked into the siphon draining the ditch! From the bridge, follow the trail through a prairie-dog town and above the shore of Boulder Reservoir to 51st Street.

This trail, a convenient hike from either direction, is especially beautiful at sunset. On the west end of Coot Lake, a cattail marsh

Coot Lake

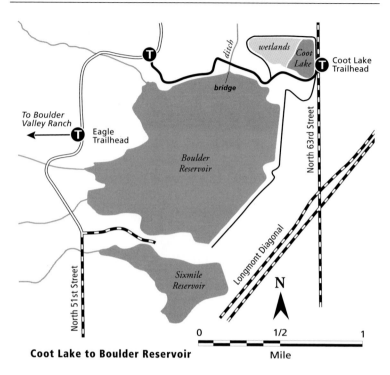

Coot Lake to Boulder Reservoir

and several small ponds usually harbor ducks, red-winged black-birds, and a northern harrier. In early spring, Easter daisies bloom here, followed by yucca, prickly pear cactus, various composites, and—finally—gayfeather in the fall. Prairie grasses, such as blue grama, and dried teasel heads remain decorative into winter. Red-tailed hawks soar frequently over the prairie-dog town, and bald eagles and northern harriers are often seen in winter.

History

Coot Lake achieved notoriety during the 1970s and early 1980s as a nude swimming hole. Later, the city closed the area to swimming because of liability problems, and now it is chiefly a haven for waterbirds such as the coots, for which it is named. (Nude bathers sometimes called themselves "cooties.")

In 1902, a nearby oil boom was sometimes called the "Haystack Field" because of its proximity to Haystack Mountain, which rises out of the plains northwest of Coot Lake. It was predicted that a "sea of derricks" would stretch to the Wyoming border, but the boom ended by the mid-1920s.

Boulder Reservoir dam, completed in 1955, measures 1.2 miles long, 48 feet high, and 265 feet thick and impounds water from Lake Granby.

Connections

- **Boulder Reservoir Loop** (about 6 miles) can start from any access point along the reservoir. Starting at the Coot Lake parking area, take the spur (1.5 miles) that has interpretive signs and that heads south past a prairie-dog colony. Although there is no official trail around the reservoir, you can connect various trails with 51st Street to make a loop.

- **Eagle Trail** and the network of trails at Boulder Valley Ranch (see below) begins on the west side of 51st Street, north of the main entrance to Boulder Reservoir.

Access

From the Diagonal Highway (SR 119) between Boulder and Longmont, turn west on CR 39 (for Coot Lake) or Jay Road (for Boulder Reservoir). On CR 39, drive 0.7 mile and park at Coot Lake. From Jay Road, turn right on 51st Street, drive 3.2 miles, and park at the northwest end of Boulder Reservoir.

Boulder Valley Ranch: Eagle Trail

Distance: 3.2 miles one way

Elevation: 5,230 to 5,533 feet

Highlights: Working ranch, wetlands, waterbirds, wildflowers, prairie dogs, raptors, and mountain views

Difficulty: Easy

Topo maps: Boulder, Niwot

Along the Sage Trail, Boulder Valley Ranch

This trail connects 51st Street and US 36 and has numerous laterals and loops. Starting at the Eagle Trailhead on 51st Street, the trail heads west (with views of the Indian Peaks) for 0.5 mile to a fork, where the Sage Trail goes to the right. Turn left and skirt the lower end of a shallow pond, and walk past a prairie-dog colony. Watch for raptors overhead, waterbirds in the pond, and great horned owls in the cottonwoods. In winter, both golden and bald eagles may be seen. In 1 mile, the trail forks again, with another section of the Sage Trail going to the right, following Farmers Ditch. Take the left fork and head uphill to Mesa Reservoir. Continue following the signs for the Eagle Trail to the Foothills Trailhead on US 36. Most of the trails in this area, which is still a working ranch, are actually farm access roads.

In spring and early summer, the wildflowers (including evening primrose, scarlet globe mallow, and several species of mustard and penstemon) bloom extravagantly along the shale cliffs. Because there is little shade, this trail is best done off-season or early or late in the day during summer.

History

Farmers Irrigation Ditch, built in 1862, provided power for the Yount-McKenzie Flour Mill near the mouth of Boulder Canyon

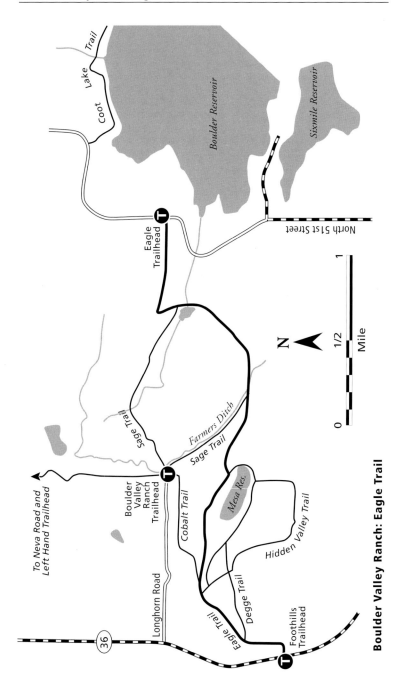

Boulder Valley Ranch: Eagle Trail

and has provided water to area farmers for more than a century. Early in the twentieth century, cattle ranchers W. W. Degge, W. W. Wolfe, Clinton Tyler, the Burger family, and the Maxwell family sometimes ran cattle from here over Rollins Pass, to as far as Steamboat Springs to take advantage of the nutritious mountain grasses. The adobe brick building at the ranch, the oldest structure still in use, was built in the early 1900s.

Connections

- **Eagle**, **Sage**, **Mesa Reservoir**, **Cobalt**, **Degge**, and **Hidden Valley trails** make various loops and permutations throughout the ranch.

- **Left Hand Trail** connects the Sage Trail to Neva Road, skirting Lefthand Valley Reservoir and the Beech Open Space picnic pavilion.

- **Coot Lake Trail** (page 7) begins 0.9 mile north of the Eagle Trailhead; walk along 51st Street to the trailhead on the reservoir side of the road.

- **Foothills Trail** (page 64) crosses under US 36 at the Foothills Trailhead, terminus for the Eagle Trail.

Access

Four trailheads give access to this area: Boulder Valley Ranch Trailhead on Longhorn Road, about 2 miles north of the intersection of US 36 and North Broadway and 1 mile east of US 36; Foothills Trailhead, 0.4 mile north of the intersection of US 36 and North Broadway on US 36; Eagle Trailhead, on the west side of 51st Street, half a mile north of the entrance gate to Boulder Reservoir; and Left Hand Trailhead on Neva Road, about 1.5 miles east of US 36.

East Boulder Trail: White Rocks and Teller Lakes Sections

Distance: 6.7 miles one way

Elevation: 5,110 to 5,415 feet

Highlights: White cliffs, mountain views, raptors (including bald eagles), waterfowl on lakes and creeks, wildlife, agricultural surroundings

Difficulty: Easy to moderate, depending on distance hiked

Topo map: Niwot

Red Tailed Hawk, Teller Lakes

Coyote, Teller Lakes

Mating Swainson's hawks

This trail on City of Boulder Open Space is well marked with signs and is divided into two sections separated by Valmont Drive. Hikers can combine the two sections or do each section separately, accessing the trail from several trailheads. From the Teller Farm North Trailhead, a short, wheelchair-accessible trail goes to Teller Lake No. 5 (North Teller Lake), where you can fish or watch birds. A half-mile path continues around the north and east sides of the lake, but the south and west sides are designated wildlife areas closed to public use.

White Rocks and Gunbarrel Hill

Distance: 4.5 miles one way

From the Teller Farm North Trailhead, go west for a short distance, cross Valmont Drive, and head north following Dry Creek (a misnomer—it's not dry). Cross the railroad track and skirt the restored gravel pit that provides habitat for many waterbirds. The White Rocks Nature Preserve, named for the cream-colored cliffs visible from the trail, supports a rare fern, miner bees, and, sometimes, nesting bald eagles and barn owls and is off-limits to the public. Faint petroglyphs created by early Native Americans, as well as names of westering pioneers, can be seen on the bluffs. For several years, a few elk have thrived in the meadows and wetlands here. This unique ecosystem was vigorously protected for many years by landowner Ricky Weiser, a Boulder environmental legend whose gadfly perseverance is still missed.

The trail circles east of the preserve and the lake, crosses Boulder Creek and an irrigation canal, climbs a couple of small ridges, and in 2.4 miles comes to a T-junction. Turn west and continue to the crest of Gunbarrel Hill, where you will have superb views of the Indian Peaks. Beyond the hill, the trail continues farther west to the Gunbarrel Hill Trailhead. Along the way, watch for raptors, coyotes, and herds of both white-tailed and mule deer.

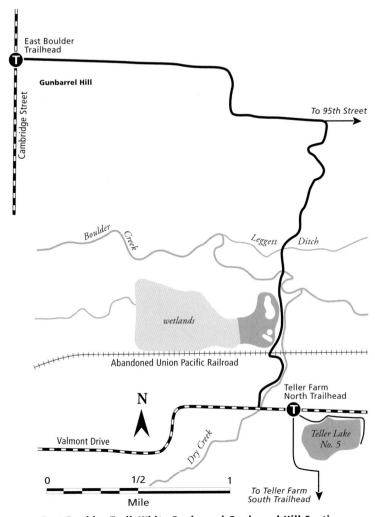

East Boulder Trail: White Rocks and Gunbarrel Hill Sections

Teller Lakes

Distance: 2.2 miles one way

Park at either the Teller Farm North Trailhead or at the Teller Farm South Trailhead. This level trail consists of old farm roads that cross two small irrigation ditches to connect Valmont and Arapahoe roads. Raptors frequently soar overhead or sit in the cottonwoods, and coyotes often prowl around the busy prairie-dog colonies. Crops are still being raised, and cattle often graze in fields leased for agriculture. A short spur from the southern end of the trail leads to one of the Teller Lakes, probably named for Henry Teller, who became Secretary of the Interior in 1882 after serving thirty years in the U.S. Senate. These lakes and a small wetland are good habitats for waterbirds, and a pier gives easy access for fishing.

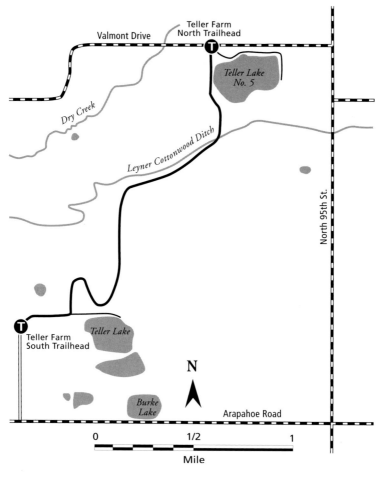

East Boulder Trail: Teller Lakes Section

A great-horned owl near the trail can often be heard at dusk, Teller Lakes

History

Winter wheat was raised on Gunbarrel Hill from the early days until the mid-1980s, when the land was purchased by the City of Boulder. Farmer Howard Morton plowed the last sod in 1938 and remembers hitting buffalo wallows with his plow. After the eroded land became open space, it was reseeded and allowed to revert to native grasses such as sideoats grama, blue grama, and bluestem.

Access

Teller Farm North Trailhead is on Valmont Drive, about a mile east of 75th and a mile west of 95th. Teller Farm South Trailhead is on Arapahoe Road, about a mile east of 75th and a mile west of 95th. Gunbarrel Trailhead is at the intersection of Cambridge and Boulderado streets in the Heatherwood subdivision.

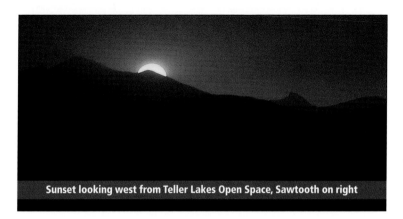

Sunset looking west from Teller Lakes Open Space, Sawtooth on right

Walden and Sawhill Ponds

Distance: 1.2 miles from Cottonwood Marsh to the west end of Sawhill Ponds

Elevation: About 5,100 feet with no elevation change

Highlights: Some of the best birding in Boulder, wildlife, fishing, mountain views reflected in ponds

Difficulty: Easy

Topo map: Niwot

Sawhill Ponds in the autumn

This network of ponds, marshes, brush, and cottonwoods is one of the best birding spots in the county and is more conducive to wandering and nature watching than to linear hiking and vigorous exercise. Watch for eagles, owls, warblers, and a great variety of shorebirds, ducks, and geese, as well as beaver, muskrat, fox, and deer. The ponds were mined for gravel from 1958 to the early 1970s, when wetlands were largely restored. Now more deer inhabit the complex than in 1900, when George Sawhill lived here as a boy and never observed them.

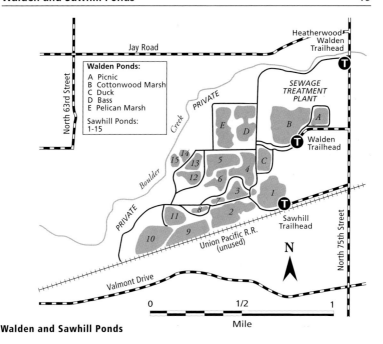

Walden Ponds:
A Picnic
B Cottonwood Marsh
C Duck
D Bass
E Pelican Marsh

Sawhill Ponds:
1-15

Walden and Sawhill Ponds

It's difficult to get lost while meandering along the old roads that are now closed to motorized vehicles. Sawhill Ponds (the southern section) is owned by the Colorado Division of Wildlife and is managed by Boulder Open Space and Mountain Parks. Walden Ponds (the northern section) is operated by the Boulder County Parks and Open Space Department. But as far as hikers and wildlife are concerned, the area is one wondrous unit.

Our favorite route starts at the Cottonwood Marsh boardwalk (Walden section), where we look for rails and other shorebirds in the shallows. At the southwest end of the marsh, head toward the administration buildings, which serve as field offices for the Boulder County Parks and Open Space Department. Cross the gravel road to Duck Pond and go through the opening in the fence into the Sawhill section. Walk west past several ponds to the cottonwood forest at the west end. You'll find lots of warblers here in the spring and fireflies in early summer. Turn south and continue until you reach the large open pond north of the railroad track. Walk east toward the Sawhill entrance. Just before you reach the large pond west of the parking lot, turn north. At this point, you can see the Walden section and can return to the Cottonwood Marsh boardwalk by walking north between several ponds.

Connections

The numerous old roads allow for a great variety of possible loops. You can also connect with the **Heatherwood-Walden Trail** at the 75th Street wastewater treatment plant north of Cottonwood Marsh and follow Boulder Creek to a parking area at 75th Street just south of Jay Road.

Access

This area is west off of 75th Street, between Jay and Valmont roads. For the Sawhill section, turn west onto the road just north of the railroad track. The Walden turnoff is also to the west and is north of the Sawhill section. It is marked by a sign between the railroad track and the sewage-treatment plant.

Cannon Loop Trail

Distance: 1 mile round trip

Elevation: 5,360 feet with negligible elevation change

Highlights: Waterbirds on Valmont Reservoir, prairie dogs, mountain views, overview of Boulder

Difficulty: Easy

Topo map: Niwot

This trail begins to the left of the cannon displayed at Legion Park (off of east Arapahoe Road) and circles below the perimeter of Goodview Hill, so called because it once served as a lookout for early Native Americans and white settlers. Excellent views of the Indian Peaks and of Valmont, Hillcrest, and Leggett-Owens reservoirs can be seen from this trail. A large prairie-dog town attracts bald eagles and other raptors. Many uncommon waterbirds, such as wood ducks, loons, and trumpeter swans, have been seen on the

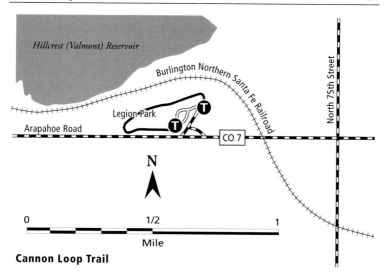

Cannon Loop Trail

Prairie dog

reservoirs. An osprey nesting box was built in 2000 after the "fish eagles" had tried unsuccessfully to nest on the power towers for several years.

Because this trail is so short and is easily accessible from Boulder, it's a good place for a lunch-hour walk and picnic.

Cannon along Cannon Loop Trail

History

In the late 1800s, Frank Weisenhorn built an icehouse here on what was then called "Owens Lake" to supply his Boulder City Brewing Company in Boulder. Townspeople came for picnicking, boating, ice-skating, dancing, and an occasional balloon ride. A dance pavilion extended over the water at the southeast corner of the lake. Public Service Company began operating the electric plant here, with one stack, in 1918. The American Legion Post No. 10 landscaped the area in 1933 as a memorial to the soldiers of World War I and installed two World War I cannons on the hilltop.

Access

Take Arapahoe Avenue east past the Valmont Power Plant and go 0.9 mile east of 63rd Street. Turn north onto a short gravel road at the Legion Park sign. Park at the turnaround on top of Goodview Hill.

Boulder Creek Path

Distance: 7 miles one way

Elevation: 5,800 feet at Fourmile Canyon to 5,200 feet at Valmont Lake

Highlights: People-, bird-, and fish-watching, tumultuous creek, catch-and-release fishing, gardens

Difficulty: Easy to moderate, depending on distance hiked

Topo map: Boulder, Niwot

Boulder Creek Path

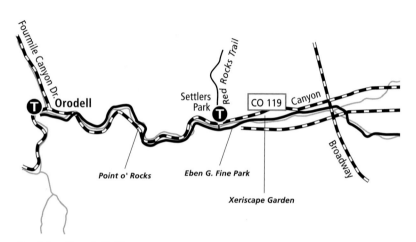

Boulder Creek Path

Stretching from east Boulder to the junction of Boulder and
Fourmile canyons, this trail along Boulder Creek cuts through the
heart of the city, attracting crowds of hikers, joggers, skaters, and
bicyclists. Because of heavy use, the trail is paved, but a parallel
gravel path in some areas is reserved for pedestrians. The section
from Point o' Rocks (one mile west of Eben G. Fine Park) to 28th
Street features signs on the history and natural history of the area.

The trail is beautiful in all seasons: Naturalized bulbs bloom in
early spring, waves of warblers arrive in May, and large willows and
cottonwoods provide summer shade and autumn color. Special
points of interest include a demonstration xeriscape garden (west of
6th Street), a children's fishing pond and a sculpture garden (west
of 9th Street), the International Peace Garden (near Boulder Public
Library), and a fish observatory (near Folsom Street).

To avoid collisions with bicyclists and rollerbladers, it's important
to keep to the right and to be aware of other users. Unless you're
feeling gregarious, the best time for this trail is early morning.
You can start at any point and go for a few blocks or for the entire
distance.

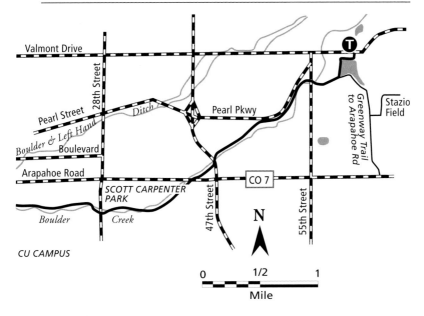

History

Although a tollroad had been built up Boulder Canyon to
Magnolia Road in 1865, it was not extended to "Middle Boulder"
(Nederland) until 1871, when silver was discovered at Caribou.
According to Boulder historian Amos Bixby, "The settlers found
Boulder Cañon so difficult of access that a man could not make his
way up it by foot.... It was a disputed question whether or not a
wagon road could ever be constructed through it." Remnants of the
tollroad and a retaining wall, built without mortar, can still be seen
at Maxwell's Pitch, named for road engineer James P. Maxwell, just
beyond the Point o' Rocks, also called Elephant Buttresses. Maxwell
was Boulder's second mayor and a member of the territorial legislature and the first state senate. During the late 1860s and 1870s,
Martha Maxwell, James's stepmother, and her husband, James A.
Maxwell, lived in the area that is now Eben G. Fine Park. Martha
was famous as one of the first female naturalists in the United States
and as a taxidermist who developed the idea of naturalistic diora-
mas in museums.

In 1883, the Greeley, Salt Lake, and Pacific narrow-gauge railroad (called the Switzerland Trail) was completed to Sunset, a town about 4 miles west of Wall Street on CR 118, and was later extended to Ward and to Eldora. The railroad washed out in 1894 during the worst flood in Boulder's history. Rebuilt in 1898, it was finally abandoned in 1919 when another flood wiped it out. Buttresses for this railroad can be seen near the Point o' Rocks.

In 1908, Frederick Law Olmsted, Jr., noted landscape architect, was brought out from Harvard University to advise the city on future planning. In his "Improvement of Boulder County" report he wrote, "[K]eeping open for public use near the heart of the city a simple piece of pretty bottom-land of the very sort that Boulder Creek has been flooding over for countless centuries . . . would give a piece of recreation ground worth a great deal to the people. And at the same time it is probably the cheapest way of handling the flood problem of Boulder Creek." Olmsted's advice was not heeded and many municipal buildings, such as a jail and the public library, were built on the creek's banks.

The west end of the Boulder Creek Path terminates at the junction of Boulder and Fourmile canyons, the former site of Orodell, a mining town that thrived during the 1870s. Much of the town burned in 1891, and the sawmill and gold mill were destroyed by the 1894 flood. The Orodell townsite is now buried under some twenty feet of rubble deposited when SR 119 was paved in 1953.

The first wheat in Colorado Territory was planted in 1860 by the Wellman Brothers (Henry, Luther, and Sylvanus) on forty acres bordering Boulder Creek at the present junction of 47th Street and Arapahoe Avenue.

Connections

- **Red Rocks Trail** can be reached from the west end of Eben G. Fine Park by walking under Canyon Boulevard to Settlers Park.

- Just beyond 17th Street, a bridge crosses Boulder Creek and a path leads up the hill to the University of Colorado campus, an attractive place to stroll—especially in autumn. Several intersecting streets (6th, 9th, Broadway, and 13th) give access to the Mapleton Historic District and to the Pearl Street Mall.

- **Greenway Trail** to Arapahoe Road (0.5 mile) merges with Boulder Creek Path east of 55th Street by a small pond.

Access

Eben G. Fine Park, at the mouth of Boulder Canyon on west Arapahoe Avenue, is the best access for the west end. Scott Carpenter Park, at 30th Street and Arapahoe Avenue, is a good access point for the middle section. A sidewalk west of the Stazio ball fields, west of 63rd Street between Valmont Road and Arapahoe Avenue, gives access to the eastern section. You can, however, pick up the trail at any point along Boulder Creek.

South Boulder Creek Trail: Baseline Road to Marshall Road

Distance: 3.5 miles one way

Elevation: 5,300 feet with little elevation change

Highlights: Tallgrass prairie, streamside habitat, tall cottonwoods and willows, white-tailed and mule deer

Difficulty: Easy

Topo map: Louisville

This trail follows South Boulder Creek through riparian corridors and wetland meadows. Part of the trail goes through the Tallgrass Prairie Natural Area, where many species of native tallgrasses and wildflowers flourish, including a rare bog orchid, *Spiranthes diluvialis*. Such uncommon birds as rails, bobolinks, and greatcrested flycatchers are sometimes seen here.

From the Bobolink Trailhead, go south. At 1.3 miles, walk through the South Boulder Road Underpass, at which point the trail becomes a gravel service road heading west for 0.3 mile, paralleling South Boulder Road. At the access gate, turn south and

continue for about 1.9 miles to Marshall Road. Cattle often graze
in the meadow beyond the access gate; avoid coming between a cow
and her calf. Wetlands and lakes near Marshall Road provide good
waterfowl viewing. Remains of the old Dorn Farm site are visible
west of the trail, just south of South Boulder Road.

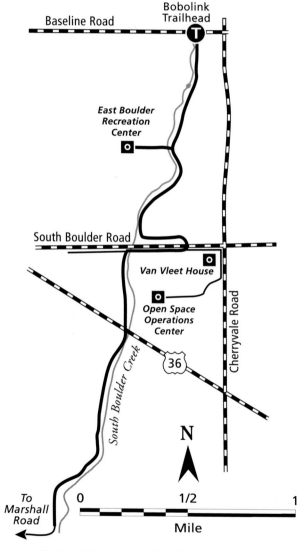

South Boulder Creek Trail

South Boulder Creek Trail

Connections

- **Centennial Trail** (about 1 mile) connects Dimmit Drive and 55th Street, skirting a llama farm and the Flatirons Municipal Golf Course and following a creek lined with willows and cotton-woods. From the Bobolink Trailhead, take the underpass beneath Baseline Road and walk a block along Gapter Road, turn left, and cross South Boulder Creek. If you turn off from Centennial Trail onto Old Tale Road, you can link with the **Boulder Creek Path** (see page 23).

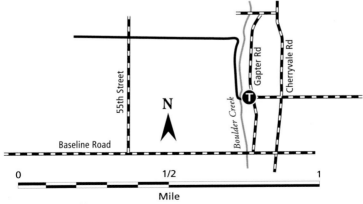

Centennial Trail

- **South Boulder Creek West** (0.7 mile) is a spur heading east from the underpass to skirt the historic Van Vleet Ranch and end at the Open Space Operation Center on Cherryvale Road.

Access

Park at the Bobolink Trailhead, 0.1 mile west of the intersection of Baseline and Cherryvale roads. You can also park at the East Boulder Community Center, where a spur trail connects to the main trail. There is a very limited amount of roadside parking at the south end of the trail at the intersection of Marshall Road and SR 93.

Dry Creek Trail

Distance: 1-mile loop

Elevation: 5,300 feet with negligible elevation change

Highlights: Views across Baseline Reservoir to snowcapped mountains; waterbirds; agricultural surroundings; prairie dogs

Difficulty: Easy

Topo map: Louisville

Hiking along the Dry Creek Trail

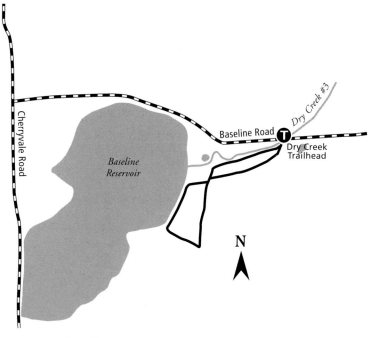

Dry Creek Trail

Follow the packed gravel trail past the prairie-dog colony to the bridge across Dry Creek (a misnomer—it's not dry). Just west of the bridge, take either branch of the loop. The left branch follows Dry Creek, and the right branch heads west, eventually paralleling the shore of Baseline Reservoir. Although the reservoir is private, you can enjoy the spectacular view across the lake to the mountains. Bring a pair of binoculars to watch the waterbirds that frequent the lake and the raptors that prey on the prairie dogs. Along the southernmost segment of trail, look to the southeast for a glimpse of the old Walburga Abbey. The Dry Creek area, sometimes called "puppy park," is a favorite for walking and training dogs, so be aware that there will be numerous "poop baggies" along the trail as well as dogs.

Access

Park at the Dry Creek Trailhead south of Baseline Road and east of the Baseline Reservoir, about a mile east of Cherryvale Road.

Carolyn Holmberg Preserve/
Rock Creek Farm: Cradleboard Trail

This working farm was purchased by Boulder County Open Space for agricultural preservation in 1980. Most of the 1,151 acres are leased, but several trails loop through the farm and past croplands. The main trailhead is at Stearns Lake, which is stocked with tiger muskie and channel catfish. It is also a good place to view shorebirds, ducks, and geese. The northwest side of the lake is a wildlife habitat, off-limits to public use.

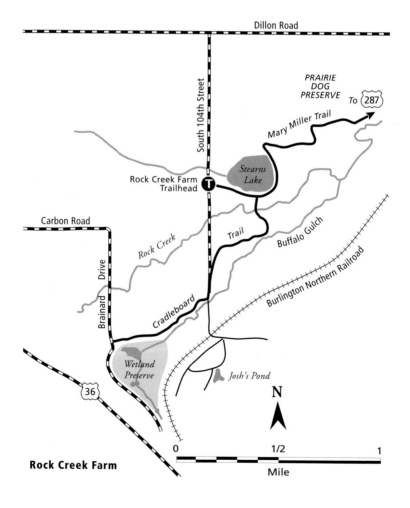

View from Rock Creek Farm

Cradleboard Trail

Distance: 1.5 miles one way

Elevation: 5,282 feet with negligible elevation change

Highlights: Stearns Lake, birdwatching, fishing, prairie dogs, panoramic views

Difficulty: Easy

Topo map: Lafayette

From Stearns Lake Trailhead, take the Mary Miller Trail around the south side of the lake. At the 0.25-mile point, the trail forks at a signpost, with the left fork following the Mary Miller Trail to US 287. The Cradleboard Trail turns right and continues south across the bridge over Rock Creek.

In a short distance, the trail heads west and eventually meets an extension of 104th Street. A right turn takes you back to the Stearns Lake Trailhead. The main trail turns left and continues past a small pond to another junction. If you continue south at this point and cross the Burlington Northern railroad tracks, you will come to various Broomfield Open Space trails, including one to Josh's Pond. Cradleboard Trail heads west along Buffalo Gulch past a prairie-dog town and a small wetland. Panoramic views of the Indian Peaks are highlights. This trail segment dead-ends at Brainard Drive, so you should retrace your route to 104th Street, which leads back to Stearns Lake.

History

An archaeological dig in this vicinity uncovered numerous Native American artifacts as well as fire pits, one of which is estimated to be 6,000 years old. The trail name pays homage to the Cheyenne and Arapaho women who formerly lived in the area and created extravagantly ornamented cradleboards.

The farm dates back to 1864, when Lafayette and Mary Miller ran a stagecoach station and a roadhouse here as well as a farm, a cattle ranch, and an apple orchard. Their grandson recalled how Mary baked 100 apple pies one day and sold them for a dollar each when the circus camped nearby. Mary founded the town of Lafayette in 1888, naming it for her husband who died from heatstroke in 1878. She helped establish the town's first school and opened Lafayette's first bank, becoming the first female bank president in the world. Legend has it that she once read a set of encyclopedias cover to cover. Many of the buildings date from 1933, when W. S. Stearns operated a dairy farm here.

The name "Carolyn Holmberg Preserve" was added to Rock Creek Farm in 2000 to honor Carolyn Holmberg, director of Boulder County Parks and Open Space from 1983 until her death in 1998. She was instrumental in preserving 40,000 acres in the county, including Rock Creek Farm.

Connections

- **Mary Miller Trail** diverges from the Cradleboard Trail 0.25 mile from the Stearns Lake Trailhead and continues east 1.25 miles to US 287. Eventually, this trail will connect to the Coal Creek Trail.

- The southward extension of the Cradleboard Trail forks several times, with one branch leading to **Josh's Pond** and another to Broomfield's **Lac Amora Open Space**.

Access

The farm is located northwest of Broomfield near the intersection of Dillon Road and 104th Street. Stearns Lake Trailhead is on 104th Street a short distance south of Dillon Road.

Coal Creek Trail

Distance: 8 miles one way

Elevation: 5,278 feet with negligible elevation change

Highlights: Streamside habitat, birdwatching, prairie dogs

Difficulty: Easy

Topo map: Lafayette

Coal Creek Trail

This urban trail extends from 120th Street in Lafayette through Louisville to town hall in Superior. The trail more or less parallels Coal Creek, traversing open space, residential, and commercial areas. Much of the trail is adjacent to noisy city streets or follows city sidewalks. However, the segment from Aquarius Trailhead to the Public Road Trailhead follows the creek through a somewhat wilder habitat and is shaded by numerous cottonwoods. From the US 287 underpass, you can continue on to 120th Street or take the

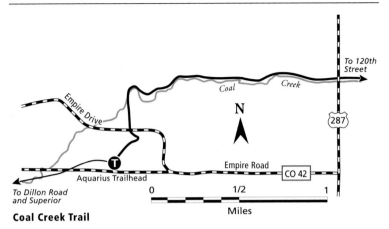

Coal Creek Trail

paved bike path to Baseline Road. Eventually, Coal Creek Trail will connect with Rock Creek Farm and the Marshall Mesa trails, creating a 20-mile network.

Grasso Park behind Superior Town Hall contains several historic buildings built in 1895 when Charles Hake, who founded the town of Superior, first homesteaded the area. Ruins of the Vulcan coal mine that operated from 1903 to 1937 and the grading for the coal-carrying train can be seen just north of the Public Road Trailhead.

Connections

- **Singletree Trail**, a newly completed 0.75-mile trail through agricultural land, will eventually link Coal Creek Trail to the Marshall Mesa trails. Singletree Trail follows the bed of the Colorado and Southern Railroad, which once served Boulder, Denver, and Eldorado Springs, and passes by the foundations of the Industrial Mine, which produced four million tons of coal between 1895 and 1945. Although the connecting links have not yet been constructed, you can catch the trail at the parking area where 2nd Avenue in Superior dead-ends and continue to 76th Street.

Access

For the east or middle section of the trail, start at Aquarius Trailhead on SR 42 (Empire Road) 1.3 miles west of US 287 or at

Public Road Trailhead where Public Road crosses Coal Creek in Lafayette. For the west end of the trail, start at the Superior City Hall. You can also access the trail from several points along the route.

Marshall Mesa, Community Ditch, Greenbelt Plateau

Distance: 2.4 miles one way

Elevation: 5,550 to 5,900 feet

Highlights: Coal-mining ruins, mountain views, grasslands, wildflowers, raptors

Difficulty: Easy

Topo map: Louisville

Mining ruins on Marshall Mesa

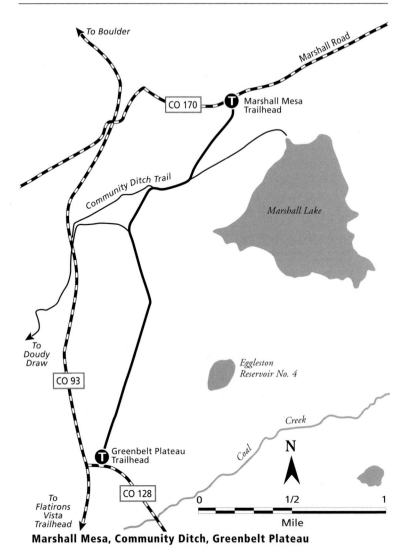

Marshall Mesa, Community Ditch, Greenbelt Plateau

You can hike this trail conveniently from either direction and make several loops and interesting detours. Starting at the Marshall Mesa Trailhead, follow the trail for 0.8 mile up to Community Ditch (built in 1885), crossing another, lower irrigation ditch along the way. (If you hike east along this lower ditch, you will find coal-mining ruins.) On top of Marshall Mesa, sandstone formations provide habitat for early wildflowers.

When you reach Community Ditch, turn west and follow the ditch to the junction for the Greenbelt Plateau, once part of the main road from Boulder to Golden. Cross the bridge and climb gently to the plateau and the wide-open spaces of the prairie, continuing on to the Greenbelt Plateau Trailhead. You can leave a car here if you want to do a one-way hike, or you can return to the Marshall Mesa Trailhead.

History

In the 1860s, shortly after coal was discovered in this area, Joseph M. Marshall built the first blast furnace to manufacture pig iron, and he purchased several of the existing mines. At various times, the coal-mining town was called Foxtown, Langford, Gorham, and, finally, Marshall. It contained eight hundred residents and three saloons—a larger metropolis than Boulder at the time. Even then, people were concerned about air pollution and complained about the smoke from a twelve-ton steam engine used to haul the coal to market. Numerous underground coal fires have flared since those early days of mining, and some are still burning. The fires may have been started by poor mining practices, by strikers, or by moonshine stills hidden in the mines; no one knows for sure. During the coal wars from 1910 to 1914, soldiers with machine guns were sometimes posted on the south slopes of the mesa. No miners were shot at Marshall, but the National Guard killed six at the Columbine Mine in Erie in 1927.

Connections

Community Ditch allows for several permutations. If you turn east at the point where the Marshall Mesa section joins Community Ditch, you will reach an overlook of privately owned **Marshall Lake** in 0.8 mile. If you continue west on Community Ditch past the Greenbelt Plateau cutoff, you reach SR 93, at which point you can cross the highway and continue along Community Ditch to **Doudy Draw** (page 125). You can also stay on the east side of the highway, cross Community Ditch, and rejoin the Greenbelt Plateau Trail in 0.3 mile.

Access

Park at the Marshall Mesa Trailhead on the south side of Marshall Road, 0.9 mile east of SR 93, or at the Greenbelt Plateau Trailhead, 0.1 mile east of SR 93 on the north side of SR 128.

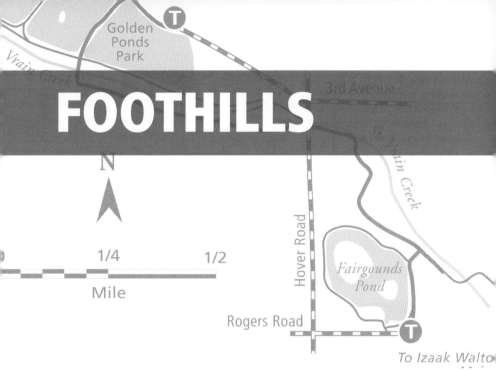

FOOTHILLS

Boulder's foothills trails, ranging in elevation from approximately 5,500 to 8,000 feet, offer a fascinating link between plains and peaks and frequently culminate in views of Boulder Valley to the east and snowcapped mountains to the west. The ecosystems extend from shrub lands to ponderosa-pine and Douglas-fir forests, supporting a wide variety of birds, mammals, and other wildlife. We prefer to hike these trails in spring and fall when temperatures are moderate, but they are also pleasant early or late in the day in summer. In winter, the more level trails are good for ski touring after a heavy snowfall.

Button Rock Preserve Loop
Via Sleepy Lion Trail

Distance: 6-mile loop

Elevation: 5,960 to 6,420 feet

Highlights: Reservoirs, wildlife, wildflowers, red and buff sandstone formations, cascading creek, waterfalls, fishing (limited permits available)

Difficulty: Moderate

Topo map: Lyons

Water spills over from Longmont Reservoir, Button Rock Preserve Loop

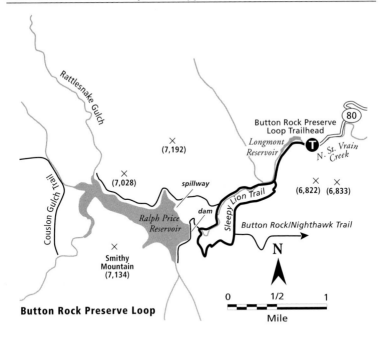

Button Rock Preserve Loop

Walking west along a gravel road (closed to traffic except for authorized vehicles), you pass a wide waterfall pouring over Longmont Reservoir Dam. A short distance beyond the long, narrow reservoir, and just before the road crosses to the right-hand side of the North St. Vrain Creek, there is a large sign for the Sleepy Lion Trail on the left. Take this trail, named for a mountain lion who once grabbed a forty-five-minute catnap there, and head up through ponderosa-pine and Douglas-fir forest to an open meadow. Just before the trail descends to the foot of the Button Rock Dam, it passes through an area of red-rock formations, where pink cacti bloom in May, and drops into a small canyon.

At the foot of Button Rock Dam, the North St. Vrain Creek blasts out from a small opening. To reach the top of the dam and the shore of Ralph Price Reservoir, take the trail that zigzags up the right side of the dam. Although no trails circle the reservoir, a 3-mile trail on the right-hand side goes to the inlet on the northwest end of the reservoir. If water is flowing over the spillway, detour around it by walking down the gravel road a short distance and following the signs back up to the ranger cottage. (Note: mileage

Pink cactus, Button Rock Preserve Loop

is given for the loop up to the reservoir and back and does not include shoreline trails.)

Returning to the parking area via the road is easier and shorter than the trail because there is no elevation gain. Brown and rainbow trout abound in North St. Vrain Creek, which parallels the road, as well as in the reservoirs. The surrounding area is a wildlife preserve open to walk-in visitors only. Look for dippers, pygmy owls, and golden eagles. In winter, bald eagles roost around the reservoir, and in summer, swallows nest along the cliffs. Bighorn sheep can be seen in some of the more remote areas.

Connections

- **Coulson Gulch Trail** (FS Trail 916) can be reached by following an old road at the northwest end of Ralph Price Reservoir. The downhill branch of Coulson Gulch drops to North St. Vrain Creek, and the uphill branch climbs to Johnny Park. It's possible to leave one car at the Coulson Gulch Trailhead (4.5 miles from US 36 via the Big Elk Meadows turnoff) and another at the Button Rock barricade for a one-way hike of about 6.5 miles. However, the trail is indistinct on the south side of Rattlesnake Gulch at the far end of the reservoir, and some rock scrambling is required. The Boulder County topo map is essential if you try this route.

• **Button Rock Trail** forks to the left just before Sleepy Lion Trail drops to the reservoir and links to **Nighthawk Trail** and **Hall Ranch**. You can do an 8-mile one-way hike by leaving cars at both Hall Ranch and Button Rock trailheads.

Access

Take US 36 north from Boulder to Lyons. From Lyons, drive 4 miles on US 36 toward Estes Park, turn left on CR 80, continue for 3 miles to the Button Rock barricade, and park along the road.

Rabbit Mountain:
Little Thompson Overlook Trail

Distance: 1 mile one way

Elevation: 5,500 to 6,000 feet

Highlights: Views from prairie to peaks, raptors, prairie dogs, tepee rings, interesting geology

Difficulty: Easy to moderate

Topo map: Carter Lake, Hygiene

Cliffs on Rabbit Mountain

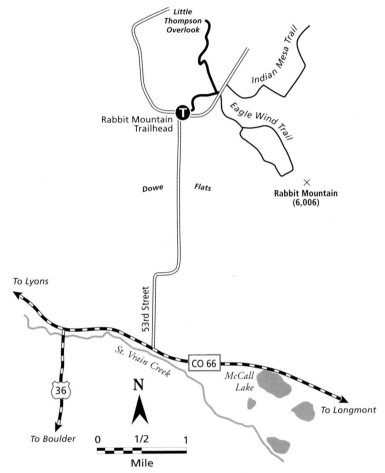

Little
Thompson
Overlook

Indian Mesa Trail

Eagle Wind Trail

Rabbit Mountain
Trailhead

T

Dowe Flats

×
Rabbit Mountain
(6,006)

To Lyons

53rd Street

St. Vrain Creek

CO 66

McCall
Lake

36

To Longmont

N

To Boulder

0 1/2 1

Mile

Rabbit Mountain: Little Thompson Overlook Trail

From the picnic pavilion, walk uphill below a colorful escarpment to a low saddle with panoramic views of the plains. At the signpost, turn left and follow the trail through stands of mountain mahogany, yucca, native grasses, and wildflowers to an overlook at the edge of a ridge. The land beyond the overlook is on private property with no public access.

This area was once called Rattlesnake Mountain—for good reasons. Watch for rattlers and also for the beautiful and harmless bull snakes. From the overlook, you can see down into the multicolored rock formations of Little Thompson Canyon. Longs Peak, Mount Meeker, and the Indian Peaks lie to the west and Pikes Peak to the south. Look for bald eagles (in winter), golden eagles, other raptors, and coyotes attracted by the prairie dogs. Also look for deer, multicolored lichen and rocks, and for evidence of faulting and earthquakes.

Return to the parking area via this same route. In the future, a connecting trail may be built to Carter Lake in Larimer County.

Mule deer along the Little Thompson Overlook Trail

History

Native Americans lived and hunted here for at least 5,000 years. Tepee rings show where the Arapaho, the most recent of the tribes, once camped. A prairie-dog colony now inhabits the main encampment. Columbus Weese, the first white settler, started farming here in 1864. His daughter married Jack Moomaw, the first National Park Service ranger on the east side of the Continental Divide. Moomaw wanted the land preserved, so his granddaughter sold it to the Boulder County Open Space Department in 1984.

Connections

- **Indian Mesa Trail** begins at the signpost on the saddle, follows the road a short distance, crosses the mesa, and dead-ends in 1.3 miles.

- **Eagle Wind Trail** follows the ridge south from the saddle to make about a 3-mile loop. The summit of Rabbit Mountain is closed seasonally to protect golden eagle nesting habitat.

Access

Turn north onto 53rd Street from the Ute Highway (SR 66) between the towns of Lyons and Longmont. Continue about 2 miles to the Rabbit Mountain Trailhead.

Hall Ranch:
Bitterbrush Trail and Nelson Loop

Distance: 9.3 miles round trip

Elevation: 5,440 to 6,820 feet

Highlights: Pink- and salmon-colored sandstone formations; mountain and canyon views; historic ranch ruins; prairie dogs, raptors, and other wildlife; wildflowers

Difficulty: Moderate to strenuous

Topo map: Lyons

Hall Ranch

Ruins of the Nelson house, Hall Ranch

The Bitterbrush Trail starts on a south-facing slope dominated by mountain mahogany and three-leaf sumac. Look north for stunning views of Hat Rock and Indian Lookout Mountain, whose orange-pink rock is dramatic in late afternoon. The trail is named for the bitterbrush, also called antelope brush, that flourishes along the trail—a sign that the area has not been overgrazed. Because this shrub is relished by both wildlife and livestock, botanists use it to evaluate range conditions.

The trail ascends through juniper and ponderosa pines to a ridge top overlooking one of the highest prairie-dog colonies in the county at 6,200 feet. At 3.5 miles, the Bitterbrush Trail joins the 2.3-mile Nelson Ranch Loop, where a short spur leads to the abandoned Nelson ranch house and a cement silo in Antelope Park. Dramatic views of Longs Peak and Mount Meeker and of the pink palisades above the North St. Vrain Valley appear to the west and north. You can return by either the same route or the Nighthawk Trail.

An important elk-migration corridor, one of the few places where elk can freely migrate from mountains to plains, runs through the ranch, which also supports mountain lions, bobcats, badgers, bighorns, wild turkeys, and prairie rattlers. Wildflowers range from lavender pasqueflowers and yellow violets in spring to lavender asters and yellow sunflowers in fall. Pink-flowering ball cactus bloom at the higher elevations in late April and May.

The trail is very popular with both hikers and mountain bikers, even on weekdays. To avoid crowds, go early in the morning, or try the Nighthawk Trail where bicyclists are prohibited. Dogs are not permitted.

History

Arapaho and Cheyenne Indians were the first known inhabitants of this area, which was homesteaded by Richard Clark in 1890. Clark later sold the ranch to the Nelson family, who built a wooden home and a concrete silo, both still standing, in Antelope Park. Hallwyn and June Hall bought the land in 1944. Their 1890 stone house and other outbuildings near the highway are currently closed to the public. Because the Hall family wanted the land preserved, they sold it to Boulder County Open Space in 1993. Many buildings on Boulder's University of Colorado campus are built from stone quarried in the area.

Connections

- **Nighthawk Trail** begins at the Bitterbrush Trailhead and in 4.1 miles joins the Nelson Loop at the far southwest corner. You can return via either the Bitterbrush Trail or the Nighthawk Trail.

- **Button Rock Trail**, a link to **Sleepy Lion Trail**, also connects to the Nighthawk Trail near the upper end. If you leave one car at the Button Rock parking area and another at Hall Ranch, you can enjoy an 8-mile trek from the North St. Vrain area to the South St. Vrain. For a longer hike, you can detour up to Ralph Price Reservoir and return via the road (see pages 43–44 for details).

Access

From Lyons, go west on SR 7 for 1.7 miles to the turnoff for the parking lot on the right side of the road.

Heil Ranch: Lichen Loop, Wapiti Trail, Ponderosa Loop

Distance: 1.3 miles round trip (Lichen Loop), 2.5 miles one way (Wapiti Trail), 5.2 miles round trip (Ponderosa Loop)

Elevation: 5,900 to 6,680 feet

Highlights: Wildlife; wildflowers; birdwatching; interesting geology and rock formations; historic ruins; views of mountains, canyons, and plains

Difficulty: Easy to moderate

Topo map: Lyons

Heil Ranch includes one of the most important elk-migration corridors in the county. Mountain lions, bobcats, black bears, mule deer, globally rare butterflies, wild turkeys, and raptors also thrive, and we once spotted two golden eagles, one of them carrying a prairie dog. Several old roads are closed to public use, and dogs are prohibited in order to protect wildlife and habitat. Various hiking permutations can be made by combining the Lichen and Ponderosa loops and the connecting Wapiti Trail.

Lichen Loop crosses an intermittent stream called Plumely Creek at Kiosk Bridge, near the upper parking area, and heads gently uphill. Soon after the trail forks, the right branch crosses over unusual examples of fossilized stromatolites, reddish rocks formed by lime-secreting blue-green algae found in marine environments. Look for ice-cream-scoop–size rocks with concentric rings. At the fork, take either branch and head up through meadows of native grasses and shrubs and past colorful lichen-covered boulders. In the ponderosa and Douglas-fir forest at the far end of the loop, a connecting trail to Wapiti branches to the right.

Wapiti Trail starts at the upper parking lot and follows an old farm road along Plumely Creek. The trail soon departs from the creek and heads uphill past a prairie-dog colony and into a ponderosa-pine forest where jays, woodpeckers, and nuthatches flourish and where spring beauties proliferate in April.

Lichen-covered rocks form "book ends" along the Lichen Trail, Heil Ranch

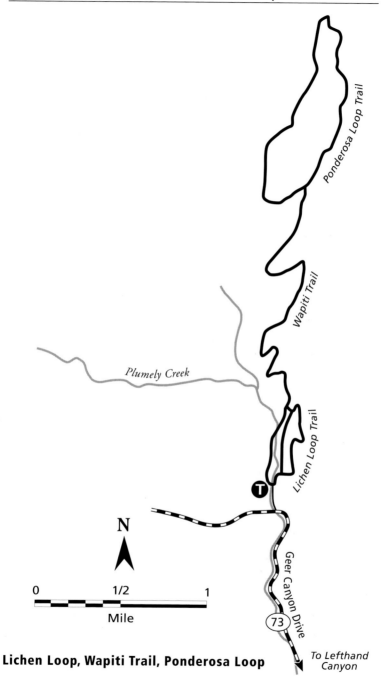

Lichen Loop, Wapiti Trail, Ponderosa Loop

Ponderosa Loop, which starts 2.5 miles up from the trailhead, balloons off of the Wapiti Trail. If you take the right branch first, you soon come to the stone foundations for several cabins, the remains of a substantial stone house, and several old quarries. Eventually, views of the South St. Vrain Canyon, Hall Ranch, and orange-pink rock formations such as Hat Rock and Indian Lookout Mountain open up below. At the high point, an overlook offers spectacular views of Longs Peak, Mount Meeker, and Sawtooth Mountain. Continue on the trail to close the loop.

History

Four prehistoric Native American sites dating back 5,000 years testify to the early use of this area. Solomon Geer, for whom Geer Canyon is named, homesteaded here in 1888. In 1996, Boulder County Open Space purchased 4,923 acres from the Heil family, who still ranch the area south of the trailhead.

Access

From US 36 north of Boulder, turn onto Lefthand Canyon Road. Go 0.6 mile and turn onto Geer Canyon Drive. Continue 1.25 miles to the parking area and trailhead.

Bald Mountain Scenic Area: Pines-to-Peak Trail

Distance: 1.5-mile loop

Elevation: 6,921 to 7,161 feet

Highlights: Views of peaks and plains, ponderosa-pine habitat, deer

Difficulty: Easy

Topo map: Boulder

Starting at the Bald Mountain picnic area, the Pines-to-Peak Trail goes through meadows and ponderosa-pine stands to Bald Mountain (7,161 feet) and loops back to the picnic area. Along the

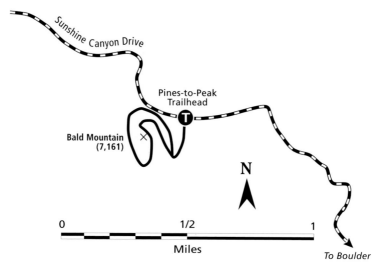

Bald Mountain Scenic Area: "Pines-to-Peak" Trail

well-marked trail are vistas of the plains and the foothills to the east and of the Continental Divide to the west. Because of its intermediate elevation, this area is good for off-season hikes. It is also a good place to take out-of-state visitors who are not yet acclimated.

History

An old corral and chute near the park entrance are historical remains of an 1886 homestead where cattle were raised. Ten years later, Frank and John Weist commenced mining in the area. Some of their exploratory pits can still be seen. The road up Sunshine Canyon was originally a military road called the Gordon-McHenry Road. It was named for the engineers who built it in the early 1860s and possibly was used by the army to intercept and attack Mormons on their way to Deseret. Intended to cross Arapaho Pass, the Gordon-McHenry Road turned west at Poorman Road and eventually petered out on the flats north of Caribou. Remnants of it can still be seen above Fourmile Canyon.

Along the Pines to Peak Trail, Bald Mountain Scenic Area

Access

The trailhead and picnic areas are 5 miles west of Boulder on the south side of Sunshine Canyon Drive. Sunshine Canyon is a continuation of Mapleton Avenue west of 4th Street.

Sugarloaf Mountain Trail

Distance: 0.5 mile one way

Elevation: 8,340 to 8,917 feet

Highlights: Spectacular views of peaks and plains

Difficulty: Easy

Topo map: Gold Hill

Sugarloaf is the symmetrical, conical mountain that dominates the foothills above Boulder. The trail provides a quick, somewhat steep workout with a reward at the top—views that encompass the Mummy Range, Longs Peak, the Indian Peaks, and Mount Evans. Below, the plains seem to stretch to infinity, and the many reservoirs sparkle like blue topazes.

Sugarloaf Mountain views

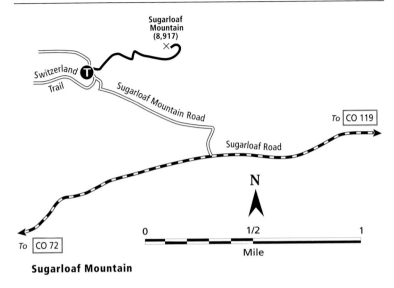

Sugarloaf Mountain

No signs mark the route, but it's easy to find. From the parking area, cross the road to the east. Go past a gate and head up the old (and stony) mining road, now closed to motorized vehicles. Douglas fir, ponderosa pine, stunted aspen groves, and lots of kinnikinnick line the road. As you near the exposed top, vegetation gives way to sandstone slabs of talus and blackened tree snags, a result of the 1989 Black Tiger wildfire that erupted after the temperature hit 100 degrees for two days in a row. The site of this raging fire that nearly destroyed the hillside community is now peaceful and teems with many species of wildflowers. Listen for nuthatches and woodpeckers.

Sugarloaf was a favorite hiking trail in the 1960s. Later, the privately owned trail was closed, and an out-of-state landowner planned to build a trophy home at the very top. Fortunately, in 1995 the county stepped in and purchased the summit.

Connections

- **The Switzerland Trail**, an old narrow-gauge railroad bed that once connected Ward to Eldora and to Boulder, intersects the Sugarloaf Mountain Road at the parking area. One of our favorite autumn hikes is along the spur that heads west toward Glacier

Lake from the parking area. There is little traffic on this stretch, and the aspen and asters are superb in late September.

Access

About a mile west of the tunnel in Boulder Canyon (SR 119), turn right onto Sugarloaf Road. Head uphill 4.9 miles to a dirt road called Sugarloaf Mountain Road. Turn right and continue another 0.8 mile to the unmarked parking area.

Anne U. White Trail

Distance: 1.7 miles one way

Elevation: 6,040 to 6,600 feet

Highlights: Lush streamside habitat, small waterfalls and pools, wildflowers, mossy rocks

Difficulty: Easy

Topo map: Boulder

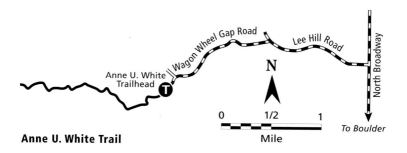

Anne U. White Trail

The trail goes gently uphill along Fourmile Canyon Creek, crossing it twenty-two times before dead-ending at private property. The stream is small, so crossings are no problem. Along the way, you pass many little pools, miniature waterfalls, and groves of aspen. Higher on the ridge, ponderosa pines and Douglas fir predominate. Pasqueflowers, shooting stars, sugarbowls, penstemon, and other wildflowers are prolific, and the running water attracts a variety of birds. Mountain lions and nesting hummingbirds have been seen here.

Shooting stars bloom along the Anne U. White Trail

Less than one mile up the trail atop a small hill, a sandstone bench invites hikers to sit and watch for wildlife along the stream below or on the rock formations across the canyon. Farther up, the trail passes through a small meadow and divides, with the left fork following the stream and the right fork climbing slightly higher. The two branches rejoin shortly before reaching a round pool fed by a small waterfall. The area is pungent with spearmint. Beyond this point, the canyon opens up a bit and the trail dead-ends below a rock outcropping.

The trail is named in memory of Anne Underwood White, who together with her husband, Gilbert White, donated twenty acres to establish the trail. In 1983, she wrote, "This steep little canyon is one of the few canyons near Boulder which has not yet had a road driven through it. It is a green and pleasant place with its rocky cliffs and ephemeral winding stream."

Access

From North Broadway, turn west onto Lee Hill Road and drive 1.1 miles to Wagonwheel Gap Road. Turn left and go 1 mile. Turn left again onto a dirt road that dead-ends in 0.2 mile. Park alongside the road.

Forsythe Canyon Creek Trail to Gross Reservoir

Distance: 1 mile one way

Elevation: 7,760 to 7,400 feet

Highlights: Waterfall, lush streamside habitat, wildflowers, secluded inlet of Gross Reservoir, views of Forsythe Rocks

Difficulty: Easy

Topo map: Tungsten

This riparian trail follows Forsythe Canyon Creek downhill through forests of pine, spruce, and Douglas fir, with occasional stands of aspen. It skirts a "secret" waterfall and dead-ends at an inlet of Gross Reservoir. Wildflowers are spectacular in late May and June, but there's a lot of deadfall along the trail; a heavy infestation of spruce budworm killed many of the Douglas firs. This area is a critical range for elk in winter, and the trail is usually icy.

From the parking area, follow an old jeep road downhill a short distance to Forsythe Canyon Creek. Just before reaching the creek, the main jeep road curves to the right. Take the branch that curves

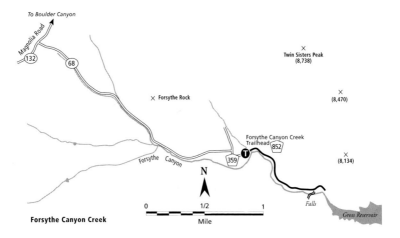

left. Descend to a sign for FS Trail 852. At the confluence of two streams, cross to the north side, and turn right. Follow the creek downstream to Gross Reservoir.

When you reach the waterfall, the trail becomes somewhat indistinct. The best route heads uphill to the left for a short distance, goes over a small hump, then descends to the foot of the falls. There is also a faint trail that crosses the boulders just to the left of the falls, but this route involves some rock scrambling. From the waterfall, return to the main trail to the left to avoid raspberry briars and stickery brush. Continue downhill to the inlet of the reservoir. Although the main trail dead-ends at the inlet, rough trails lead to several fishing spots at the reservoir itself.

Forsythe Falls

Access

From the Boulder Canyon road, take Magnolia Road (CR 132) for 6.8 miles to CR 68. Turn left and continue on CR 68 for 2.1 miles to FS Road 359, on your right. If the barricade is up, park alongside the road; otherwise, turn onto FS 359 and park in the open area at the beginning of the jeep road.

Foothills Trail

Distance: 2.8 miles (one way from Foothills Nature Center to US 36)

Elevation: 5,500 to 5,533 feet

Highlights: Wonderland Lake, Hogback Ridge, views of plains and foothills, wildflowers and native grasses, Indian game-drive wall

Difficulty: Easy

Topo map: Boulder

This area consists of rolling grasslands and a hogback that was burned over during the 1990 Olde Stage fire, started when a burning mattress was thrown from a window. The shale ridges are especially good for early wildflowers, and prairie-dog colonies attract raptors and other predators such as coyotes and, occasionally, mountain lions. Steer clear of the several unmarked paths that lead off from the main hiking trails; the main trails are well marked and easy to follow.

Although there are many possible starting points, this description begins at the Foothills Nature Center Trailhead on the south side of the center. The trail heads west, skirting the north side of Wonderland Lake, a wildlife refuge. Just beyond the lake, turn north and continue across grasslands for another 0.5 mile to an intersection with the Old Kiln Trail. The main trail forks right and crosses Lee Hill Road in 0.3 mile. Continue north and west for 0.8 mile to another junction. The right fork heads downhill 0.7 mile to the Foothills Trailhead on US 36. The left fork heads uphill to Hogback Ridge. A short distance below this fork, an unnamed trail heads

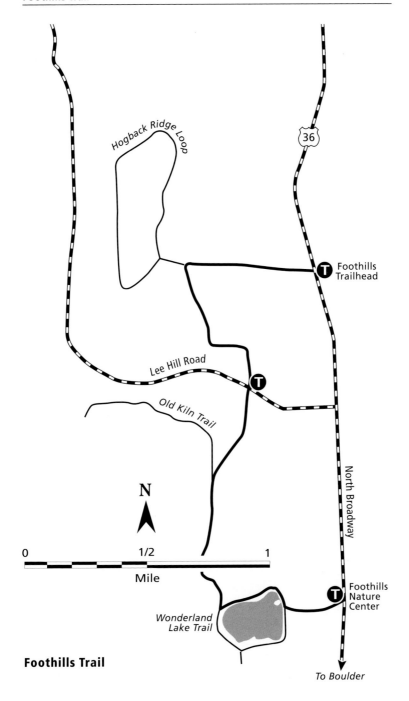

Hogback Ridge Loop

36

T Foothills
Trailhead

Lee Hill Road

T

Old Kiln Trail

N

North Broadway

0   1/2   1

Mile

T Foothills
Nature
Center

Wonderland
Lake Trail

Foothills Trail

To Boulder

Indian game drive wall along Foothills Trail

north on an old railroad grade toward the former Beech Aircraft facilities.

Before you drop down to the Foothills Trailhead, look for an old game-drive wall used by early American Indians. It looks like a crooked line of rocks to the north of the trail. Partway up the hill, the grading for the Boulder, Left Hand, and Middle Park Railroad cut through a portion of the wall in the 1880s. Although the railroad, which was projected to extend over Buchanan Pass, was not built, the grading is still visible.

Connections

- **Old Kiln Trail** branches to the left after the first half mile and dead-ends at a water tank in 0.7 mile. A lime-burning kiln, one of several that produced lime for the cement used to construct early Boulder buildings, can still be seen.

- **Hogback Ridge Loop** (1.7 miles) climbs to 6,300 feet and is worth a detour for the views and wildflowers.

Because of multiple trailheads and trail junctions, several loops or car shuttles are possible. The Foothills Trail also connects to the trail system at Boulder Valley Ranch (page 9).

Access

Trail access points are located at the Foothills Nature Center (4201 North Broadway); the Foothills Trailhead, 0.4 mile north of the intersection of US 36 and North Broadway; Fourmile Creek Trailhead on Lee Hill Road, 0.5 mile west of North Broadway; and Wonderland Lake Park at Poplar Avenue and Quince Circle.

Betasso Preserve

Betasso Preserve: Canyon Loop Trail

Distance: 3.2 miles round trip

Elevation: Starts at 6,480 feet, with a 460-foot loss and gain

Highlights: Ponderosa-pine forest, woodland birds, Abert's squirrels, views of the plains

Difficulty: Easy to moderate

Topo map: Boulder

From the east end of the Betasso Loop Road, the Canyon Loop Trail drops for about a mile through ponderosa-pine forest with Douglas fir in the moist ravines. After crossing a small, seasonal stream, the trail climbs back up through the forest into grassy meadows and joins an old fire road. Turn left (south) on this road, which leads past an old plum orchard, probably planted by Ronald McDonald who homesteaded here in 1922, and past the ruins of the McDonald cabin in a meadow below the trail.

When the fire road joins the Betasso Loop Road, turn left and return to the parking and picnic area. A slight detour near the road intersection leads up to some old farm machinery, some of which may have been used by the Blanchard family who started homesteading here in 1912, or by the Betasso family who raised cattle here starting in 1915. Ernie Betasso wanted to preserve the land, so he sold it to Boulder County Open Space in 1976.

On a hot day, you may find this trail more pleasant when done in reverse, taking advantage of the dense forest shade on the north-facing slopes for the uphill stretch. A mountain-biking link connects Betasso and Boulder Canyon. Mountain bikes are banned, however, on Wednesdays and Saturdays. Phone 303-441-4559 for current regulations.

Connections

- **Bummers Rock Trail** (0.3 mile round trip) takes off from the section of the Betasso Road that leads to the Boulder Filtration Plant and goes to a lookout point.

Betasso Preserve: Canyon Loop Trail

Access

From Boulder Canyon, turn north on Sugarloaf Road and go
0.8 mile. Turn right at the sign for the Betasso Filtration Plant and
go another half mile to where the road forks. The left fork goes to
a picnic area and trailheads, and the right fork to Bummers Rock
Trailhead and the Betasso Filtration Plant.

Biking on the Betasso Preserve

Mount Sanitas Loop

Distance: 3.1 miles round trip

Elevation: 5,520 to 6,863 feet

Highlights: Brilliantly colored sandstone formations, views of peaks and plains

Difficulty: Moderate to difficult

Topo map: Boulder

From the parking area at the mouth of Sunshine Canyon, walk behind the picnic pavilion, cross the bridge over the creek, and turn left at the Mount Sanitas sign. Follow the steep trail on the west side of the reddish sandstone formations, which are popular with

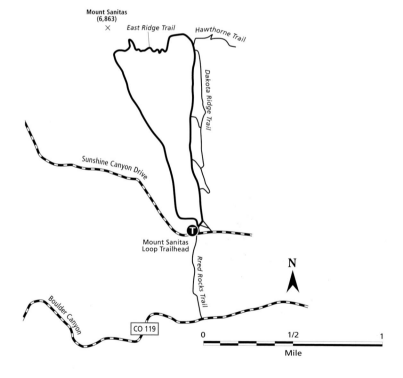

Mount Sanitas Loop

rock climbers. The trail continues to climb steeply past enormous lichen-encrusted boulders that have eroded into strange shapes and through ponderosa pines to culminate in 1.5 miles at one of the best overlooks of the City of Boulder. About halfway to the summit, the trail follows a ridge with views of snowcapped peaks to the west, the plains to the east, and Bear Peak and the Flatirons to the south. Look for raptors and listen for canyon wrens. And watch out for dog poop!

You can return via the same route or, to complete the loop, take the **East Ridge Trail** 1.8 miles. This trail drops steeply from the northeast side of the summit. It winds past sandstone slabs, passes several quarries that supplied the sandstone used in many University of Colorado campus buildings during the 1920s, and joins the **Sanitas Valley Trail**, an old fire road that was once a wagon road to the quarries. Turn right (south) on the road, which leads back through a grassy valley and returns to the parking area.

The mountain takes its name from the sanitarium, which was built in 1895 by Seventh-Day Adventists and became the present-day Mapleton Center. Some of the first hikers on Mount Sanitas were probably tuberculosis patients who came to Boulder for the good air. Although many people now emphasize the "e" sound for "i" in "Sanitas" and put the emphasis on the second syllable, the

Mount Sanitas viewed from Red Rocks Trail

name was originally pronounced "San-i-tas" as in "sanitarium," with the emphasis on the first syllable; many of us old-timers stick to the old pronunciation.

Connections

- **Dakota Ridge Trail** branches to the east of the Sanitas Valley Trail and meanders for 0.9 mile along the hogback east of Mount Sanitas. The 0.4-mile **Hawthorne Trail** is a spur connecting this trail system to Hawthorn Avenue.

- **Red Rocks** and **Anemone Hill trails** are on the south side of Sunshine Canyon and a short distance west.

Access

The trailhead is at the mouth of Sunshine Canyon, west of the Mapleton Center at Mapleton Avenue and 4th Street.

Red Rocks and Anemone Hill Loop

Distance: 2 miles round trip

Elevation: 5,440 to 6,040 feet

Highlights: Spectacular red sandstone formations, early blooming spring flowers, historical site

Difficulty: Easy to moderate

Topo map: Boulder

From Settlers Park on West Pearl Street, follow the trail that goes uphill to the east side of the red-rocks formation. Because this is a heavily used area, please stay on the designated trail.

Circle the rocks on the east side for views across the city. From the highest point on the trail, take the left-hand fork, circling the north end of the rock formation. A spur trail on the north side of the rocks and some rock scrambling will take you to the top of the formation.

The trail drops to a grassy saddle above the abandoned site of Sunshine Reservoir. At the four-way intersection, you can look down into Sunshine Canyon to the north and Boulder Canyon to the south. A depression between the saddle and Boulder Canyon is all that remains of Red Rocks Reservoir, Boulder's first reservoir, completed in 1876 and abandoned in 1906. The larger depression between the saddle and Sunshine Canyon held Sunshine Reservoir, Boulder's second water-storage facility built in 1891 and abandoned in the 1950s. Both were fed by Boulder Creek. The Sunshine Hydroelectric Facility, built in 1986, is just above the old Sunshine Reservoir.

Red Rocks formations on the Red Rocks-Anemone Hill Loop

From the saddle, continue uphill to the southwest. The trail ascends up the south side of Anemone Hill, named for the pasqueflowers that were once abundant here. The official trail ends at the aqueduct where Arapaho Peak suddenly looms into view. This trail is especially lovely in spring because of the many early blooming flowers in the irrigation ditches. We have seen phlox, flax, thimbleberry, evening primrose, spiderwort, and geraniums as early as April. Brush-loving birds also like to hide out in the wild plums and other shrubbery along the ditches.

Retrace your route back down Anemone Trail. When you return to the grassy saddle, take the trail to the south, which descends to Settlers Park and avoids the climb back up to the red rocks.

History

The first settlers in Boulder County were gold seekers from Nebraska, led here by Thomas A. Aikins. They camped near the red rocks. Uncertainty exists regarding the exact date of their arrival. October 17, 1858, was long accepted as the arrival date of the first settlers, based on an account written in 1880 by Amos Bixby. However, historian Tom Meier has done extensive research into letters and newspaper accounts written at the time of settlement and believes the party could not have arrived before December 21, 1858. Accounts also vary regarding the number and names of the first settlers.

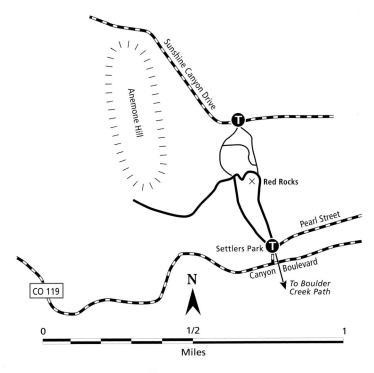

Red Rocks and Anemone Hill Loop

Several irrigation ditches built in the 1880s cut across this area. In the early 1900s, Frederick Law Olmsted recommended that the red rocks become a public park, and he called the city irrigation ditches "a veritable treasure of municipal decoration" that should be incorporated into "promenades."

Connections

- **Boulder Creek Path** (page 23) can be reached by following the sidewalk through the underpass beneath Canyon Boulevard to Eben G. Fine Park.
- **Mount Sanitas Trail** (page 71) begins north of the red rocks and on the north side of Sunshine Canyon.

Access

Start from Settlers Park at the west end of Pearl Street. You can also do this trail "backwards" by starting from the trailhead on the south side of Sunshine Canyon, almost directly across from Mount Sanitas, and taking the old service road up to the grassy saddle.

Flagstaff Trail

Distance: 1.5 miles one way

Elevation: 5,720 to 6,820 feet

Highlights: Views of mountains, plains, and city; coniferous forest, wildlife, wildflowers

Difficulty: Moderate

Topo map: Boulder, Eldorado Springs

Although this trail takes you across busy Flagstaff Road five times, it does lead you to the top of Flagstaff Mountain, one of Boulder's best-known landmarks, and offers good views of the Flatirons and the plains. The long straight line that stretches east, seemingly to infinity, is Baseline Road. It marks the fortieth parallel and is historically important because it once divided Nebraska Territory (a free state) from Kansas Territory (a slave state). It still marks the boundary between those states today.

The rather steep trail starts on the left side of Flagstaff Road at the turnoff for Baird Park. Along the trail, several side trails lead to popular rock climbs and viewpoints, but the main trail is always obvious. Spring and summer wildflowers are magnificent, and deer, squirrels, chipmunks, and birds are abundant. The trail culminates across the road from an old well built by the Civilian Conservation Corps (CCC) during the Great Depression.

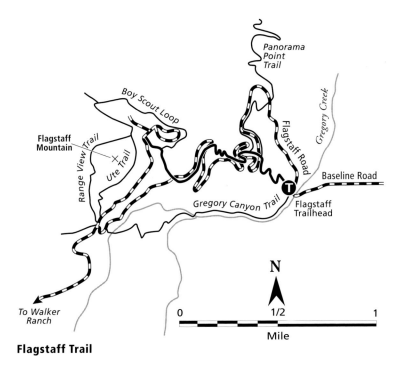

Flagstaff Trail

Follow the paved road up to the picnic area and the Sunrise Circle Amphitheater, also built by the CCC and often used for weddings. On summer weekends, stop to see the nature displays at the Flagstaff Summit Center. The best views of the Front Range are from Mays Point, which is connected to Artists Point by a short path leading downhill from the west end of Flagstaff Road. The

Views along the Flagstaff Trail

unmarked summit of Flagstaff Mountain (6,872 feet) is just south of the picnic area and about sixty additional feet in elevation.

History

In 1910, there was talk of building an amusement park on top of Flagstaff Mountain, to be reached by an inclined railway. Landscape architect Frederick Law Olmsted objected: "The scenery of Flagstaff Mountain is too noble, too magnificent, too precious to be wasted in serving as an almost unneeded accompaniment to the fun of roller coasters, moving pictures and vaudeville shows." He urged that it be left as "a place of quiet mountain scenery, remote and vast, where the weary can find peace."

Several stories exist explaining the name "Flagstaff." According to Martin Parsons, a park ranger in 1916 who patrolled the area on horseback, two men got into an argument. One man lost his shirt, and the victor tied it to the top of a dead pine tree visible from the city. From the turn of the century to 1947, flag contests were held annually by students from the Boulder Preparatory School. The "Onies" (freshmen) had two hours to plant a flag on the mountain while the "Toots" (sophomores) tried to wrest it from them. The first United States flag, a wooden one, was officially flown on Flagstaff Mountain on June 1, 1918.

Connections

(All of these trails are clearly signed.)

- **Range View Trail** or **Ute Trail** (page 80), starting near the picnic area, and **Gregory Canyon Trail** (page 82) can be combined with Flagstaff Trail for a loop hike. Descend to Realization Point, cross Flagstaff Road, and descend Gregory Canyon to Baird Park.

- **View Point** (or **Panorama Point**) **Trail** (1 mile; 560-foot gain) starts at 3rd Street and Arapahoe Avenue and joins the Flagstaff Trail near Panorama Point.

- **Boy Scout Trail** (0.8 mile; 140-foot gain) connects the Sunrise Circle Amphitheater and the picnic area, with a spur to Mays Point and Artists Point.

Access

Park at Baird Park and walk back down the road to the Flagstaff Trailhead near the spot where Baseline Road becomes Flagstaff Road.

Range View Trail

Distance: 0.6 mile one way

Elevation: 6,748 to 6,800 feet

Highlights: Views of the Indian Peaks, wildlife

Difficulty: Easy

Topo map: Boulder, Eldorado Springs

Most foothills trails provide "windows" through which we can peek at the Indian Peaks, but Range View Trail from Flagstaff Road to Artists Point offers one continuous view. The coniferous forest you pass through provides habitat for Abert's squirrels, blue grouse, crossbills, and other conifer-loving creatures but does not block the view. From Realization Point, the trail climbs up the west side of Flagstaff Mountain. At the summit, the trail connects with the Boy Scout Trail, which goes along a dirt road for a short distance to Artists Point, where a spur leads northwest to Mays Point.

Connections

- **Tenderfoot Loop** (2.1 miles; 250-foot elevation gain) branches to the left almost immediately and goes uphill and downhill through coniferous forest.

- **Ute** and **Boy Scout Trails** join Range View Trail near the summit and can be combined for an easy loop. Ponderosa pines growing in an almost perfect, hundred-foot-long row delineate a section of trail once used by the Utes, possibly as far back as the sixteenth century. See map on page 77 for Boy Scout Trail.

- **Gregory Canyon** (page 82), **Greenman**, and **Ranger trails** (page 87) begin across the road from Realization Point. You can make

View from Flagstaff

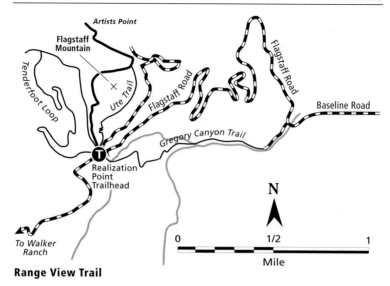

Range View Trail

a long loop by combining Flagstaff, Range View or Ute, and Gregory Canyon trails.

Access

Park at Realization Point 3.4 miles up Flagstaff Road, where the road intersects with Chapman Drive.

Gregory Canyon Trail

Distance: 1.1 miles one way

Elevation: 5,800 to 6,680 feet

Highlights: Wildflowers, brush-loving birds, red-rock formations, streamside habitat

Difficulty: Moderate

Topo map: Eldorado Springs

This short but steep trail climbs above Gregory Creek and offers edge-on views of the Flatirons. In springtime, it's one of the best wildflower hikes in the county. Apple and plum trees (and lots of poison ivy) are thick at the beginning of the trail and give way to pine trees near the top. Listen for canyon and rock wrens and other brush-loving birds. Chipmunks and golden-mantled ground squirrels are common.

About halfway up, the trail crosses a side creek, ascends through ponderosa pines to a grassy meadow, and ends at a dirt road across from Realization Point, where several trails diverge.

History

The canyon is named for John Gregory, an early gold miner who in the 1860s built a road up the canyon to his mines at Black Hawk. This canyon was the main route to Black Hawk for many years. Gregory's "corduroy road" consisted of logs placed close together across the route and was almost impassable. Several other attempts were made to build a road up the canyon, and finally, in 1873, a rough road was built and used until Flagstaff Road was completed in 1906.

Many old apple trees along this trail were probably planted by Ernest Greenman. (See Green Mountain Loop Via E. M. Greenman and Ranger Trails for more information on Ernest Greenman.)

Mariposa Lily

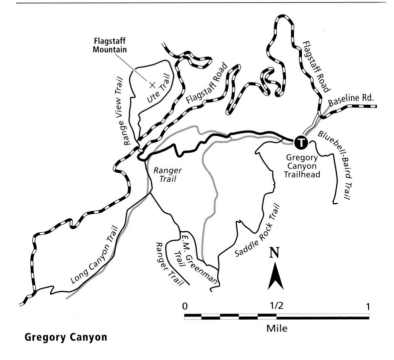

Gregory Canyon

Connections

- **Greenman** and **Ranger trails** (page 87) begin a short distance to the left of the meadow below Realization Point; continue up these trails for a strenuous climb of Green Mountain.

- **Range View** and **Ute trails** (page 80) begin across the road from Realization Point. To return to the trailhead via a different route, combine these trails with Flagstaff Trail (see page 76).

- **Bluebell-Baird** (page 90) and **Saddle Rock trails** (page 85) also start from Baird Park.

Access

At the spot where Baseline Road becomes Flagstaff Road, turn left onto a road that promptly dead-ends at Gregory Canyon Trailhead in Baird Park. The Gregory Canyon Trail begins to the left of the outhouse.

Saddle Rock and Amphitheater Loop

Distance: 1.3 miles one way

Elevation: 5,800 to 7,050 feet

Highlights: Red-rock formations, dense coniferous forest

Difficulty: Moderate to strenuous

Topo map: Eldorado Springs

This short but steep trail provides a good workout and leads to a prominent rock formation. For much of the distance it follows Contact Canyon, which contains remnants of old logging roads and was used for conditioning by skiers training for the Olympics in the 1960s. The trail starts together with the Gregory Canyon Trail (see above) but almost immediately forks to the left, crosses Gregory Creek, and heads uphill through a dense Douglas-fir and ponderosa-pine forest. Shortly after leaving a tributary of Gregory Creek, the trail joins the Amphitheater Trail. For a short loop, you can turn left at this point and descend back to the trailhead.

The Saddle Rock Trail continues to zigzag up to another junction. The left branch goes to the First Flatiron, and the right branch enters a more open area with good views of the First Flatiron, edge-on, and of the City of Boulder. Continue on the right branch. Although aptly named Saddle Rock is conspicuous from many points in the city, it's easy to miss from the trail, which actually

Green Mountain and Saddle Rock from Flagstaff Trail

passes above it. At the crest of the ridge where the Indian Peaks become visible, there are some rather insignificant rocks on the right. Saddle Rock is north of these rocks and is reached by a short, easy scramble.

Return via this same route until you reach the marked junction of the Amphitheater and Saddle Rock trails. Continue down the right branch, which passes under a semicircle of sandstone formations called "the Amphitheater," a popular area for rock climbing, to reach the trailhead.

Connections

- **E. M. Greenman Trail** (page 87) is a short distance beyond Saddle Rock. Continue along the crest and drop down to join Greenman, at which point you can either turn left to climb

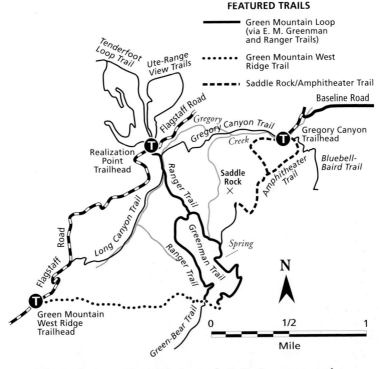

Saddle Rock, Green Mountain Loop via E. M. Greenman and Ranger Trails, and Green Mountain West Ridge Trail

Green Mountain or turn right to return to the trailhead via Gregory Canyon (see page 82).

- **Bluebell-Baird Trail** (page 90) joins the Amphitheater Trail just before Baird Park.

Access

At the spot where Baseline Road becomes Flagstaff Road, turn left onto a road that promptly dead-ends at the Gregory Canyon Trailhead in Baird Park. Both the Saddle Rock and the Gregory Canyon trails begin to the left of the outhouse.

Green Mountain Loop
Via E. M. Greenman and Ranger Trails

Distance: 3.3 miles round trip

Elevation: 6,748 to 8,144 feet

Highlights: Views of peaks and plains from the top, coniferous-forest habitat, ladybugs on the summit

Difficulty: Moderate

Topo map: Eldorado Springs

From the west end of the parking area across from Realization Point, walk a short distance down the dirt road to a small meadow. Turn right and follow the old road to the Green Mountain Lodge. A sign for the Ranger Trail is on the left side of the lodge. Follow this trail up through a moist, coniferous forest thick with bracken fern, moss, and various species of wintergreen. Several unusual plants, including rare orchids, grow on the north slopes of this mountain, and numerous species of butterflies nectar on the flowers in the meadow below the lodge.

In 0.3 mile, the Ranger Trail forks to the right. Turn left onto the Greenman Trail, which contours into another gulch and is soon joined by the Saddle Rock Trail; both junctions are well marked. Shortly after the Saddle Rock sign, Greenman Trail crosses a small stream below Greenman Springs and begins to climb steeply, mak-

Green Mountain from Flagstaff Road

ing numerous switchbacks up to the Green Mountain summit. A viewfinder identifies the peaks from Mount Evans to Longs Peak, and in autumn and early spring, ladybugs sometimes congregate here.

From the summit, drop down to the west on the Green Mountain West Ridge Trail. Very soon the Ranger Trail branches to the right and drops steeply via switchbacks to the junction with the Greenman Trail, ending at Green Mountain Lodge.

History

The Greenman Trail is named for Ernest Greenman, Boulder's "Johnny Appleseed" who arrived in 1896 and planted hundreds of apple trees. The descendants of these trees still bear fruit throughout the foothills. His niece, Dorothy Greenman, recalled that when they walked in the mountains, he carried seeds of all kinds in his pockets and scattered them around the springs. He was one of the founders of the Rocky Mountain Climbers Club and led more than a hundred climbs of the Third Flatiron and more than thirty trips to Arapaho Peak. His photo collection, stored in the Carnegie Library, shows climbers standing atop Longs and other local peaks. According to Greenman, a trail existed on Green Mountain "as far back as 1917." The Ranger Trail is named for Martin Parsons, an early park ranger who patrolled on horseback and probably built the trail. His photo collection is also an important historic source.

Connections

- **Gregory Canyon Trail** (page 82) turns east at the meadow below Flagstaff Road. You can do a strenuous hike to Green Mountain by starting at the Gregory Canyon Trailhead.

- **Saddle Rock Trail** (page 85) branches east from the E. M. Greenman Trail shortly below the springs.

- **Range View, Ute,** and **Tenderfoot trails** (page 80) begin across Flagstaff Road at Realization Point.

- **Long Canyon Trail** (1.1 miles; 740-foot gain) begins on the right side of Green Mountain Lodge and follows upper Gregory Creek through lush wildflower gardens to emerge on Flagstaff Road just south of Cathedral Park picnic area.

- **Green Mountain West Ridge Trail** (1.4 miles; 640-foot gain) is the easiest route up Green Mountain and provides an almost continuous, unobstructed view of the Front Range to the west. It's also snow-free much earlier in the spring than either the Greenman or the Ranger trails. Starting on Flagstaff Road 1.6 miles southwest of Realization Point, the trail goes gently down and up, down and up to a junction below the summit of Green Mountain. At this point, the Ranger Trail descends to the left, and the Green Bear Trail heads to the right (southwest) to Bear Canyon. The main trail ascends steeply to the summit of Green Mountain. If you use two cars, you can ascend this trail and descend via either the Greenman or the Ranger trails.

Access

Drive up Flagstaff Road 3.4 miles to a three-way intersection and park in the area to the left, opposite Realization Point.

Bluebell-Baird Trail

Distance: 0.7 mile one way

Elevation: 5,800 to 6,000 feet

Highlights: Ponderosa pines, spring wildflowers, colorful fall shrubs

Difficulty: Easy

Topo map: Eldorado Springs

Starting at the south side of Baird Park, this trail crosses Gregory Creek, diverges from the Amphitheater Trail, climbs through a meadow filled with native grasses, continues through a ponderosa-pine forest, and ends at the Bluebell Shelter. Bluebell-Baird serves primarily as an access trail to several other trails. However, about halfway along the trail in autumn, a red sumac patch frames an outstanding view of the First Flatiron and, in spring, some of the best stands of coralroot orchids grow here.

History

The trail and the park are named for Dr. and Mrs. William Baird, who donated 160 acres in Gregory Canyon to the city in 1908. In the 1930s, the Civilian Conservation Corps built a trail connecting Gregory Canyon with Bluebell Canyon. In 1948, Harris Thompson built a 200-foot rope tow (later extended another 850 feet uphill), powered by a Dodge gasoline engine. He and Steve Bradley, University of Colorado ski coach, operated the Mesa Ski Slope for a few seasons. You can still see the grass-covered mound that served as a ski jump.

Flatirons framed in sumac, from Chautauqua meadow

Connections

- **Amphitheater Trail** (page 85) branches to the right after the Gregory Creek crossing.

- **Chautauqua Trail** (0.6 mile; 440-foot elevation loss) branches to the left and terminates at Chautauqua Park.

- **Ski Jump Trail** (0.2 mile; 160-foot loss) also branches left and goes past the site of the Mesa Ski Slope to join Chautauqua Trail.

Author in sumac along the Bluebell-Baird Trail

- **Bluebell Mesa Trail** (0.6 mile; 340-foot loss) also branches left and joins the Chautauqua Trail. To make a loop trip, walk down the road from the Bluebell Shelter to the Chautauqua Trail and take one of these three trails back up to the Bluebell-Baird Trail.

- **First** and **Second Flatiron Trail** (1.1 miles; 960-foot elevation gain) makes steep switchbacks up the hill to the right just before the Bluebell Shelter and leads to the famous Flatiron formations.

- **Mesa Trail** (page 96) begins just below the Bluebell Shelter.

Access

Turn left onto a road at the point where Baseline Road becomes Flagstaff Road. The road promptly dead-ends at a small parking area at the Gregory Canyon Trailhead in Baird Park.

Royal Arch Trail

Distance: 1.4 miles one way

Elevation: 5,680 to 6,950 feet

Highlights: Large sandstone arch, views of the plains and of flat-iron formations, coniferous forest

Difficulty: Moderate

Topo map: Eldorado Springs

This is a short, steep trail that frequently ascends via stone "stairs" or log risers. The reward at the end is a twenty-foot sandstone arch framing views of Boulder Valley to the southeast and red-rock formations to the north. From the Chautauqua Park parking lot, walk 0.6 mile up the old Bluebell Road (closed to traffic) to the Bluebell Shelter. The Royal Arch Trail begins just above the shelter, veers to the left, and continues through a ponderosa-pine forest. After crossing Bluebell Creek, which is often dry, the trail zigzags uphill past a viewpoint at a rock outcropping and continues to a saddle, called Sentinel Pass, with excellent views of the south face of the Third Flatiron and of the two "ironing boards." In spring, falcons and

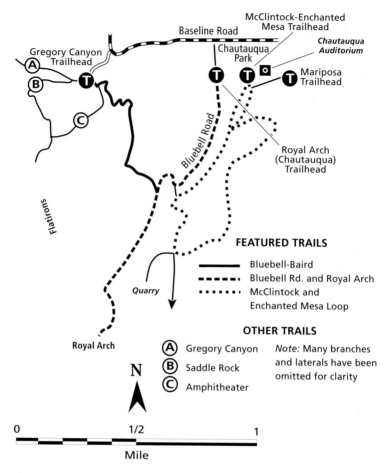

FEATURED TRAILS

──────── Bluebell-Baird

━ ━ ━ ━ ┅ Bluebell Rd. and Royal Arch

• • • • • • • McClintock and
Enchanted Mesa Loop

OTHER TRAILS

(A) Gregory Canyon

(B) Saddle Rock

(C) Amphitheater

Note: Many branches
and laterals have been
omitted for clarity

0   1/2   1

Mile

**Bluebell-Baird Trail, Royal Arch, and McClintock
and Enchanted Mesa Loop**

other raptors often nest in the Flatirons. Listen for their shrill cries
as well as the cascading song of the canyon wrens.

At the saddle, the trail drops abruptly to the left for about one
hundred feet into another gulch and then climbs very steeply up to
the arch. When you come to a slot cave and a small spring, you are
almost there. Parts of this trail may be rerouted in the future.

Royal Arch

History

For many years, this arch, which looks like two kissing marmots, was an annual goal for climbers from Chautauqua. Early photos show ladies in long skirts and gentlemen in coats and ties resting beneath the window. According to Pat Ament and Cleve McCarty in *High Over Boulder*, the arch was discovered by Lawrence Bass of Boulder, and the first trail to it was built about 1898 by "Rocky Mountain Joe" Sturtevant, an early Boulder photographer and hiking guide. It was named by Edwin Chamberlin, one of the founders of the Rocky Mountain Climber's Club, who was studying for his Masonic Royal Arch Degree at the time. The city purchased the land in 1920, and the present trail was built the following year by the Boulder Rotarians, with help from the Boy Scouts, Ernest Greenman, and Eben G. Fine.

Connections

• Third Flatiron Trail (0.3 mile; 480-foot elevation gain) veers right about 0.1 mile up from the trailhead and is chiefly an access trail for rock climbers.

Access

Start at the Bluebell Shelter, approaching it either from Chautauqua Park or from the Bluebell-Baird Trail at Baird Park. Mileage for this hike is determined from Chautauqua Park.

Mesa Trail

Distance: 6.9 miles one way

Elevation: 5,680 to 5,600 feet (north to south), with many ups and downs totaling about 1,400 feet of elevation loss and gain

Highlights: Views of the Flatirons and other rock formations; a variety of habitats, wildflowers; wildlife; access to many other trails

Difficulty: Moderate

Topo map: Eldorado Springs

Hiking the Mesa Trail

Because this trail goes through habitats ranging from ponderosa-pine forests to grasslands to wetlands, the variety of wildflowers and wildlife is exceptional, even though there is little elevation change. Deer are abundant, and black bears, coyotes, foxes, and mountain lions are sometimes sighted. Golden eagles and prairie falcons nest in the cliffs, and in 1991, peregrine falcons returned to nest near the Flatirons after an absence of more than thirty-five years.

Although you can hike the trail from either direction, this description starts on the north end, at the Chautauqua parking area. Walk 0.6 mile up the paved road (closed to traffic) to a point just below the Bluebell Shelter where the Mesa Trail veers left. It goes up and down hills, across mesas, and into canyons. Occasionally, an old road remnant strays off to the left or right, going to an abandoned cabin or a stone quarry.

En route, you cross six major canyons. Lateral trails drop down Bluebell, Shanahan, and Skunk canyons and head up Bear, Fern, and Shadow canyons. You hike below such well-known rock formations as the Flatirons, Seal Rock, Devils Thumb, the Maiden, and the Matron. See below for a description of our favorite lateral trails, all of which are clearly signed.

The main trail heads in a generally southerly direction. Near Shadow Canyon, the trail forks, but the two branches soon rejoin, and the trail meanders down past the historic Doudy-Debacker-Dunn House, ending at the South Mesa Trailhead on Eldorado Springs Drive.

History

When Boulder mountaineer Ernest Greenman was in his eighties, Cleve McCarty published his reminiscences in *High Over Boulder*. Greenman remembered working with the Rocky Mountain Climber's Club and the Boulder Chamber of Commerce to place two hundred cairns between Boulder and Eldorado Springs: "We blazed trees, trimmed limbs, and made a little trail clear across there in '24." Long before this, however, there had been primitive tollroads and quarry roads that were later incorporated into the Mesa Trail. The old Anderson Quarry, which supplied stone for the historic Boulder Depot, is at the turnoff for Skunk Canyon, and the Wood-Bergheim Quarry is a short distance from the Enchanted Mesa intersection.

Several cabins are moldering away along the trail. Harriet and Frank Roosa built a tiny stone hut a short distance before the Anderson Quarry, and near the south end of the Mesa Trail, domestic iris still grow beside a fallen-down wooden shack called the School-marm's Cabin. According to Dock Teegarden, who has unearthed a wealth of local history, it was used by Miss Florence Lane, a red-headed Denver schoolteacher who drove her Model T Ford up the road for weekend and summer retreats in the 1920s and 1930s.

When Andrew Doudy first settled in the area around 1859, there were still traces of Native American camps, tepee rings, and arrowheads. Doudy, the first settler here, built a gristmill, sawmill, and a wooden house near South Boulder Creek. The flood of 1864 washed out the mills but not the house, which was purchased, along with the surrounding land, by John Debacker in 1869 for five hundred dollars. Debacker added the two-story stone house that still stands on the site and used water from an irrigation ditch to power a waterwheel that drove a cream separator and a washing machine.

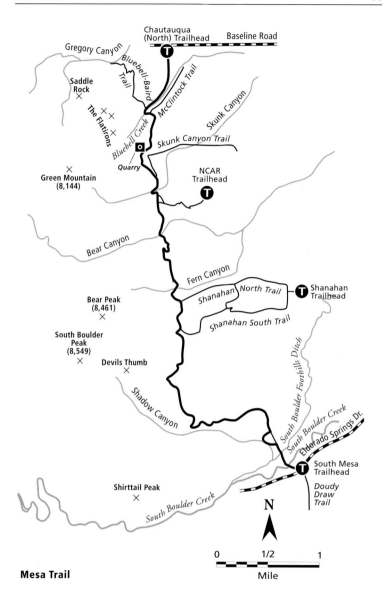

Mesa Trail

In 1901, Debacker turned the property over to his daughter Emma and her husband, John Dunn, who raised dairy cattle here until John Dunn's death in 1953. The City of Boulder purchased the property in 1969 and demolished the wooden portion of the house for safety reasons. The stone walls in the area were built by out-of-work miners who, in the 1870s, removed rocks from Debacker's fields in exchange for food and lodging.

See the lateral trails below for additional historic tidbits.

Connections (North to South)

- **Bluebell-Baird Trail** (page 90) begins at the Bluebell Shelter near the north end of the Mesa Trail.

- **Royal Arch Trail** (page 93) begins at the Bluebell Shelter.

- **McClintock** and **Enchanted Mesa Loop** (page 103) begins at the picnic shelter south of Chautauqua Auditorium.

- **Skunk Canyon** (1.3 miles; 550-foot elevation loss) drops to the east from the Mesa Trail 1.3 miles from the Bluebell Shelter and crosses two gullies where brush-loving birds shelter, to end at the west end of Deer Valley Road. About halfway down, a trail to Kohler Mesa branches to your left and joins a network of trails on Enchanted Mesa.

- **Mallory Cave Trail** (page 107) joins the Mesa Trail just south of the intersection with the Dakota Trail.

- **Bear Canyon**, **Bear Peak**, **Fern Canyon Loop** (page 111) heads up Bear Canyon a short distance southwest of NCAR.

- **Shanahan North** and **South trails** (1.6 miles each) branch to the east. North Trail splits off 0.6 mile south of Bear Canyon and loses about 880 feet; South Trail splits at 1.1 miles and loses 660 feet. The trails cross a mesa and descend through a ponderosa-pine forest that is rich in penstemon and arnica in June and join a short distance above Hardscrabble Drive.

- **Big Bluestem Trail** (page 115) heads east 1.8 miles south of Bear Canyon.

- **South Boulder Creek Trail** (page 27) forks east 0.7 mile from the South Mesa Trailhead.

- **Shadow Canyon to South Boulder Peak** (page 118) branches west from the Mesa Trail near the upper intersection of Towhee and Homestead trails.

Devils Thumb along Shadow Canyon Trail

- **Towhee and Homestead Loop** (page 122) begins at the Doudy-Debacker-Dunn House.

Access

The two main access points are the ranger cottage at Chautauqua (the turnoff is one block west of Baseline and 9th Street) and the South Mesa Trailhead on Eldorado Springs Drive, 2 miles west of SR 93. There are several other access points, such as NCAR at the

Cross-country skiing below the Flatirons

west end of Table Mesa Drive, the Shanahan Trailhead beyond the end of Hardscrabble Drive, the Enchanted Mesa Trailhead at the Chautauqua Picnic Area, and the South Boulder Creek Trailhead at SR 93 and Thomas Lane.

McClintock and Enchanted Mesa Loop

Distance: 2.5 miles round trip (See map on page 94)

Elevation: 5,730 to 6,160 feet

Highlights: Self-guided nature trail, wildflowers, brush-loving birds, deer

Difficulty: Easy

Topo map: Eldorado Springs

This trail starts in plum and hawthorn thickets and climbs into an open, parklike forest of ponderosa pines where early spring pasqueflowers and spring beauties abound. The ponderosa pines are good places to look for Abert's squirrels. From the picnic shelter south of Chautauqua Auditorium, the McClintock Trail descends to cross Bluebell Creek. Almost immediately it forks, with the left branch descending to Mariposa Avenue. Take the right branch that climbs to intersect the Enchanted Mesa Road, which is closed to traffic. Cross the road and continue uphill, paralleling Bluebell Creek. The interpretive plaques are in memory of Henry H. Mc-Clintock, for whom the trail is named. He was a former member of the park board.

When the McClintock Trail reaches the Mesa Trail, turn left (south) and continue 0.3 mile to a major trail intersection. The Mesa Trail continues straight ahead, and the right fork goes 0.3 mile to the abandoned Woods-Bergheim Sandstone Quarry. Take the left fork and go downhill past a covered city reservoir to the Enchanted Mesa Road. This road again intersects the McClintock Trail at Bluebell Creek. Return to Chautauqua Park via either the McClintock Trail or the Enchanted Mesa Road, which is very good for ski touring when there is sufficient snow.

Pasqueflower, McClintock and Enchanted Mesa Loop

"Save Enchanted Mesa" was the rallying cry for environmentalists when the mesa was threatened by a proposal for a luxury hotel in the early 1960s. At that time, it became obvious that the Blue Line (a line above which the city would not provide water or sewer service) would not prevent development of the mountain backdrop. Boulder citizens passed a bond issue to purchase the mesa.

Connections

- **Kohler Mesa Trail** (various permutations, all short and easy) branches south from Enchanted Mesa Trail a short distance below the Mesa Trail intersection. It later splits. A left branch goes downhill to the **Four Pines Trail**, which ends at the corner of 17th Street and King Avenue. A right branch heads uphill to join the Mesa Trail. The straight-ahead branch goes down to Skunk Canyon.

Access

Park near the Chautauqua Park picnic pavilion south of the auditorium. The turnoff for Chautauqua is 1 block west of 9th Street off of Baseline Road.

Walter Orr Roberts Nature Trail

Distance: 0.2 mile one way

Elevation: About 6,000 to 6,051 feet

Highlights: Views of Flatirons and plains, access to NCAR, deer, wildflowers, interpretive weather signs

Difficulty: Easy

Topo map: Eldorado Springs

This red gravel trail was named for Walter Orr Roberts, a conservationist and a world-renowned physicist who was instrumental in founding the National Center for Atmospheric Research (NCAR). The trail starts on the northwest side of NCAR and goes to the west end of Table Mountain Mesa, looping around the plateau with spectacular views of the Flatirons, Bear Peak, and Boulder Valley. It's an ideal place to take out-of-town guests who don't have much time or are not acclimated for hiking. To prevent erosion caused by heavy use, please stay on the trail.

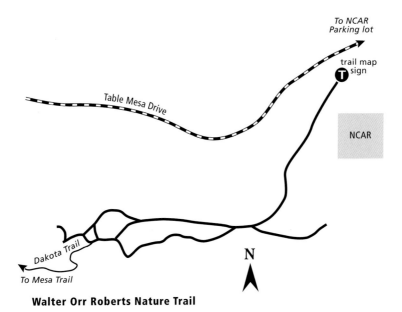

Walter Orr Roberts Nature Trail

Walter Orr Roberts Trail in the winter

Herds of mule deer can almost always be seen, and wildflowers are spectacular in spring. Along the way, interpretive signs explain weather and climate phenomena. When you read the "brown cloud" sign, look east to observe the real thing. The award-winning NCAR building, designed by I. M. Pei, simulates the pink sandstone of the Flatirons. Crushed Lyons sandstone was mixed with the concrete to tint it pink. Inside, you can view additional exhibits on the sun, atmospheric phenomena, climate, and the flora and fauna of the mesa as well as changing art exhibits.

Connections

- **Dakota Trail** forks to the south at the far end of the loop, connecting NCAR to the Mesa Trail in about half a mile. If you take this link, look for wild iris in late May in the dip before climbing to the water tank.

Access

Take Table Mesa Drive west to where it dead-ends at the NCAR parking lot. Public parking is permitted.

Mallory Cave Trail

Distance: 1.1 miles one way

Elevation: 6,080 to 7,020 feet

Highlights: One of few accessible caves in Boulder County, views of Boulder Valley, colorful rock slabs, bats

Difficulty: Moderate to strenuous (tricky rock scramble at end)

Topo map: Eldorado Springs

Don't expect stalactites, stalagmites, or crystals in Mallory Cave. It's a fairly small, shallow, sandstone cave blackened by smoke, but since there are so few caves in the area, it's exciting to find. The shortest approach is to take the Walter Orr Roberts Trail, starting on the west side of NCAR, and then the Dakota Trail, which crosses over the Dakota Formation to a water tank. Just before reaching the Mesa Trail, you come to a fork. The left fork leads down to the Mallory Cave sign.

The Mallory Cave Trail climbs through Douglas-fir and ponderosa-pine trees along the flank of Dinosaur Mountain. About halfway between the Mesa Trail and the cave, the trail goes up a stone "staircase" between slabs of pink sandstone. Eventually, you come to a fork with a sign indicating the right branch goes to climbing rocks and the left branch to the cave. Beyond this sign you begin the final scramble up a slab and through a keyhole to the cave. There is mild exposure on the last fifty feet, but there are plenty of hand- and footholds. Technical climbing skills are not needed. The stone tower above the cave is called Sharks Fin. Seasonal closings in summer and early fall protect the Townsend's big-eared bats that sleep upside down on the roof of the cave during the day.

History

Mallory Cave was discovered by E. C. Mallory in August 1932 when he was eighteen years old and just out of the State Preparatory School. "I always wanted to explore where no one else went," he says. So one night his friend Martin Parsons, a ranger in Boulder Mountain Parks, suggested the area on Dinosaur Mountain. Mallory, on a solo hike, was searching for a trail through the ridges when he found the cave. Two huge stumps, obviously cut by saws, were in front of the cave. Parsons said that many years earlier, two men cutting lumber had talked about a cave, but it was not recorded and had been lost until Mallory came upon it. For many years, Mallory kept the cave a secret. Eventually, at Parsons' urging, he put up a sign saying, "Rediscovered 1932 by E. C. Mallory."

Access

Park at NCAR at the west end of Table Mesa Drive. Any access point for the Mesa Trail will also work.

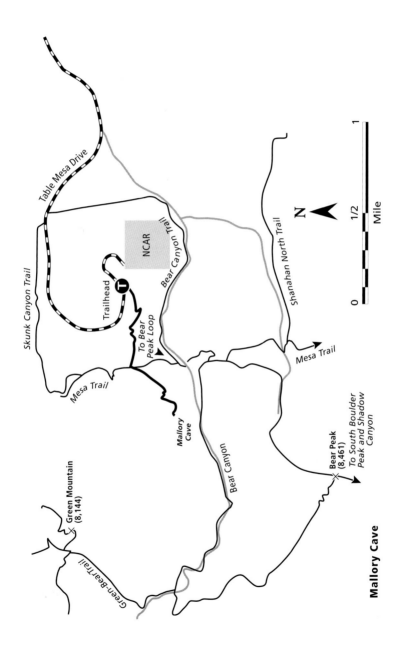

Mallory Cave

Mallory Cave

Bear Peak Loop Via Bear Canyon, Bear Peak West Ridge, and Fern Canyon

Distance: 7.7 miles round trip

Elevation: 6,080 to 8,461 feet

Highlights: Views of peaks and plains, cascading creek, lush canyons, rock slabs

Difficulty: Strenuous

Topo map: Eldorado Springs

Bear Peak, with rounded shoulders and a pointy summit, is one of Boulder's most prominent landmarks. Several routes lead to the top, but this is one of the prettiest. Take the Walter Orr Roberts Trail from the west side of NCAR to the Dakota Trail, which intersects with the Mesa Trail. Turn left (south) on the Mesa Trail, which soon drops to Bear Canyon Road (closed to traffic). Continue across Bear Creek and go partway up the next hill where a sign points to Bear Canyon on your right (north). Follow the Bear Canyon Trail past a utility tower, and continue uphill paralleling the creek, which the trail crosses numerous times. Poison ivy grows luxuriantly along the lower part of this trail along with wildflowers. Willows, cottonwoods, aspen, and flowering shrubs also grow along the creek bottom.

At 1.7 miles up the canyon, you come to a junction. Take the left fork up the Bear Peak West Ridge through a coniferous and scattered aspen forest. This ridge walk offers views of the Indian Peaks, Walker Ranch, a sawtooth ridge on Green Mountain, and the plains. Near the summit, the trail becomes quite steep, and there is a bit of a rock scramble at the top—but the view is worth it. In late spring and summer, swallows dart so near you can hear the swoosh of their wings.

Just below the summit, a sign points to the Fern Canyon Trail, which descends the northeast ridge to a fern-filled gulch where raptors often nest in dramatic rock formations, such as Seal Rock. This trail is shorter than the route up but is extremely steep, losing more than 2,000 feet of elevation in 1.2 miles. If you have knee problems, retrace your steps, taking the Bear Canyon route down. When the Fern Canyon Trail rejoins the Mesa Trail, turn left to complete the loop.

History

In 1861, just three years after the first white encampment in Boulder, Henry Norton, a road builder, and George Williamson, a miner, built a wagon road up Bear Canyon to Black Hawk and Central City. The road soon washed away. Others also tried, but storms destroyed their efforts five times. In 1885, the route was abandoned.

Connections

- **South Boulder Peak** (8,549 feet) is separated from Bear Peak by 0.7 mile, so both can be climbed in a single outing. Just below the summit of Bear Peak on the northwest side, a sign marks the route to South Boulder Peak and to Shadow Canyon, which descends to the Mesa Trail in 1.7 miles.

- **Green-Bear Trail** (0.9 mile) forks to the right at a trail junction and leads to the Green Mountain West Ridge Trail, which climbs Green Mountain. If you park one car at NCAR and another at the Green Mountain West Ridge Trailhead, you can make a one-way hike by connecting these trails through Bear Canyon.

Access

Park at NCAR at the west end of Table Mesa Drive. Any access point to the Mesa Trail will also work but will be a longer hike.

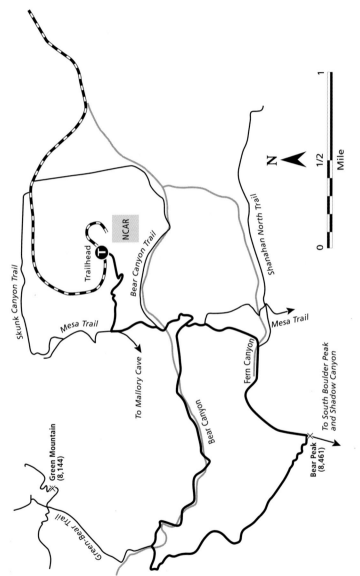

Bear Peak Loop via Bear Canyon, Bear Peak West Ridge, and Fern Canyon

Bear Peak in the winter

Big Bluestem and South Boulder Creek Loop

Distance: 4.3 miles (short loop), or 7.1 miles (long loop)

Elevation: 5,490 to 5,800 feet (short loop), or to 6,200 feet (long loop)

Highlights: Native grasses, sumac, views of Flatiron formations

Difficulty: Easy to moderate

Topo map: Eldorado Springs, Louisville

From the parking area at the pond, walk up Thomas Lane to where it dead-ends at a gate. Go through the gate and follow the trail uphill through fields of big bluestem and other native grasses, including switchgrass, Indian grass, and blue grama. (Bluestem, also called "turkey foot," is blue only in spring; in autumn, it's a cross between burgundy, peach, and mauve.)

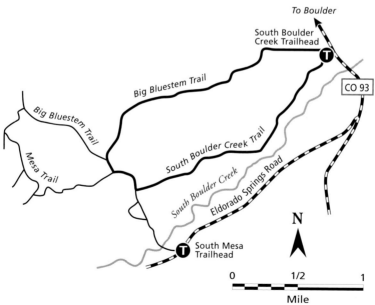

Big Bluestem and South Boulder Creek Loop

Big Bluestem Trail

In 2.3 miles, you come to a junction where you must decide whether to take the short loop or the long loop. For the short loop, take the left fork to connect with the Mesa Trail in 0.1 mile. Turn left on the Mesa Trail and go another 0.1 mile to the South Boulder Creek Trail. Turn left again and follow this trail downhill to complete the loop. In fall, stands of sumac blaze like fire just below the intersection of the South Boulder Creek and Mesa trails. Near the end of the trail, you pass a boggy area filled with cordgrass, a grass used by early settlers for roofing sod houses.

If you want to take the long loop, take the right fork, which heads uphill past the ruins of an old homestead to connect with the Mesa Trail in 0.8 mile. Follow the Mesa Trail to the left for 0.4 mile. Take the first fork to the left, which heads downhill to connect with the South Boulder Creek Trail in 1.7 miles and completes the loop previously described.

It's possible to continue on the Mesa Trail (page 96) to either end if you do a car shuttle.

Access

Turn west off of SR 93 at Thomas Lane, 1.8 miles south of Table Mesa Drive. Immediately after turning, head into the parking lot for the South Boulder Creek Trailhead.

Blue grama grass, a native short grass, thrives along the foothills

South Boulder Peak Via Shadow Canyon

Distance: 2.5 miles one way

Elevation: 5,600 to 8,549 feet

Highlights: Views of peaks and plains, rock formations, shady coniferous forest

Difficulty: Strenuous

Topo map: Eldorado Springs

Abert's squirrels live in ponderosa pine forests

Although this peak is slightly higher than Bear Peak, its profile is less familiar because it lies farther west and is hidden by Bear Peak from most vantage points. However, the views from the top are equally spectacular, and the trail up Shadow Canyon offers unique perspectives of Devils Thumb and Devils Thumb Ridge.

From the Mesa Trail South Trailhead, follow the Mesa Trail until it enters the ponderosa pines, where the trail splits. Take the left branch past the McGillvray Cabin, now almost hidden by European poplars and overgrown shrubs. Beyond this cabin where the Mesa Trail veers north, turn left (south) and continue on the old service road that curves up to the Stockton cabin. The

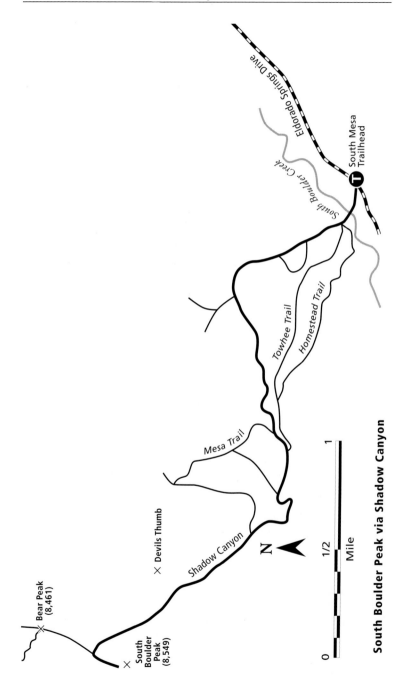

South Boulder Peak via Shadow Canyon

McGillvray Cabin

springs and a small pool above this cabin are good for bird and animal watching, and in early October the sumac turns a vivid red.

Just beyond the Stockton Cabin is another signpost. A right turn leads back to the Mesa Trail and is an alternative return route. A left turn leads into Shadow Canyon, a narrow, fern-filled canyon where flammulated owls and raptors nest. From here, the trail climbs very steeply, gaining 1,620 feet in elevation in about a mile, frequently ascending via stone "stairs" past huge red boulders.

When the trail reaches the saddle between Bear Peak and South Boulder Peak, turn left (southwest) at the signpost and continue climbing. A bit of easy rock scrambling brings you to the summit, where the views stretch from Longs Peak to Pikes Peak. Gross Reservoir and Walker Ranch lie below, and the plains, dotted with innumerable lakes, seem to fade into infinity to the east. You can enjoy raspberries that ripen near the summit in autumn, but leave some for the bears!

History

In October 1920, six members of the Boulder chapter of the Colorado Mountain Club stumbled upon this canyon and wrote about it in the club's magazine, *Trail & Timberline*: "Shadow Canyon—as we are trying to name it, since it has no other name that we can discover—is a very deep, long canyon cutting in between Bear Mountain and South Boulder Peak.... It is rimmed with huge, upstanding rocks 'about and all around,' whose great shadows are cast almost any time of day upon the opposite mountainside.... We found it heavily wooded with spruce, cedar and pine and full of beautiful kinnikinnick patches."

The Stockton Cabin at the mouth of the canyon was probably built in the 1890s as a miner's shack. West of the cabin, a mining tunnel goes into the hillside for about twelve feet, and there is another tunnel north of the cabin. Roscoe Stockton, a teacher, historian, and writer, bought the land and cabin in 1910, and his family held it until it was purchased by the city. The McGillvray Cabin, probably built by homesteader Seth Prudens in the 1870s, is a little lower than the Stockton Cabin, near the point where the Mesa Trail turns north. Hugh McGillvray bought it in 1906, and the gingerbread was probably added around 1917. The outhouse, which is almost impossible to find now, was noted for its large, south-facing windows and was hauled up from the plains where it had served as a child's playhouse.

Access

Park at the Mesa Trail South Trailhead on Eldorado Springs Drive, 2 miles west of SR 93.

Towhee and Homestead Loop

Distance: 2 miles round trip

Elevation: 5,600 to 6,080 feet

Highlights: Ponderosa-pine forests, brushy ravines, bird and animal watching, views of plains and foothills, historic buildings

Difficulty: Easy

Topo map: Eldorado Springs

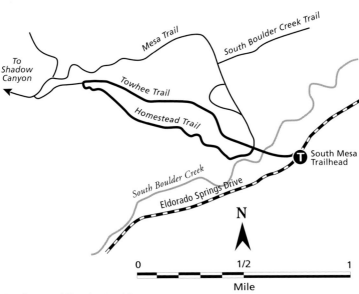

Towhee and Homestead Loop

Doudy-Debaker-Dunn House from the Homestead Trail

Although this trail is equally attractive from either starting point, this description starts with the Homestead section on the north side of the Doudy-Debacker-Dunn House. The Homestead Trail cuts behind an old apple orchard and follows South Boulder Creek a short distance before heading up the open, south slope of a small ridge. When you think you have gained the top of the ridge, you are actually on a gentle plateau. The trail continues up through ponderosa-pine forest and open grassy areas. Look for Abert's squirrels and mule deer. At the point where the plateau steepens rather sharply, the trail heads down the north side of the ridge, crosses Shadow Canyon Creek, and joins the Towhee Trail.

The Towhee Trail turns east and stays above the creek, which may be dry in late summer and fall, for a short distance before dropping down and crossing the creek again. The trail continues down, crosses a low stone wall and irrigation ditch, and ends back at the house. Look for marmots and chipmunks around the wall and for towhees and other brush birds in the chokecherries, hawthorns, and hackberries. In the spring, listen for boreal chorus frogs in the wet areas.

History

See Mesa Trail (page 96) for homesteading information.

Connections

- **Mesa Trail** (page 96) connects to the upper end of the loop a short distance above where Towhee and Homestead join, allowing for several permutations. If you keep heading west on the Mesa Trail, you will connect with **Shadow Canyon Trail** (page 118).

Access

Park at the South Mesa Trail Trailhead on Eldorado Springs Drive, 2 miles west of SR 93. Follow the Mesa Trail for approximately 0.1 mile to the Doudy-Debacker-Dunn House.

Doudy Draw to Flatirons Vista

Distance: 3.3 miles one way

Elevation: 5,680 to 6,220 feet (on the ridge) and down to 5,900 feet

Highlights: Views of foothills and Flatirons, wildflowers, birds, variety of habitats from riparian to grassland to pine forest

Difficulty: Easy to moderate

Topo map: Eldorado Springs, Louisville

Easter daisies on the Doudy Draw Trail

Starting at the Doudy Draw Trailhead, this trail follows a small creek through stands of wild plum, hackberry, and hawthorn—habitat for brush-loving birds such as lazuli buntings, towhees, tanagers, grosbeaks, and orioles. In early spring, gravelly ridges near the trail support some of the first pasqueflowers, and on New Years Day 2004, Easter daisies were in bloom.

The first 0.3 mile is paved, ending in a cottonwood-grove picnic area, at which point the trail becomes dirt. It crosses Community Ditch and continues up the draw to the southwest. At about 1.5 miles, the trail climbs the ridge to the east and flattens out on top

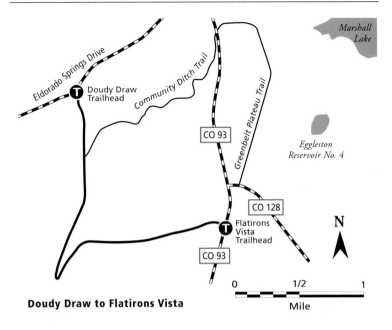

Doudy Draw to Flatirons Vista

of the mesa in an open ponderosa-pine forest. When you crest the ridge, turn and look west for spectacular views of snowcapped peaks framed by the Eldorado Springs "gateway rocks." Continue east across the grassy plateau to the Flatirons Vista Trailhead. By leaving

View of Arapaho Ridge from the Doudy Draw Trail

a car at both trailheads, you can make this a one-way hike in either direction.

History

Named for early homesteaders Andrew and Sylvester Doudy, upper Doudy Draw narrowly escaped becoming the site for two hydroelectric dams in 1993. An alert reader of the *Federal Register* noticed that a California company had applied for a permit to build two dams on open space. (A 1920s law allows companies to apply for a hydroelectric dam permit without notifying private land-owners and to condemn the land.) The city found out about the proposal in time to oppose the project successfully.

Connections

For a 6-mile loop hike, connect the two ends of Doudy Draw Trail with the **Greenbelt Plateau Trail** and **Community Ditch**. However, this loop involves crossing heavily traveled SR 93 twice.

Access

Park at either the Flatirons Vista Trailhead on the west side of SR 93, just south of SR 128, or at the Doudy Draw Trailhead about 2 miles west of SR 93 on Eldorado Springs Drive.

South Boulder Creek Loop (Walker Ranch Loop)

Distance: 7.5 miles round trip

Elevation: 7,200 feet, with a total elevation gain of more than 1,000 feet via several ups and downs

Highlights: Variety of habitats, from tumultuous creek to meadows to forests; wildflowers; birds; historic buildings; regeneration after fire

Difficulty: Strenuous

Topo map: Eldorado Springs

South Boulder Peak from Walker Ranch

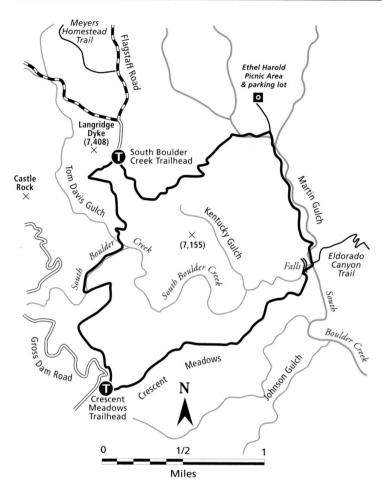

South Boulder Creek or Walker Ranch Loop

Several trails and old ranch roads can be combined for an up-and-down loop variously called Walker Ranch or South Boulder Creek Loop. From the South Boulder Creek Trailhead, descend on an old road to the creek, with views of Langridge Dyke and Castle Rock on your right. At the creek, turn right and follow it upstream to a bridge. Immediately after crossing the bridge, the trail forks. The right fork continues along the creek for a short distance and dead-ends at private property.

Take the left fork, which climbs rather steeply to Crescent Meadows and has outstanding views of the snowcapped Front Range. Turn left onto the **Crescent Meadows Trail**, where you enter the upper end of Eldorado Canyon State Park and drop steeply to South Boulder Creek. Severe erosion makes this section hazardous, so be careful. After crossing the creek, the trail connects with the **Eldorado Canyon Trail**. At this intersection, a spur trail leads to the Ethel Harold Picnic Area and another parking lot. Take the left branch and climb to the **Columbine Gulch Trail**. Turn left onto this trail, which completes the loop in another 1.25 miles. Because this trail, a favorite for mountain bikers, is crowded on weekends, it is best hiked on weekdays.

History

James and Phoebe Walker ran the largest cattle ranch in the Front Range in the late nineteenth and early twentieth centuries. In spite of several fires, most of the outbuildings are still intact and are open to the public on designated Living History Days, when volunteers show what daily life was like in the late 1800s. The most recent wildfire in September 2000 burned more than 1,000 acres on Walker Ranch and adjacent areas. It took 5 days, 500 firefighters, and $1.5 million to bring it under control. The rebirth of the forest and the resurgence of wildflowers are fascinating to observe.

Connections

- **Eldorado Canyon Trail** intersects the Walker Ranch Loop and goes over several ridges to Eldorado Canyon State Park in 4.4 miles.
- **Meyers Homestead Trail** (see below) starts across Flagstaff Road from Walker Ranch. Eventually, the county hopes to link this trail and Walker Ranch.

Access

At Realization Point, 3.4 miles up Flagstaff Road, turn left and drive 4.5 miles to the South Boulder Creek Trailhead on the east side of the road. You can also start at the Crescent Meadows Trailhead on the east side of the Gross Dam Road (a continuation of Flagstaff Road).

Meyers Homestead Trail

Distance: 2.5 miles one way

Elevation: 7,200 to 7,880 feet

Highlights: Wildflowers, wildlife, woodlands, scenic overlook, ruins of historic barns

Difficulty: Easy to moderate

Topo map: Eldorado Springs

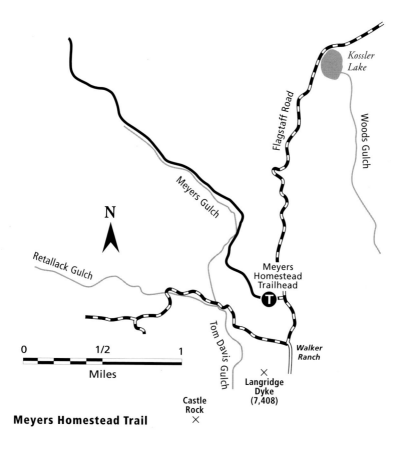

Meyers Homestead Trail

One of the barns built by James Walker on the Meyers Homestead Trail

Starting at the picnic area a short distance northwest of Walker Ranch, an old road (closed to motorized vehicles) drops down to a meadow containing the ruins of one of James Walker's old barns. From the meadow, take the road that heads west, following a small stream (the road that goes to the barn dead-ends at private property in about 0.3 mile). Near the top, the road veers away from the stream and curves around an upper meadow to an overlook with views of the Indian Peaks and Boulder Canyon. There are several aspen groves and flower-filled meadows along the way. In spring, bluebirds, attracted by the row of birdhouses along the fence, seem to sing from every fence post, and in autumn elk may bugle.

Andrew R. Meyers patented this homestead in 1890 and logged most of the trees, using portable sawmills, before selling the land to James Walker. Walker was more successful than most cattlemen of his time because he fenced the cattle, fed them in winter, and used a hardy Scottish breed. Some of the ruins of his seventeen hay barns can be seen from the Meyers Homestead Trail.

Connections

- **South Boulder Creek Loop** begins across Flagstaff Road at the top of the small hill.

Access

At Realization Point, 3.4 miles up Flagstaff Road, turn left and drive 4.4 miles to the Meyers Homestead Trailhead on the west side of the road.

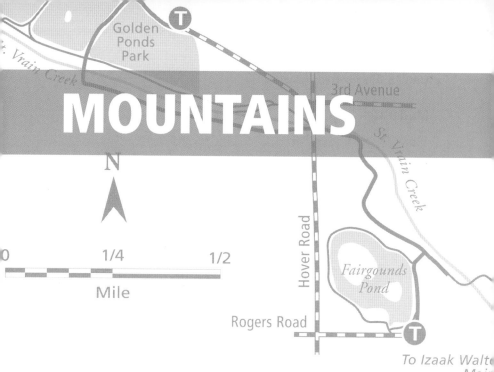

A t higher elevations the foothills turn to mountains, the reason why many of us are addicted to hiking. Ecosystems include aspen woodlands, lodgepole-pine forests, spruce and fir forests, mountain meadows and wetlands, and the tundra. Most of these trails are on U.S. Forest Service land and are maintained by the U.S. Forest Service. They are best hiked in summer and early fall, as snow may not melt until late June and may cover the trails again by October. In winter, many of the trails and access roads are superb for ski touring.

Most of the trails described here are strenuous if you hike the entire distance. However, the first segments are often easy to moderate, so check the topo maps and hike only as far as is fun. Here are a few especially beautiful, but easy, sections of longer trails:

Easy

- Copeland Falls (page 137)
- Mitchell Lake (page 160)
- Long Lake, Jean Lunning Trail (page 161)
- Hessie Falls (page 184)

Caribou Ranch Trails (page 171)

Moderate

- Isabelle Lake (page 161)
- Fourth of July Mine (page 179)
- Calypso Cascade, Ouzel Falls (page 134)
- Timberline Falls (page 140)
- South St. Vrain Trail to Baptist Camp Road (page 152)

Wild Basin Area

W ild Basin, in the southeastern corner of Rocky Mountain National Park (RMNP), lies in Boulder County. You'll find numerous lakes, waterfalls, peaks, and many miles of trails in the Wild Basin area, all of which are covered extensively in several books and RMNP brochures. We have limited coverage in this guide to just one trail—our favorite. Pick up a park brochure and explore others.

Ouzel Lake Via Calypso Cascade and Ouzel Falls

Distance: 4.9 miles one way

Elevation: 8,520 to 10,000 feet

Highlights: Waterfalls, lakes, cascading creek, wildflowers, coniferous forests, snowcapped mountain views

Difficulty: Strenuous

Topo maps: Allens Park, Isolation Peak

This is one of the best waterfall trails in Colorado, and it is a popular ski tour in winter. For most of its length, it follows North St. Vrain Creek (so wild it looks like one continuous waterfall)

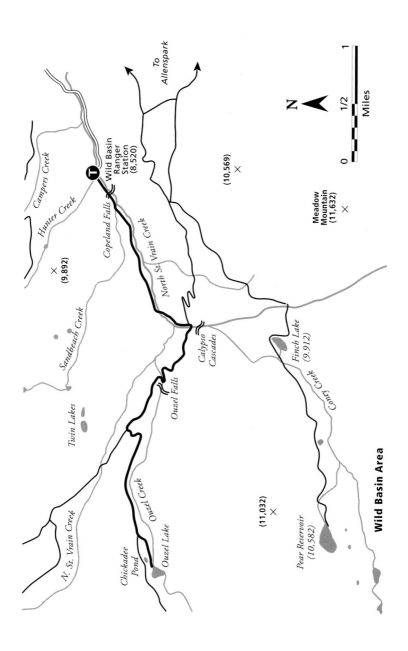

N

0   1/2   1
Miles

To Allenspark

Wild Basin Ranger Station (8,520)

(10,569)

Meadow Mountain (11,632)

Campers Creek

Hunter Creek

Copeland Falls

North St. Vrain Creek

(9,892)

Sandbeach Creek

Calypso Cascades

Finch Lake (9,912)

Coney Creek

Twin Lakes

Ouzel Falls

N. St. Vrain Creek

Chickadee Pond

Ouzel Creek

Ouzel Lake

(11,032)

Pear Reservoir (10,582)

Wild Basin Area

Ouzel Falls

through shady coniferous forests mixed with aspen. Near the end, it rewards hikers with a high mountain lake surrounded by jagged peaks. Of course, you don't have to hike the whole distance; any of the waterfalls are delightful destinations in their own right.

Rocky Mountain National Park trails are well-maintained, providing signs giving mileage at every junction and bridges across every creek. The trail to Ouzel Lake and connecting trails start at the south end of the Wild Basin Ranger Station parking lot. Your first stop should be at upper and lower Copeland Falls. A side trail makes a short detour to them, whetting your appetite for the even wilder falls to come. Just beyond the falls, a rock garden on the right is filled with wildflowers in spring and summer.

The main trail climbs 1.8 miles to Calypso Cascade, named for the fairyslipper orchids *(Calypso bulbosa)* that are abundant along the trail in late May and early June. These falls and many other Wild Basin features were named by botanist William Cooper when he mapped the area in 1911; his map sold for only fifteen cents. At Calypso Cascade, the trail to Finch Lake and Pear Lake veers to the left. Take the Ouzel Lake Trail to the right. At 2.7 miles, Ouzel Falls thunders on your left. There are good views from the bridge, but it's worth taking the muddy side trail a short distance for full frontal views of this forty-foot fall, named for the water ouzels or dippers that often nest here.

From the bridge, the trail skirts a cliff and climbs to another junction, with the right fork heading to Thunder Lake and Boulder–Grand Pass, and the left fork continuing on to Ouzel Lake. The Ouzel Lake Trail goes up a ridge that was swept by the 1978 Allenspark forest fire, which took a month to contain. Small shrubs, a few aspen and pine, and extensive blueberry patches are revegetating the burned area, and snags of the incinerated forest still stand. The fire did open up spectacular views of Longs Peak and Mount Meeker on the right, Copeland Mountain on the left, and jagged peaks in between.

The trail continues along the ridge to another junction, where the right fork goes to Bluebird Lake and the left fork drops slightly for half a mile to Ouzel Creek and the outlet for Ouzel Lake. There are actually two lakes at the end of the Ouzel Lake Trail, but Chickadee Pond, hidden by a lateral moraine, is easy to miss unless you walk to the burned-over moraine behind the outhouse at the Ouzel Lake campsite.

Connections

- **Bluebird Lake** (6.3 miles), **Thunder Lake** (6.8 miles), **Finch Lake** (5.3 miles), and **Pear Lake** (7.3 miles) trails all branch off from the Ouzel Lake Trail. Mileages are from the Wild Basin Trailhead.

Fairyslipper orchid for which Calypso Cascade is named

Access

From Boulder, take US 36 north to Lyons. Turn left onto SR 7 and continue to the Wild Basin turnoff, about 2 miles northwest of Allenspark. Turn west, drive past Wild Basin Lodge, and turn right onto a dirt road that dead-ends in 2.3 miles at the Wild Basin Ranger Station parking lot. The lot fills up during the summer, so plan to arrive early. In winter, the road is usually closed about 2 miles before the ranger station.

St. Vrain Area

Buchanan Pass Trail to Gibraltar Lake, St. Vrain Glaciers, Red Deer Lake, Buchanan Pass, and Sawtooth Mountain

Sawtooth Mountain, Buchanan Pass Trail

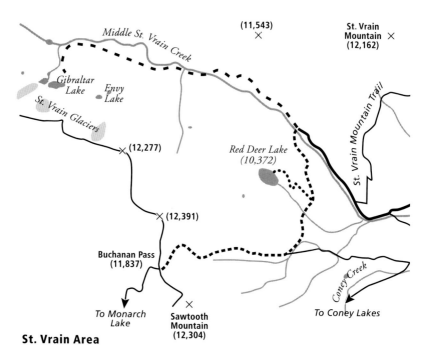

St. Vrain Area

Starting at the parking area west of Camp Dick, walk for a short distance along the road to the Buchanan Pass Trail sign. Deposit your wilderness permit in the box here if you are backpacking. (Note: This trail was formerly called the Middle St. Vrain Trail, and some signs still show this name.) Drop down to cross Middle St. Vrain Creek on the bridge. The Buchanan Pass Trail, closed to motorized vehicles, climbs gently through a mixed conifer and aspen forest, paralleling the north side of the creek for about 2 miles to Timberline Falls. Because the trail is used in winter for ski touring and snowshoeing, it is marked with blue diamonds.

If you have a rugged 4-wheel-drive vehicle with high clearance, you can drive the extremely rough road, FS 114, which parallels the south side of the creek for about 3.5 miles and ends across a bridge from the trail, near the Indian Peaks Wilderness boundary.

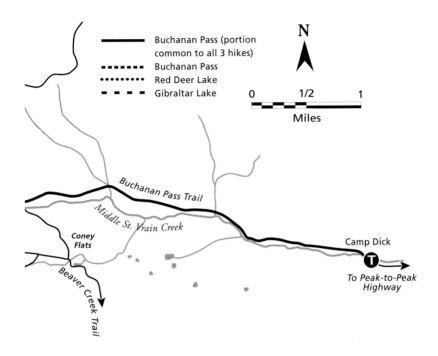

About half a mile beyond the first sign for the Indian Peaks Wilderness, good campsites abound in a flower-filled meadow. When we were last there, the meadow was inhabited by many ground squirrels and a long-tailed weasel. At the upper edge of the meadow, the St. Vrain Mountain Trail branches to the right.

Continue straight ahead on the Buchanan Pass Trail for about 1 mile to another meadow with good campsites. Logging was extensive here prior to the 1930s, and you can still see stumps more than three feet across, traces of old cabins, machinery, and even solidified cement bags bearing the imprint of the wrapping material. At the upper end of this meadow, a trail junction sign points straight ahead for Gibraltar Lake and the St. Vrain Glaciers and to the left for Red Deer Lake, Buchanan Pass, and Sawtooth Mountain. Mileages in the following descriptions are from Camp Dick.

Gibraltar Lake and St. Vrain Glaciers

Distance: 8.4 miles one way

Elevation: 8,638 to 11,200 feet

Highlights: Glaciers, alpine lakes, cascading creek, wildflowers, views of Elk Tooth Mountain, craggy ridges

Difficulty: Strenuous

Topo map: Allens Park, Isolation Peak

Looking up St. Vrain Valley with a distant view of Elk Tooth

The St. Vrain Glaciers and the topography created by them form some of the wildest, most beautiful scenery in the Indian Peaks Wilderness. It's a place of splendor. Because of its length, we recommend this trip as an overnight backpack outing rather than as a day hike. Better yet, set up a base camp for a day or two, giving yourself a chance to explore and savor the scenery and solitude.

At the trail junction mentioned above, continue up the St. Vrain Glacier Trail with a jagged, gray rock ridge to your right, the creek to your left, and Elk Tooth Mountain (elevation, 12,848 feet) dominating the end of the valley. A variety of wildflowers is reclaiming the old corduroy road, and at higher elevations, glacier lilies turn the slopes a buttery yellow at the edge of melting snowfields in late spring and early summer.

Glacier lilies

This old logging road narrows to a footpath that leads to the first creek crossing. Descend to the creek and *carefully* traverse the rickety logs. Continue following the left-hand side of the creek even though the trail seems to disappear at times.

Eventually, you come to a lovely, shallow lake dotted with wooded islands. This lake, not on the maps, seems almost enchanted. Perhaps, like Brigadoon, it will not be there when we go again. The trail crosses a logjam at the lower end of this lake, then climbs fairly steeply, crossing several small streams, to emerge at an alpine meadow above an unnamed lake we call "Lower Gibraltar." A massive cairn at this point is a good spot to stop to enjoy the view of Elk Tooth and to take your bearings, as the official trail seems to end here.

A short climb up either side of a braided creek brings you to Lake Gibraltar, which is shaped like a dumbbell with a small rocky rib separating the two halves. Two of the St. Vrain Glaciers plunge into the lake. Above the lake, a waterfall springs suddenly from the scree slope, falls for about ten feet, and is absorbed again by the scree.

Climb the gentle ridge southeast of the lake for wonderful views of Lake Envy below as well as views of Elk Tooth and the basin containing the Gibraltar Lakes and the St. Vrain Glaciers.

Red Deer Lake

Distance: 6.9 miles one way

Elevation: 8,638 to 10,372 feet

Highlights: Timberline lake, cascading creek, wildflowers, views

Difficulty: Strenuous

Topo map: Allens Park, Isolation Peak

Red Deer Lake, set in a rocky bowl under jagged cliffs, is surrounded by wind-flagged conifers, aspen, and wildflowers and is fed by snowfields and a small waterfall. The terrain is rough and rocky, but a few camping sites can be found in the trees. At the trail junction (mentioned on page 141), turn left on the Buchanan Pass

Trail and cross the bridge over the Middle St. Vrain Creek. Contour for about 1 mile and turn right onto Red Deer Lake Trail. A short, steep climb brings you to the lake. Several old roads and trails, now out of service, are shown on the USGS topo maps. However, the main trail is obvious and well-marked.

Buchanan Pass and Sawtooth Mountain

Distance: 9.5 miles one way

Elevation: 8,638 to 11,837 feet at Buchanan Pass, and 12,304 feet at Sawtooth Mountain

Highlights: Spectacular views, alpine wildflowers, wildlife

Difficulty: Strenuous

Topo map: Allens Park, Isolation Peak

Sawtooth Mountain looks like a giant snaggletooth rising from the rolling tundra and is the extreme eastern point of the Continental Divide in the United States. It dominates the skyline for many miles but is easier to climb than it appears. However, a long hike with considerable elevation gain is necessary before actually starting the summit climb; therefore, backpacking into the general vicinity makes for an easier trip.

Follow the Buchanan Pass Trail past the turnoff for Red Deer Lake, and contour around the ridge to the Beaver Creek Trail junction. Turn right and head up the valley over several easy stream crossings, with the main creek staying to your left. As the subalpine habitat shifts to krummholz and tundra, look for the low point on the ridge ahead. That's Buchanan Pass. The trail zigzags around the left side of a small buttress into a small alpine meadow and crosses to the other side of the basin, where it makes a switchback and then continues on up to the pass. Large snowfields persist until late in the season and may conceal parts of the trail.

From the pass, turn left (southeast) and climb the ridge half a mile to the summit of Sawtooth. No technical skills are needed, and the route is obvious.

View of Sawtooth Mountain

History

Archaeologist Jim Benedict has identified many prehistoric hunting blinds and game-drive walls near Buchanan Pass. The walls make a rough, upside-down V to funnel the animals uphill toward the narrow end, where the hunters crouched behind blinds. Benedict directed the excavation of a hunting camp and butchering stations below nearby Coney Lake and found stone points dating to about 5,700 years ago. Bighorn sheep, formerly plentiful here, have been reintroduced into the North St. Vrain Creek drainage and are spreading back.

The pass, probably named for President Buchanan, who signed the 1861 bill creating the Colorado Territory, was used as a stage road in the early 1890s. Fortunately, a proposal in 1967 to build a tollroad and tunnel was defeated.

Connections

- **St. Vrain Mountain Trail** forks to the north at the lower end of the meadow where the Buchanan and the St. Vrain Glacier trails diverge.

- **Buchanan Pass Trail** continues west and downhill to Monarch Lake for a long but beguiling backpacking trip.

- **Beaver Creek Trail** to the Mitchell Lake parking area, with other junctions to Mount Audubon and to Coney Lake, heads southeast from the Buchanan Pass Trail about a mile from the pass.

Access

From the Peak-to-Peak Highway (SR 72), turn west at Peaceful Valley onto FS Road 114. Park just beyond the west side of the Camp Dick Campground. An alternative route is to turn west onto CR 96 from SR 72 and drive to Coney Flats Road at the northwest end of Beaver Reservoir, just beyond the spillway. From Coney Flats, you can easily hike the Beaver Creek Trail to its junction with the Buchanan Pass Trail. However, the Coney Flats Road (high-clearance, 4-wheel drive only) is so bad that it's almost easier to hike it than it is to jeep it.

St. Vrain Mountain Trail

Distance: 4.5 miles one way

Elevation: 8,900 to 12,162 feet

Highlights: Aspen to alpine habitats; wildflowers; views of Longs Peak, Wild Basin, the Indian Peaks, and the plains

Difficulty: Strenuous

Topo map: Allens Park

Starting in a forest of lodgepole pine and aspen, the St. Vrain Mountain Trail reaches the Indian Peaks Wilderness boundary in about half a mile. It parallels a branch of Rock Creek up through a more open hillside to an old burn area, where it zigzags away from the creek. Eventually, the trail returns to and crosses the creek, then climbs the opposite hillside through a mixed conifer forest to an alpine saddle between Meadow Mountain to the east and St. Vrain Mountain to the west.

At the saddle, the trail swings south across the tundra, offering great views of Longs Peak, the surrounding mountains, and Wild

St. Vrain Mountain

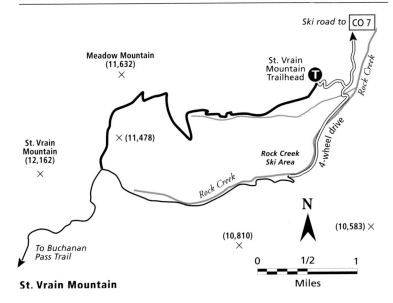

St. Vrain Mountain

Basin. The easiest route to the summit of St. Vrain Mountain starts on the east flank of the mountain. There is no official trail to the top, but it's not difficult to see the route that climbs about 700 additional feet, partly across talus, to the summit. Beyond the saddle, the St. Vrain Mountain Trail continues for 3 miles to the Buchanan Pass Trail.

For hikers not interested in peak-bagging, the trail section up to the alpine saddle between St. Vrain and Meadow mountains (about 3 miles and 2,400 feet of elevation gain) is well worthwhile—especially in late June and early July when the tundra is in bloom. This part of the trail goes up a south-facing bowl that gets very warm and is good for early flowers. Deep snowdrifts may persist in the spruce/fir forest below the saddle, even as flowers bloom above and below them. In mid-August, mushrooms are usually plentiful along the lower portion of the trail, and in late September, the aspens turn to gold.

According to some stories, the Rock Creek Ski Area predated World War II and was operated with a single rope tow. The unplowed part of the Ski Road and the lower trail section still offer good ski touring.

Connections

- Although there is no official trail up **Meadow Mountain** (elevation of 11,632 feet), the route is obvious from the saddle, and the final ascent is quite easy. At the RMNP boundary sign, turn right and climb until you're there.

- St. Vrain Mountain Trail intersects two other trails, **Buchanan Pass** (page 139) and **Rock Creek**, either of which can be combined for long loops.

Access

From Boulder, take US 36 north to Lyons. Turn left onto SR 7 and continue to Ferncliff. Turn left onto old SR 7 (now the business loop between Ferncliff and Allenspark). Follow the old highway to Ski Road (CR 107), just east of Allenspark. Turn left and continue to a fork in 1.7 miles. Take the right fork, which dead-ends in half a mile at the St. Vrain Mountain Trailhead.

South St. Vrain Trail to Brainard Lake

Distance: 5 miles one way

Elevation: 8,760 to 10,440 feet

Highlights: Mixed aspen and conifer forests, wildflowers, some streamside habitat

Difficulty: Strenuous

Topo map: Ward, Gold Hill

Starting at the South St. Vrain Trailhead, FS Trail 909 is well-marked with signs and blue diamonds. It parallels South St. Vrain Creek through meadows and aspen groves and then leaves the creek to continue uphill through a mixed aspen and coniferous forest. At various points, the trail swings back to the creek, but this first section is the best riparian area and is especially nice in late spring and early summer when columbine and paintbrush bloom, and in September when the aspens turn golden. In about 2 miles, the trail

South St. Vrain Trail with snow sculpture on the sign

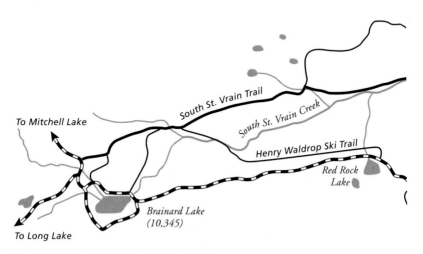

South St. Vrain Trail to Brainard Lake

joins a dirt road leading to the Baptist Camp. For a short, easy hike, turn around at this point and retrace the route down.

To continue to Brainard Lake, walk up the road to a U.S. Forest Service sign and turn right onto a trail that bypasses private property. Continue on this trail past two signs pointing to the right for Stapp Lakes. At the second Stapp Lakes sign, a third trail joins the main trail from the Baptist Camp on the left. Continue on the main trail up to a major trail intersection where the Sourdough and the South St. Vrain trails join—the halfway point on the South St. Vrain route to Brainard Lake.

The left fork at this intersection goes up to the Red Rock Trailhead. Stay on the main trail, which heads up to a T-junction. The right fork goes to Beaver Reservoir. Take the left fork and continue past three more junctions (the Waldrop Ski Trail enters and later exits from the left, and a third branch goes to the Brainard Lake

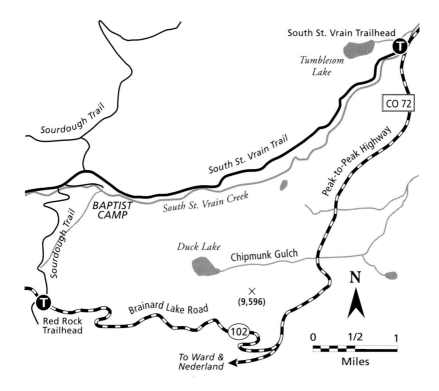

parking area). The main trail ends at a small parking area above the Brainard Lake Road, near the Colorado Mountain Club cabin built in 1928. (It's recorded that during one 1929 CMC outing, the men, clad only in boots and skis, followed a track near the cabin and skinny-dipped in a seven-foot drift at the bottom of the hill.) Except for a narrow, icy section near the beginning, this trail is good for ski touring and snowshoeing in winter.

Connections

The trail lends itself to one-way hikes or ski tours if you leave one car at the Red Rock Trailhead or at Brainard Lake and another at the South St. Vrain Trailhead. You can connect with either the **Sourdough Trail** (page 164) or the **Henry Waldrop Ski Trail**, which begins a short distance above the Red Rock Trailhead at a gate that closes the road in winter and goes to the CMC cabin above Brainard Lake. You can also take either the **Baptiste** or the **Wapiti trails** that form a loop off the Sourdough Trail but are maintained only for winter use.

Access

From the intersection of the Brainard Lake Road and the Peak-to-Peak Highway (SR 72), drive north 2.7 miles on the Peak-to-Peak Highway. Turn west at the sign for the Tahosa Boy Scout Camp and park along the road just west of the bridge.

Ceran St. Vrain Trail to Miller Rock

Distance: 3 miles one way

Elevation: 8,330 feet to 7,960 feet, and on to 8,646 feet

Highlights: Cascading creek, rock formations, wildflowers

Difficulty: Moderate

Topo map: Raymond, Gold Hill

Ceran St. Vrain Trail

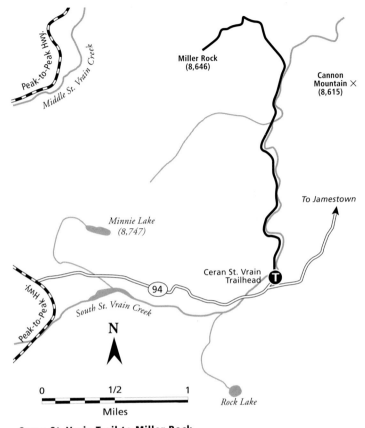

Ceran St. Vrain Trail to Miller Rock

Starting at a bridge that crosses a swirling cascade, this trail, which is named for an early fur trader, follows South St. Vrain Creek 2 miles downhill to an old jeep road, losing about 400 feet. In spring, this section of the trail is almost like a rain-forest path passing through pine, Douglas fir, spruce, and aspen trees, never losing sight or sound of the roaring creek. In late May and early June, it's one of the best places to find large clusters of fairyslipper orchids.

When the trail intersects the jeep road, turn left and follow the road uphill (away from the creek) to the top of a ridge. Continue on the road, which drops slightly, crosses two intermittent streams, and climbs again to a small plateau in a ponderosa-pine stand. At this point, several old jeep roads intermingle, and it's easy to get confused. Continue on the main road to a sign for Miller Rock. Turn left at this intersection and continue steeply uphill to another fork. The left fork drops back down to the plateau, so take the right fork, which continues uphill past a smallish rock outcropping and on to Miller Rock, a massive granitic formation with splendid views of the Indian Peaks. A faint trail circles the base of the rocks, and it's fairly easy to scramble to the top.

Access

From Lefthand Canyon (CR 106), take CR 94 to Jamestown. From the Jamestown post office, continue another 4.7 miles to the large sign for Ceran St. Vrain. Turn right on the dirt road that dead-ends at the trailhead. The trail can also be reached from the Peak-to-Peak Highway (SR 72) by turning east on CR 94.

Brainard Lake Area

Brainard Lake is the hub for many trails leading into the Indian Peaks Wilderness and up to the tundra. The area west of Brainard Lake is managed for day use only. Permits from the U.S. Forest Service are required for overnight backpacking trips into other parts of this heavily used wilderness. The entire area is superb for wildflowers and alpine scenery. To reach Brainard Lake, take CR 102, which heads west off the Peak-to-Peak Highway just above Ward. There is a small fee during the summer to use the area beyond Red Rocks Lake. Here are some of our favorite trails originating near Brainard Lake, probably named for Colonel Wesley Brainard, who prospected here in the late 1800s.

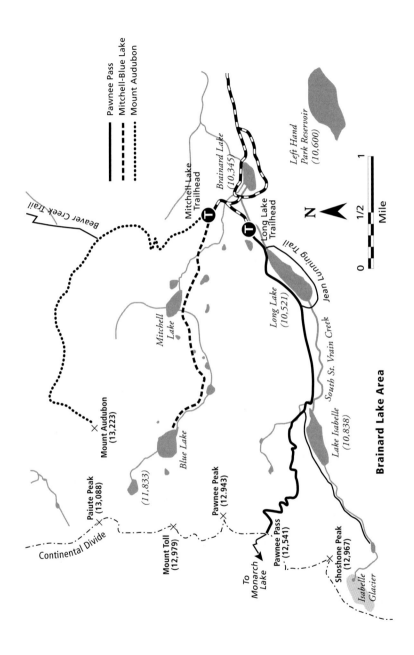

Pawnee Pass
Mitchell-Blue Lake
Mount Audubon

Beaver Creek Trail

Mitchell Lake Trailhead

Brainard Lake
(10,345)

Left Hand
Park Reservoir
(10,600)

Long Lake Trailhead

N

0   1/2   1
Mile

Mitchell
Lake

Long Lake
(10,521)

Jean Lunning Trail

South St. Vrain Creek

Mount Audubon
(13,223)

Lake Isabelle
(10,838)

Blue Lake

(11,833)

Paiute Peak
(13,088)

Pawnee Peak
(12,943)

Continental Divide

Mount Toll
(12,979)

To
Monarch
Lake

Pawnee Pass
(12,541)

Shoshone Peak
(12,967)

Isabelle
Glacier

Brainard Lake Area

Mount Audubon

Distance: 3.8 miles one way

Elevation: 10,480 feet to 13,223 feet

Highlights: Dramatic views of peaks and plains, alpine wildflowers

Difficulty: Strenuous

Topo map: Ward

This prominent mountain, which can be seen from many points in Boulder County, looks like a dish of ice cream with one spoonful taken from the side. Because it is one of the many Indian Peaks, the views from the summit are especially dramatic. Imagine looking down on Mount Toll! Two-thirds of the trail lies above timberline, so the views and the alpine wildflowers en route are also magnificent.

Mount Audubon

Starting at the Beaver Creek Trailhead on the north side of the Mitchell Lake parking area, climb gently through coniferous forest and krummholz to emerge above timberline in 1.5 miles at a junction. The Beaver Creek Trail continues another 3.7 miles to Coney Flats. Take the left fork, which climbs steeply for another 2 miles to the summit of Mount Audubon. Cairns mark the trail above timberline and are helpful when snowfields cover parts of the trail early in the season. The final scramble to the top involves some talus, but the route is well-marked by cairns. The summit is flat and fairly large, with several waist-high stone windbreaks. This is one of the easier 13,000-foot peaks to climb, and the rewards are well worth the effort. Plan to get to the top before noon to avoid afternoon thunderstorms.

History

Botanist C. C. Parry and zoologist J. W. Velie climbed the mountain in 1864, naming it for the famous naturalist and painter, who never visited Colorado. In 1914, Ellsworth Bethel drew a sketch map of the Indian Peaks for the U.S. Board of Geographic Names and suggested naming the peaks for Western American Indian tribes. Eleven of his proposed names were accepted, including Apache, Arikaree, Navajo, Ogalalla, Pawnee, Paiute, and Shoshone.

Connections

- At the junction of the Mount Audubon and **Beaver Creek trails**, you can take the right fork for another 3.7 miles to Coney Flats. From Coney Flats you can climb another 1.7 miles to the **Buchanan Pass Trail** (page 139).

- **Mitchell** and **Blue Lake trails** (see next trail description) also begin at the Mitchell Lake parking area.

Access

Take CR 102 west from the Peak-to-Peak Highway (SR 72). At the end of CR 102, circle Brainard Lake to the junction for the Long and the Mitchell Lake parking areas. Turn right and continue past the Long Lake turnoff to the Mitchell Lake parking area.

Blue Lake Via Mitchell Lake

Distance: 2.5 miles one way (See map page 157)

Elevation: 10,480 to 11,320 feet

Highlights: Lakes, creeks, spectacular views, wildflowers, forest

Difficulty: Moderate

Topo map: Ward

Blue Lake is one of the gems of the Indian Peaks Wilderness Area. Mount Toll (elevation, 12,979 feet) rises majestically above it, a waterfall cascades into its upper end, and wildflowers surround it. Starting at the Mitchell Lake Trailhead, the well-marked trail climbs through a coniferous forest to Mitchell Lake in 1 mile. It skirts the left-hand side of the lake, crosses a creek, and climbs through subalpine terrain to Blue Lake, which nestles into tussocky knolls at timberline. Parry primrose, mertensia (chiming bells), and candy-tuft are especially luxuriant at the creek crossing just beyond Mitchell Lake, and several tarns grace the way between the two lakes. Just before the final climb to Blue Lake, a lovely, broad cascade flows from beneath a snowbank.

Blue Lake and Mount Toll

Connections

• A steep, difficult climb from the upper end of Blue Lake involving talus-scrambling and getting over snowfields leads to a saddle between **Pawnee Peak** and **Mount Toll**, and from there to either summit. Although you can see occasional signs of a trail along this route, it is not officially maintained, and the snowfield on Mount Toll can be dangerous. It's possible—but strenuous—to cross the saddle, drop down to the **Pawnee Pass Trail** (page 161), and return to the Mitchell Lake parking area via Isabelle and Long lakes. However, the section between Blue Lake and Pawnee Pass Trail is off-trail and difficult. Take along a topo map.

• **Mount Audubon Trail** (page 158) also begins at the Mitchell Lake parking area.

Access

Use the same parking area as for Mount Audubon; see previous description.

Pawnee Pass Via Long Lake and Lake Isabelle

Distance: 4.6 miles one way

Elevation: 10,520 feet to 12,541 feet

Highlights: Spectacular views, wildflowers, lakes, cascading creeks, tundra

Difficulty: Strenuous

Topo map: Ward

Surrounded by craggy peaks and pointy gendarmes, this pass is one of our favorites. However, it's not necessary to hike all the way to the pass to enjoy the trail. The quarter-mile stroll to Long Lake affords unsurpassed views across the lake to Navajo (note the "organ player" on the west side) and Apache peaks.

Pawnee Pass from Niwot Ridge

Starting at the Long Lake Trailhead, the trail goes through spruce/fir forests and crosses the wilderness boundary at Long Lake where the Jean Lunning Trail branches to the left. Even if you don't take this trail, walk a short distance on it to the outlet of Long Lake for a magnificent view. Pawnee Pass Trail skirts the right-hand side of Long Lake and climbs gently through the forest, making a couple of switchbacks before reaching Lake Isabelle in 2 miles. Early in the season, a broad, rippling cascade gushes out of a snowbank below this lake. Just before reaching Lake Isabelle, cross the South St. Vrain Creek on stepping stones and climb a small ridge, emerging slightly above the lake. Lake Isabelle is usually drained in late August, so if this is your destination, check with the U.S. Forest Service to determine whether it still holds water.

At the first view of Lake Isabelle, the trail splits, with the Isabelle Glacier Trail leading straight ahead and the Pawnee Pass Trail climbing to the right. The trail crosses the creek three times before zigzagging through the last outposts of trees into fields of tundra and talus. The views looking down into Lake Isabelle, often tinted a jade green by glacial milk, are luscious. En route, you pass several tarns, bogs, and meadows and go through several miles of alpine flowers. Snowfields often persist until late in the season, especially the large snowfield across the trail just before the pass.

Upon reaching Pawnee Pass, it's worth descending the other side for a few switchbacks or so to see the dramatic gendarmes on the west side. If you continue to drop, you will reach Pawnee Lake in 2 miles, Crater Lake in 5 miles, and Monarch Lake in 11 miles. From the pass, you can climb Pawnee (elevation, 12,943 feet) or Shoshone (elevation, 12,967 feet) peaks, or several other Indian Peaks. It's possible (but difficult) to make a loop trip, crossing Pawnee Peak and dropping down between Pawnee Peak and Mount Toll to Blue and Mitchell Lakes, and then back to the Long Lake Trailhead. There are no marked trails to the peaks, so a topo map and backcountry experience are essential.

History

When the pass was surveyed for a railroad route in 1882, Canadian Native Americans carried in bread and other supplies; hence the trail's former name of "Breadline Trail." The present trail was built by the Civilian Conservation Corps. Fred Fair, Boulder city engineer in the early 1900s, discovered Isabelle and Fair glaciers early in the twentieth century and named Isabelle Glacier and Lake for his wife. After he died in 1935, his ashes were scattered over the two glaciers.

Long Lake

Connections

- **Jean Lunning Scenic Trail** (about a 2.5-mile loop circling the lake) branches to the left at the lower end of Long Lake and rejoins Pawnee Pass Trail shortly beyond the upper end of the lake.

- **Niwot Ridge Trail** branches off from the Jean Lunning Trail at the upper end of the first meadow. Niwot Ridge was established as one of only seventeen long-term ecological research stations in the country in 1980 and is famous for alpine research.

- **Isabelle Glacier Trail** skirts the right-hand side of Lake Isabelle and climbs to the glacier in 1.7 miles.

Access

Take CR 102 west from the Peak-to-Peak Highway (SR 72). At the end of CR 102, circle Brainard Lake to the junction for the Long and Mitchell Lake parking areas. Turn right and continue to the Long Lake turnoff (to the left) and parking area.

Sourdough Trail

Distance: 14.6 miles one way (some trail work is still in progress, so mileages are subject to change)

Elevation: 8,638 feet (Camp Dick) to 9,160 feet (Beaver Reservoir) to 9,960 feet (Brainard Lake Road) to 9,200 feet (Rainbow Lakes Road)

Highlights: Good ski touring, shady coniferous forest

Difficulty: Strenuous for entire trail; moderate for individual segments

Topo map: Allens Park, Ward

Three segments, described in the following paragraphs from north to south, comprise this long trail (FS 835) that stretches from Peaceful Valley to the Rainbow Lakes Road, with many ups and downs. This is not one of our favorite hiking trails as it lacks the breath-stopping beauty of most mountain hikes. Because it was

Sourdough Trail in the winter

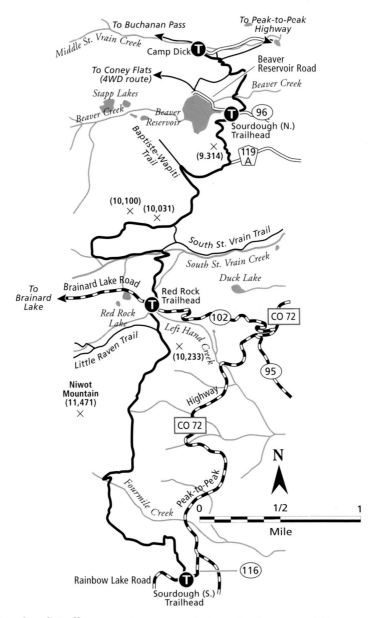

To Buchanan Pass

To Peak-to-Peak Highway

Middle St. Vrain Creek

Camp Dick

Beaver Reservoir Road

To Coney Flats (4WD route)

Beaver Creek

Stapp Lakes

Beaver Creek

Beaver Reservoir

96

Sourdough (N.) Trailhead

× (9.314)

119 A

Baptiste-Wapiti Trail

(10,100) ×   (10,031) ×

South St. Vrain Trail

South St. Vrain Creek

Duck Lake

To Brainard Lake

Brainard Lake Road

Red Rock Trailhead

Red Rock Lake

102

CO 72

Left Hand Creek

Little Raven Trail

× (10,233)

95

Niwot Mountain (11,471) ×

Highway

CO 72

N

1/2   1

0

Mile

Fourmile Creek

Peak-to-Peak

116

Rainbow Lake Road

Sourdough (S.) Trailhead

Sourdough Trail (Courtesy of Harlan Barton and the Colorado Mountain Club) built chiefly for ski touring and mountain biking, the route stays mainly in the forest, where it is protected from the worst winds, and it is clearly marked with blue diamonds. You can do a two-car, one-way trip on any of the segments or combine the Sourdough with other trails for a variety of loops.

Camp Dick Campground to Beaver Reservoir (about 2 miles one way; 522-foot elevation gain). From the parking area at the west end of the Camp Dick Campground, walk along FS Road 921 for a short distance to where the Buchanan Pass Trail crosses the road. At the trail sign, turn left onto the Buchanan Pass Trail, which goes gently up and down past several small stream crossings and through a lush coniferous forest. The mile-long stretch of this trail between Camp Dick and Peaceful Valley campgrounds is a lovely walk with many blue columbines blooming in July. About halfway between the two campgrounds, the Buchanan and Sourdough trails intersect. Turn right and climb up to a T-junction. The right branch goes to the north end of Beaver Reservoir, connecting to the Coney Flats Road. The main Sourdough Trail continues to the left and meanders up and down in a generally east-to-southeast direction, eventually crossing Beaver Creek. From the bridge, the trail contours around a small hill up to the Beaver Reservoir Road.

In winter, the road into Camp Dick is not plowed, so start at the parking area where the Peak-to-Peak Highway crosses Middle St. Vrain Creek and ski up the unplowed road a short distance to the Buchanan Trail. Continue on the trail to the intersection with Sourdough, adding about a mile to the distance.

Beaver Reservoir to Brainard Road (6.8 miles one way; 800-foot elevation gain). The second segment of the trail starts at the sign just before you reach Beaver Reservoir, across the road from the previous section. The trail climbs through an area that burned in 1988. The stark, dead trees are now enveloped in a profusion of wildflowers in summer, and small aspens are thriving. The proliferation of trails and old roads in this vicinity can be confusing, so keep an eye out for blue diamonds.

Follow the diamonds up through a mixed coniferous and aspen forest, past a sign for the Wapiti Ski Trail, and on up to a large meadow with two small ponds and views of the Indian Peaks. Continue up to the intersection with South St. Vrain Trail, cross the creek, and ascend to Brainard Road below Red Rock Lake.

Brainard Road to Rainbow Lakes Road (5.8 miles one way; 760-foot elevation loss). The third segment starts across the road from the Red Rock Trailhead, dropping to a bridge across Left Hand Creek. In about half a mile, the **Little Raven Trail**, an excellent ski-touring trail to Brainard Lake, branches to the right. Sourdough Trail contours around the lower flanks of Niwot Mountain, eventually crossing Fourmile Creek. The trail stays mostly in coniferous forest, mixed with some aspens, and generally follows the 10,000-foot contour line until near the end, where it drops rather steeply to Rainbow Lakes Road (CR 116).

History

Camp Dick was a Civilian Conservation Corps camp in the 1930s. CCC workers built forty-five miles of trails in addition to building roads and dams and fighting fires in the Indian Peaks area. Sourdough Trail is partly a collection of some of these old roads.

Access

All trailheads are west of the Peak-to-Peak Highway (SR 72). The four main access points are:

- Camp Dick Campground on the Middle St. Vrain Road (turnoff is 5.8 miles north of Ward).

- Beaver Creek and Beaver Bog trailheads, about 2 miles west of SR 72, on CR 96, east of Beaver Reservoir (turnoff is 2.5 miles north of Ward).

- Red Rock Trailhead, on the right-hand side of CR 102 just east of Red Rock Lake at the winter closure gate (2.6 miles west on Brainard Lake Road).

- Sourdough Trailhead, on CR 116, the Rainbow Lakes Road, 0.4 mile west of SR 72 (turnoff is 4.7 miles south of Ward, or 7 miles north of Nederland).

Caribou and Rainbow Lakes Area

Caribou Town Site

Topo map: Nederland

Silver was discovered in Caribou in 1869, and by the following year, more than thirty-five mines were in operation. Over the years, more than $20 million worth of silver was taken from these mines. In 1872, a solid silver-brick walk from the main street of Central City to the Teller House was built from Caribou silver to welcome President Ulysses S. Grant.

During its heyday, the town supported several hotels, saloons, a millinery, and a photographic studio. However, the town was a

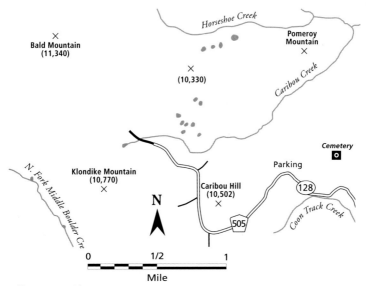

Caribou Town Site

magnet for tragedy. Winters were hard, and fires were frequent. Many children died from scarlet fever and diphtheria. Some families lost all their children within a week. After the catastrophic fire of 1879, the town began to die, and only a few foundations remain today. Even the cemetery has been almost leveled by vandals.

The town may literally have been a magnet, as it was built next to a "magnetic dike" that seems to attract electrical storms. In *A Look at Boulder*, Phyllis Smith reports that when children wrote on the blackboard, static electricity gave them a nasty shock and that men wearing rubber boots became weak. Because of its exposed location, hikers should be especially wary of lightning around Caribou during the summer thunderstorm season.

Our favorite thing to do in this historic area is to wander with no particular destination, looking at ruins and wildflowers. Most of the area lies in Roosevelt National Forest, but some private inholdings and working mines are closed to the public. Many intersecting jeep roads make good hiking routes, but there are no officially maintained or marked trails.

To see the Caribou Cemetery, walk northeast uphill from the parking area. To climb Caribou Hill and see the nearby mining ruins, climb FS Road 505 until it starts to drop; turn right (west) and continue uphill. A benchmark gives the elevation (10,502 feet) on the summit. A more strenuous climb starting in this area is an unmarked route up Bald Mountain, the stony lump on Arapaho Ridge below the Arapaho Glacier overlook. If you try this, get a topo map!

Access

Take CR 128 west from SR 72 just northwest of Nederland. The road is rough. Park at the top where the road branches in four different directions.

Caribou Ranch: DeLonde Trail and Blue Bird Loop

Distance: 4.2 miles round trip

Elevation: 8,560 feet to 8,860 feet

Highlights: Aspen, wildlife (including moose, elk, and beaver), historic buildings

Difficulty: Easy to moderate

Topo map: Ward, Nederland

    The 1.2-mile DeLonde Trail climbs gently through mixed conifer forests, meadows, and aspen groves to a junction with the 1.8-mile Blue Bird Loop. At the junction, drop down on an old ranch road to the DeLonde Homestead, set in a rolling meadow with beaver ponds and willow carrs. Because of the plentiful aspens, this stretch is a colorful autumn walk. After sightseeing around the historic homestead, continue on the Blue Bird Trail, which goes uphill to the right of the old barn. At the upper end of the loop, a 0.1-mile spur leads to the Blue Bird Mine. The main Blue Bird Trail crosses two small creeks before reaching the junction with the DeLonde Trail, which returns to the trailhead. The stretch from the trailhead

Caribou Ranch, DeLonde Homestead

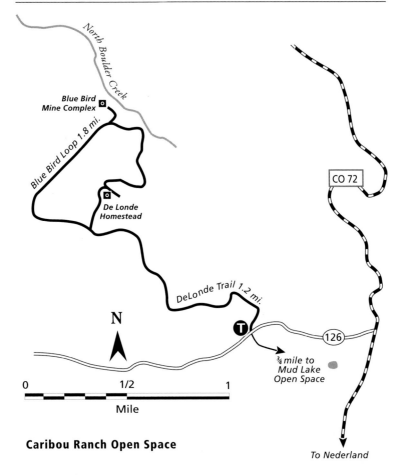

Caribou Ranch Open Space

to the Blue Bird Mine follows the Switzerland Trail railroad grade and is an easy ski tour.

The 2,180-acre open-space property is home to a wealth of wildlife, including an elk herd. To protect the calving elk and migrating birds, the ranch is closed from April 1 through June 30. The area will also be restricted in September (time of the elk rut) for a few years until a study on human impacts is completed. Mountain lions, black bears, bobcats, short-tailed weasels, Townsend's big-eared bats, and moose are among the fifty mammal species that share the territory.

History

The Switzerland Trail served the Blue Bird Mine, named after azurite found in the silver ore, from 1904 to 1919. The mine site includes the bunkhouse, used as a stage stop in the 1965 remake of *Stagecoach*, and remains of other historic buildings. Several owners have run the ranch over the years. Two of the most notable are Lynn Van Vleet, who purchased the ranch in 1936 for the first Arabian horse-breeding operation in Colorado, and James Guericio, who renamed the ranch Caribou when he bought it in 1971 as a recording base for rock groups, such as the Beach Boys, Frank Zappa, and Elton John. John Lennon is said to have recorded "Lucy in the Sky with Diamonds" in a converted barn on the property.

Connections

- A 0.75-mile trail leads to the **Mud Lake Open Space** and a trail circling the lake.

- Future plans call for an extension along the **Switzerland Trail** to the old mining town of Batesville and on to the **Sourdough Trail**.

Caribou Ranch

Access

From Nederland, drive 1.8 miles north on SR 72 (Peak-to-Peak Highway) and turn west on CR 126. Continue 1 mile to the parking lot.

Rainbow Lakes Trail

Distance: 1 mile to upper lakes

Elevation: 9,920 to 10,280 feet

Highlights: Lakes, beaver ponds, coniferous forest, wildflowers

Difficulty: Easy

Topo map: Ward

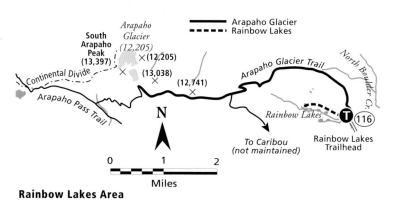

Rainbow Lakes Area

The Rainbow Lakes Trail climbs gently through a mixed coniferous and aspen forest and past limber pines twisted into shapes like lyres and candelabras. The trail leads to a string of small lakes containing brook trout. How lucky we are that the envisioned road along this route to Arapaho Pass and Grand Lake never materialized!

Starting at the west end of the Rainbow Lakes Campground, the trail (an old road that narrows to a trail) soon passes a wilderness boundary sign and veers to the left, away from the old road. The trail rejoins the road and reaches the first lake, partly filled with

Rainbow Lakes

pond lilies, in about half a mile, then continues on to the second lake. After the second lake, you come to a boggy area and a small creek crossing. A short climb up a rocky ridge brings you to a double lake, separated by a narrow band of rocks. The trail eventually peters out above these lakes.

Connections

• **Arapaho Glacier Trail** also begins at the campground.

Access

From the Peak-to-Peak Highway (SR 72) halfway between Nederland and Ward, turn west onto CR 116 at the University of Colorado Mountain Research Station sign. This rough, gravel road dead-ends in 5 miles at the Rainbow Lakes Campground. The road is closed in winter and is good for ski touring.

Arapaho Glacier Trail
to Arapaho Glacier Overlook

Distance: 6 miles one way (See map page 174)

Elevation: 9,920 to 12,720 feet

Highlights: Views of glacier, peaks, plains, and lakes; alpine wild-flowers; mushrooms

Difficulty: Strenuous

Topo map: Ward, Monarch Lake

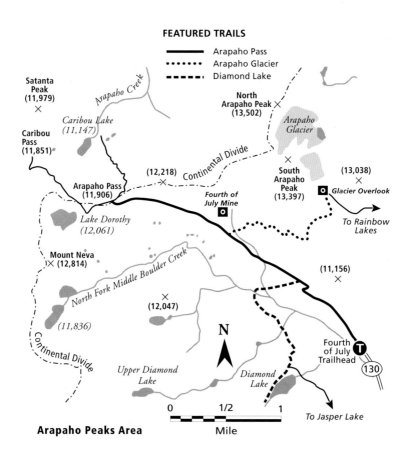

FEATURED TRAILS

——— Arapaho Pass
••••••• Arapaho Glacier
▬ ▬ ▬ Diamond Lake

Satanta
Peak
(11,979)

Arapaho Creek

North
Arapaho Peak
(13,502)

*Arapaho
Glacier*

*Caribou Lake
(11,147)*

Caribou
Pass
(11,851)

Continental Divide

(12,218)

South
Arapaho
Peak
(13,397)

(13,038)

Glacier Overlook

Arapaho Pass
(11,906)

*Fourth of
July Mine*

To Rainbow
Lakes

*Lake Dorothy
(12,061)*

Mount Neva
(12,814)

North Fork Middle Boulder Creek

(12,047)

(11,156)

(11,836)

Continental Divide

N

Fourth
of July
Trailhead

130

*Upper Diamond
Lake*

*Diamond
Lake*

To Jasper Lake

0   1/2   1

Arapaho Peaks Area

Mile

South Arapaho Peak

The Arapaho Glacier Trail, formerly called the Glacier Rim Trail, skirts Boulder's watershed (closed to the public) and climbs to the glacier overlook. The best views of the lush, forbidden basin that contains Albion, Goose, and Silver lakes are seen from this trail. At timberline, you can look down into the Rainbow Lakes as well as the Boulder watershed. The plains stretch out to the east, and the Arapaho Peaks loom ahead. The higher you climb, the better the views become.

Starting at the Arapaho Glacier Trailhead, the trail climbs through a mixed coniferous forest where mushrooms proliferate in August. In about 2 miles, just before a wilderness boundary sign, the trail passes through the last outposts of twisted limber pine and onto the tundra. A barbed-wire fence and frequent no-trespassing signs separate the watershed from U.S. Forest Service land. Ignoring these signs can result in large fines.

The trail circles below a 10,000-foot-plus knob and climbs the north-facing slope of Arapaho Ridge, eventually crossing the ridge to the south-facing slope. From the south side, there are views down into Diamond Lake and across to Mounts Evans and James, Grays, and Torreys peaks. On a clear day, you can see Pikes Peak, far to the south. Early in the season, snowfields may cover parts of the trail at this point, but cairns show the way to go. About a mile from the overlook, a faint, unmarked route descends a shallow valley on the left to the Caribou town site.

At the glacier overlook, views in every direction are superb. Sliding down the glacier, a popular sport in the old days, is forbidden. Cairns on the south-facing side of the peak indicate the best route up the talus to the summit of South Arapaho Peak.

Connections

- **Arapaho Pass Trail** (page 178) can be combined with the Arapaho Glacier Trail for a "key exchange" hike. If one party parks at Rainbow Lakes Campground and the other at Buckingham Campground, each party can make an 8.5-mile, one-way hike on the combined trails.

- **Rainbow Lakes Trail** (page 174) also begins at Rainbow Lakes Campground.

Access

See the description for Rainbow Lakes Trail, above.

Arapaho Pass Area

Arapaho Pass Trail to Arapaho Pass, Diamond Lake, and South Arapaho Peak

Distance: Arapaho Pass, 3.3 miles; Diamond Lake, 2.6 miles; South Arapaho Peak, 3.9 miles

Elevation: 10,121 at trailhead to 11,906 feet at Arapaho Pass; 10,960 feet at Diamond Lake; 13,397 feet on South Arapaho Peak

Highlights: Spectacular views, wildflowers, alpine lakes, waterfalls, glacier, historic and prehistoric sites

Difficulty: Moderate to strenuous, depending on distance hiked

Topo map: Monarch Lake, East Portal

Hikers can make several separate day trips to the destinations above, saunter along just the lower portion of the trail, or do a strenuous combination, possibly packing into the backcountry. (A permit is required for the Indian Peaks area.)

An annual July trek to the Arapaho Pass Trail is a tradition for many hikers who claim the wildflowers here are the best in the county. Blue columbine and scarlet paintbrush line the trail at mid-elevations; mertensia, mimulus, and monkshood mass along creek crossings; fields of yellow glacier lilies, uncommon on the eastern side of the Continental Divide, bloom at the edge of retreating snowfields; and alpine flowers carpet the tundra.

Arapaho Pass Trail

Starting in the spruce/fir forest at the Fourth of July Trailhead, the Arapaho Pass Trail crosses several small streams before fording a larger stream and then a tumbling creek that will probably wet your boots. In 1.2 miles, the Diamond Lake Trail branches to the left, and the Arapaho Pass Trail makes a switchback and opens out into lush flower gardens.

Globeflower meadow near Diamond Lake

In 2.1 miles, you reach the site of the Fourth of July Mine, where the Arapaho Glacier Trail goes to the right and the Arapaho Pass

Trail contours up to the pass following the route of an old wagon road. Pikas and marmots usually squeak and whistle along this section of the trail, which is quite stony and crosses some snowfields early in the season. At the pass, you can look down onto Caribou Lake and Coyote Park, or you can seek shelter from the wind behind prehistoric hunting blinds.

History

The basin around the Fourth of July Mine was one of the largest Paleo-Indian hunting camps on the Front Range and was used most recently by Ute and Arapaho tribes. Archaeologist Jim Benedict has identified several hunting blinds and game-drive walls near the pass and has excavated ancient steam pits. He says this pass was the only important prehistoric travel route across the Continental Divide between Devils Thumb Pass and Buchanan Pass.

C. C. Alvord discovered silver in the area in 1875 and established the Fourth of July Mine. A wagon road crossed the pass late in the 1800s, and in 1904, the state appropriated $5,000 to build a road but only completed the east side. In the 1960s, a tollroad was proposed and defeated.

Marmot on Arapaho Pass

Indian game wall taken from Rollins Pass

Connections

- **Arapaho Pass Trail** continues on down to **Caribou Lake** and follows Arapaho Creek down to Monarch Lake, making a good 13.5-mile backpack route.

- **Lake Dorothy Trail** (0.5 mile) continues up from the pass. At 12,061 feet, this lake is one of the deepest and coldest in the region.

- **Caribou Trail** continues beyond Lake Dorothy and over Caribou Pass, offering good views of Columbine Lake. A snowfield persists across this poorly maintained trail until midsummer, and the path, narrow with exposed stretches, is slowly sliding away. It is therefore considered dangerous.

Diamond Lake

Diamond Lake lies almost at timberline and is reached via a trail that passes through a variety of habitats. Bog aficionados revel in the numerous marshy areas filled with bog orchids, little red elephants, and flowers that like wet feet. Hikers can keep their feet dry (mostly) thanks to boardwalks across the wettest areas.

From the trailhead, follow the Arapaho Pass Trail for 1.2 miles to the junction with the Diamond Lake Trail, which veers to the left. From here, you drop about 240 feet to the North Fork of Middle Boulder Creek, crossing several small streams en route. Cross the creek on the double log bridge and follow the trail up through a spruce/fir forest and across several small streams. Just before you reach the lake, a large meadow brims with rosy paintbrush in summer. Continue straight ahead for a diamond-shaped lake that sparkles with diamonds on a sunny day.

White-tailed ptarmigan

Connections

- **Devils Thumb Bypass Trail** branches to the left just before you reach Diamond Lake. By leaving one car at Hessie, you can make a one-way, one-day hike down, or you can continue up to **Jasper Lake** and **Rollins Pass** and down via the **King Lake Trail**, connecting several trails for a spectacular backpack ending at Hessie.

- The main trail skirts the right-hand side of Diamond Lake to two inlets at the upper end. Climb the trail beside the first inlet creek to a willow bog for a view of a braided cascade that originates at **Upper Diamond Lake**. From here, faint user trails not maintained by the U.S. Forest Service lead to Upper Diamond Lake and to a tarn old-timers called "Banana Lake" because of its shape. These lakes, high in an alpine basin, involve cross-country hiking, so take a topo map if you go.

South Arapaho Peak

Starting at the Fourth of July Trailhead, follow the Arapaho Pass Trail to the Fourth of July Mine. Turn right and follow the Arapaho Glacier Trail around the south-facing shoulder of South Arapaho Peak and onto the tundra. A large rock shelter at the glacier overlook protects hikers from the usually fierce wind and provides a good lunch spot.

Arapaho Glacier—the largest in Colorado—is a major source of Boulder's water. In fact, Boulder is the only city in the United States to own a glacier. During the Pleistocene Epoch, the glacier may have been 10 to 15 miles long and 1,000 feet deep. Like glaciers worldwide, Arapaho Glacier is shrinking as the climate warms and now measures only 0.5-mile square and 200 feet deep.

Cairns on the south-facing side of the peak indicate the best route up the talus to the summit.

History

In 1897, botanists Darwin M. Andrews (for whom Boulder's arboretum is named) and Herbert N. Wheeler of the U. S. Forest

South Arapahoe Peak

Service were botanizing on the east side of Arapaho Pass, looking for dogtooth violets (glacier lilies). They hiked across what Boulderites then called "the big snowbank" and recognized it as a true glacier, which they reported to the University of Colorado. On July 14, 1900, Eben Fine, early Boulder druggist and outdoorsman, made a solo ascent of South Arapaho Peak and also found the glacier, which he publicized widely. Possibly the first settlers to climb the Arapaho Peaks were three prospectors (W. C. Andree and two unnamed Hungarians), who climbed one of the peaks in 1861, thinking it was Longs Peak.

City Engineer Fred Fair developed much of Boulder's watershed beginning in 1904 and was one of the early promoters of tourism in the Indian Peaks area. For many years, Fair and the Boulder Chamber of Commerce championed the idea of a road to the glacier overlook and received an initial appropriation from Congress. Fair was even given a concessioner's permit to build shelters and refreshment stands at the overlook. As a publicity stunt, the Denver and Interurban Railroad in 1923 offered $1,000 to any aviator who landed a plane on the St. Vrain Glacier, which provided a smoother landing field than Arapaho Glacier. Charles Lindbergh accepted the challenge. However, the offer was withdrawn when Fair considered the unfavorable publicity that would ensue if Lindbergh crashed.

Fortunately, the road to the glacier was never built, and in 1927, the City of Boulder bought 3,685 acres of watershed, including the glacier, from the federal government for $4,606. From 1938 to 1974, the Boulder Chamber of Commerce sponsored an annual August hike up to the glacier. Forty-eight people made the hike in 1938; 600 in 1974. Too many people and heavy environmental damage brought these megahikes to an end.

Connections

- Strong, experienced climbers can continue another 0.75 mile along the ridge (with some exposure) to **North Arapaho Peak** (13,502 feet).

- If one party parks at Rainbow Lakes Campground and another party at Buckingham Campground, an 8.5-mile, one-way hike along the **Arapaho Glacier Trail** with a key exchange can be made (page 176).

Access

From the southwest end of Nederland, take CR 130 past the town of Eldora to the Hessie junction. Take the right branch for another 4 miles to Buckingham Campground (also called the Fourth of July Campground). At the campground, take the right fork up to the parking lot at the Fourth of July Trailhead.

Hessie Area

Hessie, a town founded in the 1890s by Captain J. H. Davis and named for his wife, was the largest mining camp in this area. Gold and silver mining was prominent throughout the region, especially at Lost Lake and around Jasper Creek. Today, you often stumble upon ruins of mines and cabins. The trails described here go through moist coniferous forest with globeflowers, buttercups, and marsh marigolds blooming in early summer, and columbines, locoweed, and paintbrush a bit later. In autumn, the aspen groves around Hessie turn golden, and in winter, the road into the town site and beyond makes a good ski tour, as does the road up to Buckingham Campground.

Devils Thumb Bypass Trail to Jasper Lake, Devils Thumb Lake, and Devils Thumb Pass

Distance: 4.5 miles to Jasper Lake, 5.5 miles to Devils Thumb Lake, and 7.1 miles to Devils Thumb Pass

Elevation: 9,000 to 10,814 feet at Jasper Lake, to 11,160 feet at Devils Thumb Lake, to 11,747 feet at Devils Thumb Pass

Highlights: Waterfalls, cascading creeks, lakes, spectacular views, tundra, wildflowers

Difficulty: Strenuous

Topo map: Nederland, East Portal

From the town site of Hessie, take the old jeep road up to the bridge across the North Fork of Middle Boulder Creek. Cross the bridge and continue up the road, which is closed to motorized vehicles at the bridge. When you hear the roar of a waterfall, take a short detour to your left to see one of the best waterfalls in the county. Dippers nest behind these falls in June, and a rainbow is usually visible in the morning mist.

Beyond the falls, the road continues to a trail junction at the bridge across the South Fork of Middle Boulder Creek. At the bridge, two routes to Devils Thumb Pass diverge. The original Devils Thumb Pass Trail crosses the bridge, follows the road up to Woodland Flats, and crosses the South Fork of Middle Boulder Creek a second time. It then continues along the west side of Jasper Creek to a bridge and rejoins the Devils Thumb Bypass Trail on the east side of the bridge across Jasper Creek.

We prefer the Devils Thumb Bypass Trail because it is less swampy and more flowery. For the Bypass Trail, do not cross the bridge, but hike up the right-hand side of the creek through a moist coniferous forest that opens out into a flower-filled meadow below

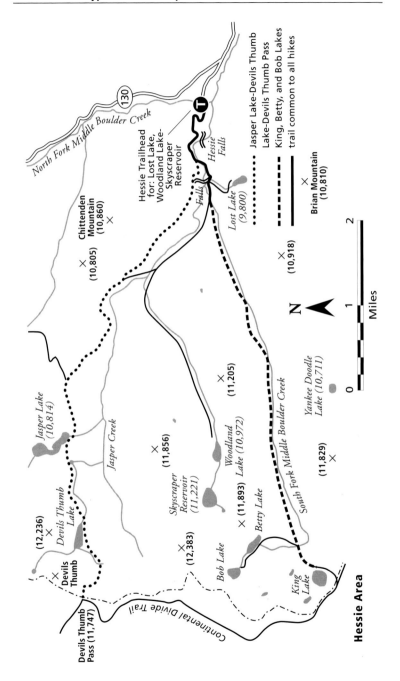

130

North Fork Middle Boulder Creek

Hessie Trailhead for: Lost Lake, Woodland Lake-Skyscraper Reservoir

Hessie Falls

Falls

Jasper Lake-Devils Thumb Pass
Lake-Devils Thumb Pass
King, Betty, and Bob Lakes
trail common to all hikes

Brian Mountain (10,810)
×

Chittenden Mountain (10,860)
×

×
(10,805)

Lost Lake (9,800)

×
(10,918)

N

Miles

Jasper Lake (10,814)

×
(11,205)

2

×
(11,856)

Yankee Doodle Lake (10,711)

Jasper Creek

Woodland Lake (10,972)

1

(12,236)
×

Devils Thumb Lake

Skyscraper Reservoir (11,221)

× (11,893)

Betty Lake

South Fork Middle Boulder Creek

×
(11,829)

Devils Thumb
×

×
(12,383)

Bob Lake

King Lake

0

Devils Thumb Pass (11,747)

Continental Divide Trail

Hessie Area

Devils Thumb Lake

Chittenden Mountain. About half a mile beyond the Indian Peaks Wilderness boundary sign, the Devils Thumb Bypass Trail rejoins the other fork of the Devils Thumb Trail that comes in from the left. This fork is an alternate route back to Hessie.

To reach Jasper Lake, continue uphill, staying on the right-hand side of Jasper Creek for about 2 miles. You can either follow the road, which is straightforward but stony and hard on the feet, or you can take a trail, which crisscrosses the road a few times and is marked with cairns. Several old road remnants may be confusing, but they are usually blocked with branches.

At the ruins of an old log cabin, the trail forks. Both forks cross Jasper Creek on logs just below Jasper Lake. An attractive waterfall flows across a logjam at the outlet of the lake, another waterfall cascades into the upper end, and a rock rib creates the illusion that there are two lakes. The trail skirts the lower end of Jasper Lake and climbs on to Devils Thumb Lake, nestled at the base of Devils Thumb, in another mile, passing several alpine tarns along the way. The best view of Devils Thumb, the prominent gendarme visible from many spots in the Hessie area, is from the outlet of Devils Thumb Lake. The trail crosses the creek at the outlet and skirts the southern edge of the lake. It climbs past a grassy tarn and then zigzags steeply up to a ridge top that is actually south of the pass. Views in all directions are superb, especially to the north and

Hessie Falls

west, where the Never Summer and the Gore ranges dominate the skyline.

A corniced snowfield across the trail lasts until late in the season and, in some years, never melts. This snowfield may be impassable for inexperienced hikers during some seasons. From the top of the ridge, you can drop 0.6 mile to the pass.

Connections

- From the pass, follow the ridge south to pick up the **High Lonesome Trail**, a segment of the **Continental Divide National Scenic Trail**, which leads to Rollins Pass and is marked with cairns. This trail crosses the tundra at about 12,000 feet on the west side of an east-facing escarpment, below a jagged ridge. If the weather is good, we prefer to follow the ridge, looking down into the lake basins to the east. Shortly before reaching Rollins Pass, there are views of King, Bob, and Betty lakes framed in the pinnacles of the ridge. A good two-day backpacking loop can be made by following the Continental Divide National Scenic Trail 3 miles south to Rollins Pass, and returning via the **King Lake Trail** (see below). This loop offers several miles of alpine gardens for flower enthusiasts as well as possible sightings of ptarmigan and elk.

- A hard-to-find trail to **Diamond Lake** (page 182) branches to the right 0.6 mile below Jasper Lake and is marked with cairns.

Access

Take CR 130 past the town of Eldora (west of Nederland and north of the Eldora Ski Area) to the sign for Hessie, 1.5 miles beyond Eldora. A rough cobblestone road to Hessie drops to the left. To reach the parking area, you must drive through water that may be fairly deep. High-clearance, 4-wheel-drive vehicles are helpful. If you decide to hike rather than drive this last bit of road, take the quarter-mile Columbine Trail that bypasses the wet section. If you're tempted to ignore "No Parking" signs along CR 130, don't. Fines are stiff and cars have been towed.

King Lake Trail to King, Betty, and Bob Lakes

Distance: 5.2 miles to King Lake, with a half-mile spur to Betty and Bob lakes

Elevation: 9,000 to 11,431 feet at King Lake, to 11,440 feet at Betty Lake, to 11,600 feet at Bob Lake

Highlights: Waterfalls, turbulent creek, lakes, mountain views, alpine flowers

Difficulty: Strenuous

Topo map: Nederland, East Portal

From the town site of Hessie, take the old jeep road up to the bridge that crosses the South Fork of Middle Boulder Creek where the Devils Thumb Bypass Trail veers right. See the previous trail description for details on this stretch. Cross the bridge and follow the road up to Woodland Flats. At the sign for the Lost Lake Trail, which turns left, continue straight ahead for a short distance to another bridge across the South Fork of Middle Boulder Creek. Just beyond the bridge, the trail forks again, with the right fork going to Woodland Lake, Jasper Lake, and Devils Thumb Lake and Pass.

Betty Lake

The King Lake Trail turns left and parallels the creek through coniferous forest and meadows. At the upper end of the valley, the trail zigzags steeply up a head wall to cross the creek. There's no bridge, but you can either jump or use stepping stones.

Just before this creek crossing, at 11,200 feet, a small path branches to the right. At present, the trail is obscure and may be hard to find; a topographic map is helpful. Follow the faint trail marked by cairns up a ridge through krummholz, willows, and alpine flowers to Betty Lake. From the ridge, look south for views of the old Moffat railway and the Devils Slide trestles. The trail continues along the left-hand side of Betty Lake, crosses a creek, and climbs a lateral moraine to Bob Lake, a beautiful glacial lake fed by a small waterfall. Between these two lakes, the trail virtually disappears but is marked by occasional cairns.

Descend via this same route (an elevation loss of about 400 feet) back to the King Lake Trail. This trail climbs up to King Lake, which is nestled in a glacial cirque.

Connections

- **Lost Lake Trail** branches left from the jeep road at Woodland Flats 1.1 miles from the trailhead and climbs 0.5 mile to the lake and some mine ruins. This is an excellent ski-touring trail.

- **Devils Thumb Pass Trail** (see previous description) continues straight ahead at Woodland Flats, with a later branch leading to Woodland Lake and Skyscraper Reservoir.

- A good, two-day backpacking loop (about 15 miles) can be made by continuing on the King Lake Trail up to the **Continental Divide National Scenic Trail.** Continue north to connect with the **Devils Thumb Trail**, which comes up a side ridge south of Devils Thumb Pass. Complete the loop via **Devils Thumb Bypass Trail.** Use a topographic map for this loop, as some of the connections may not be obvious. This loop offers miles of alpine gardens for flower enthusiasts. Watch for marmots, ptarmigan, pika, and pipits on the tundra.

Access

See the trail access for Devils Thumb Bypass Trail to Jasper Lake, Devils Thumb Lake, and Devils Thumb Pass (page 186).

Woodland Lake, Skyscraper Reservoir

Distance: 4.3 miles one way to Woodland Lake, 4.8 miles one way to Skyscraper Reservoir

Elevation: 9,000 to 10,972 feet at Woodland Lake to 11,221 feet at Skyscraper Reservoir

Highlights: Waterfalls, turbulent creek, lakes, mountain views

Difficulty: Strenuous

Topo map: Nederland, East Portal

From the town site of Hessie, take the old jeep road up to Woodland Flats, crossing both the North Fork and the South Fork of Middle Boulder Creek. (See page 186 for more details on this section of the hike.) Just beyond the bridge across the South Fork, the trail branches, with the left branch leading to King Lake. Continue straight ahead past the Indian Peaks Wilderness boundary sign and

Moss campion

through a meadow filled with wildflowers in summer (this is the same as the original Devils Thumb Pass Trail). This section of the trail also passes by old beaver ponds and through some marshy areas where bog orchids and little red elephants bloom profusely.

In about a mile, the trail makes another fork, with the right branch going to Jasper Lake and Devils Thumb Pass, and the left fork to Woodland Lake and Skyscraper Reservoir. At this point, it's worth stopping at the small waterfall below the bridge over Jasper Creek to look for dippers (water ouzels). Continue up the Woodland Lake Trail, climbing steeply on the left side of the creek (a tributary of Jasper Creek) that drains Woodland Lake. After the trail crosses the creek (no bridge), it makes a wide sweep to the right and eventually returns to parallel the creek up through a spruce/fir forest to Woodland Lake.

The trail continues on the right-hand side of the lake and climbs steeply for about a half-mile up the remnants of an old road to Sky-scraper Reservoir. This last segment of the trail is somewhat faint and may be covered by snowfields early in the season. If you lose the trail, stay high on the right-hand side of the valley, avoiding the boggy area near the creek that flows out of the reservoir.

Everett Long (whose family started Long's Iris Gardens on North Broadway in 1905) built Skyscraper Reservoir for irrigation between 1941 and 1947. He sold the reservoir and water rights to the City of Boulder in 1966.

Access

See the Devils Thumb Bypass Trail (page 186).

Rollins Pass Area

Although most of this area lies in Gilpin County, we're including it because it's just barely over the county line, and it includes especially beautiful lakes, trails, wildflowers, and views as well as historic railroad artifacts. Traditionally, several of the trails described here have started at the East Portal of the Moffat Tunnel. However,

Trestles on Rollins Pass

we have described alternative trails, which are actually easier than starting from East Portal and which lead to popular destinations in the James Peak area of Roosevelt National Forest.

The route over Rollins Pass was first used by Native Americans, and stone hunting blinds and game-drive walls can still be seen in various places. John Fremont's party crossed the pass in the 1840s and left two men buried at Deadman's Gulch, now part of the Eldora Ski Area. The first road over the Continental Divide into Middle Park was opened in 1866 by General John Q. Rollins, who improved an old army route and ran it as a tollroad. Rollins also established the town of Rollinsville, refusing to allow saloons, gambling, or dance halls within the city limits.

David H. Moffat built his famous railroad across the pass in 1903. Railway workers called the town site at the summit "Corona—The Crown of the Top of the World." It was the highest railroad station in the world. A railroad station, hotel, and restaurant thrived here until 1928, when the Moffat Tunnel was completed and the line over the pass was closed. You can still see rail ties, remnants of the old snowsheds that protected the trains from avalanches, and some building foundations at the top of the pass. Although the pass is officially known as Rollins Pass, many of us still call it "Corona Pass."

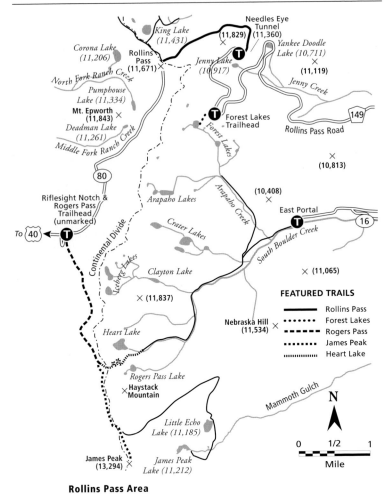

Rollins Pass Area

Forest Lakes

Distance: 0.5 mile one way to the second lake

Elevation: 11,000 to 10,680 feet

Highlights: Alpine lakes, sheer cliffs, moist coniferous forest, wildflowers, mushrooms

Difficulty: Easy

Topo Map: East Portal

From the ridge above Rollins Pass, we have counted eight lakes and tarns in the Forest Lakes basin, ranging from alpine glacial tarns to large, heavily wooded lakes, and ranging in color from turquoise to near-black. However, most of these can be reached only by rough fishing trails. The two largest lakes are reached by FS Trail 809, a well-defined trail starting at the Forest Lakes Trailhead. This trail is different from most because you reach the lakes by going down.

The trail drops from the Rollins Pass Road through a moist coniferous forest (good for mushrooming in August) to the first lake. A rough trail circles the lake, which nestles beneath dramatic cliffs and gendarmes and below a cascade bordered with wildflowers. We like to make the complete circuit of the lake, but the shorter route is to turn left when you reach the lake and go directly to the outlet, where another fishing trail leads down the east side of the creek. This trail leads past another small pond to the second of the Forest Lakes.

If you circumnavigate a large bog near this lake, look to the west side for the remains of a small red-and-white plane that crashed here many years ago. Mushrooms and wildflowers are especially profuse in this area—and so are bogs.

Forest Lakes

Connections

- If you start at the East Portal of Moffat Tunnel, we recommend using a topo map, even though the first section is easy. Hike about 1 mile west from the tunnel to a large meadow where two trails diverge. The left trail climbs steeply (and often obscurely) to **Heart Lake** (3.5 miles), and the right trail (not quite as steep) leads to the lowest Forest Lake in about 4 miles. Beyond the meadow, the **Forest Lakes Trail** follows an old road for a while, but the route is not marked and is easy to lose once the road peters out. Both trails are excellent for ski touring, and you can usually follow in someone else's tracks.

- A short distance beyond the Forest Lakes parking area, the road is closed to both vehicular and foot traffic at the **Needles Eye Tunnel**. However, if you walk the faint trail above the tunnel, you can continue up the ridge through tundra wildflowers and look down into the Forest Lakes. If you ascend this ridge, look for Native American game-drive blinds and walls.

Access

From Boulder, take SR 119 to Rollinsville. Turn west onto CR 16. In 7.5 miles, the road forks, with the left fork leading to the East Portal of the Moffat Tunnel. Continue right on the Rollins Pass Road for another 11 miles. The road gets fairly rough, passing Yankee Doodle and Jenny lakes en route. The parking area for Forest Lakes is on a hairpin curve just above Jenny Lake.

James Peak Via Rogers Pass Trail

Distance: 3.5 miles one way

Elevation: 11,000 to 13,294 feet

Highlights: Spectacular views, tundra flowers

Difficulty: Strenuous

Topo map: East Portal, Empire

Hiking across the tundra toward James Peak

Views from a thirteener are as spectacular as from a fourteener, and the climb is a bit easier. From James Peak, the prominent thirteener visible from many points in Boulder County, you can see all the way from Pikes Peak to the south, to Longs Peak to the north. Some additional fourteeners seen from the summit include Mounts Evans and Bierstadt, Grays and Torreys peaks, and Mount of the Holy Cross.

Starting in the spruce/fir forest at the Rogers Pass Trailhead at Riflesight Notch, the trail (actually an old road) contours gently up the hill toward Rogers Pass at 11,860 feet. Shortly after you reach timberline, another old road comes in from the left. (If you just want a wildflower walk, this is a pleasant road to explore.) At about 1.5 miles, you cross an old ditch, and soon the Continental Divide National Scenic Trail (marked by massive cairns as well as white posts with blue insignia) joins the Rogers Pass Trail from the left.

Continue for a short distance on this merged trail, but don't go all the way to Rogers Pass. Just before Rogers Pass, the route to James Peak drops slightly to the right and contours around Haystack Mountain before climbing to a slight saddle below the summit ridge of James Peak. Look for an ancient Native American hunting blind and a game-drive wall on this saddle. The Continen-

tal Divide Trail continues to follow the divide south all the way to
Berthoud Pass and beyond. At the saddle, leave the Continental
Divide Trail and follow the large stone cairns straight up the talus
slope to the summit.

History

Dr. Edwin James, a member of Major Stephen H. Long's expedi-
tion, was the first man on record to climb a 14,000-foot peak in the
United States. He and two companions climbed Pikes Peak (which
Pike never climbed) in 1820. Long, in the early 1820s, was prob-
ably the first white explorer to enter Boulder County. Later, James
Peak was named for Edwin James and Longs Peak for Stephen
Long.

The trestle at Riflesight Notch was part of the "Loop" on David
Moffat's railroad line. At this point, the train crossed the notch on
the trestle, circled the hill, went through a tunnel (now collapsed)
beneath the trestle, and descended to Middle Park.

Connections

- **South Boulder Creek Trail** (a continuation of Rogers Pass Trail)
  to **Heart Lake** drops down 1 mile from Rogers Pass to Heart
  Lake. You can continue another 3 miles down to East Portal.

- **Continental Divide National Scenic Trail** joins the Rogers Pass
  Trail and offers seemingly limitless tundra walking in either direction.

Access

From US 40, take the Rollins Pass turnoff (CR 80) about 1.5
miles below the Winter Park Ski Area and drive 12 miles up to the
Rogers Pass Trailhead, which begins on the right-hand side of the
road across from the trestle over Riflesight Notch. Park in wide
spots along the road. James Peak can also be climbed from James
Peak Lake Trailhead, from St. Mary's Glacier, and from South Boulder Creek Trail, starting at the East Portal of Moffat Tunnel.

NEARBY STATE
AND COUNTY PARKS

S everal state parks and a Jefferson County park are within an
hour of Boulder and offer excellent hiking trails. The ones
described here are our favorites.

Eldorado Canyon State Park

This canyon is internationally renowned for its rock climbing and
for the dramatic red-rock formations. A required state parks pass is
available at the park entrance and at the visitor center at the end of
the road.

Rattlesnake Gulch Trail

Distance: 1.9 miles to hotel ruins

Elevation: 6,050 to 6,760 feet

Highlights: Views of red-rock formations and rock climbers, hotel ruins, woodland and canyon birds

Difficulty: Moderate

Topo map: Eldorado Springs

At the Rattlesnake Gulch Trailhead sign, follow the trail to your left and enjoy views of the red-rock walls that form a spectacular gateway to Eldorado Canyon. At the first switchback, the **Fowler Trail** (0.7 mile; 40-foot elevation gain) goes behind the Bastille rock formation to the eastern park boundary.

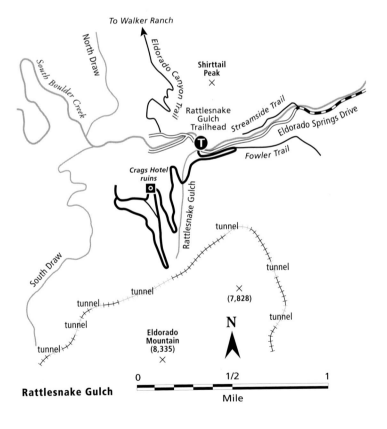

Rattlesnake Gulch

Eldorado Canyon State Park

From the switchback, the main trail climbs to a flat area below an aqueduct. It then drops down to cross a small stream, which may be dry in summer. From here, the trail zigzags up an east-facing slope to the ruins of the Crags Hotel. Only the foundations, a fireplace, and the basin of an ornamental fountain remain. Junipers, Douglas firs, and ponderosa pines now grow out of the crumbled brick and crockery shards, while sumac thrives in the fountain. This hotel opened in 1908 and burned down in 1912. Possibly some of the guests watched Ivy Baldwin, who walked a seven-eighths-inch cable strung between the Bastille and Wind Tower at a height of 685 feet. From 1906 until his eighty-second birthday in 1948, he crossed the high wire eighty-nine times.

At the south (upper) end of the ruins plateau, the trail forks, making a 0.8-mile loop up to the Santa Fe and Rio Grande Railroad at 7,220 feet. If you time your hike to coincide with the schedule of the train, you can watch it emerge from one tunnel and enter another one. A short distance up the right branch, a spur goes to a viewpoint for the Continental Divide.

Other Park Trails

- **Streamside Trail** (0.3 mile; 20-foot elevation gain) near the park entrance goes along the north side of South Boulder Creek, giving access to various rock-climbing routes such as the Wind Tower and Redgarden Wall.

- **Eldorado Canyon Trail** (4.5 miles: 970-foot elevation gain) starts on the north side of the road at the upper end of the park and goes up and down hill to connect with the Walker Ranch Loop (page 127).

Access

Turn west from US 93, 4 miles south of Boulder, onto Eldorado Springs Drive and continue to the west end of El Dorado Springs. From the park entrance, drive 0.6 mile up the road to a small parking area at the Rattlesnake Gulch Trailhead.

White Ranch County Park

   White Ranch Park in Jefferson County covers 3,040 acres and includes more than 18 miles of multi-use trails. To sort out the many intersecting trails, be sure to get a map at the west parking lot. Be aware of possible changes, as trail building and realigning are currently underway. The rock formations throughout the park are rich in mica, and many of the trails glitter like gold because of this mineral.

White Ranch Park

Rawhide Loop

Distance: 4.5 miles round trip

Elevation: 7,500 feet, with losses and gains of several hundred feet

Highlights: Views of Denver and the plains, wildlife, wildflowers, historic farm equipment

Difficulty: Easy to moderate

Topo map: Ralston Buttes, Golden

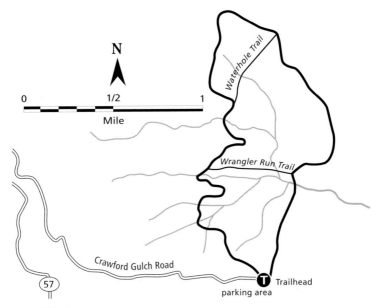

Rawhide Loop

We like to start at the west end of this loop, which follows an old ranch road downhill in a northerly direction. The trail goes up and down through open meadows and ponderosa-pine forests. At 1.1 miles, the **Wrangler's Run Trail** forks to the right, and at the Sourdough Springs Equestrian Camp, the **Waterhole Trail** also forks to the right. Both of these trails reconnect with the Rawhide Trail, making shorter loops possible.

In about 2.5 miles, the Rawhide Trail turns east, narrows, and begins the return part of the loop through Douglas-fir and ponderosa-pine trees, with views of the Ralston Buttes and of Denver.

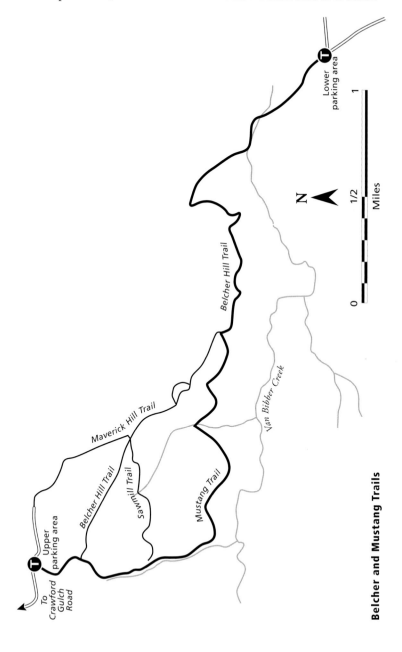

Belcher and Mustang Trails

This section is especially lovely in late April and early May when pink-flowering cacti bloom and blue grouse boom. Just before reaching the parking lot, you pass through an "open-air museum" with interpretive signs, featuring nineteenth-century harrows, seed drills, and other farming machinery, similar to that used by the Paul White family when they homesteaded here in the early 1900s.

Other Park Trails

- **Belcher Trail** can be combined with **Mustang Trail** for a one-way, 4.7-mile descent to the lower parking area 1 mile west of SR 93. This trail passes through numerous life zones with views of cliffs, grasslands, and a deep canyon formed by Van Bibber Creek.

Access

Take SR 93 south from Boulder and turn west on CR 70 (Golden Gate Canyon Road), 0.5 mile before reaching Golden. Continue 4 miles. Turn right on CR 57 (Crawford Gulch Road) and follow the signs for White Ranch Park. Park at the second parking lot.

Golden Gate Canyon State Park

More than 35 miles of trails crisscross this state park, which is one of our favorite places for early spring flowers and for autumn aspens. Many of the trails, labeled with signs depicting wildlife tracks, eventually lead to Frazer Meadow, a grassy opening surrounded by aspens and containing the ruins of an old homestead. Stop at the visitor center to purchase the required state parks pass and to see the excellent displays. Also, pick up a trail map and bird and flower lists.

Horseshoe Trail to Frazer Meadow

Distance: 1.8 miles one way

Elevation: 8,200 to 9,200 feet

Highlights: Aspen, wildflowers, grassy meadows

Difficulty: Easy

Map: Golden Gate Canyon State Park map

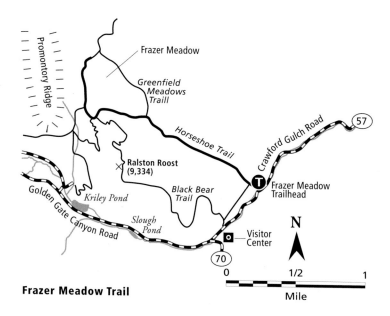

Frazer Meadow Trail

Autumn aficionados delight in this trail, which passes through aspen groves and an understory of shrubs and herbaceous plants that turn scarlet, crimson, and gold in September. Starting at the Frazer Meadow Trailhead, the trail (designated by a horseshoe symbol on the signs) parallels a small seasonal stream, crossing it several times. A short distance from the trailhead, **Black Bear Trail** to Ralston Roost takes off to the left. Continue up on Horseshoe Trail. In a little more than a mile, a trail to **Greenfield Meadows** and some backcountry camp sites veers to the right. To make a loop, take this branch to Frazer Meadow, returning via the Horseshoe Trail.

Frazer Meadow Trail

Otherwise, continue on Horseshoe Trail, which crosses and then leaves the stream. The trail climbs past the Ground Squirrel Trail and merges with the Mule Deer Trail. At the Mule Deer intersection, turn right, cross the stream again, and stop at the ruins where John Frazer homesteaded in 1880. Aspens circle the meadow, and beyond the aspens, a coniferous forest cloaks craggy rock formations.

History

This area was once famous for bootlegging—an operation commemorated by the place-name "Bootleg Bottom." Some seventeen stills were said to be active in the 1920s when local farmers were the principal suppliers for Denver and Central City. The chief entrepreneur and his driver transported whisky (made from corn, sugar, water, and yeast) and gin (flavored with juniper berries) in a wagon labeled "Smith's Breadwagon." To confuse the lawmen, they flipped a coin to determine their route and ran cattle behind the wagon to obliterate the tracks.

Connections

So many trails interconnect in this park that hikers can make almost endless permutations, looping in whatever direction fancy takes. By doing a car shuttle, you can hike from one end of the park to the other—from Bootleg Bottom to the Frazer Meadow Trailhead, for instance. Check the park map for possibilities.

Access

Take SR 93 south from Boulder to Golden Gate Canyon Road (CR 70). Turn west and continue for about 14 miles to the visitor center. Frazer Meadow Trailhead is about half a mile east of the Golden Gate Canyon State Park Visitor Center, on the north side of the road.

Barr Lake State Park

From the 1940s through the 1960s, pollution from Denver sometimes created rafts of white, soapy-looking bubbles that were more common than rafts of white pelicans. A new sewage-treatment plant improved the water quality, and Barr Lake opened as a state park in 1977. The southern half of the lake is now a wildlife refuge, and the northern half is open to boating and fishing.

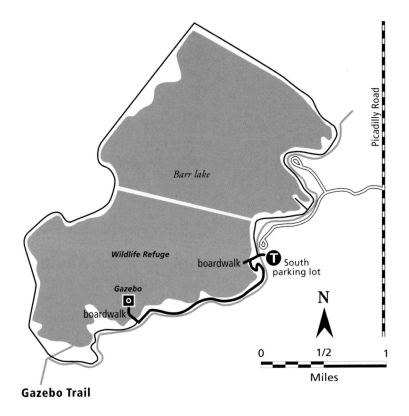

Gazebo Trail

Three hundred and forty-six species of birds have been seen in the park, which serves as the headquarters for the Colorado Bird Observatory, a nonprofit organization for research on western birds. Stop at the nature center to see the displays and to check a bulletin

Bald eagle

board that lists recently observed species of birds and mammals. Park naturalists often give guided walks.

Gazebo Trail

Distance: 1.5 miles one way

Elevation: About 5,150 feet, with no elevation gain

Highlights: Birdwatching, nature study, lake and mountain views

Difficulty: Easy

Map: Barr Lake State Park

From the south parking lot and picnic area, cross the bridge over the Denver and Hudson Canal and turn left (south). Almost immediately, you have a choice: the left branch stays high, whereas the right branch takes a short detour on a boardwalk out over the water. If you're birdwatching, take the boardwalk!

The boardwalk soon rejoins the main trail, which follows the lakeshore around to another boardwalk leading across the water to a gazebo that is usually equipped with a viewing scope. From here, you can watch a rookery populated by great blue herons and cormorants. For several years, a pair of bald eagles has nested in the vicinity of this rookery and can often be seen in spring, along with white pelicans, western grebes, and various other waterbirds. From May until fall migration, warblers, orioles, and other colorful birds can be seen in the cottonwoods along the shoreline.

Connections

• A 9-mile, unnamed trail, including the Gazebo Trail, circles the entire lake.

Access

From Boulder, take SR 7 to Brighton. Just before reaching Brighton, turn right onto US 85. In a few blocks, turn left onto Bromley Lane. Continue east on Bromley Lane to Picadilly Road. From here, large brown signs direct you to Barr Lake, which is located at 13401 Picadilly Road. Stop at the entrance for the required state parks pass and for a brochure and map. For more information on activities at Barr Lake State Park, call 303-659-6005.

WHEELCHAIR-ACCESSIBLE TRAILS

St. Vrain Creek

Golden Ponds Park

3rd Avenue

St. Vrain Creek

Hover Road

Fairgounds Pond

0   1/4   1/2

Mile

Rogers Road

To Izaak Wa

This section is dedicated to Tom and Maddy Goldhawk for their courage and gallantry.

M ost Greenways trails are wheelchair accessible and are described in a free Greenways Trails map; call 303-441-3266. *Boulder Area Accessible Trails and Natural Sites*, by Topher Downham, Steven Mertz, and Dinah Pollard (free at the Chautauqua ranger cottage and at Boulder recreation centers) is an invaluable resource that includes detailed maps. Consult this book for more details on the trails below and for additional trails and sites.

These selected wheelchair-accessible trails are described in more detail earlier in our book:

- **Boulder Creek Path** (page 23) is either paved or has a hard surface for the entire distance.

- **Centennial Trail** (page 29) is paved.

- **Coal Creek Trail** (page 35) is mostly crusher fines and hard-packed gravel, but access from Aquarius Trailhead is difficult; park along Elysian Field Drive instead.

- **Coot Lake Trail** (page 7) has a good surface and a fishing pier but involves a bridge if you circle the lake.

- **Doudy Draw Trail** (page 125) is paved for the first 0.3 mile to a picnic area in a cottonwood grove. The southern end of the **Mesa Trail** across the road can be negotiated by wheelchair but is difficult.

- **Dry Creek Trail** (page 30) has a crusher fines surface.

- **East Boulder Trail, Teller Farm Section**, and **Teller Lake No. 5** trails (page 13) have good surfaces and lead to fishing access. The White Rocks Section is negotiable for about 1.5 miles but is often muddy.

- **Foothills Trail** (page 64) has a crusher fines surface for the 0.75-mile section connecting Locust Avenue and Lee Hill Drive. The upper section connecting to Wonderland Lake is not recommended, but you can reach the lake via the lower trail starting at Foothills Nature Center. The **Wonderland Lake Trail** can be extended by taking paved walks through the adjoining neighborhood.

- **Fowler Trail** (page 202) has a slight uphill grade, but the crusher fines surface can be negotiated to the point where it ends behind the Bastille.

- **Gazebo Trail** at Barr Lake State Park (page 214) follows an old dirt road for most of the distance, with a boardwalk leading out to the gazebo.

- **Long Lake** (page 161), the first segment of the **Pawnee Pass Trail**, is dirt and would be feasible for wheelchairs only when the trail is dry. The grade is slightly steeper than 6 percent in places.

- **Mary Miller Trail** (page 33) at Rock Creek Farm has a good surface and offers fishing access at Stearns Lake.

- **Pella Crossing** (page 5) skirts several lakes with fishing access.

- **Sage Trail** (page 10) has a good surface but some grades of 12 percent.

- **South Boulder Creek Trail** (page 27) between Baseline Road and the East Boulder Community Center, and between Valmont Lake and Arapahoe Road, is paved. The segments continuing to South Boulder Road and on to Marshall Road are either crusher fines, gravel, or hard dirt.

- **St. Vrain Greenways Trail** in Longmont (page 2) is paved and includes a loop around Fairgrounds Lake.

- **Walden** and **Sawhill Ponds trails** (page 18) are level and consist of either crusher fines, hard gravel, or hard dirt. Heatherwood-Walden Trail is paved to the boundary with Walden Ponds.

- **Walter Orr Roberts Nature Trail** (see page 105) has a good surface and spectacular views.

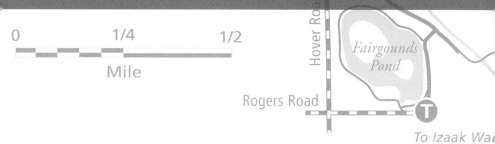

OUTDOOR ETHICS

Adapted from the *Boulder County Nature Almanac*

There's no shortage of hiking trails or outdoor places to go in Boulder County. But now there's also a superabundance of people, many of whom frequent these trails and places. To put things in perspective, according to naturalist Steve Jones, there are 250,000 humans and only a couple of dozen black bears; 110,000 human dwellings and only about 10 golden eagle nest sites; 60 retail florists and only a half-dozen known specimens of white adder's-mouth, one of our rarest orchids.

Whenever we go out into nature, we run the risk of loving it to death. Although anyone who would use this book probably already "treads lightly" on the land, here are a few suggestions to help us all preserve the places we cherish.

- Leave wildflowers, plants, and even rocks for others to enjoy.

- Leave archaeological and historical artifacts undisturbed.

- Comply with signs regarding pets, and keep dogs leashed where required.

- Comply with signs regarding vehicles and mountain bikes, which are prohibited on some trails because of problems with erosion.

- Do not shortcut trails. Shortcuts destroy vegetation and cause erosion.

- Build campfires only when and where they are permitted, and never leave one unattended.

- Bury human waste and bury or burn toilet paper or carry it out.

- Leave gates open or closed, as they are found.

- Give right-of-way to horses, keeping to the downhill side. Horse riders should keep to trails.

- Do not disturb nesting birds, and comply with closures designed to protect plants or animals. Keep all pets out of these areas, too.

- When hiking on trails used for ski touring, avoid stepping in the ski tracks. Your steps can leave "post-holes" that are dangerous for skiers.

- Do not leave trash or food behind. Carry out your litter, and, if you want to do a good deed, carry out litter left by others.

- Respect no-trespassing and private-property signs. Explore only where permitted.

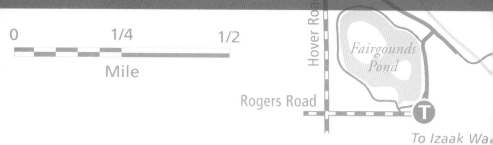

OUTDOOR SAFETY

Adapted from the *Boulder County Nature Almanac*

Taking precautions against hazardous conditions you may meet along any trail—from the plains to the mountains—can help make every hiking experience safe and pleasant. Here are a few tips on preparing for a safe hike in Boulder's outdoors.

- Dress appropriately for the weather, which can change quickly, especially in the mountains. Even in summer, a light jacket and poncho may be needed. In winter, dress in layers for added insulation and to facilitate quick adjustments. Use a broad-brimmed hat or visor in summer and a warm cap in winter. Be aware of the symptoms of hypothermia.

- Use a sunscreen lotion with a rating of 15 or higher, and wear dark, UV-protecting glasses—Colorado's sun is fierce.

- Always take plenty of water, maps, emergency food, and basic first-aid supplies, except for the easiest strolls.

- Don't hike alone. If you insist on going solo, be sure someone knows where you're going and when you'll return.

- Newcomers need time to acclimate to the high altitude. Be aware of the symptoms of altitude sickness. If you feel altitude sickness, return immediately to a lower elevation.

- In winter, be aware of avalanche danger and avoid areas where avalanches may occur.

- Anticipate thunderstorms on summer afternoons, especially at high elevations. If you are caught in a thunderstorm, get to a lower elevation quickly and avoid seeking shelter under isolated trees, rock formations, fences, and power lines. If lightning is actually striking around you, squat in the lowest area you can find.

- If a flood warning is issued, climb to the highest ground possible. Don't try to drive out of a canyon ahead of a flood.

- Don't drink water from lakes or streams. *Giardia lamblia*, a parasite that attacks the intestinal system, is widespread. Backpackers should treat water by boiling it for twenty minutes or use a filter pump.

- Check for ticks, which can carry several diseases, during spring and summer. Brush them off if they have not yet embedded in your skin. If they are embedded, cover the tick with heavy oil and wait for half an hour. If it hasn't disengaged by then, use tweezers.

- Be extra careful around waterfalls, rushing streams, and irrigation ditches. Watch children in such circumstances.

- Be alert for hazards such as poison ivy, rattlesnakes, and mine openings and shafts.

- Do not eat mushrooms, berries, or plants unless you are absolutely positive of their identification.

- Be prudent around wildlife. Don't feed or pet wild animals, and don't come between a mother and her young. Although bear and mountain-lion sightings are uncommon, they have been increasing in recent years. Back slowly away if a bear or mountain lion is sighted, avoid direct eye contact, and speak calmly. An attack is most unlikely. However, if a mountain lion stalks you, respond aggressively and make yourself appear as large as possible; don't run. If either a bear or lion attacks, fight back.

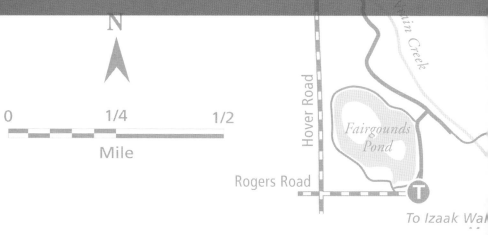

BIBLIOGRAPHY

Maps

Available at Boulder sporting-goods stores or from the issuing agency.

- Boulder County Road Map. Available from Boulder Chamber of Commerce, 2440 Pearl Street.

- Boulder Greenways Self-Guided Tour Map, 2004. Available free from the Boulder Greenways Coordinator, (303) 441-3266.

- City of Boulder Open Space and Mountain Parks Lands Trails Map, 2004.

- Colorado Mountain Club, Boulder Group. Ski Trail Map: Brainard Lake–Middle St. Vrain, 1996.

- Colorado Mountain Club, Boulder Group. Trail Map: Boulder Mountain Parks and Nearby Open Space, 2004.

- U.S. Forest Service. Arapaho and Roosevelt National Forests, 1997.

- U.S. Geological Survey. Boulder County, Colorado. 1:50,000-scale Topographic Map, 1980.

- U.S. Geological Survey. 7.5 minute series USGS topographic maps for smaller units, as noted in trail descriptions, various years.

Books

Most are available at the Carnegie Library or Boulder Public Libraries.

Ament, Pat, and Cleve McCarty. *High Over Boulder*. Boulder, Colo.: March Press, 1976.

Arps, Louisa Ward, and Elinor Eppich Kingery. *High Country Names*. Boulder, Colo.: Johnson Publishing Co., 1972.

Benedict, James B. *Arapaho Pass*. Ward, Colo.: Center for Mountain Archaeology, 1985.

———. *Archaeology of the Coney Creek Valley*. Ward, Colo.: Center for Mountain Archaeology, 1990.

Bixby, Amos. "History of Boulder County." *History of Clear Creek and Boulder Valleys, Colorado*. Chicago: O. L. Baskin & Company, 1880.

Bridge, Raymond. *Geology of Boulder County*. Boulder, Colo.: Lone Eagle, 2005.

Crossen, Forest. *Western Yesterdays: David Moffat's Hill Men*. Fort Collins, Colo.: Robinson Press, 1976.

Cushman, Ruth Carol, Stephen R. Jones, and Jim Knopf. *Boulder County Nature Almanac*. Boulder, Colo.: Pruett Publishing Co., 1993.

Downham, Topher, Steven J. Mertz, and Dinah S. Pollard. *Boulder Area Accessible Trails & Natural Sites*. Boulder, Colo.: Boulder County Parks and Open Space, 2000.

Eberhart, Perry. *Guide to the Colorado Ghost Towns and Mining Camps*, 4th ed. Chicago: Sage Press, 1969.

Exploring Boulder County, 2nd ed. Boulder, Colo.: Boulder County Parks and Open Space Department, 1993.

Helmuth, Ed, and Gloria Helmuth. *The Passes of Colorado*. Boulder, Colo.: Pruett Publishing Co., 1994.

Hudson, Suzanne. *History of Boulder's Parks and Recreation, or How We Got to Be So Pretty.* Boulder, Colo.: Boulder Parks and Recreation Department, 1993.

Meier, Tom. "It Ain't Necessarily So." *The Early Settlement of Boulder: Set in Type—Cast in Bronze—Fused in Porcelain.* Boulder, Colo.: Boulder Creek Press, 1993.

Mitchell, Mark F., and Peter J. Gleichman. "Cultural Resource Inventory of the Contiguous Boulder Mountain Parks." Unpublished manuscript, on file at City of Boulder Mountain Parks Department, 1996.

Olmsted, Frederick Law. "The Improvement of Boulder County: Report to the City Improvement Association." Boulder, Colo.: Boulder City Improvement Association, 1910.

Ormes, Robert M. *Guide to the Colorado Mountains*, 9th ed. Edited by Randy Jacobs. Denver, Colo.: Colorado Mountain Club, distributed by Cordillera Press, 1992.

Pettem, Silvia. *Boulder: Evolution of a City.* Niwot, Colo.: University of Colorado Press, 1994.

Roach, Gerry. *Colorado's Indian Peaks Wilderness Area: Classic Hikes and Climbs.* Golden, Colo.: Fulcrum Publishing Co., 1989.

———. *Flatirons Classics: A Guide to Easy Climbs and Trails in Boulder's Flatirons.* Golden, Colo.: Fulcrum Publishing Co., 1987.

Robertson, Janet. *The Front Rangers.* Boulder, Colo.: Colorado Mountain Club, 1971.

Schoolland, John. *Boulder in Perspective.* Boulder, Colo.: Johnson Publishing Co., 1980.

———. *Boulder Then and Now.* Boulder, Colo.: Pruett Publishing Co., 1979.

Smith, Phyllis. *A Look at Boulder: From Settlement to City.* Boulder, Colo.: Pruett Publishing Co., 1981.

Wolle, Muriel Sibell. *Stampede to Timberline.* Boulder, Colo.: Self-published, 1949.

Websites

Numerous websites give useful information; surf the Internet under keywords and under various governmental agencies. Here are three of the most useful for Boulder:

www.fs.fed.us/arnf (click on Recreation)

www.ci.boulder.co.us/openspace

www.co.boulder.co.us/openspace (click on Recreation)

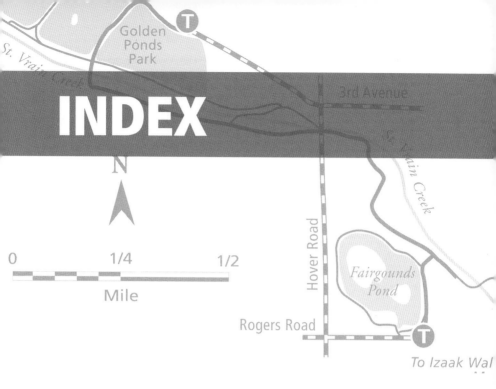

Leadership in Business Education

National Business Education Association
1914 Association Drive
Reston, VA 20191–1596

ISBN: 0-933964-79-X

Leadershi
Business Education

National Business Education Association Yearbook, No.

2014

Co-Editors
Marcia Anderson
Barbara Hagler
Southern Illinois University Carbondale

Published by

National Business Education Association
1914 Association Drive
Reston, VA 20191-1596
(703) 860-8300 • Fax: (703) 620-4483
www.nbea.org

PREFACE

Leadership for the business education profession has never been more critical than now. Profound changes have occurred for the profession in the past several decades requiring new thinking and leadership approaches to assure that business education remains on the forefront in education. Authors for this 2014 NBEA Yearbook, *Leadership in Business Education*, are recognized leaders in the profession and have shared numerous ideas and strategies for all business educators for their varied leadership roles in the profession.

Chapters in this yearbook are organized into three parts:

Part 1: Approaches to Leadership includes four chapters: *Chapter 1: Nature of Leadership* addresses leadership traits and styles, leaders as vision creators, and current leadership models. *Chapter 2: Educational Administrators' Leadership for 21st Century Business Education* focuses on research relating to the effectiveness of business education, including career and technical education, administrators at all levels to bridge the gap among education, workforce training, and economic development. *Chapter 3: The Leader as Motivator and Communicator* discusses the importance of the human element in organizations, including practical methods for motivating and communicating in educational environments, technology applications, and the use of social media. *Chapter 4: Leadership Profiles of Business Educators* presents results of interviews with individuals who are recognized for their varied business education leadership roles regarding their perceptions on how the profession prospers through strategic leadership.

Part 2: Leadership for the Business Education Profession contains the following chapters: *Chapter 5: Leadership for Advancing Research in Business Education* covers the fundamental role of research and scholarship in the advancement of the profession and how scholarly journals serve to document the past and disseminate current scholarly research that develops the profession's knowledge base. *Chapter 6: Leadership in Professional Associations for Business Education* discusses leadership roles and trends in professional organizations given their obligation to ensure the quality of professional preparation, practice, and continuing professional education. *Chapter 7: Business Teacher Education Program Leadership* outlines the process for entering the business education profession as a certified teacher and the leader's role in innovative teacher preparation program delivery, assuring quality clinical placement as well as local, state, and national professional involvement. *Chapter 8: Leadership for Legislative Impact and for Business Education Partnerships* stresses the involvement of business education professionals and their advocacy for the profession in legislative arenas and in creating partnerships.

Part 3: Business Education Program Leadership: Roles and Responsibilities has five chapters: *Chapter 9: Leadership in State-Level Business and Career and Technical Education Divisions* identifies roles and responsibilities of the business education state supervisor in interpreting state and federal educational legislation, statewide curriculum dissemination, student organizations, integration of the academic curriculum, and teacher certification. *Chapter 10: Leadership for the Elementary/Middle School Business Education Curriculum* stresses business education emphasis at this level, discussing career guidance and exploration opportunities, curricular offerings, and program articulation. *Chapter 11: Leadership in Secondary Education Business Programs* presents the leadership perspective for the secondary education business and academic curriculum using state, national, and professional standards, as well as student organizations, program funding, professional development, advisory boards, student recruitment, and articulation. *Chapter 12: Leadership in Community College Business Programs* outlines community college leaders' responsibilities in student recruitment, business course and program development, staffing and faculty development, business student organizations, budgeting, student job placement, community resources, advisory boards, and articulation. *Chapter 13: Leadership in College and University Business Programs* provides leadership views related to undergraduate and graduate academic programming, students and quality assurance, faculty development and research responsibilities, and program funding and accreditation.

Part 4: Business Teachers and Business Students as Leaders includes three chapters: *Chapter 14: The Business Teacher as Leader* addresses the teacher leader development process of participating in high-quality professional development, building effective relationships, navigating challenges, effecting change, and guiding the advancement of the profession. *Chapter 15: Developing Business Students' Leadership Characteristics for Workforce Roles* identifies leadership characteristics needed by future business workers—decision making, reasoning, critical thinking, oral/written communication skills—and instructional strategies for developing these traits in secondary/postsecondary students. *Chapter 16: Business Student Organization Leadership* discusses the role of business student organizations in developing leadership, communication, and team skills among students, along with requisite advisor leadership for developing and retaining a quality business student organization.

Chapter authors were encouraged to integrate relevant policy statements enacted by the Policies Commission for Business and Economic Education into the chapter's leadership content. As reflected in the October 2013 NBEA *Business Education Forum* article entitled "A Legacy of Leadership: PCBEE's Impact on Business and Economic Education," this commission "provides leadership in defining the parameters of the discipline, recommending action to improve the discipline, and serving as a voice for the discipline" (p. 42). PCBEE policy statements indicate philosophies and foundations for the business education profession and are referenced by business education leaders.

The 23 contributing authors to this yearbook are to be lauded for their willingness to make the commitment to share their leadership expertise in their chapters to make this publication a reality. These authors represent all NBEA regions and a variety of business education backgrounds.

Leadership in Business Education is a refereed publication. Chapter organization and chapter thesis statements for the publication were initially reviewed by the NBEA Publications Committee. Committee members also provided input on potential authors for each chapter. Each chapter was reviewed by three or more business educators specially selected for their knowledge and background on the chapter's topic.

And a special note of appreciation goes to Pamela S. Cubberly, NBEA editor, for her attention to detail as she worked to bring the chapters of this yearbook together; her spirit of teamwork in communicating with chapter authors and with us in making this yearbook the best possible publication was indeed admirable.

Marcia Anderson, Co-Editor
Barbara Hagler, Co-Editor
Southern Illinois University Carbondale

BOARD OF REVIEWERS

Special thanks to the members of the review board, for their time and talent graciously given to reviewing the 16 chapters of the 2014 NBEA Yearbook, *Leadership in Business Education*.

Nature of Leadership

Priscilla Y. Romkema
Black Hills State University
Spearfish, SD

To better understand and appreciate the "nature of leadership" in business education, the development of leaders, the qualities of leaders, and the conditions necessary for leaders to emerge must be examined within the complexities of leadership. Researchers, authors, and journalists since before the 20th century have provided a wealth of perspectives and insights into the "art and science" of the field. Today, a substantial body of literature exists to examine and build on so that leadership and leaders may be better understood, identified, and developed. This chapter will address definition(s) of leadership, leadership theories, and styles of leadership, as well as the leadership commitment shared by business educators, as evidenced in selected statements from the Policies Commission for Business and Economic Education (PCBEE).

KEY ELEMENTS AND CONCEPTS

What is leadership? This section will discuss some key elements and concepts of leadership, as well as traits, attributes, qualities, and characteristics of leaders.

Since the late 19th century, individuals from various disciplines, including psychology, business, and sociology, have generated theories, models, and studies to create a substantive body of literature in the broad area of leadership. Leaders themselves have become the focus of articles, books, and chapters as leadership models and theories are applied to styles and situations. Harvard Business School, among others, maintains an online database of leaders. As stated on the school's Web site, "This database was compiled in an effort to identify and chronicle the lives of 20th century men and women whose business leadership shaped the ways that people live, work, and interact" (Harvard Business School, n.d., p. 1). This database serves as a visual timeline of leaders who have risen to address challenges in their industry, served as leaders in various geographic locations, and responded to the economic, political, social, and cultural realities of the particular time in history in which they lived.

Definitions of leadership are as varied in depth and breadth as the body of literature itself. The leadership quotes below, each excerpted from Kruse (2012), concisely reflect the variations of leadership theories and models. They are listed as examples of leadership perspectives held by cultural, political, business, and social leaders over the decades.

- "He who has never learned to obey cannot be a good commander." (Aristotle)

- "A leader is a dealer in hope." (Napoleon Bonaparte)

- "Lead me, follow me, or get out of my way." (General George Patton)

- "You manage things; you lead people." (Rear Admiral Grace Murray Hopper)

- "Outstanding leaders go out of their way to boost the self-esteem of their personnel. If people believe in themselves, it's amazing what they can accomplish." (Sam Walton)

- "Effective leadership is putting first things first. Effective management is discipline, carrying it out." (Stephen Covey)

- "Before you are a leader, success is all about growing yourself. When you become a leader, success is all about growing others." (Jack Welch)

- "A leader is one who knows the way, goes the way, and shows the way." (John Maxwell)

- "Effective leadership is not about making speeches or being liked; leadership is defined by results not attributes." (Peter Drucker)

- "The key to successful leadership today is influence, not authority." (Kenneth Blanchard)

- "Leadership and learning are indispensable to each other." (John F. Kennedy)

- "You gain strength, courage, and confidence by every experience in which you really stop to look fear in the face. You must do the thing you think you cannot do." (Eleanor Roosevelt)

In 2010 Northouse stated the following:

Leadership is a process whereby an individual influences a group of individuals to achieve a common goal...leadership is a process, includes influence, occurs in groups, involves common goals...defining leadership as a process means that it is not a trait or characteristic that resides in the leader, rather a transactional event that occurs between the leader and the followers. (p. 3)

In a review of literature on leadership, it is not uncommon to see the following areas identified, examined, analyzed, and measured in order to better understand the nature of leadership: action, attributes, attitude, accomplishments, assertiveness, discipline, flexibility, and transformation. Although common threads appear in the literature, a vast array of perspectives and positions exists.

Those who are or will be engaged in research, scholarship, and creative activity in leadership are well positioned to enhance the depth and breadth of an already vibrant field of research.

LEADERHIP TRAITS: POSITIVE AND NEGATIVE

Bass and Bass (2008) stated that "a trait is a construct based on consistent individual differences between people; personality is the organized pattern of distinctive traits of a specific person" (p. 103). Traits have a lasting nature. Although a trait may be noted in an individual in a given moment or during a brief period, the trait's true impact is experienced and noted over an extended period and, therefore, is continuous and recurring.

According to the educational portal *Management Study Guide* ("Trait theory," n.d.), it is stated that the

trait model of leadership is based on the characteristics of many leaders—both successful and unsuccessful—and is used to predict leadership effectiveness. The resulting lists of traits are then compared to those of potential leaders to assess their likelihood of success or failure. (n.d., p. 1)

Leaders may exhibit positive and/or negative traits over the course of their lives and a given leader's construct may be perceived by followers or other leaders in a positive or negative manner.

Students in leadership courses at Woodbury University in Los Angeles (Marques, 2007) worked with their respective professors to use the phenomenological approach to examine qualities of world-renowned leaders. The review and analysis of the six leaders chosen was based solely on the skills of these leaders and the impact of these skills on others and themselves. As the students conducted their research, the qualities of the leaders were grouped as either positive or negative. Examples of positive qualities identified in this study follow: motivating, independent, resilient, courageous, communicative, visionary, motivational, charismatic, and determined. Negative qualities noted in this study were overconfident, mismanaging, ruthless, inflexible, intolerant, unethical, disrespectful, stubborn, authoritarian, and coercive.

In the final analysis of Marques's study, the qualities that surfaced as common threads among all six leaders were confidence, hard work, empathy, risk taking, communication, strategic insight, intelligence, determination, resilience, passion, and respect for close relatives. Multiple theories must be considered when drawing conclusions about leadership. In addition, "leaders can utilize their skills, traits, and behaviors in positive and negative ways with equal success" (Marques, 2007, p. 100). The research study further demonstrated that adaptability and flexibility are both important from leaders. Thus, it should be noted that there are challenges in drawing on one theory only to classify a given leader.

LEADERSHIP ATTRIBUTES, QUALITIES, AND CHARACTERISTICS

Leaders are often referenced regarding the attributes, qualities, and characteristics they exhibit. Although the three terms reflect common perspectives, there are some distinctive aspects regarding each. Definitions for attributes, qualities, and characteristics follow:

- **Attributes:** things noted as belonging to a person (quality, character, characteristic, or property) ("Attributes," 2013)

- **Qualities:** essential or distinctive characteristics, properties, or attributes ("Qualities," 2013)

- **Characteristics:** distinguishing features or qualities ("Characteristics," 2013)

The *attributes* of leaders symbolize the core or essence of those individuals. Many attributes are noted and detailed in the literature. A compilation of leadership information at Texas Tech University (Clark, 2000) yielded three primary attributes that must be possessed and exhibited by leaders: standard bearers, developers, and integrators:

- **Standard bearers.** Leaders establish the ethical framework of an organization and model this on a daily basis. This ethical framework creates and fosters a culture that defines the organization going forward. When situations and challenges arise in an organization, how leaders respond serves as an example to others.

- **Developers.** Leaders serve as teachers, trainers, and coaches in the organization. In doing so, they lay the foundation for a learning, growing organization. Development of others by seizing opportunities, leading, following, working with others, and taking risks provides the environment that embodies development.

- **Integrators.** A leader is similar to the conductor of an orchestra in understanding the macro picture of the organization and creating and articulating a vision so that others understand their roles and contributions. Using an orchestra as an illustration serves as a visualization of the desired unity, momentum, and anticipation. Leaders who are integrators are proactive and sense where there may be issues and concerns going forward. Because of this, they are able to navigate themselves and others in a unified fashion through challenging times.

The terms *qualities* and *characteristics* are sometimes used interchangeably with *traits*, *properties*, or *features*, even though there are slight variations in meaning. Terms such as dependable, decisive, tactful, courageous, loyal, enthusiastic, judicious, and knowledgeable or phrases such as uses good judgment, takes the initiative, or operates with integrity are also used to describe a leader.

LEADERSHIP THEORIES: CORE PARADIGMS AND MODELS DEFINED

Leadership theories may be grouped into five main categories or classifications. Although variations exist within classifications, these categories are well understood and accepted by those engaged in leadership development and research.

Trait Theory
Are leaders born or made? Is leadership an art or a science?

The trait theory or approach is based on the premise that leaders and followers have innate qualities (physiological, intellectual, social, and personality) and that leaders may be identified through an understanding of the traits of leaders. This theory had its roots in the "great man theory" of the 19th and early 20th centuries when existing cultural, political, military, and social leaders were studied on their traits, qualities, or dispositions. The notion that great leaders *are born, not made* was the essence of this leadership thought, which also sought to explain leadership emergence and effectiveness. Scottish historian Thomas Carlyle (1849) remarked in the 19th century that "The history of the world is but the biography of great men" (p. xv).

Psychologist Gordon Allport (1927) developed a trait theory of personality in the early to mid-1900s. He examined the dictionary and noted every term that referred to a personality trait, resulting in a list of more than 4,400 different traits, which he classified into the following three trait categories:

- **Cardinal traits:** traits that dominate an individual's entire personality.

- **Central traits:** common traits that make up our personalities, such as kindness, honesty, and friendliness.

- **Secondary traits:** traits that only present under certain conditions and circumstances, for example, getting nervous before delivering a speech to a large group of people. (Cherry, 2013; "Gordon Allport's Career and Theory," para. 1)

Although the trait theory focused on common traits of current leaders, researchers began to note that leadership did not necessarily extend to all situations or contexts. The idea that a leader may not be a leader in all situations was further explored. One example is from Stogdill (1948) who concluded that leadership is not due to single traits but better explained in terms of the relationship of the leader to other members of an organized group. He stated that "leaders' traits must bear some relevant relationship to the characteristics of the followers. An adequate analysis of leadership needs not only a study of the leader, but of the situation" (as cited in Bass, 1990, p. 54). Stogdill spurred additional research regarding a larger context in which to understand leaders.

In Herbert Spencer's Critique of "Great Man Theory" from *The Study of Sociology* (1873), he noted that leaders were products of the society in which they lived:

> You must admit that the genesis of the great man depends on the long series of complex influences which has produced the race in which he appears, and the social state into which that race has slowly grown…Before he can re-make his society, his society must make him. (para. 4)

Thus, the trait theory of leadership was based on the idea that successful and unsuccessful leaders possessed distinctive traits and that traits may be used to predict who will emerge as a leader and who will be an effective leader.

Behavioral Theory

Do leaders alone determine and assign what needs to be done and expect cooperation? Do leaders engage their teams in participating in decision making and encouraging support and follow through?

Behavioral theories focus on how people/leaders behave or *live out* their beliefs. The belief that the behavior of the leader determines the performance of the leader and/or the followers is central to these theories. It is assumed that the leader has the necessary discernment to behave in the most appropriate manner in a given situation. Perhaps, it could be stated that a behavior may be chosen and balance may be attained in terms of concerns for human resources and productivity.

In the 1930s German-American psychologist Kurt Lewin used a leader's behavior to conceptualize and build a leadership framework. He identified three types of leaders: autocratic, democratic, and laissez-faire:

- **Autocratic** leaders make decisions without consulting their teams. This style of leadership is considered appropriate when decisions need to be made quickly, when there is no need for input, and when team agreement is not necessary for a successful outcome.

- **Democratic** leaders allow the team to provide input before making a decision, although the degree of input can vary from leader to leader. This style is important when team agreement matters, but it can be difficult to manage when there are lots of different perspectives and ideas.

- **Laissez-faire** leaders do not interfere; they allow people within the team to make many of the decisions. This works well when the team is highly capable, is motivated, and does not need close supervision. However, this behavior can arise because the leader is lazy or distracted. This is where this approach can fail. (Brooks, 2012).

Contingency Theory

What qualities of a leader determine how a decision is made and the impact of that decision? How involved must the leader be in an organization or group's performance?

In 1967 Fiedler published his "A Theory of Leadership Effectiveness" model. In four decades, the model has been thoroughly reviewed and re-examined by other researchers. Fiedler's theory was that the leader's motivational system and the control and influence the leader has on a decision determines or is contingent on the effectiveness of the leader in getting high group performance ("Fiedler's Contingency Model," 2013) Thus, style of leadership as well as the situation of the group are paramount.

Managers or leaders needed to be selective in identifying employees (who are either task or people oriented) to lead specific efforts in the organization. The relationship between the leader and the employees, the task/activity to be addressed, and the specificity of the process and goals comprise the group's situation. Fiedler's theory was based on the belief that "an impersonal but task-oriented leader can be effective in a group as long as the group is highly structured and has clearly defined tasks" (Latham, n.d., "Prescriptive," para. 1).

How should a manager identify a leader within the organization for a given task? Fiedler's theory includes a least-preferred coworker scale. This scale is used to identify the human relations orientation and task orientation of potential leaders. For example, in situations in which there will be a high level of control in order to accomplish clear tasks, a manager might select a leader with a task orientation when a high level of control is needed to accomplish clear tasks and, in contrast, a highly relational employee to help facilitate a complex task with difficult issues.

Contingency refers to a possibility that is conditional on something that is uncertain ("Contingency," 2013). Thus, a contingency theory such as Fiedler's is not a highly prescriptive that must be followed in every context; rather, it provides a ballpark direction to the leader with a large measure of flexibility embedded for any given situation.

Power and Influence Theory
What approach is the best way for leaders to get things done in an organization? Which is most appropriate: the use of position power or influence/people power?

Raven (2008) summarized his initial work with John R. P. French dating back to 1959 in which they developed an organizational study on power and arrived at five forms of power (sometimes informational power is included): legitimate, coercive, reward (positional), expert, and referent (personal). Many leaders and those who conduct research in this arena believe that referent and expert power are the two most advantageous forms.

- **Legitimate.** The target person complies because he or she believes the agent has the right to make the request and the target person has the obligation to comply.

- **Reward.** The target person complies in order to obtain rewards he or she believes are controlled by the agent.

- **Expert.** The target person complies because he or she believes that the agent has special knowledge about the best way to do something.

- **Referent.** The target person complies because he or she admires or identifies with the agent and wants to gain the agent's approval.

- **Coercive.** The target person complies in order to avoid punishments he or she believes are controlled by the agent. (Raven, 2008)

The value of understanding the impact of power and influence is in understanding and using the forms of power and influence for good and in developing and encouraging leadership skills in others.

Integrative Theory

Should a leader draw on multiple leadership theories in a given situation? Is it possible to integrate various aspects of primary leadership theories into one theory?

Yukl (1989) reviewed and summarized major theories of leadership. Topics included leadership versus management, leader traits and skills, leader behavior and activities, leader power and influence, situational determinants of leader behavior, situational moderator variables, and transformational leadership. In addition, he included an integrating conceptual framework to show how the different theories and lines of research fit together. He stated that, in recent decades, the number of studies that "straddle" multiple theories is increasing and theories in ongoing research are converging.

Yukl said that aspects of various theories are, in fact, interrelated. Thus, his conceptual framework depicts the interconnectedness of leader characteristics, managerial behavior, intervening variables, situational variables, personal power, and end-result variables. In simple terms, the end results or ultimate effectiveness of an organization depend on a myriad of other variables. Leaders have tremendous impact in that they can shape and influence actions and challenges, create choices, etc.

An integrative approach embraces a more inclusive tapestry of leadership and recognizes the complexity of leadership, including intrapersonal and interpersonal factors and the external environment. Therefore, using Yukl's theory, leaders must recognize that, because of numerous factors that impact an organization, their leadership could at times almost appear to be overwhelmed by the situation. Research in this field continues to transform how individuals see theories intersecting and overlapping. New integrative approaches are on the horizon.

STYLES OF LEADERSHIP: SELECT APPROACHES REVIEWED

How are the various forms of leadership styles defined? What is an example of each style?

The usefulness of a review of leadership-related definitions is that well-understood terminology and concepts enhance the broader discussion on leadership (theories and application). One way to define leadership is according to the style exhibited by the leader and the activities or responses of those with whom the leader interacts.

In each of the following selected leadership styles—as defined by Businessdictionary. com (2013)—the working definitions serve as a concise statement on the individuals and situations so that the style will be recognized when it is seen or experienced.

- **Transactional:** "Style of leadership that is based on the setting of clear objectives and goals for the followers as well as the use of either punishments or rewards in order to encourage compliance with these goals" ("Transactional Leadership," 2013).

- **Authoritarian/autocratic:** "A leadership style in which the leader dictates policies and procedures, decides what goals are to be achieved, and directs and controls all activities without any meaningful participation by the subordinates" ("Authoritarian Leadership," 2013).

- **Bureaucratic:** "An established, habitual, logical, or prescribed practice or systematic process of achieving certain ends with accuracy and efficiency, usually in an ordered sequence of fixed steps" ("Bureaucratic Leadership," 2013).

- **Charismatic:** "The guidance provided to an organization by one or more individuals seen as heroic or inspiring and who have therefore been granted the organizational power to make dramatic changes and extract extraordinary performance levels from its staff. For example, a business manager imbued with charismatic leadership could be enlisted to orchestrate a turnaround or launch a new product line" ("Charismatic Leadership," 2013).

- **Democratic:** "Involves a team guided by a leader where all individuals are involved in the decision-making process to determine what needs to be done and how it should be done. The group's leader has the authority to make the final decision of the group" ("Democratic Leadership," 2013).

- **Laissez-faire:** "Laissez-faire leaders try to give the least possible guidance to subordinates, and try to achieve control through less obvious means. They believe that people excel when they are left alone to respond to their responsibilities and obligations in their own ways" ("Laissez-faire," 2013).

- **Servant:** "A method of development for leaders that stresses the importance of the role a leader plays as the steward of the resources of a business or other organization, and teaches leaders to serve others while still achieving the goals set forth by the business" ("Servant Leadership," 2013).

- **Transformational:** "Style of leadership in which the leader identifies the needed change, creates a vision to guide the change through inspiration, and executes the change with the commitment of the members of the group" ("Transformational Leadership," 2013).

- **Affiliative:** "A type of leadership that promotes harmony among his or her followers and helps to solve any conflict. This type of leader will also build teams that make sure that their followers feel connected to each other. Typically the followers will receive much praise from this style of leader; however, poor performance tends to go unchecked" ("Affiliative Leadership," 2013).

Glanz (2002) defined seven quality leadership styles specifically for educators: dynamic aggressives, dynamic assertives, dynamic supportives, adaptive aggressives, adaptive assertives, adaptive supportives, and creative assertives. In addition, Glanz provided a list of virtues (courage, impartiality, empathy, judgment, enthusiasm, humility, and imagination) that should be expected of educators, as well as a section on enhancing the qualities and virtues in oneself and others. Gaining a better understanding of leadership styles enables those in leadership positions, those aspiring to become leaders, and those who are being led to better understand others as well as themselves.

LEADERSHIP ROLES FOR BUSINESS EDUCATION AT ALL EDUCATIONAL LEVELS

Subsequent chapters of this 2014 NBEA Yearbook discuss leadership on the basis of approaches, the business education profession in general, and roles and responsibilities of those in business education leadership positions at state-level business and career and technical education divisions, elementary/middle schools, secondary schools, community colleges, career colleges, and colleges and universities. This yearbook also discusses business teachers and students as leaders.

The following four leadership-related policy statements from PCBEE establish the groundwork and common thought process regarding the business education profession and the importance of leaders and leadership development. The table below provides excerpts from each of the four statements (italics added by author for emphasis), and the reference list provides the direct links.

SUMMARY

The "Nature of Leadership" is as complex as the theories that have been developed, reviewed, challenged, and enhanced from the 19th century to the present. Leadership theories are understood more clearly with a foundation in relevant terminology and basic concepts in the field of leaders and leadership development. Leadership theories may be grouped into five categories that capture various periods in the 19th and 20th centuries and researchers in the fields of psychology, sociology, and business, among others: trait, behavioral, contingency, power and influence, and integrative. The last category merges aspects of multiple theories to reflect the dynamic and complex environment surrounding leadership. In addition, leadership styles are exhibited in a variety of ways, including transactional, authoritarian, bureaucratic, charismatic, servant, and affiliative. These styles are well defined and provide a compelling statement on the respective style and its relationship to leadership theories.

With history as a predictor of the future, it is clear that leadership theories and styles will continue to evolve as new academic and cultural interests emerge, researchers

Table 1. Policies Commission for Business and Economic Education: Selected Leadership-Related Policy Statements

Policy Statement 60: This We Believe About the Profes- sional Development of Business Educators (PCBEE, 1997)	"**We Believe That** professional development is the process that improves the *job-related knowledge, skills, and attitudes* of business educators. The goals of professional development are to advance a student's learning and to improve the practice of teaching. The professional development of business educators is a process that begins with recruitment, progresses through initial preparation, induction or entry year, and licensure; the development process continues through advanced certification and career-long learning. Renewal is at the heart of each of these phases of the *professional development* continuum" (p. 1).
Policy Statement 64: This We Believe About the Role of Business Education at all Educational Levels (PCBEE, 1999)	"**We Believe That** all persons regardless of age, gender, and career aspirations can benefit from participating in business education. Meeting the needs of the Net generation, who in the year 2000 will be between the ages of two and twenty-three, will be a primary focus of our profession. They will *influence* how each of us will interact in the world. Thus, busi- ness educators must recognize that there is a major difference between Net generation learners and those from previous generations. Powerful technology has enabled the Net generation to develop different mindsets about work" (p. 1).
Policy Statement 83: This We Believe About the Transfor- mation and Future of Business Education (PCBEE, 2008)	"While business educators honor the heritage that has provided a framework for our endeavors, **we believe that** vibrant, *forward-looking* professional business educators urgently need to initiate a *significant transformation of the business education profession*" (p. 1). "In order for business education to thrive, **we believe that** concerted actions must be taken to ensure the *continuing development of relevant, authentic business education for all learners*. The transformation of the profession needs to reflect the change in learners, social context, and business education" (p. 1).
Policy Statement 90: This We Believe About Civility in Educational Environments (PCBEE, 2012)	"*Civility*, defined as courtesy and politeness, is critical in all settings, whether educational, business, personal, or social. Concern about the effects of incivility in society is evident both in the educational and popular literature. The rise of incivility is often attributed to the ubiquitous nature and use of technology, insufficient parental supervision, students' sense of entitlement, and lack of tolerance among diverse student populations. Lack of civility disrupts the learning environment as well as negatively impacts workplace, social, and personal interactions" (p. 1). "**We believe** everyone deserves the opportunity to learn in a civil educational environment" (p. 3). "**We believe** civility should be fostered through • engaging in lifelong learning of civil behaviors; • practicing empathy, respecting diversity, and being considerate of others; • encouraging civility in homes, classrooms, online environments, all institutional settings, and the community; • developing a policy addressing appropriate behaviors and responses; and • monitoring, reporting, and correcting inappropriate conduct. Therefore, **we believe** business education has the opportunity and responsibility to weave the tenets of civility into its curriculum" (pp. 3–4).

continue to explore the field and build on the past, and new studies are undertaken to enhance and further develop the body of literature in the area of leadership.

REFERENCES

Affiliative leadership. (2013). In *Businessdictionary.com*. Retrieved from http://www.businessdictionary.com/definition/affiliative-leadership.html

Allport, G. (1927, May). Concepts of trait and personality. *Psychological Bulletin, 24*(5), 284–293. doi:10.1037/h0073629

Attributes. (2013). In *Dictionary.com*. Retrieved from http://dictionary.reference.com/browse/attribute?s=t

Authoritarian leadership. (2013). In *Businessdictionary.com*. Retrieved from http://www.businessdictionary.com/definition/authoritarian-leadership.html

Bass, B. B., & Bass, R. (2008). *The Bass handbook of leadership: Theory, research, and managerial applications* (4th ed.). New York, NY: Free Press.

Bass, B. M. (1990). *Bass & Stogdill's handbook of leadership: Theory, research, and managerial applications* (3rd ed.). New York, NY: Free Press.

Brooks, C. (2012, June 18). What are leadership styles and skills? *Business News Daily.* Retrieved from http://www.businessnewsdaily.com/2704-leadership.html

Bureaucratic leadership. (2013). In *Businessdictionary.com*. Retrieved from http://www.businessdictionary.com/definition/bureaucratic-leadership.html

Carlyle, T. (1849). *On heroes, hero-worship, and the heroic in history*. Boston, MA: Houghton-Mifflin.

Characteristics. (2013). In *Dictionary.com*. Retrieved from http://dictionary.reference.com/browse/characteristics?s=t

Charismatic leadership. (2013). In *Businessdictionary.com*. Retrieved from http://www.businessdictionary.com/definition/charismatic-leadership.html

Cherry, K. (2013). Gordon Allport biography. Retrieved from http://psychology.about.com/od/profilesal/p/gordon-allport.htm

Clark, Donald. (2000). Leadership–character and traits. Texas Tech University. Retrieved from http://www.depts.ttu.edu/aged/leadership/leadchr.htm

Contingency. (2013). In *Dictionary.com*. Retrieved from http://dictionary.reference.com/browse/contingency?s=t

Democratic leadership. (2013). In *Businessdictionary.com*. Retrieved from http://www.businessdictionary.com/definition/democratic-leadership.html

Fiedler's Contingency Model: Matching leadership style to a situation. (2013). In *Mind tools: Essential skills for an excellent career*. Retrieved from http://www.mindtools.com/pages/article/fiedler.htm

Glanz, J. (2002). *Finding your leadership style: A guide for educators*. Alexandria, VA: Association for Supervision and Curriculum Development.

Harvard Business School. (n.d.). Leadership: American business leaders of the twentieth century. Retrieved from http://www.hbs.edu/leadership/database

Kruse, K. (2012, October 16). 100 best quotes on leadership. Retrieved from http://www.forbes.com/sites/kevinkruse/2012/10/16/quotes-on-leadership

Laissez-faire leadership. (2013). In *Businessdictionary.com*. Retrieved from http://www. businessdictionary.com/definition/laissez-faire-leadership.html

Latham, A. (n.d.). The advantages of Fiedler's Contingency Model. *Chron: Small business*. Retrieved from http://smallbusiness.chron.com/advantages-fiedlers-contingency-model-18368.html

Marques, J. (2007). On impassioned leadership: A comparison between leaders from divergent walks of life. *International Journal of Leadership Studies, 3*(1), 98–125. Retrieved from http://www.regent.edu/acad/global/publications/ijls/new/vol3iss1/marques/marques.htm

Northouse, P. G. (2010). *Leadership: Theory and practice* (5th ed.). Thousand Oaks, CA: Sage Publications, Inc.

Policies Commission for Business and Economic Education (PCBEE). (1997). *This we believe about the professional development of business educators* (Statement No. 60). Retrieved from http://nbea.org/newsite/curriculum/policy/no_60.pdf

Policies Commission for Business and Economic Education. (1999). *This we believe about the role of business education at all educational levels* (Statement No. 64). Retrieved from http://nbea.org/newsite/curriculum/policy/no_64.pdf

Policies Commission for Business and Economic Education. (2008). *This we believe about the induction and mentoring of new business teachers* (Statement No. 83). Retrieved from http://nbea.org/newsite/curriculum/policy/no_83.pdf

Policies Commission for Business and Economic Education. (2012). *This we believe about civility in educational environments* (Statement No. 90). Retrieved from http://nbea.org/newsite/curriculum/policy/no_90.pdf

Qualities. (2013). In *Dictionary.com*. Retrieved from http://dictionary.reference.com/browse/quality?s=t

Raven, B. (2008, December). The bases of power and the Power/Interaction Model of Interpersonal Influence. *Analyses of Social Issues and Public Policy, 8*(1), 1–22. Retrieved from http://onlinelibrary.wiley.com/doi/10.1111/j.1530-2415.2008.00159.x/pdf

Servant leadership. (2013). In *Businessdictionary.com*. Retrieved from http://www.businessdictionary.com/definition/servant-leadership.html

Spencer, H. (1873). Herbert Spencer's critique of "Great Man Theory," from *The Study of Sociology*. Retrieved from http://history.furman.edu/benson/fywbio/fywbio_spencer_excerpts.htm

Stogdill, R. M. (1948). Personal factors associated with leadership: A survey of the literature. *Journal of Psychology, 25*(1), 35–71. doi:10.1080/00223980.1948.9917362

Trait theory of leadership. (n.d.). In *MSG: Management study guide*. Retrieved from http://www.managementstudyguide.com/trait-theory-of-leadership.htm

Transactional leadership. (2013). In *Businessdictionary.com*. Retrieved from http://www.businessdictionary.com/definition/transactional-leadership.html

Transformational leadership. (2013). In *Businessdictionary.com*. Retrieved from http://www.businessdictionary.com/definition/transformational-leadership.html

Yukl, G. (1989). Managerial leadership: a review of theory and research. *Journal of Management, 15*(2), 251–289. doi:10.1177/014920638901500207

Educational Administrators' Leadership for 21st Century Business Education

Sandy Braathen and Glenda Rotvold
University of North Dakota
Grand Forks, ND

Administrators and educational leaders at all levels—from building-level principals to district superintendents and career and technical education (CTE) directors to state supervisors of business education—directly impact the quality of business education. The quality of business education relies on the support and guidance of these administrative leaders.

Effective leadership is essential to building and sustaining successful business education programs. Effective leadership has been found to be the most important factor when looking at what attracts teachers to "challenged" schools and also what makes them stay at those schools. Leadership has also been found to be second only to teaching in directly impacting student learning (Leithwood, Louis, Anderson, & Wahlstrom, 2004; Shelton, 2010).

This chapter focuses on many of the ways in which effective leaders can influence and impact business education. The sections in this chapter will include the following items for which effective leaders are responsible: developing personnel, facilitating collaboration, planning and setting direction, implementing standards, initiating and implementing change, and integrating technology.

DEVELOPING PERSONNEL
The demands on all CTE programs, including business education programs, continue to increase as school reforms take place, educators are held accountable for

student learning, new initiatives are implemented, and technology continues to change and impact programs. Professional development is one means of ensuring that the knowledge and skills needed to be effective in the school environment will be met. "Continuous high-quality professional development and support strengthens a school leader's capacity to improve instruction and creates a school culture of shared leadership, collaboration, and high expectations for all students" (Shelton, 2010, pp. 9–10).

Recognizing the Need for Professional Development

In 1997 the Policies Commission for Business and Economic Education (PCBEE) recognized the importance of professional development for business educators:

> **We Believe That** through professional development, teachers learn to think and teach differently; policy makers learn about the complexities of transforming ideas into realities; and administrators learn about the support necessary to facilitate teacher change. Thus, professional development based on a collaborative network among business educators, administrators, policy makers, and business and community representatives, leads to positive change. (p. 2)

The need for professional development continues to expand, and business education leaders must recognize the importance of providing development opportunities, as stated by Sass and other members of the Professional Development Joint Working Group (2011):

> Secondary CTE serves a large segment of secondary students and must contribute to their academic as well as technical learning. Most CTE teachers will need considerable professional development to broaden their teaching skills and to learn to use data for program improvement. (p. iii)

Sass et al. also stressed that the professional development should relate to the courses being taught and that the duration and intensity of professional development should be sufficient to influence the instruction.

Offering and Supporting Professional Development

Administrators and business education leaders can support business educators not only by recognizing the need for professional development opportunities but also by seeking opportunities and supporting education and training when necessary. Providing funding for professional development is one aspect of supporting professional development, whether it means paying registration fees; covering costs of substitute teachers; offering release time; providing transportation, lodging, books, or other materials; or covering the costs associated with bringing professional consultants or speakers to the teachers.

Another aspect of supporting professional development is assisting staff with finding appropriate professional development opportunities. If appropriate professional development opportunities are not available, leaders at all levels should seek out the needed opportunities and may even need to develop the appropriate training. As recommended in PCBEE's (2010) Policy Statement 87, virtual environments should also be considered when seeking development opportunities. Virtual training environments eliminate most of the costs associated with travel, reduce time out of the classroom (and hours paid for substitute teachers), and allow flexibility and convenience for the users.

Building and Developing Future Leaders

An important component of professional development is developing leaders for the future. Good leaders will recognize current teachers as future leaders as well. In addition to preparing teachers to lead in the future, Marks and Printy (2003) found that cultivating teacher leadership was important for school performance. Shelton (2010) also discussed the need for mentoring teachers as potential leaders. He indicated that mentors should have high performance standards, clearly defined responsibilities, and high-quality training.

FACILITATING COLLABORATION

In addition to developing personnel, a second responsibility of successful leaders is to build and support a community of collaboration.

The concept of shared leadership is one that has been strongly embraced in the literature on leadership (Lambert, 2002; Marks & Printy, 2003; Robinson, Lloyd, & Rowe, 2008). "A key characteristic of effective school leaders is that they create an environment of shared responsibility, authority, and decision making in the school so faculty and staff have ownership over decisions that affect student learning" (National Comprehensive Center for Teacher Quality, 2008, p. 4).

Administrators who recognize this and take a collaborative approach to improving their schools will take advantage of the many partnerships that exist within the school system as well as those that link the school system with outside entities.

Local School and District Partnerships

Within the school building alone, business educators will have a continuing need to develop partnerships with others in the building. Many initiatives that focus on school improvement, such as career clusters, will require the coordination of academic subject areas such as English, math, and science with career and technical subjects, including business education. When teachers in these areas form partnerships, it will lead to more cohesive schools where students are the immediate beneficiaries. Local-level administrators at this level should encourage the partnerships and provide opportunities for the teachers to combine their efforts. Coordinating planning time, rewarding collaborative efforts, recognizing success, and facilitating professional development are some of the ways in which administrators can foster collaboration.

Beyond the individual school walls, district leaders should look to collaborate with other schools and districts. Forming consortia will often provide the strength in numbers that is lacking in an individual school or district. Consortia allow schools to work together to share ideas, resources, and administration of programs. Additionally, consortia can assist with assessment efforts.

Local and district leaders will also be tasked with fostering partnerships with state leadership. Participating in statewide initiatives can benefit local programs in several ways. Statewide initiatives can help programs to remain on the leading edge, increase student enrollment and participation, build community partnerships, and assist with securing funding for new programs and initiatives at the state and national levels. State-level administrators can also help local administrators with interpreting guidelines and ensuring compliance in order to receive federal funding.

State and National Partnerships

State-level administrators can take advantage of consortia and professional association partnerships such as the National Association of Supervisors of Business Education and National Association of State Directors of Career and Technical Education Consortium (NASDCTEc) and through professional associations such as the National Business Education Association (NBEA) and Association for Career and Technical Education. These associations are instrumental in setting policies and direction at the national level. Being part of such associations can help state leaders remain on the leading edge of new initiatives and allow them to be change agents.

Involvement in professional associations can provide additional opportunities for leaders at all levels to serve their profession, learn from others, set direction for the profession, and develop a network of support. One important example of how professional associations can be helpful is NBEA's *National Standards for Business Education* (NBEA, 2013). The standards provide a guide for educators and specify what business education students at various levels should know and be able to do. Several states have already cross-referenced their state requirements with previous editions of the business education standards.

Business and Industry Partnerships

Recent emphasis on students being both career and college ready necessitates a close relationship between business education programs and workforce partners. NASDCTEc indicated that active partnerships with industry are what set career and technical education apart from other programs and allow for high-quality programs. NASDCTEc (2010a) noted the importance of maintaining industry partnerships:

As the pace of technological change increases, CTE must keep up with the ever-changing demands of the economy. That means CTE must work with employers to ensure that programs provide students with experiences that are current and relevant to economic demands. (p. 10)

Work-based learning links classroom learning with workplace experience through both paid and nonpaid experiences and is at the foundation of many business education partnerships with community businesses (PCBEE, 2005b).

The PCBEE (2005b) noted that, in order for business educators to be successful as agents of change using work-based learning,

> support must come from appropriate stakeholder groups (i.e., state department of education staff, local administrators, university teacher educators, and cooperating business partners). To ensure acceptance of WBL [work-based learning], all stakeholders should work collaboratively to document and disseminate examples of best WBL practices. (p. 2)

In addition to work-based learning, partnerships with business and industry can benefit business education in many other ways as well. Those noted by NASDCTEc (2010, September) include creating training facilities and/or providing equipment, establishing apprenticeships, participating in advisory committees, developing industry standards, developing curricula, developing assessments, developing certifications, providing internships for students, providing externships for teachers, supporting student organizations, serving as mentors or adjunct faculty, being an advocate, and working with counselors to raise awareness of career opportunities.

PLANNING AND SETTING DIRECTION

A third responsibility of successful leaders is to plan for the future and set the direction programs will take.

The goal of most educational reform is to improve teaching and student learning. Whatever the approach to school reform, success depends on the capacities and motivations of local leadership who agree with its purposes, understand what will make the reform efforts successful, help colleagues understand how to integrate reform, and provide the supports needed to see the reform or initiative meet its goals (Leithwood et al., 2004).

Making decisions about how to implement changes and plan for the future will present constant challenges for leaders. Two important steps that administrators at any level should seriously consider in the planning phase are identifying opportunities and setting priorities and incorporating data into decision making.

Identifying Opportunities and Setting Priorities

Leaders at all levels need to be aware of potential opportunities and constantly be seeking and creating opportunities. For example, Alabama and South Carolina are two states that have demonstrated leadership in taking advantage of opportunities to connect education and economic development. According to NASDCTEc (2010b), both of these states

> have used their investments in career technical education (CTE) to lure and retain international companies, and prepare students to vie for jobs across the globe.

Their forward-thinking approach has helped them partner with leaders of major, burgeoning industries to develop programs that train their students for the jobs of tomorrow, and secure employment and high-wage opportunities for their states' residents. (p. 1)

Furthermore, CTE programs can provide the education needed locally to prevent industries from seeking workers from abroad. CTE is viewed as critical for U.S. global competitiveness (NASDCTEc, 2010, July).

Setting priorities is an equally important component for successful leadership. Leaders' contributions to and positive influence on student learning will depend on their careful choice of what features of their organization on which to spend their time and attention and realizing what the optimal condition of these features should be (Leithwood et al., 2004).

Today's school leaders not only face challenges with limited financial and human resources but also many more demands and varied responsibilities than ever before. Local school administrators must make decisions and implement action related to school reform, such as improving teaching and learning, resource planning, curricula development, technology integration, professional development, and human resource management, just to name a few. Consequently, top priorities need to be identified to ensure allocation of adequate resources and time for successful accomplishment. Data should be used to help identify the priorities.

Incorporating Data into Decision Making

Data-driven decision making is another powerful tool for effective leadership. "Schools must understand the value of a data-driven approach to education. Having performance systems will contribute to informed decision-making" (West, 2012, p. 10). Using data for decision making can assist *entire* organizations, leaders, and/or teachers at all levels to identify and solve problems.

One of the contributing forces driving the use of data and analytics for decision making is the trend toward requiring increased accountability for educational institutions (Dietz-Uhler & Hurn, 2013; Hilliard & Jackson, 2011; West, 2012). This increased accountability can be attributed to a number of factors, including legislation such as the No Child Left Behind Act of 2001, reporting requirements for accreditation, and accountability to parents and the local community (Coburn & Turner, 2012).

In addition to having concrete data and documentation to meet the above requirements, data and analytics can improve operational efficiency, cut costs, and improve teaching and learning (Dietz-Uhler & Hurn, 2013; Messelt, 2004; Nastu, 2010); offer promise in moving toward more personalized instruction (Dietz-Uh ler & Hurn, 2013; Nastu, 2010); and optimize college recruitment and retention, classroom scheduling, and alumni donation efforts (Nastu, 2010). Data-driven decision making can also be used to help narrow achievement gaps, motivate students, and improve curriculum, teacher quality, and communication with key stakeholders (Messelt, 2004). Furthermore, ways to use those data as a support tool include improving observations and providing better feedback to teachers, using results and feedback to determine needed professional development, and using results to determine the needed instructional services for individual students (Hilliard & Jackson, 2011).

Available technology, such as learning management systems, data analytics software, and data mining, makes it easy for leaders to gather and summarize data to be used in the decision-making process (Long & Siemens, 2011). Technology and the use of data mining and data analytic software can provide systematic, real-time data and feedback for teachers and administrators to help improve academic performance, identify trends and problem areas, and allocate resources efficiently (Long & Siemens, 2011; West, 2012).

Data collection should be planned carefully and involve multiple types of data such as achievement, demographic, program, and perception data (Learning Point Associates, 2004). Multiple data types and sources are needed to ensure that complete and accurate results are obtained on which to base a variety of decisions and achieve the maximum improvement and benefit for all students.

IMPLEMENTING STANDARDS

A fourth responsibility of successful leaders is implementing, maintaining, and evaluating progress toward standards.

Implementing standards in a program is closely aligned with setting program direction. The standards to be met by a program define the direction the program will take. Program standards can be defined by and imposed at federal, state, and local levels. Initiatives at all levels will impact the standards adopted for the specific local-level business education programs. Examples of initiatives and the importance of setting the direction are included for each level in the following sections: federal, state, and local.

Federal Level

School reform is an ongoing topic of discussion and has led to implementation of numerous initiatives at the federal level. These initiatives and directives also impact the state level and, ultimately, the local district and program levels. Two recent initiatives impacting business education are the Career Clusters Initiative and the Common Core State Standards (CCSS).

The vision of the Career Clusters Initiative is to enable learners to transition successfully from education to careers by providing a framework connecting secondary with postsecondary education; academic with career and technical education; and education with business, workforce development, and economic development communities. (PCBEE, 2008, p. 1)

The Common Core State Standards (CCSS) are

a single set of English-Language arts and mathematics standards designed to ensure that all students graduate high school prepared to enter college or the workforce. The standards clearly define the knowledge and skill students need to thrive in entry-level, credit-bearing, academic college courses and in workforce training programs. (NASDCTEc, 2011b, p. 1)

NASDCTEc supports both of these initiatives and has been working to further the success of both career clusters and Common Core State Standards at the state and local levels. However, the consortium has noted that, although the standards address academic coursework, they do not completely address the career component. Therefore, it becomes necessary for leaders to align their career and technical program standards with the CCSS. The employability skills and career-specific skills that CTE provides need to be aligned with the CCSS (NASDCTEc, 2011b).

According to NASDCTEc (2011b), the standards provide an opportunity to integrate CTE content and practices through the various programs of study, embedding credit opportunities, aligning learner levels, and providing accelerated learning. Implementation of the CCSS standards will require CTE leaders to work with the academic discipline leaders to ensure that students are engaged in both academic and CTE courses (Meeder & Suddreth, 2012). The teachers, principals, and other administrators will determine the best means for meeting the standards.

State Level

Although initiatives and standards typically are developed at the national level, individual states must determine how the standards will be met within programs. State career and technical directors, state supervisors of business education, and state education department leaders are charged with the task of working with federal-level administrators as well as local-level administrators and educators to determine how to implement the standards. These administrators are also instrumental in determining how to assess progress toward meeting the standards.

The state-level leaders are often responsible for assessing local programs' compliance with national standards. State leaders must also ensure that local programs are meeting the requirements for other funding sources, which flow from the federal government through the state agencies to local districts and programs.

One example of a state aligning its state standards for both academic and CTE standards to national standards is how Kansas has incorporated the CCSS standards. After adopting CCSS in 2010, Kansas aligned the new CCSS standards with its CTE curriculum (NASDCTEc, 2011a). The Kansas State Department of Education links the Kansas standards with databases containing a variety of resources including student demographics and student achievement data.

The resulting system provides various assessment tools, suggestions for instructional decisions, and information on multiple initiatives targeting school improvement. The broader goal is to increase student engagement in the learning process with greater support and opportunity for teachers to alter and improve instructional practices. (NASDCTEc, 2011a, p. 3)

Local Level

Local-level administrators and leaders will need to help guide local programs through the process of compliance with state and national standards. When federal funding is channeled from the federal level through the state departments to local districts and agencies, not meeting the set standards or not complying with the requirements can be costly for local programs, resulting in a loss of funding dollars.

Local leaders will also need to constantly look for new opportunities, including seeking consortia or other groups to partner with for new initiatives, taking advantage of new funding opportunities, incorporating new training and professional development opportunities, and identifying unmet needs and developing programs to meet those needs. It is especially important for leaders at the local level to be champions for the teachers in their programs and to encourage shared leadership.

INITIATING AND IMPLEMENTING CHANGE

A fifth responsibility of successful leaders is to serve as a change agent, both initiating and implementing change.

As mentioned above, the CTE landscape continues to change; astute leaders will not only embrace the change but initiate it. As Boateng (2012) noted,

the nature of work is changing; technology keeps changing rapidly; there is increased public demand on [the] vocational technical education system to produce individuals with more opportunities for present and future prospects in multiple industries, and offer the individuals with enough skills for personal development and success in the changing society. (pp. 50–51)

In response to the changing demands, the survival of business education depends on managing these changes effectively. Recognizing changing demographics and maintaining flexibility are key factors to consider in managing change.

Recognizing Changing Demographics

Educational delivery, instructional strategies, and educational support systems need to be designed to fit the learning styles and needs of the audience. Education needs to change as the world around it changes in order to be effective in meeting its goals. Therefore, the importance of recognizing today's changing student demographics should not be underestimated. How to deliver instruction in the most effective ways must be a strong consideration for administrators as they consider the changing demographics of learners. The background and language needs of students should be part of planning for effective instructional delivery. Because changes also typically impact budgets, part of administrators' considerations should also cover what taxpayers would be willing to support (Hilliard & Jackson, 2011).

In 2008 the Policy Commission for Business and Economic Education recognized the diversity of today's students, the transforming learning environment, and the need for business educators to facilitate diverse learner engagement in this global, connected world (PCBEE, 2008).

Maintaining Flexibility

Flexibility is needed to thrive in such a dynamic environment in order to respond effectively to input from constituents, findings from data analysis and trends, students' needs, continuous improvement plans, or whatever other challenges or opportunities arise. Leaders must remain flexible enough to choose from a variety of best practices as needed (Leithwood et al., 2004). Overbay, Mollete, and Vasu (2011) recommended the following: "Plan for the short term and the long term, but be flexible enough to realize when the schedule needs to change" (p. 57).

Additionally, as more courses are becoming graduation requirements for students, elective courses, such as many business courses, are difficult for students to fit into their schedules. "Therefore, we believe that administrators, counselors/advisers, and teachers must work together to create opportunities for students to have flexible schedules for completing a meaningful business course sequence" (PCBEE, 2005a, p. 1).

If goals and positive results are to be achieved, leaders must inspire and motivate their teams to action. A plan with no action achieves nothing; action with no plan or direction is chaos. In either case, goals cannot be achieved without action.

INTEGRATING TECHNOLOGY

A sixth responsibility of successful leaders is to manage and integrate technology in order to maximize its effectiveness.

When considering new technology initiatives, Overbay et al. (2011) recommended that administrators follow these guidelines: solicit input throughout the entire process, plan with the educational needs of the individual schools in mind, provide training and professional development for teachers, establish a collaborative environment for planning, and become turnover-proof by not only developing teachers' expertise but also sharing some of the leadership for the technology initiative. Leaders must also ensure that there is a good reason or significant benefit to the teaching and learning process by implementing the technology.

In 2001 the Collaborative for Technology Standards for School Administrators created a set of technology standards that identified what principals should know about technology to be effective in supporting, integrating, and using technology in schools (McCampbell, 2001). These standards became the International Society for Technology in Education (ISTE) National Educational Technology Standards for Administrators (NETS-A), which were updated in 2009.

According to ISTE's (2012) NETS-A,

transforming schools into digital age places of learning requires leadership from people who can accept new challenges and embrace new opportunities. Now more than ever, the success of technology integration depends on leaders who can implement systemic reform in our schools. ("Digital Age Leadership," para. 2)

The first NETS-A standard is Visionary Leadership, which states that "educational administrators inspire and lead development and implementation of a shared vision for comprehensive integration of technology to promote excellence and support transformation throughout the organization" (International Society for Technology in Education [ISTE], 2009). The shared vision should use digital resources to meet learning goals, support instruction, and maximize performance. The vision should also be part of strategic plans that include technology. Leaders should advocate for policies and programs at all levels that support the infusion of technology (ISTE, 2009).

Identifying Technology Goals and Needs

Planning for technology begins by identifying technology goals and needs. Identifying technology goals and requirements should be a team effort. This team effort can create a win-win situation for the principal, teachers, technology coordinators, and students. First, the principal can draw from the expertise of other internal leaders, such as technology coordinators who can serve as technology translators; technology coordinators can also serve on the school's leadership team, helping the principal make technology decisions that can positively impact teaching and learning in addition to searching for other ways to enhance and support the school's vision (Sugar & Holloman, 2009).

Second, teachers should be included in this collaborative team effort. Administrators can assist overloaded teachers by devoting work time to collaborative planning and setting the direction for those planning sessions.

Third, leaders must face the reality of and plan for staff turnover. Although it can be detrimental to a technology initiative, turnover will happen; so administrators should plan for it (Overbay et al., 2011).

Selecting Appropriate Technologies

A clear vision for technology is essential in order to make wise information, communications, and technology purchases lasting several years (Flanagan & Jacobsen,

2003). Input from a variety of constituents will help school leaders create a shared vision that has support of staff and faculty. When selecting appropriate technologies, Overbay et al. (2011) offered two important guidelines:

- **Let the plan fit the individual school.** The needs and resources of each school are different and the plan should also differ.

- **It is not just about the technology**. "Technology initiatives are about people—the people who plan with, teach with, and learn with the technology" (p. 56). Administrators must actively listen to teachers in each phase of implementation. Before making purchase decisions and planning professional development, administrators must consider what teachers know, what teachers need to know, and what teachers will actually use.

Planning, Designing, and Implementing Technology Solutions

Good planning mandates that each principal know as much as possible about the school's infrastructure and the specific teaching needs of the faculty…Planning must reflect the instructional needs of the school as well as a realistic timeframe for implementation. (Overbay et al., 2011, p. 57)

To accomplish needed change and improvement, administrators will want to retain competent, technology savvy personnel, as well as maintain the appropriate technology infrastructure. The infrastructure must be able to handle the integrated technology systems necessary to support all aspects of the school's needs, from management to teaching and learning (ISTE, 2009).

Providing Training Opportunities

Technology training opportunities should encompass all school personnel, including teachers, technology support staff, principals, and other local and district administrators. Findings from a recent study by Schrum, Galizio, and Ledesma (2011) indicated that many states or institutions do not require any formal preparation in technology or technology implementation for school leaders, even though school leaders recognize that supporting technology is essential to effectively leading their schools in today's world. "If school principals are to effectively inspire and lead a staff in integrating technology across the curriculum, then professional development opportunities must be available for principals to develop these skills and dispositions" (Flanagan & Jacobsen, 2003, p. 140). Without professional development opportunities for administrators, they are left to learn these skills on their own, or not at all.

Overbay et al. (2011) discussed the importance of planning for training teachers to use new equipment. They noted that training is often overlooked when planning to purchase equipment. However, training is crucial for the new equipment to be used to enhance instruction. "A vital aspect of professional development is timing and 'dosage.'

Additional professional development should be paced throughout the school year so teachers have time to digest what they learn and try out new skills in the classroom" (Overbay et al., 2011, p. 58). The importance of professional development and training for technology was echoed by PCBEE (1997) in Policy Statement 60.

SUMMARY

Educational leaders significantly impact the quality of business education, recruitment and retention of quality teachers, and student learning. Research has found that effective educational leaders implement the following strategies: (a) develop people by supporting professional development and offering professional development opportunities, (b) facilitate collaborative teams and partnerships at all levels, including business and industry and local, state, and national, (c) use a variety of data and data types, in addition to input from faculty, staff, and constituents to inform decision making, (d) initiate and implement change that recognizes changing demographics, maintains flexibility, and motivates people to action, and (e) effectively integrate technology by identifying technology goals and needs, seeking valuable input from faculty and staff, selecting appropriate technologies, and designing and implementing technology solutions and infrastructure.

A key point to consider when applying this approach is that the above strategies not only are interdependent but also need to work seamlessly together, rather than in isolation, to synergistically produce positive outcomes and derive the greatest benefits. For example, data should be used to drive decision making, including decisions on what professional development opportunities should be offered or decisions related to student learning. As data are frequently obtained from various technological solutions or information systems, effective technology solutions and infrastructure must be in place for that data collection and analysis to occur. Educational leaders, faculty, and staff need the knowledge to make those technology decisions and then be able to use the technology to collect, report, and analyze the data. Consequently, appropriate professional development opportunities for all teachers, staff, and leaders are essential to ensure that educational professionals are adequately equipped to use the technology, make the best decisions possible, and provide the optimal learning environment for today's diverse student population.

A second point—or tip—to consider is that, because change will be constant, educational leaders should pay attention to changing demographics, maintain flexibility, and plan for turnover to ensure relevancy and continued success.

Last, but certainly not least, due to the great demands put on educational leaders today, including wise allocation and management of resources, increased student learning outcomes, accountability, and numerous other decisions, educational leaders cannot do it all alone. Research has shown that effective leadership also includes using a collaborative approach that accepts and uses valuable input from all stakeholders and develops various strategic partnerships. Partnerships with business and industry and close relationships with agencies, departments, and leaders from the local, state, and federal levels can not only help to provide support for existing programs but also provide opportunities for growth that will help schools adequately prepare students for successful careers in the 21st century.

REFERENCES

Boateng, C. (2012, August). Evolving conceptualization of leadership and its implication for vocational technical education. *World Journal of Education, 2*(4), 45–54.

Coburn, C. E., & Turner, E. O. (2012, February). The practice of data use: An introduction. *American Journal of Education, 118*(2), 99–111. doi:10.1086/663272

Dietz-Uhler, B., & Hurn, J. (2013, Spring). Using learning analytics to predict (and improve) student success: A faculty perspective. *Journal of Interactive Online Learning, 12*(1), 17–26. Retrieved from http://www.ncolr.org/jiol/issues/pdf/12.1.2.pdf

Flanagan, L., & Jacobsen, M. (2003). Technology leadership for the twenty-first century principal. *Journal of Educational Administration, 41*(2), 124–142. doi:10.1108/09578230310464648

Hilliard, A., & Jackson, B. T. (2011, January). Current trends in educational leadership for student success plus facilities planning and design. *Contemporary Issues in Education Research (CIER), 4*(1), 1–8.

International Society for Technology in Education. (2009). ISTE.NETS-A: Advancing digital age leadership standards. Retrieved from http://www.iste.org/docs/pdfs/nets-a-standards.pdf?sfvrsn=2

International Society for Technology in Education. (2012). Standards. Retrieved from http://www.iste.org/standards/nets-for-administrators

Lambert, L. (2002). A framework for shared leadership. *Educational Leadership, 59*(8), 37–40.

Learning Point Associates. (2004, December). *Guide to using data in school improvement efforts.* Naperville, IL: North Central Regional Educational Laboratory. Retrieved from http://www.learningpt.org/pdfs/datause/guidebook.pdf

Leithwood, K., Louis, K. S., Anderson, S., & Wahlstrom, K. (2004). *How leadership influences student learning.* New York, NY: The Wallace Foundation.

Long, P. D., & Siemens, G. (2011, September). Penetrating the fog: Analytics in learning and education. *EDUCAUSE Review Online, 46*(5), 30–40. Retrieved from http://www.educause.edu/ero/article/penetrating-fog-analytics-learning-and-education

Marks, H. M., & Printy, S. M. (2003, August). Principal leadership and school performance: An integration of transformational and instructional leadership. *Educational Administration Quarterly, 39*(3), 370–397. doi:10.1177/0013161X03253412

McCampbell, B. (2001, May/June). Technology standards for school administrators. *Principal Leadership, 1*(9), 68–70. Retrieved from http://nassp.org/portals/0/content/48168.pdf

Meeder, H., & Suddreth, T. (2012, May). *Common Core State Standards and career and technical education: Bridging the divide between college and career readiness.* Washington, DC: Achieve Inc.

Messelt, J. (2004). *Data-driven decision making: A powerful tool for school improvement.* Minneapolis, MN: Sagebrush Corporation. Retrieved from https://www.erdc.k12. mn.us/promo/sage/images/Analytics_WhitePaper.pdf

Nastu, J. (2010, September). Advanced analytics: Helping educators approach the ideal. eSN Special Report, *eSchool News*, 17–23. Retrieved from http://www-935.ibm.com/ services/ie/gbs/pdf/Smarter_Education_Advanced_Analytics.pdf

National Association of State Directors of Career Technical Education Consortium. (2010, July). *Career technical education: A critical component of states' global economic strategy.* Issue Brief. Retrieved from link under "Jobs and Economy" from http://www.careertech.org/legislation/briefs-papers.html

National Association of State Directors of Career Technical Education Consortium. (2010, September). *Career and technical education and business partners: Bridging education and the economy.* Issue Brief. Retrieved from link under "Jobs and Economy" from http://www.careertech.org/legislation/briefs-papers.html

National Association of State Directors of Career Technical Education Consortium. (2011a, May). *CTE and college and career ready standards: Preparing students for further education and careers.* Issue Brief. Retrieved from link under "Standards and Education" from http://www.careertech.org/legislation/briefs-papers.html

National Association of State Directors of Career Technical Education Consortium. (2011b, May). *CTE and the Common Core Standards.* Issue Brief. Retrieved from link under "Standards and Education" from http://www.careertech.org/legislation/ briefs-papers.html

National Business Education Association (NBEA). (2013). *National standards for business education: What America's students should know and be able to do in business* (4th ed.). Reston, VA: Author.

National Comprehensive Center for Teacher Quality. (2008). *Enhancing leadership quality TQ source tips & tools: Emerging strategies to enhance educator quality.* Washington, DC: Author. Retrieved from http://www.gtlcenter.org/sites/default/ files/docs/EnhancingLeadershipQuality.pdf

Overbay, A., Mollette, M., & Vasu, E. S., (2011, February). A technology plan that works. *Educational Leadership, 68*(5), 56–59. Retrieved from http://eric.ed.gov/ ?id=EJ972032

Policies Commission for Business and Economic Education (PCBEE). (1997). *This we believe about the professional development of business education* (Statement No. 60). Retrieved from http://nbea.org/newsite/curriculum/policy/no_60.pdf

Policies Commission for Business and Economic Education. (2005a). *This we believe about business education as core academic content* (Statement No. 76). Retrieved from http://nbea.org/newsite/curriculum/policy/no_76.pdf

Policies Commission for Business and Economic Education. (2005b). *This we believe about work-based learning* (Statement No. 77). Retrieved from http://nbea.org/news-ite/curriculum/policy/no_77.pdf

Policies Commission for Business and Economic Education. (2008). *This we believe about the value of career clusters in business education* (Statement No. 82). Retrieved from http://nbea.org/newsite/curriculum/policy/no_82.pdf

Policies Commission for Business and Economic Education. (2009). *This we believe about the induction and mentoring of new business teachers* (Statement No. 84). Retrieved from http://nbea.org/newsite/curriculum/policy/no_84.pdf

Policies Commission for Business and Economic Education. (2010). *This we believe about virtual professional development* (Statement No. 87). Retrieved from http://nbea.org/newsite/curriculum/documents/PCBEEStatement87_000.pdf

Robinson, V. M. J., Lloyd, C. A., & Rowe, K. J. (2008, December). The impact of leadership on student outcomes: An analysis of the differential effects of leadership types. *Educational Administration Quarterly, 44*(5), 635–674. doi:10.1177/0013161X08321509

Sass, H. B., Bottoms, G., Pritz, S. G., Kelley, P., Foster, J. C., Hodes, C., & Lewis, M. V. (2011, March). *Improving secondary career and technical education through professional development: Alternative certification and use of technical assessment data.* Louisville, KY: National Research Center for Career and Technical Education. Retrieved from http://www.nrccte.org/sites/default/files/publication-files/improving_ed_through_pd.pdf

Schrum, L., Galizio, L. M., & Ledesma, P. (2011, March). Educational leadership and technology integration: An investigation into preparation, experiences, and roles. *Journal of School Leadership, 21*(2), 241–261.

Shelton, S. (2010). *Strong leaders, strong schools: 2009 school leadership laws.* Denver, CO: National Conference of State Legislatures. Retrieved from http://www.wallacefoundation.org/knowledge-center/school-leadership/state-policy/Documents/2009-School-Leadership-Laws.pdf

Sugar, W., & Holloman, H. (2009, November). Technology leaders wanted: Acknowledging the leadership role of a technology coordinator. *TechTrends, 53*(6), 66–75.

West, D. M. (2012, September). *Big data for education: Data mining, data analytics, and Web dashboards.* Washington, DC: The Brookings Institution. Retrieved from http://www.brookings.edu/research/papers/2012/09/04-education-technology-west

The Leader as Motivator and Communicator

Virginia Hemby
Middle Tennessee State University
Murfreesboro, TN

Effective leaders possess certain skills and abilities: recognizing what action needs to be accomplished and moving forward to make things happen, believing in what they are doing, and motivating and inspiring others throughout the process (Hersey, Blanchard, & Johnson, 2013). Moreover, Adair (2011) theorized that leadership and motivation share a symbiotic relationship. One cannot lead without the ability to motivate others. Thus, effective leaders focus on the human element in organizations by identifying individual needs and motivation (Adair, 2011).

This chapter focuses on the importance of the human element in organizations, emphasizing motivation and communication, including theories of motivation and behavior, communication models, as well as practical methods of motivating and communicating in educational environments. International communications, technology applications, and social media are also addressed. Also included in this chapter is the work of the Policies Commission for Business and Economic Education, including the "This We Believe" statements that address business education leadership.

THE HUMAN ELEMENT IN ORGANIZATIONS

When asked to define leadership, Peter Drucker, the father of management as a discipline, reportedly stated that no such construct existed; therefore, leadership could not be defined. Drucker further espoused that leaders were labeled as such merely because they had people who followed them (Balda, 2009).

However, upon a more detailed review of Drucker's work, one finds that Drucker did believe that leadership existed. Drucker often mentioned the writings of Xenophon, the Greek general of the eighth century B.C. and how those writings teach leadership skills. Specifically, Drucker hypothesized that leadership exists through an absence of power. Thus, an effective leader can be described as an individual who can motivate or persuade others with something other than power (Balda, 2009).

Drucker's belief is particularly applicable to professional associations because individuals volunteer to contribute their time and energy without the use of power. The executive director of the National Business Education Association (NBEA), for example, does not order members to serve nor do the president of NBEA or presidents of any of its affiliate organizations. These individuals lead in the absence of power. So, why do members choose to participate? What motivates members of organizations, employees, teachers, administrators, and students to work toward the greater good or an ever-increasing bottom line and to do so by working harder and better?

Adair (2011) suggested that an effective leader should possess knowledge, both of a technical or specialist variety, as well as general knowledge. As part of general knowledge, leaders must understand people and what motivates them. Thus, motivating people involves an understanding of what makes those individuals want to perform, and the anticipated behavior is a direct result of the motivating factors employed by leaders.

Motivation and Behavior

People leave organizations because of bad leadership. When people are asked to rank the reasons why they left or would leave their jobs or positions, the resulting data reveal the highest-ranked reason to be leadership. Leaders who are seen as insecure, unclear, overinvolved, or unavailable create a great deal of damage in an organization and are the main culprit behind employee dissatisfaction (Hersey et al., 2013).

A review of existing literature clearly demonstrates that researchers have long tried to identify and understand motivational factors behind individual behaviors (Cunningham, 2011; Hassard, 2012; Kopelman, Prottas, & Falk, 2012; Levitt & List, 2011; Zhong & House, 2012). Leaders are no different in this regard because possessing the ability to identify what motivates individual members or employees ultimately results in the achievement of organizational goals (Hersey et al., 2013).

Professional organizations are also interested in what motivates individuals to join the organization and what leaders can do to motivate these individuals to engage in the organization's activities and to remain productive members. Because professional organizations encourage and shape educational leadership (Policies Commission for Business and Economic Education [PCBEE], 2006), understanding the motivation for individuals to join and to remain members of an organization is vital to the continual success of that organization. Effective leaders also recognize that their organizations offer an opportunity for advocacy, particularly in professions such as business education, and want to develop other leaders to become voices for that purpose (PCBEE, 2006).

An example of a research project designed to elicit responses from active and inactive members regarding their motivation for membership in the Delta Pi Epsilon professional association was conducted by McCroskey and O'Neil (2010). In their findings, the authors stated that individuals were motivated to be and remain members of Delta Pi Epsilon because of a very high level of commitment to their profession, business education.

Definitions of Motivation

From a psychological perspective, motivation is defined as "a dynamic factor that directs behavior toward an objective" (Bruno, 2013, p. 136). Motivation can be either extrinsic or intrinsic. Behavior motivated by extrinsic factors includes those activities in which individuals engage because they are instrumental to the receipt of awards, recognitions, and praise or to the avoidance of punishments or unpleasantness. People do not find these actions inherently satisfying in themselves (van Steenkiste, Ryan, & Deci, 2008). Intrinsic motivation, however, stems from an individual's desire to engage in a behavior because the activity itself is challenging and rewarding. Individuals derive satisfaction from the activity without the need for outside recognition (Bruno, 2013).

In studying the field of motivation, Adair (2011) theorized that the Pareto Principle had applicability to motivation in terms of leadership and individual motives. Adair termed his theory the Fifty-Fifty Rule and attributed 50% of a person's motivation to intrinsic (comes from inside the individual) factors and 50% to extrinsic (comes from the individual's environment and especially from the leadership in that environment). However, Adair stated that these proportions (50/50) were not mathematical and varied by individual. In the end, the most critical factor in the Fifty-Fifty Rule was the quality of leadership; therefore, the strongest link was between leadership and motivation.

Both individual motives and goals play a role in overall motivation, whether intrinsic or extrinsic. To understand how motives and goals affect individual motivation, one needs to know the meaning of these terms.

Motives. Motives are the reasons behind individual behavior—what propels an individual to satisfy basic needs or wants. Motives have been defined as reasons for a course of action, both conscious and unconscious ("Motive," 2009). Motives are also called felt needs, something that causes an individual to act ("Motive," n.d.). These needs drive individuals to be interested in something, to maintain or diminish that interest, and to determine the direction of individuals' behaviors (Pardee, 1990).

Copious research involving the use of motives in numerous fields is available. Examples include the following:

- De Jong and Schalk (2010) identified three motives for engaging in temporary employment: the autonomous or voluntary motive, the stepping-stone motive, and the controlled or involuntary motive.

- Diseth and Kobbeltvedt (2010) investigated the relationship among achievement motives, achievement goals, learning strategies, and academic achievement.

- Gable (2006) examined the processes and outcomes associated with approach and avoidance social motives and goals in two short-term longitudinal studies and one cross-sectional study.

- Williams and Frymier (2007) used a modified version of the student communication motives scale developed by Martin, Myers, and Mottet (1999) to measure student motives for engaging in out-of-class communication.

Motives can be both internal and external. Intrinsic motivators come from inside the individual. Examples of intrinsic or internal motivators include professional growth, increasing responsibility, meaningful work, or autonomy. Extrinsic motivators are those factors outside the individual such as money, benefits packages, or work environment. Organizations have long believed that extrinsic motivators are most important to individuals. However, Ping, Bruene, and Chen (2005) dispelled this belief through research findings that revealed intrinsic motivators are stronger and of longer duration than extrinsic motivators.

Goals. Psychologists often refer to goals as incentives (Hersey et al., 2013). Using the term incentives as a synonym for goals can be confusing, however. On the one hand, the word incentive makes people think of tangible rewards, especially monetary ones. Goals, on the other hand, are outside the individual and can be intangible, as in praise or power. For example, if individuals desire to be recognized for their work in an organization, they may be content with the public praise of the leader and that incentive may be sufficient to ensure that those individuals continue working for the good of the organization.

Motives, goals, and behavior have a symbiotic relationship. For a goal to be effective, it must align with the highest-strength need (motive) of the individual. The need with the greatest strength at the moment is the one that will receive the most action. Once a need has been satisfied, it decreases in strength and no longer motivates behavior.

In addition, goals must be attainable. Goals should be high enough to require individuals to stretch to reach them, but they should also be realistic and achievable. If people attempt to reach a goal without success or after working toward the goal realize that the goal is within their grasp, the degree of motivation and effort decreases. When individuals view a goal either as almost impossible to achieve or as easily attainable, they will stop trying. People are not highly motivated to continue toward the final goal (Hersey et al., 2013).

An educational example demonstrating the importance of attainable goals involves group or team assignments. In group projects, students are often expected to achieve a final goal—the completion of a report and oral presentation on a specific topic or product. Students are judged by their instructors (the class/course leaders) only in terms of reaching that final goal. A better approach to a group project would be for instructors to set interim, short-term goals that are realistic. Group members would then receive positive reinforcement along these milestones, thus building confidence and commitment of those individuals to reach the final goal of project completion.

Theories of Motivation

Theories of motivation are classified into content theories and process theories. Content theories of motivation focus on people and what motivates them. Process theories deal with the *how-to* perspective—what actions an effective leader can use to motivate people.

Content theories. Content theories include the hierarchy of needs (Maslow, 1954), achievement-power approach (McClelland, 1961; 1971), theory X and theory Y (McGregor, 1960), and motivation-hygiene theory (Herzberg, Mausner, and Snyderman, 1959).

Hierarchy of needs. Most people are familiar with Maslow's hierarchy of needs based on the premise that individual needs can be ranked by importance from the most basic—physiological—to the highest—self-actualization (Maslow, 1954). However, leaders who attempt to motivate members of an organization with the promise of money via raises or benefits packages may find themselves in a quandary when those same people fail to be motivated about the leaders' goals. If these individuals have their basic physiological and safety needs met, they have no motive to seek additional money with which to acquire what they already possess.

- Effective leaders recognize the need to have mechanisms in place to help employees with emotional and mental well-being, and to offer a range of retirement options as well as disability and life insurance coverage. These benefits encourage employees to feel safe and help organizations to build employee trust.

- Effective leaders can use the social need in individuals to establish teams and groups that work toward organizational goals. When people congregate to accomplish a common work goal, they can satisfy their need for affiliation as well. Other programs that effective leaders may implement to assist employees in developing a sense of belonging include a "bring-your-pet-to-work policy"; company luncheons, banquets, or retreats; open work spaces; and/or company-sponsored sports teams and clubs.

- Effective leaders recognize that people in their organizations need to have their esteem needs met and use various strategies (aside from awards for recognition) to do so: reserved parking spaces and all-expense-paid luxury vacations for winning competitions.

- Effective leaders recognize that meeting the self-actualization needs of employees is good for the organization, because inspired people will perform at their highest levels. An effective leader can help people within the organization meet their self-actualization needs through the following: tuition-reimbursement programs, educational assistance plans, paid sabbaticals, partnerships with humanitarian or philanthropic organizations that allow organizational members to get out of the office and partner with co-workers on charity events, or an organizational match program that agrees to donate dollar-for-dollar (or a percentage) of employees' contributions to charitable organizations.

Notwithstanding the information presented above, when discussing needs, one must be aware of the environment in which people are living and working. For example, in a developing country, physiological needs may take precedence over any other, followed by safety and social needs. In a developed society, however, the most pressing need may be social because both esteem and safety are equally important. When standards of living and education rise, individuals' behaviors tend to be dominated by esteem and self-actualizing activities (Hersey et al., 2013).

Achievement-power approach. McClelland (1961; 1971) worked from Maslow's hierarchy of needs to create a new theory termed the achievement-power approach. Although still focused on the personal needs of individuals, his achievement-power approach replaced the hierarchical structure of Maslow with interacting and occasionally competing needs. McClelland (1971) theorized that needs are learned and that achievers want to find solutions to problems, take calculated risks by setting moderate achievement goals, and desire concrete feedback on their performance.

Theory X and theory Y. Based on an examination of individual behavior in the work environment, McGregor (1960) asserted that leaders hold two opposing views of workers. Theory X leaders believe workers to be inherently lazy and that their goal is to avoid work. In theory Y, workers are assumed to have an intrinsic motivation that compels them to look for accountability and to solve problems independently of their leaders.

McGregor identified more closely with theory Y, hypothesizing that, when people have their basic physiological needs and safety needs met and their social, esteem, and self-actualization needs start to dominate, a controlling management style would be ineffective in motivating them to perform. He also believed that leaders need to refine their approach to managing people based on this more accurate concept of human nature and motivation.

Motivation-hygiene theory. Herzberg, et al. (1959) interviewed engineers and accountants to identify motivating factors related to their work environment. This research led to the motivation-hygiene theory in which the authors postulated that intrinsic factors lead to overall job satisfaction, whereas extrinsic or external factors create overall dissatisfaction. Herzberg, et al. labeled these two factors as motivation factors and hygiene factors (1959).

Examples of hygiene or maintenance factors, as Herzberg et al. (1959) described them, include company policies, administration, supervision, working conditions, interpersonal relations, money, status, and security. These factors have no relationship to employee productivity but are merely conditions under which a job is performed. When hygiene factors are satisfied, employees are also satisfied, but the resulting satisfaction does little to motivate those individuals toward better performance.

Motivators are those factors that people can experience in a job, such as feelings of achievement, professional growth, and recognition. These factors, Herzberg et al. claimed, do have an impact on employee productivity because they affect job satisfaction (1959).

The work of Herzberg et al. (1959) serves as the foundation for content theories of motivation. The authors were able to discern that satisfaction comes from the work itself and that dissatisfaction results from external environmental influences.

As described in the foregoing section, content theories of motivation focus on people and what motivates them. Effective leaders need to have a basic understanding of content theories—the motives people have in pursuing goals. The following section introduces process theories of motivation. These theories deal with the *how-to* perspective, what actions an effective leader can use to motivate people.

Process theories. Process theories emerged in the 1960s when cognitive psychology theories merged with work motivation theories (Griggs, 2011). Four major theories emerged during this period: reinforcement theory (Skinner, 1987), expectancy theory (Vroom, 1964), goal-setting theory (Locke & Latham, 1990), and equity theory (Adams, 1965). Table 1 briefly presents and explains each of these process theories.

Reinforcement theory. After reviewing the process theories, one may suggest that reinforcement theory might apply when business teachers introduce students to keyboarding. As classroom leaders, teachers desire to reward appropriate behavior when possible. With the proliferation of technology and the early ages at which students are introduced to various technologies, many learn poor and improper keying techniques. Attempting to help students learn (or re-learn) proper finger placement and technique may necessitate employment of one or more of the five reinforcement schedules: continuous schedule, fixed interval schedule, variable interval schedule, fixed ratio reinforcement, and/or variable ratio schedule. The choice will depend on whether the business teacher desires the behavior to be sustained over time (variable ratio schedule) or simply to have students rapidly learn the new techniques while discontinuing improper or incorrect ones (continuous schedule) (Skinner, 1987).

Table 1. Process Theories of Motivation

Reinforce-ment Theory (Pavlov and Skinner)	• System of behavior modification through use of rewards and punishments. • Uses a reinforcement schedule (five schedules; each has varying degrees of impact on learning and extinction). • Consequences are reinforcement (positive and negative), punish-ment, and extinction.	• Positive reinforcement occurs when desired behavior is exhibited. • Negative reinforcement (punishment) is applied when adverse behavior or consequence arises. • Both positive and negative reinforce-ment have desired effect of increasing appropriate behavior.
Expectancy Theory (Vroom)	• Uses hierarchical needs system. • Connection between effort, reward, and performance. • Relies heavily on reinforcement of behavior. • Consistency and scheduling rewards are of paramount importance; with-out both, trust is eroded in both the system as well as the leader.	• High motivation will be achieved if individuals perceive high probability that greater effort will result in valuable rewards. • Perceived ability and desirability of the reward are proportional. • The more positive the reward, the higher the level of motivation.
Goal-Setting Theory (Locke)	• Based on McGregor's Theory Y and Maslow's Hierarchy of Needs. • Goals are immediate regulators of behavior. • Relationship exists between diffi-culty of goal and the performance. • Rewards are of paramount importance. • Money is considered primary incentive in goal setting.	• Ideal goal is difficult yet attainable. • If goal is not sufficiently challenging, em-ployee will not put forth maximum effort. • If goal is too difficult (or not attainable), employee will shut down. • Feedback, knowledge of results, partici-pation in decision-making, competition, and incentives only affect individual performance from perspective of setting and committing to specific high goal.
Equity Theory (Adams)	• Focuses on perception of individual. • People are motivated to maintain re-lationships with others when those relationships are deemed to be fair. • When relationships are perceived to be unfair, individuals want to rectify the situation and to make relationships fair. • When comparing themselves with others, individuals want their efforts and achievements to be judged fairly. • When employees view the ratio of effort (inputs) to reward (outputs) as balanced, equity occurs. • Individuals are motivated to reduce inequity, whether it exists or is imagined.	• Experience, age, education, skill, and contributions are considered inputs (anything the employee feels should be valued that he/she brings to the organization). • Rewards (outputs) can be both nega-tive (poor evaluations and/or work conditions, demotion) and positive (pay, status, and bonus). • Referent is created by comparing outputs to inputs (as related to the individual employee). • If personal referents are perceived as disproportional to those of another employee, inequity exists. • Fairness is still important to the individual employee and can affect employees' performance.

Sources: Latham, Ganegoda, & Locke, 2011; Whittington & Evans, 2005; Pinnington & Edwards, 2000; Locke & Latham, 1990; Skinner, 1987; Vroom, 1964; and Adams, 1965.

Expectancy theory. Effective leaders who employ the expectancy theory of motivation need to design a system of rewards that demonstrate to employees or members of the organization that effective performance will result in outcomes (or rewards) that the employees or members desire. Effective leaders must also be consistent and schedule rewards. In addition, the evaluation system must be credible and visible to all members of the organization. Trust is at the heart of this theory of motivation; if employees or members of an organization do not believe that promised extrinsic rewards will materialize, they have little motivation to perform or to achieve (Vroom, 1964).

Goal-setting theory. The goal-setting theory guides leaders to establish goals and rewards for meeting those goals. However, this theory directs effective leaders to know what each employee or organizational member desires so that effective incentives and rewards for goal accomplishment can be designed on individual bases (Locke & Latham, 1990).

Equity theory. Adams (1965) conducted the original research and presented the theory that an individual is motivated by his or her perception of fairness, equity, and justice exercised by management. However, since the original research, the desire for social equity has waned (Lerner, 2003). Nonetheless, effective leaders must continue to support this theory because workers and organizational members still see fairness as an important component potentially affecting performance.

Regardless of the theories on what motivates people, the one piece of advice that effective leaders take from them is that people are individuals and individuals respond to different motivating factors. Effective leaders, therefore, cannot take the *one-size-fits-all* approach to motivation.

COMMUNICATION IN ORGANIZATIONS

Previous research has reported a link between effective communication and leadership (de Vries, Bakker-Pieper, & Oostenveld, 2010). The de Vries et al. research uncovered several noteworthy findings related to leadership style and communication. Specifically, the researchers found that charismatic and human-oriented leadership styles result in more communication. Task-oriented leadership, however, results in less communication.

In 2011 Google conducted a study (Project Oxygen) involving 10,000 observations about managers that resulted in a list of best manager behaviors. Fifth on the list was "Be a good communicator and listen to your team" (Bock, as cited in Bryant, 2011). Although manager and leader are not synonymous terms, the actions they represent are complementary. Therefore, both leaders and managers must be effective communicators and engage in listening behaviors that demonstrate interest in others' success and well-being.

School leaders, for example, are charged with choosing the right words for the situation when communicating with their constituents. Haycock (2011) stated that effective education leaders employ proper filters for messages they need to share with their teachers, staff, students, and parents/guardians. Effective leaders know their words have an impact on the way people respond to challenges. So, they learn to choose their words carefully and to send clear, consistent, and mission-focused messages. Effective leaders also remind their staff of their importance to the mission and to the students they serve (Murphy, Goldring, Cravens, Elliott, & Porter, 2011).

School leaders must also be able to communicate clearly and genuinely and to listen responsively. The ability to connect with parents/caregivers and to communicate clearly helps to foster the proper environment for parental involvement to support student achievement. Also, leaders must be open and genuine in their communication with teachers to encourage a positive instructional environment. Listening is an important skill that all leaders must develop. If a leader is unable to listen responsively to students, staff, teachers, and parents/caregivers, he or she will struggle to ensure the school environment is meeting the needs of all involved (Dotger, 2011).

During his time as headmaster of Brookline High School in Boston, Weintraub (2012) developed some guidelines for effective leadership. One of his overarching goals involved responding to phone calls and e-mail. Weintraub labeled the process as one of his six Rs—responsiveness. As an effective leadership practice, Weintraub responded to every phone call and e-mail message each day.

Communication Models

Because communication skills are vital to success in the workplace, leaders need to have an understanding of the models of communication and what fundamentals work best when establishing and maintaining rapport with their organizational members.

Components of communication. People do not always consider communication as comprising parts or components; they talk, write, or give a speech, and that is communication. However, communication is a process that involves an idea that is encoded into a message using a system of shared language so that the receiver of the message will be able to decode it and understand the message as the creator/sender intended it to be understood.

In the middle of this process, however, the creator or sender of the message has to make decisions on the channel by which to send the message (i.e., face to face, e-mail, letter, memo, or text). In addition, the creator or sender must consider potential barriers that could arise in this communication process (bypassing, physical or psychological issues, cultural differences, perception, and nonverbal cues) and attempt to circumvent or avoid them.

Effective leaders are effective communicators and recognize that the communication process is riddled with challenges. Intentional or unintentional slights, such as directing more eye contact to male attendees in a meeting or other subtle cues involving gestures, proximity, or position in a physical environment, can impact trust (Hersey et al., 2013).

The Linear Model. This model of communication does not involve the receiver but is one sided: one-way communication through the use of Web sites, YouTube videos, television commercials, flyers, and signs. The use of the Linear Model in communication involves the hope that the receiver will actually open, view, read, and understand the communication. The sender/creator, however, has no accurate method for determining if such is taking place (Gerbner, Shannon, & Weaver, 1990).

The Interactional Model. The model involves feedback from the receiver, in a give-and-take scenario much like a tennis match. This model is not very effective in face-to-face situations as only minimal interaction is occurring (Gerbner et al., 1990).

The Transactional Communication Model. This model of communication is the best for describing the face-to-face process. In the model, "noise" (both internal and external) as part of the communication process is included. Noise refers to verbal communication barriers such as differences in interpretation and language as well as nonverbal signals that are inappropriate or send conflicting messages (Newman, 2015). Effective leaders recognize that to bridge the communication divide that results because of external and internal noise, they must diminish any external noise and clarify terminology in their communications in order to decrease internal noise (Wood, 2009a).

Patterns of Communication

Effective leaders recognize the need for varying communication patterns depending on the people with whom they are communicating. For example, if a leader is working with an experienced group of individuals, he or she might find structuring the communication pattern in a more democratic, freewheeling fashion to be the best approach. However, if the leader is dealing with an inexperienced novice group, he or she would be more likely to operate in a more autocratic manner. As these two groups are at different levels of motivation, commitment, and responsibility, an effective leader will employ a different kind of communication pattern for each (Hersey et al., 2013).

Gender and generational communication differences. Communication differences between genders have long been a source of conflict and confusion (Wood, 2009b). For example, in a question session following a presentation, men are more likely to ask the first questions and to ask more and longer questions than women. Women prefer a one-on-one setting where they can engage in more individual conversation. Women prefer "rapport" talk; men prefer "report" talk (Wood, 2009b).

Today's workforce comprises at least four different generations of people: Radio Babies (or Silent Generation), born 1930–1945; Baby Boomers, born 1946–1964; Generation Xers (or Baby Busters), born 1965–1976; and Generation Ys (or Generation Why), born 1977–1990 (Gravett & Throckmorton, 2007). Each generation has specific values and norms; each generation has a different preference for communication and motivation. Effective leaders must understand each generation so that they can communicate with the always-connected Generation Y members and manage the frustration of the Baby Boomers as they deal with annoying e-mail and text messages and the disrespectful 24/7 demands of Generation Y (Hersey et al., 2013).

Communication across cultures. Organizations are no longer classified as national but are part of the international business community proliferated by the explosion of the Internet and e-commerce. Therefore, effective leaders must develop their intercultural skills because the activities in which they engage (negotiating, motivating, and leading) are subject to cultural differences.

For example, nonverbal communication cues vary by culture. A gesture considered appropriate in Western culture can be seen as totally inappropriate in another. In addition, greetings, eye contact, facial expressions, sentence structure, word meaning, personal contact, forms of address, gifts, and negotiation protocols all differ from culture to culture (Siftar, 2013).

Leaders must recognize that organizations comprise people from a myriad of cultures, each with unique perceptions and expectations. These individuals expect their cultural traditions and beliefs to be considered when working with others. The ultimate goal for an effective leader is to create a culture of inclusion within the organization (Hersey et al., 2013).

Social media and communication. Changes in technology have led to an increased need for embracing new opportunities to communicate, connect, and collaborate. Effective leaders realize that they have the responsibility of leading by example. However, one of the first issues a leader must consider is the implementation of an acceptable use policy for social media. Because of the ease with which people can access various social media tools, their use of these programs could easily increase exponentially to the point that the organization experiences problems with connectivity. The work of the organization can be affected when access is slow or nonexistent.

School leaders, in particular, have an imperative to model the appropriate behaviors inherent in the use of social media for communication. If administrators hesitate to use unfamiliar tools and programs, teachers will also model that same behavior. Social media tools can improve communication by increasing opportunities in which to communicate and by encouraging contact between teachers and students and between teachers and administrators. In addition, social media can open a world of possibilities for teachers to communicate with their counterparts around the globe and to bring classroom experiences to life for their students by including these communication opportunities (Joosten, 2012).

School leaders want students to be prepared for the next phase of their lives, whether that involves college or the workplace. To best prepare students, leaders recognize the need to improve their own skills. Accomplishing that goal can be done through the use of social media tools for collaboration: personal learning networks, blogs, and Twitter (Larkin, 2011).

Regardless of the medium by which great leaders communicate, the goal is to increase effectiveness through the ways in which they communicate. Anders (2013) has spent 25 years studying corporate leaders in action. He has learned that great leaders communicate in the following ways: (a) bring the vision to life (translate the mission statement into concrete actions), (b) ask smart questions (questions can be more powerful than statements), (c) take time to read the room (careful listening equates with winning people's trust), (d) create a climate in which things get done (prioritize and set interim mileposts), (e) use stories to get points across (share teaching anecdotes), (f) be mindful of what you do not know (on-the-job learning), and (g) make people feel they work for a winner (employees need to believe they are working for the best company in its field).

PRACTICAL METHODS OF MOTIVATING AND COMMUNICATING IN EDUCATIONAL ENVIRONMENTS

As reported by the Council of Chief State School Officers (CCSSO) in presenting the Educational Leadership Policy Standards, very little research had been conducted regarding effective education leadership and ways to evaluate that leadership (2008). In the decade preceding the release of these standards, however, numerous research projects led to a proliferation of data and the resulting literature had grown exponentially.

As a result of these research studies, the National Policy Board for Educational Administration's Interstate School Leaders Licensure Consortium revised the Educational Leadership Policy Standards to better reflect the crucial connection between school leadership and student achievement (CCSSO, 2008). The consortium believed that effective leaders promote better teaching and that "leadership is second only to classroom instruction among school-related factors that influence student outcomes" (CCSSO, 2008, p. 9). Effective leaders are able to hire and retain the best, most capable teachers. These leaders provide support and model best practice.

Elementary and Secondary Education

Administrators. Effective leaders at elementary and secondary levels should be focused on ensuring that *every* student achieves success. They should involve all stakeholders in the process of (a) developing and implementing a vision and a mission, (b) creating a personalized learning environment for students, one that also motivates students, (c) ensuring proper management of resources to promote a safe and effective learning environment, (d) building relationships with all constituents (teachers, families/caregivers, and community partners), (e) modeling principles of fairness, integrity, transparency, and ethical behavior, (f) advocating for students and their families/caregivers; and (g) assessing and anticipating trends in order to make necessary adaptations (CCSSO, 2008).

These expectations exert tremendous pressure on administrators, especially in light of today's continually connected society. Harsh criticism of educational leaders and school systems is much easier to disseminate via tweets, texts, and e-mail. In addition, because of these technology trends, school leaders find themselves interacting more frequently with a computer than with people. Hoerr (2011) recommended that principals make an effort to return to their roots: making the effort to consciously and personally connect with teachers, parents/guardians, staff, and students. Part of this process involves asking questions and actively listening to the responses: What do you see as the strengths of our school? What are the challenges? What suggestions do you have to help the school and to help you, the teacher?

Weintraub (2012) suggested that existing school leaders might hone their skills by teaching or coteaching a class and doing so with a regular teaching assignment. School leaders who teach classes are able to connect with students and demonstrate to teachers their goal of understanding teachers' day-to-day duties and responsibilities.

In a research study designed to identify deficits of new principals as perceived by public school superintendents, Cray and Weiler (2011) found new principal candidates were noted to have little to no understanding of basic personnel supervision issues. On a more troubling note, however, these new principals were found to completely lack training on best practices in the classroom (i.e., quality instruction). In their conclusions, Cray and Weiler recommended that university programs need to adequately address necessary skills for educational leadership positions as these programs are not meeting identified needs for new administrators. These findings are even more vital as the federal government begins to include the evaluation of school leaders as a new requirement in its funding calculations (House, 2012).

Teachers. As reported by Stein (2009/2010), the educational system in the United States has a leadership shortage at all levels—including the classroom. Unfortunately, most individuals who enter the teaching field do not describe themselves as leaders. Most teachers believe that their training prepared them to manage the classroom but not to serve in a leadership capacity. Because, by their very definitions, leadership and management are not the same, one can understand how teachers view themselves as managers, as they have little to no knowledge and skills associated with leadership (training in motivation theories, organizational and human behavior, or team building) but as managers can work with students to accomplish the goals of an educational institution (Stein, 2009/2010).

School administrators, however, consider teachers to be informal leaders (Roby, 2009). As such, Stein (2009/2010) argued that teachers must be taught leadership basics. They must also be expected to demonstrate these leadership skills and be held accountable for doing so successfully. As Stein so accurately stated, "a teacher who leads students gives them hope for the future" (2009/2010, p. 86).

In 2001 the PCBEE stated that business educators should serve as mentors to new professionals entering the field. In this regard, current business teachers serve in the role of leader, effectively mentoring students and new professionals as well. PCBEE members also challenged business teachers to accept a leadership role in political advocacy for the field of business education, stating that business teachers should participate in school governance as well.

Whether discussing leadership at the elementary and secondary levels or in higher education, business teachers have a responsibility for providing leadership (PCBEE, 2009). Veteran teachers should assist new teachers by helping them to develop their own leadership skills as well. An organization (and profession) relies on the leadership of its members to create continuity of purpose and mission. Therefore, teachers should embrace the leadership mantle and use their skills to shape the future of education while leading by example.

Higher Education

Today's leadership challenge in academia includes "changing expectations, unclear goals, conflict between professional and administrative authority, dual control systems, and faculty loyalty to the discipline-specific organizations to which they belong" (Czech & Forward, 2010, p. 433). The leader who plays the greatest role in managing these higher education issues is the department chair. These individuals are involved in nearly every aspect of departmental activities even while being viewed as neither faculty nor administration but rather as occupying the territory between the two.

In a 2007 literature review focused on effective leadership in higher education, Bryman uncovered 13 behaviors associated with effective departmental leaders. Two behaviors are notable for college department chairs: foster a collegial atmosphere and advance the department's cause.

According to Cleveland-Innes (2012), in order to effect change at the college level, leadership must include everyone, including the rank-and-file employees. In other words, leadership must be collaborative and distributed. However, most postsecondary cultures prevent interaction and collaboration (Gano-Phillips et al., 2011).

In identifying leadership themes in the context of general education reform, Gano-Phillips et al. (2011) stated that many institutions of higher learning have climates of distrust, suspicion, and secrecy that span disciplines and academic departments. Therefore, effective leaders must prioritize the establishment of trust and ensure that their focus transcends the emphasis on their own programs and departments.

SUMMARY

As stated in the introduction to this chapter, the human element plays a major role in leadership in organizations. Understanding the needs, motivations, and behavior of individuals is important to the success of any leader. Effective leaders embrace the fact that organizational members are individuals with various motives and needs. In addition, a good leader also recognizes that organizational members' needs change as one goal is met and another defined. Effective leaders are dynamic, open with their communication, and unafraid to seek assistance when needed. Their behaviors reflect the human element in their organizations.

In summary, effective leaders should follow a framework for motivation built on the following pillars: "(1) be motivated yourself; (2) select only highly motivated people; (3) treat each person as an individual; (4) set realistic and challenging targets; (5) remember that progress motivates; (6) create a motivating environment; (7) provide fair rewards; and (8) give recognition" (Adair, 2011, p. 109). A good leader also knows that he or she is ultimately effective only because of the people who follow.

REFERENCES

Adair, J. (2011). *Leadership and motivation: The fifty-fifty rule and the eight key principles of motivating others.* London, UK: Kogan Page.

Adams, J. S. (1965). Towards an understanding of inequity. *Journal of Abnormal and Social Psychology, 67,* 422–436.

Anders, G. (2013, January 20). How great leaders communicate. Retrieved from http://www.linkedin.com/today/post/article/20130120173044-59549-how-great-leaders-communicate

Balda, W. (2009, June 1). There is no such thing as leadership. *Managing turbulence. The Simeon Institute.* Retrieved from http://managing-turbulence.org/2009/06/02/there-is-no-such-thing-as-leadership [blog post].

Bruno, B. (2013). Reconciling economics and psychology on intrinsic motivation. *Journal of Neuroscience, Psychology, and Economics, 6*(2), 136–149.

Bryant, A. (2011, March 12). Google's quest to build a better boss. *The New York Times.* Retrieved from http://www.nytimes.com/2011/03/13/business/13hire.html

Bryman, A. (2007). Effective leadership in higher education: A literature review. *Studies in Higher Education, 32*(6), 693–710.

Council of Chief State School Officers (CCSSO). (2008). *Educational Leadership Policy Standards: ISLLC 2008.* Retrieved from http://www.ccsso.org/Documents/2008/Educational_Leadership_Policy_Standards_2008.pdf

Cleveland-Innes, M. (2012). Who needs leadership? Social problems, change, and education futures. *International Review of Research in Open & Distance Learning, 13*(2), 231–235.

Cray, M., & Weiler, S. C. (2011). Principal preparedness: Superintendent perceptions of new principals. *Journal of School Leadership, 21*(6), 927–945.

Cunningham, R. A. (2011, September). Douglas McGregor: A lasting impression. *Ivey Business Journal, 75*(5), 5–7.

Czech, K., & Forward, G. L. (2010). Leader communication: Faculty perceptions of the department chair. *Communication Quarterly, 58*(4), 431–457.

De Jong, J., & Schalk, R. (2010). Extrinsic motives as moderators in the relationship between fairness and work-related outcomes among temporary workers. *Journal of Business Psychology, 25*(1), 175–189. doi:10.1007/s10869-009-9139-8

De Vries, R. E., Bakker-Pieper, A., & Oostenveld, W. (2010). Leadership = Communication? The relations of leaders' communication styles with leadership styles, knowledge sharing, and leadership outcomes. *Journal of Business Psychology, 25*(3), 367–380.

Diseth, A., & Kobbeltvedt, T. (2010). A mediation analysis of achievement motives, goals, learning strategies, and academic achievement. *British Journal of Education Psychology, 80*(4), 671–687. doi:10.1348/0007099/0X492432

Dotger, B. H. (2011). The school leader communication model: An emerging method for bridging school leader preparation and practice. *Journal of School Leadership, 21*(6), 871–892.

Gable, S. L. (2006). Approach and avoidance social motives and goals. *Journal of Personality, 74*(1), 175–222. doi:10.1111/j.1467-6494.2005.00373.x

Gano-Phillips, S., Barnett, R. W., Kelsch, A., Hawthorne, J., Mitchell, N. D., & Jonson, J. (2011). Rethinking the role of leadership in general education reform. *The Journal of General Education, 60*(1), 65–83.

Gerbner, G., Shannon, C. E., & Weaver, W. (1990). Other models. In J. Fiske (Ed.), *Introduction to communication studies* (pp. 24–38). London, UK: Routledge.

Gravett, L., & Throckmorton, R. (2007). *Bridging the generation gap: How to get Radio Babies, Boomers, Gen Xers, and Gen Yers to work together and achieve more.* Franklin Lakes, NJ: Career Press.

Griggs, H. L. E. (2011). *Influence of job satisfaction of small high school and large high school principals in the state of California* (Doctoral dissertation). Retrieved from ProQuest, UMI Dissertations Publishing (UMI No. 3502220).

Hassard, J. S. (2012). Rethinking the Hawthorne Studies: The Western Electric research in its social, political, and historical context. *Human Relations, 65*(11), 43–46. doi:10.1177/0018726712452168

Haycock, B. (2011). Sounding the charge for change: How leaders communicate can inspire or defeat the troops. *Phi Delta Kappan, 93*(4), 48–51.

Hersey, P. H., Blanchard, K. H., & Johnson, D. E. (2013). *Management of organizational behavior: Leading human resources* (10th ed.). Upper Saddle River, NJ: Prentice Hall.

Herzberg, F., Mausner, B., & Snyderman, B. (1959). *The motivation to work* (2nd ed.). New York, NY: Wiley.

Hoerr, T. R. (2011, October). Pretend you're new again. *Educational Leadership*, 88–89.

House, J. (2012, November). Evaluating school leadership. *THE Journal*, 19–22.

Joosten, T. (2012). *Social media for educators: Strategies and best practices*. San Francisco, CA: John Wiley.

Kopelman, R. E., Prottas, D. J., & Falk, D. W. (2012). Further development of a measure of theory X and Y managerial assumptions. *Journal of Managerial Issues, XXIV*(4), 450–470.

Larkin, P. (2011, September). Getting connected: Social media tools offer principals powerful ways to connect to their peers and model productive technology use. *Principal Leadership*, 22–25.

Latham, G. P., Ganegoda, D. B., & Locke, E. A. (2011). Goal-setting: A state theory, but related to traits. In T. Chamorro-Premuzic, S. von Stumm, & A. Furnham (Eds.), *The Wiley-Blackwell handbook of individual differences* (pp. 579–587). Hoboken, NJ: Wiley-Blackwell.

Lerner, M. J. (2003). The justice motive: Where social psychologists found it, how they lost it, and why they may not find it again. *Personality & Social Psychology Review, 7*(4), 388–399.

Levitt, S. D., & List, J. A. (2011). Was there really a Hawthorne Effect at the Hawthorne Plant? An analysis of the original illumination experiments. *American Economic Journal: Applied Economics, 3*(1), 224–238. Retrieved from http://www.aeaweb.org/articles.php?doi=10.1257/app.3.1.224

Locke, E. A., & Latham, G. P. (1990). *A theory of goal setting and task performance*. Englewood Cliffs, NJ: Prentice Hall.

Martin, M. M., Myers, S. A., & Mottet, T. P. (1999). Student's motives for communication with their instructors. *Communication Education, 48*(2), 155–164.

Maslow, A. H. (1954). *Motivation and personality*. New York, NY: Harper

McClelland, D. C. (1961). *The achieving society*. New York, NY: Van Nostrand Reinhold.

McClelland, D. C. (1971). *Assessing human motivation*. Morristown, NJ: General Learning Press.

McCroskey, S., & O'Neil, S. L. (2010). Factors leading to membership in professional associations and levels of professional commitment as determined by active and inactive members of Delta Pi Epsilon. *Delta Pi Epsilon Journal, 52*(3), 111–137.

McGregor, D. (1960).*The human side of enterprise*. New York, NY: McGraw-Hill

Motive. (2009). In *The American heritage dictionary of the English language* (4th ed.). Retrieved from http://www.thefreedictionary.com/p/motive

Motive. (n.d.). In *Merriam-Webster's online dictionary*. Retrieved from http://www.merriam-webster.com/dictionary/motive

Murphy, J. F., Goldring, E. B., Cravens, X. C., Elliott, S., & Porter, A. C. (2011). The Vanderbilt Assessment of Leadership in Education: Measuring learning-centered leadership. *Journal of East China Normal University, 29*(1), 1–10.

Newman, A. (2015). *Business communication: In person, in print, online* (9th ed.). Belmont, CA: Cengage Publishing.

Pardee, R. L. (1990). Motivation theories of Maslow, Herzberg, McGregor, and McClelland: A literature review of selected theories dealing with job satisfaction and motivation. Retrieved from ERIC database. ED 316 767.

Ping, X., Bruene, A., & Chen, A. (2005). Interactive impact of intrinsic motivators and extrinsic rewards on behavior and motivation outcomes. *Journal of Teaching in Physical Education, 24*(2), 179–197.

Pinnington, A., & Edwards, T. (2000). *Introduction to human resource management.* New York, NY: Oxford University Press.

Policies Commission for Business and Economic Education (PCBEE). (2001). *This we believe about the emerging roles of the business educator* (Statement No. 68). Retrieved from http://nbea.org/newsite/curriculum/policy/no_68.pdf

Policies Commission for Business and Economic Education. (2006). *This we believe about the value of professional associations* (Statement No. 79). Retrieved from http://nbea.org/newsite/curriculum/policy/no_79.pdf

Policies Commission for Business and Economic Education. (2009). *This we believe about the induction and mentoring of new business teachers* (Statement No. 84). Retrieved from http://nbea.org/newsite/curriculum/policy/no_84.pdf

Roby, D. E. (2009). Teacher leadership skills: An analysis of communication apprehension. *Education, 129*(4), 608–614.

Siftar, M. (2013, April 1). Cultural awareness training: A new "must" for business. *Philadelphia Business Journal.* Retrieved from http://www.bizjournals.com/philadelphia/blog/guest-comment/2013/04/cultural-awareness-training-a-new.html

Skinner, B. F. (1987). Whatever happened to psychology as the science of behavior? *American Psychologist, 42*(8), 780–786.

Stein, L. (2009/2010). Lead students: Don't just manage them. *Phi Delta Kappan, 91*(4), 82–86.

Van Steenkiste, M., Ryan, R. M., & Deci, E. L. (2008). Self-determination theory and the explanatory role of psychological needs in human well-being. In L. Bruni, F. Comim, & M. Pugno (Eds.), *Capabilities and happiness* (pp. 187–223). Oxford, UK: Oxford University Press.

Vroom, V. H. (1964). *Work and motivation.* New York, NY: Wiley.

Weintraub, R. J. (2012). 15 lessons on leadership. *Phi Delta Kappan, 93*(7), 80.

Whittington, J. L., & Evans, B. (2005). General issues in management. *Problems & Perspectives in Management, 2*, 114.

Williams, K. D., & Frymier, A. B. (2007). The relationship between student educational orientation and motives for out-of-class communication. *Communication Research Reports, 24*(3), 249–256. doi:10.1080/0882409701446625

Wood, J. T. (2009a). *Communication in our lives* (4th ed.). Belmont, CA: Thomson-Wadsworth.

Wood, J. T. (2009b). *Gendered lives: Communication, gender, and culture* (8th ed.). Belmont, CA: Wadsworth.

Zhong, C. B., & House, J. (2012). Hawthorne revisited: Organizational implications of the physical work environment. *Research in Organizational Behavior, 32*, 3–22. doi:10.1016/j.riob.2012.10.004

Leadership Profiles of Business Educators

Peter Meggison
Massasoit Community College
Brockton, MA

Robert B. Mitchell
University of Arkansas at Little Rock
Little Rock, AR

In today's increasingly challenging educational environment, business education depends on quality leadership for articulating new vision and directing goal attainment. As stated by the Policies Commission for Business and Economic Education (2008),

In order for business education to thrive, we believe that concerted actions must be taken to ensure the continuing development of relevant, authentic business education for all learners. The transformation of the profession needs to reflect the change in learners, social context, and business education…Transformation and survival of relevant business education depends upon quality leadership. (p. 1)

The business education profession must learn from its history and build on the contributions of past and present leaders in order to keep business education vibrant and at the forefront of the global world in which we live. Many leadership scholars recognize that, although individuals may have certain innate leadership abilities, leaders can be developed (Nohria & Khurana, 2010). The leadership profiles in this chapter illustrate the varied leadership skills found among business educators and varied paths to the development of these leadership capabilities.

QUALITIES OF LEADERS: LEADERSHIP TRAITS

No one best model of leadership fits the business education profession. The leadership profiles highlighted here illustrate that leadership approaches change based on situational variables in play at any one time: variables such as the challenges faced, characteristics of the persons involved, and the culture of the environment.

Research has identified the following leader traits as differentiators between leaders and nonleaders (Lussier & Achua, 2007); the business education leaders profiled in this chapter clearly evidence the following traits:

- **Dominance:** Leaders want to be in positions of leadership, will develop their leadership skills, and view leadership as enjoyable.

- **High energy:** Leaders conscientiously seek to achieve goals.

- **Self-confidence:** Leaders are self-assured in their abilities and effectiveness.

- **Locus of control:** Leaders feel in control of their performance and work to succeed.

- **Stability:** Leaders are emotionally in control of the situation and positively use strengths and overcome weaknesses to assure success.

- **Integrity:** Leaders are trustworthy.

- **Intelligence:** Leaders have the ability to think critically and problem solve.

- **Flexibility:** Leaders adjust to contingent situations.

- **Sensitivity to others:** Leaders understand others as individuals and know how to influence them on an individual basis.

Effective leaders often have varying degrees of these nine leadership traits, and a leader does not need to possess each trait to be successful. Goleman (2004) found, however, that most effective leaders have one commonality: high emotional intelligence. Focusing on the impact of intelligence on understanding and managing relationships, Goleman concluded that other characteristics or dimensions of leadership are important overall, but emotional intelligence must be highly developed for leadership success. He identified five components of emotional intelligence:

- **Self-awareness**, including self-confidence

- **Self-regulation**, including trustworthiness and integrity and openness to change

- **Motivation**, including a strong drive to achieve, optimism, and organizational commitment

- **Empathy**, including expertise in building talent and sensitivity

- **Social skill**, including effectiveness in leading change, persuasiveness, and expertise in team leadership

He emphasized that emotional intelligence can be learned, can be improved with training and practice, and usually increases with maturity.

TRANSFORMATIONAL LEADERSHIP BEHAVIORS

As business education faces the growing challenge of developing leaders, the theory of transformational leadership has increased relevance. Simic (1998) described transformational leaders as those who advance change by helping followers increase their feelings of self-importance and motivating them to perform beyond expectations by putting the needs of the organization first. Leaders who demonstrate these characteristics are entrepreneurial, innovative, flexible, open and sincere, led by values, and visionary. Four behaviors are observed among transformational leaders (Barling, Christie, & Hoption, 2011):

- **Idealized influence:** Transformational leaders create vision and collective mission while focusing on what is best for all. They go beyond self-interest and act with integrity.

- **Inspirational motivation:** Transformational leaders encourage others to accomplish goals not thought possible by inspiring and fostering self-resilience.

- **Intellectual stimulation:** Transformational leaders encourage others to be innovative, to develop personal strategies, to question the status quo, and to overcome resistance.

- **Individualized consideration:** Transformational leaders provide mentorship by caring and focusing on the personal needs of others.

The following profiles of recognized leaders in business education, while sharing commonalities, are at the same time quite diverse and clearly reflect the behaviors of transformational leaders.

LEADERSHIP PROFILES OF BUSINESS EDUCATORS IN THE UNITED STATES

June S. Atkinson, State Superintendent of Public Instruction, North Carolina

When June Atkinson became North Carolina's State Superintendent of Public Instruction in 2005, the state's high school graduation rate was about 68%. Today, that rate has skyrocketed to more than 80%—an all-time high. In no small part, this accomplishment is related to the deliberate, focused work that has taken place under June's leadership to make improvements and recognize schools and districts contributing to that accomplishment.

A "tried and true" business educator, June understands the importance of improving teaching and learning by creating school environments that encourage student success, keeping education modern and relevant, and ensuring that every high school graduate is both career and college ready. June has business education degrees from Radford University, Virginia Tech, and North Carolina State University, all of which she has put to good use in her nearly 40 years of experience in education. During her career, she has served as a chief consultant and director in the areas of business education, career and technical education, and instructional services with the North Carolina Department of Public Instruction. A former business education teacher, June has been involved with instruction and curriculum development throughout her career and served as president of the National Business Education Association in 1990–1991.

In leading the North Carolina Department of Public Instruction, June currently directs the groundbreaking initiative, the Accountability and Curriculum Reform Effort, to revitalize the state's curriculum and accountability programs. The landmark Race to the Top Grant supports this work in addition to several other key initiatives such as transforming low-performing schools. As a creative and attentive leader, June's focus is on ensuring students have the opportunity to learn the technical skills that are important in today's global economy. Partnerships with numerous corporations have enabled North Carolina to advance the skills of both teachers and students as, ultimately, learning is transformed and student achievement improves. In her position as state superintendent, June oversees almost 1.5 million students in more than 2,500 public schools.

In reflecting on her own professional life, June believes that her mentors served as models for how to negotiate to get objectives accomplished and to work with people who have differing ideas and strategies. These mentors helped June to develop her own style of leadership based on the best practices she has observed.

June suggested these ideas for those who aspire to leadership positions:

- Be as knowledgeable as possible about the field.

- Ask good questions and listen to other points of view.

- Read books or material from fields other than one's own.

- Listen to others without interrupting.

- Establish good relations with people, regardless of position, authority, or power.

- Continue to learn.

- Forgive yourself and others when mistakes are made.

- Focus more on the future than the past.

- Always look toward the future and ascertain patterns.

- Be specific about what you want to accomplish.

- Use "we" much more often than "I."

- Strive to be results oriented.

As a contextual leader, June continues to adapt to situations, goals, and circumstances as they arise.

Kathleen A. DeKalb, Fort Plain (New York) Central School

As president of the Business Teachers Association of New York State, Kathleen (Kathie) DeKalb has made positive impacts in improving the status of business education in New York State, not the least of which have been increased conference participation, improved member benefits, and greater communication with members in one of the most diverse states in this nation. Serving as leader of the Business Teachers Association for four years (in 2002–2004 and 2009–2011), Kathie has been in a position to actively participate in projects generated through the New York State Education Department, including curriculum development, lobbying for various programs, development of the Department-of-the-Year Awards, refining test questions for high-stakes testing in business, determining the scope and sequence of business education throughout the state, and serving as the official liaison between the Education Department and the business teachers in the state.

Kathie's reflective personality, which emits a very calm exterior, does not betray her passionate commitment toward the emerging role business education should play in the overall development of American youth. And this commitment is contagious. Recently, at a particularly stressful meeting that would have an impact on the availability of statewide business education resources in her state, Kathie was trying to persuade a colleague to join a team to work on a project. The colleague turned to Kathie and said, "You make it difficult to say, 'No' to you!" And the colleague accepted this challenge. Kathie's sensitive, yet idealistic, personality makes others want to be part of Kathie's team. Kathie readily admits, however, that she does have high expectations for herself as well as those around her.

Having reasonable, attainable goals, Kathie believes, is the cornerstone of a broader vision because if you do not know where you are going, how can anyone follow you there? Kathie's style of leadership views service as an opportunity, which at times, includes sitting back and listening to people and thinking about what could motivate them to achieve a particular goal. Working side by side is important for a leader because it enables one to experience what others are experiencing and is of great help in the decision-making process.

Kathie believes that there are many people she has met in her personal and professional life who have acted as her mentors. Finding the strengths of others and transferring those strengths into her own life has made an important difference for her. It is especially important, Kathie recognizes, for a person in a leadership position to be willing to really listen and learn from others. As a leader, it is equally important to find ways to maintain those sparks of enthusiasm in one's professional life that allow the passion to shine through in all that one does.

Kathie cautions that being a natural leader does not mean that one must have all the requisite skills needed to be a *good* leader. Undergraduate course work in business administration and graduate work in educational leadership have all contributed to Kathie's leadership skill development process. In the long run, however, a good leader cannot be something he or she is not: one has to be true to himself/herself and reflect that attitude toward others. In recognition of her numerous and significant contributions in her state, in 2011 Kathie was awarded the Clinton A. Reed Outstanding Business Educator Award by the Business Teachers Association of New York State.

Diane J. Fisher, The University of Southern Mississippi

Diane Fisher is very well qualified to serve in her role as a teacher of teachers at The University of Southern Mississippi. Her teaching experience, as a business educator, has been at the middle school, high school, community college, and university levels. She has taught a wide variety of business subjects in her career and currently teaches business education methods courses and supervises student teachers of business subjects.

Diane's commitment to the preparation of future business teachers grew out of her awareness of the important role business education—at both the secondary and post-secondary levels—plays in the overall career and professional/personal development of students engaged in American education. As past president of the National Association of Business Teacher Education (2012–2013), Diane continues to be instrumental in ensuring that graduates of business teacher education programs throughout the United States are not only well versed in business content but also able to demonstrate the most effective characteristics of superior educators. Diane also served as president of her state business education association and was awarded the NBEA Collegiate Teacher-of-the-Year Award. She has written numerous articles for professional publications and is a frequent speaker at conferences for business teachers.

In the classroom, in her work with colleagues, and in her dealings with professionals in various teachers' organizations, Diane exhibits a democratic style of leadership, one that can be viewed as transformational. Even though she requires her students to adhere to high standards of performance, she is recognized as a caring teacher and leader. Diane believes it is necessary for people—whether students or colleagues—to be involved in the decision-making process in order to be productive. This style, for Diane, has been effective because it has enabled her to produce quality work and to support others in doing likewise. A big part of leadership, Diane thinks, involves believing in one's self and in the abilities of others. It is necessary, Diane believes, to attempt to see one's self as others see you; in this way, one becomes more confident and, therefore, more apt to become involved and to give back to the profession.

Through the years, Diane has surrounded herself with people who have believed in her and also inspired her. Unknowingly, these individuals' encouragement of her to believe in herself served as a catalyst for her to develop a passion for teaching, which she now tries to instill in her students.

In addition to her role as a teacher educator, Diane has also been able to develop future leaders through her work in sponsoring Future Business Leaders of America and Phi Beta Lambda events in which her students have won first-place awards in both national and state events.

As a teacher of teachers, Diane is passionate about business education and believes the profession needs "the best" teachers possible to help students obtain positive learning outcomes. Witnessing her students place first and second in the "Future Business Teacher" competitive event at the National Phi Beta Lambda convention, in particular, was especially rewarding for both Diane and the students involved. In fact, the first-place winner was named Teacher-of-the-Year by her school district after her third year of teaching.

When Diane enters the classroom each day, she says she strives to be the very best she can be; similarly, she views this as an opportunity to encourage students to be the very best they can be. This passion, for Diane, becomes her legacy.

Maurice S. Henderson, Business Professionals of America State Director, Michigan

Maurice Henderson has always been proactive, rather than reactive. As a professional, he has never placed himself in a position where others would need to tell him how to get a task accomplished. Instead, if something becomes obvious to Maurice that will benefit the profession, he wants to be part of the venture; he is inherently drawn to be part of its success. Maurice enters such ventures with a passion for accomplishment because he is totally committed to advancing business education in every way possible. Rather than trying to get other people to change, Maurice approaches situations by attempting to discover how his own natural strengths complement those with whom he is working, as he believes that in unity there is strength.

Like many value-driven leaders, Maurice encourages those aspiring to fulfill positions of leadership to "jump right in." Action-oriented leaders can attest to this, as in reality, it simply means taking the steps necessary to obtain and achieve the results to which one may aspire. To those interested in leadership through NBEA state/territory/province positions, Maurice advises attendance at the NBEA Leadership Academy held each year in conjunction with the NBEA Convention.

Maurice has been successful in various positions of leadership because he is open minded, a nurturer, and a good listener. These three unique characteristics have enabled him to facilitate productive meetings and bring a group together in one accord. No matter how tough the task or how controversial the issue, by maintaining an open mind and being careful and thoughtful while listening to both the verbal and non-verbal cues of others, a leader can ensure that all voices are heard and respected.

Maurice was instrumental in bringing about the establishment of the NBEA-sponsored National Business Honor Society for high school business students. He served on the original task force with seven other dedicated NBEA members to establish the honor society and continues to serve as chair of the National Business Honor Society Governing Council. He is proud that he has been an important player in this service to business education as he hears about the success and excitement that the honor society has brought to the students in the schools where chapters have been established.

For many years Maurice has also been thoroughly immersed with the work of the student organization, Business Professionals of America (BPA), at both the state and national levels. In his position as Michigan State Director of BPA, Maurice mentors students to become leaders. Countless students have advanced to prominent positions in business because of his continuous support and encouragement. In addition, he has served on the BPA National Board of Trustees and served as chair of the BPA State Association Advisory Council. Through these positions, Maurice has been able to assist BPA in developing programs and services that have benefited business students throughout America.

Through all these activities and associations, Maurice has demonstrated leadership skills resulting in positive relationships with people. As Maurice serves the profession as president of the National Business Education Association in 2014–2015, his excellent organizational, technical, and human relations skills will enable him to continue to transform the profession.

Mary Ann Lammers, Linn-Benton Community College, Albany, Oregon

Mary Ann Lammers knew she wanted to be a business teacher when she was a sophomore at Colstrip High School in rural Montana. In fact, she feels her leadership abilities were developed early through participating in 4-H, as well as other educational experiences in the small 75-student high school. Opportunities for leadership, even though she really did not view it that way at the time, continued to abound for Mary Ann while she majored in business education at Montana State University–Bozeman.

Today, while reflecting on her days as a student, she believes that her parents, teachers, and a variety of mentors encouraged her and made her feel that she was making a difference in the activities in which she was involved. Mentors for Mary Ann included prominent national leaders in business education: Harvey Larson from Montana State University and Lloyd Bartholome and Ted Ivarie from Utah State University. These educators encouraged, guided, and assisted Mary Ann whenever she sought insight or when she needed concrete guidance on a problem that needed resolution, not only as a student but well into her professional career. For Mary Ann, she knew that she could call on them at any time, discuss a situation, and leave the discussion with a plan of action, whether it was comfortable or not!

Mary Ann describes herself as a "nuts and bolts" type of person who actually enjoys making lists and getting things done in an orderly fashion. She believes being tolerant and respectful of others—both superiors and subordinates—has enabled her to excel at being a teacher and leader in business education. She expects others to be loyal, honest, and productive and believes that she has exhibited these same traits with those with whom she has had contacts.

Mary Ann's leadership and impact on professional business education associations is extensive and varied. Being elected to serve as consultant for the Oregon Business Education Association for more than 10 years attests to the level of confidence her colleagues have in her expertise and wisdom. In fact, this association decided to institute a special scholarship in her honor. The Lammers Professional Development Scholarship is given each year to an Oregon business teacher to help defray the costs of his/her attendance at the annual NBEA Convention. In the span of 10 years, Mary Ann served twice as president of her state business education association.

Mary Ann was elected to serve as the Oregon representative to the Western Business Education Association. She served as association president and its representative to the NBEA Executive Board. Her colleagues recognized her outstanding leadership qualities, and in 2004–2005 she was elected to serve her profession as NBEA president. Mary Ann believes that to be a successful leader, one has to have one's house in order. Time management and efficient use of resources that are at one's disposal are essential qualities one must possess in order to serve in a leadership role. In addition, one must understand one's own communication and personality style and recognize and understand how others communicate and respond to situations. A good leader, according to Mary Ann, needs to be a good listener and able to acknowledge that there are always at least two sides to a story or a conflict. Sometimes this puts leaders in a "lonely" place, but they must know what their standards and values are and hold true to those even when public sentiment may seem to be against them.

Beryl C. McEwen, North Carolina A&T State University

Anyone who has ever met Beryl McEwen immediately recognizes her as a calm, open, and consistent person, one who is willing to listen to others' points of view. Beryl believes that almost any problem can be solved with negotiation, as long as all participants are willing to listen and compromise, and this philosophy is probably her greatest attribute as a leader.

Currently vice provost for strategic planning and institutional effectiveness at North Carolina A&T State University, Beryl has also served her university as associate vice chancellor for academic affairs, associate dean of the School of Business and Economics, and professor and chairperson of the Business Education Department.

Mentors have encouraged and supported Beryl over the years and have enabled her to develop confidence as a professional. She credits her dissertation advisor at Southern Illinois University, Marcia Anderson, as well as a professor, Heidi Perrault, with assisting Beryl in becoming grounded in the ever-changing discipline of business education and in helping her to develop the confidence to be of professional service to this discipline. Beryl has learned much from good leaders, and she is willing to jump into a project and learn from her mistakes, although she readily admits that she does have a severe aversion to failure. Yet, she continues to look for opportunities to grow professionally and personally and to make contributions to the business education profession.

In turn, Beryl has served as a role model to many, including numerous young African Americans just entering the business education profession. She counts as her mentees not only secondary school business educators but also media directors, school principals, a school superintendent, several attorneys, and many mid-level managers and corporate trainers. Beryl says it always brightens her day when, from time to time, she receives unsolicited notes from these professionals she has nurtured.

In the work environment, Beryl recommends having a willingness to accept responsibilities and challenges and always do the very best work in the job that one has. Beryl's philosophy is that it is better to be known for the quality of one's work, rather than for the ability to target and pursue leadership positions. In other words, the "proof is in the pudding." At her own university, Beryl has "grown" into positions of leadership because of her demonstrated leadership abilities and skills in the positions she has held. Her work ethic speaks for itself.

Beryl has received many awards during her professional career in which she has been recognized as an outstanding administrator, teacher, researcher, and writer. She has served as national president of Delta Pi Epsilon, as well as her state business education association and the Office Systems Research Association. Numerous research-based presentations by Beryl at professional conferences have been recognized as important contributions to improving the methodology of business education.

It is even more important, Beryl feels, to treat others with respect and to acknowledge and reward the good work of others, because leaders never lead alone! Those who work with Beryl recognize her as a focused leader who provides sound guidance when she asks others to be involved with projects. She has never been afraid to be in the trenches, however, doing the hard work, and that is why others say she leads by example—a compliment that she most cherishes.

Beryl advises those entering the profession to be good at something but, even more so, to be very, very good at something and to be willing to give more than you get.

John J. Olivo, Bloomsburg University of Pennsylvania

A self-admitted extrovert and optimist, John Olivo's participative and democratic approach to leadership has won him the admiration and respect of his peers, students, and administrators. Through John's leadership as professor and chair of the Business Education Department at Bloomsburg University of Pennsylvania, the retention rate for students in the business teacher education program is consistently more than 70% and the placement rate for program graduates is always 100%.

Dynamic in the classroom, philosophical about learning, and totally involved with any project that he encounters—these are the reasons accounting for John's success as a college professor of business and business teacher education. John has succeeded in securing more than $1 million in grants through several funding agencies in Pennsylvania. These grants have serviced business educators throughout the state in updating their skills in the areas of new technology and instructional strategies. Other grants have benefited the Bloomsburg region by providing training for the unemployed in the area of information processing. John has represented his university as a visiting scholar in both China and Poland.

Two mentors, in particular, have served as role models for John. Gloria Payne of Davis and Elkins College and Robert Poland of Michigan State University both possessed similar characteristics according to John. Each of them cared about students *first* and encouraged John not to be insular but to go beyond his "comfort zone" and to realize that his decisions will not please all people all of the time.

John believes that true leadership is dynamic and transformational. It means having the ability to get people—colleagues, students, administrators—to work for and with you because they want to. For John, this means a diplomatic and adaptable approach to problem solving. When working with other professionals, valuing their input on decisions—both big and small—is an absolute must. Along the way, however, it can also mean admitting when one is wrong and recognizing that one does not have all the answers. It also means giving credit when credit is due. Those who have worked with John would certainly say that he is trustworthy, energetic, inspiring, fair, and emphatic.

Responsibilities at his own university as well as involvement with professional organizations have enabled John to mentor and be a positive influence on the lives of many business teachers—both neophytes and those already in the profession. John served as president of the National Business Education Association in 2011–2012 and has held positions of leadership in other professional organizations at the local, state, regional, and national levels. He has also presented workshops on a variety of topics of interest to business teachers at conferences of these associations.

Bloomsburg University has recognized John as a teaching scholar and, likewise, professional organizations have honored John for his teaching, leadership, and professional contributions to the discipline. He was named Outstanding Post-Secondary Educator of the Year by the Pennsylvania Business Education Association, Collegiate Educator of the Year by the Eastern Business Education Association, and Collegiate Teacher of the Year by the National Business Education Association.

Eric Swenson, Montana Office of Public Instruction

As business education specialist with the Montana Office of Public Instruction, Eric Swenson's leadership role is multifaceted. He exercises leadership and general supervision under applicable laws, rules, and regulations pertinent to business education and career and technical education. Eric also conducts professional development training for teachers, counselors, and administrators in all areas of business education and serves as the state advisor for the secondary and postsecondary divisions of the Montana Association of Business Professionals of America. Activities that fall into Eric's typical workday include managing federal and state grants, ensuring compliance requirements of local education agencies are met, facilitating program improvement, and providing assistance in the development and integration of technology, pathway development, and standards development. Most of all, however, Eric enjoys his position of leadership when he is working "hands-on" with the teachers in his state by providing technical assistance to those professionals who are interested in successful instructional designs for implementation in their classrooms.

Although Eric has held multiple positions of leadership within business education, Eric readily admits that he actually prefers working behind the scenes. Eric feels that it is a distinctive honor to be able to witness the accomplishments others have made as a result of participation in activities in which Eric has played a leadership role. Eric recognizes he tends to be outgoing but can also be reserved at times. As a person who is detail oriented but who still likes to see the "bigger picture," Eric relishes new adventures and gaining fresh ideas. Eric cited Business Professionals of America as a major player in his own professional career. He believes this student organization has afforded him an opportunity to hone his leadership skills. He recognizes, too, the value of BPA in developing leadership abilities of business students. Now Eric has an opportunity to "give back" to the organization in his role as a member of its board of trustees.

Likewise, as an officer with the Montana Business Education Association, Eric has worked to encourage new and young professionals to become involved, so that they, too, can be of service to the profession. Whether it is by serving on a committee, presenting a workshop, or seeking positions of leadership within the organization itself, Eric believes that opportunities for leadership training and development abound. Eric is always excited when he has seen teachers he has encouraged advance through the ranks and begin taking part in the activities and opportunities available through various leadership roles.

Eric recognizes that the biggest challenge for these individuals is frequently getting them to overcome the fear of being overwhelmed by responsibilities. Yet, these teachers view Eric as a point of reference who can be counted on to help them with whatever challenge needs to be resolved. He encourages those he mentors to move at their own pace and to accept the opportunities when they feel comfortable or when the time is right. Even though his own leadership experiences have often been the result of "jumping in with both feet first" or "trial and error," he has always known that other professionals were available for support and advice. His mentors include Linda Wise Miller and Martha C. Yopp, both from the University of Idaho. These prominent and professionally active leaders not only provided Eric with the methods, tools, and resources to be a successful business educator but also modeled the importance of active involvement in professional organizations and lifelong learning.

For those moving into leadership positions, Eric encourages them to start small. He feels that growing by incremental steps gives the person an opportunity to learn, to ask questions, to observe protocols or norms, and to begin to develop relationships with members of the organization and the organization's leaders.

Judee A. Timm, Monterey Peninsula College, Monterey, California

A person who enjoys a challenge is probably the best way to describe Judee Timm, a community college international business professor in Monterey, California. If things become too routine, Judee has a reputation for shaking things up, and this tendency is why Judee has a passion for international business. According to Judee, it is an area that does not allow one to become too comfortable. In fact, like so many areas of business education, international business is an area where there's always something new to learn as well as something that will challenge one's thinking and learning.

Judee's dedication to the international business scene prompted her and Jane Thompson to establish the *Journal for Global Business Education*, the professional journal of the International Society of Business Education. In addition, Judee has served as a writer, editor, and speaker on various international business topics presented worldwide. Being true to her commitment to keep students and teachers informed, engaged, and excited about international business, Judee was also called to serve as president of the International Society of Business Education.

Judee has had many mentors in her professional life, and she says that she wanted to be just like them! These were people who were thoroughly engaged in their profession and truly loved and believed in what they were doing. These mentors, Judee believes, enabled her to get connected with the right people who assisted her in advancing her interests in international business.

Judee has sage advice to those who aspire to leadership positions. She says: just do it! Do not be afraid to say "yes," even when an assignment seems daunting. The successful leader, Judee believes, allows others to succeed and is willing to work hard and to go the "extra mile." She has always enjoyed sharing ideas, projects, opportunities, and connections and enjoys recognizing the successes of others. Along the way, Judee has learned that not everyone is going to like what she does or how she does it; but she takes such criticism with the proverbial "grain of salt."

The effective leader, according to Judee, does not ask people to do things that he or she would not do or has not done in the past. For Judee, this means being assertive at times but still inclusive. People who work with Judee recognize that she knows how to get things done by setting a cohesive direction and getting the right people together to make things happen. She recommends keeping the final goal constantly in the forefront of the project, whatever it may be. Judee's leadership style has given her the reputation of someone who will get results, while at the same time, getting people motivated to be a part of a team that will get results.

Leadership for Judee has always been a "work in progress." It starts with honing one's competence in a given area (for Judee, international business) and sharing this expertise with others. Judee can cite many "success stories" that can be attributed to her leadership abilities. One, however, directly relates to student success. A highly motivated student enrolled in one of Judee's international business classes found out that his dream of attending a university was dashed due to his family's difficult financial situation. Shortly after learning this, Judee received an announcement regarding a study-abroad program in South Korea that was being offered "all expenses paid" for member institution community college students. The student immediately processed the application, and Judee wrote a letter of reference and assisted him with the laborious application process. Things seemed to be moving in the right direction until Judee discovered that the college, due to budget constraints, did not pay its annual dues. This would have precluded her student from applying. Undeterred, Judee felt that the student should not miss this unique opportunity as it was out of his control. She offered to pay the dues herself; but the college did, at this point, find the money to pay the dues and the student had the experience of a lifetime and he was hooked on international business. This student went on to graduate from Cornell University, experience another internship in Dubai, and achieve a rewarding career in international business.

As a leader, success stories like this make the life of an international business educator a true joy.

Janet M. Treichel, Executive Director, National Business Education Association, Reston, Virginia

In her position as executive director of the National Business Education Association for 24 years, Jan Treichel has guided the association—and for that matter the entire business education field—through times of challenge and curriculum redirection. Chief among these ventures has been leading the business education community in re-establishing its role and responsibility for the entire business curriculum through the development and nationwide acceptance of NBEA's *National Standards for Business*

Education. In addition to maintaining the office of the association, including the association's budget, publications, staff, and a myriad of other day-to-day activities, Jan is liaison with NBEA members and the association's affiliates across the United States and internationally.

In Jan's own professional life, she has always been competitive and confident in confronting issues and challenges. With her strong values of honesty, loyalty, and integrity, Jan demonstrates a sense of urgency in accomplishing goals and is not tolerant of the "when we get around to it" attitude. Daring to be different and moving away from a conformist mentality means taking chances and risking failure to achieve outcomes that will make a difference for our profession.

Jan believes that people get where they are by standing on someone else's shoulders, and she readily admits that she has been blessed to have many people who have mentored her throughout her life and career. Although her parents did not attend college, they were—and still are—the most influential people in her life. They both believed that education was important, and they wanted it for their daughters. Strength, confidence, humor, determination, and decency are just some of the values that were sacred to Jan's parents and that she has incorporated into her own life through their example. Colleagues and teachers, early in her career, also recognized Jan's potential and encouraged her to take positions of responsibility and leadership. It was they who opened the doors for Jan, but she was courageous enough to walk through them. Jan was the recipient of the 2013 John Robert Gregg Award in recognition of her outstanding contributions to the business education profession.

Jan's good sense of humor and her ability to relate to all kinds of people—the diverse membership of NBEA in particular—have placed her in a position of working with business educators to become more involved with the association and to move into positions of leadership. Jan firmly believes the chief way to develop leadership in our field is to empower people and to give them a role in the decision-making process, thereby helping them to develop their own leadership potential.

Jan offers these insights for leadership development:

- Believe in yourself and who you are.
- Be persistent, passionate, and demonstrate excellence in everything you do.
- Never accept less than your best.
- Be fair, honest, decent, and courageous.
- Get up when you fall down, brush yourself off, and try again.
- Find the joy in life.
- Always give more than you take.
- Do not waste another day before you start becoming what you were meant to be.

Although Jan can offer many "success stories" concerning her positions of leadership and prominence over many years in business education, Jan recalls one that is especially endearing to her. In 1999 a meeting of several leaders in business education was convened at NBEA headquarters. The national board chair of one of the student organizations brought with her a young man who was relatively new to the profession. During the meeting, Jan recognized the young man was someone special and began to encourage him to get involved at regional and national levels. He began accepting various committee and board positions, provided exemplary leadership in each endeavor, and will be president of the National Business Education Association in 2014–2015.

SUMMARY

The educators featured in this chapter come from throughout the United States and include a prominent researcher, a state superintendent of public instruction, a business teacher educator, a student organization leader, a college provost, a state department supervisor, an international business educator, an executive director of a professional association, and department chairs from high school, community college, and university levels. The professional lives of these individuals have all taken different paths, yet they have all viewed service as an opportunity to transform the business education profession.

Business education continues to meet the challenge of transforming the profession through the development of leaders who are visionary and whose actions will enable the field to prosper in a complex, technologically dependent global environment. Commonalities among the leaders include the influential role of professional organizations in their lives, the need to constantly maintain a positive attitude, the desire to be of service to the profession, and the importance of mentorship.

REFERENCES

Barling, J., Christie, A., & Hoption, C. (2011). Leadership. In Zedeck, S. (Ed.), *APA handbook of industrial and organizational psychology: Building and developing the organization* (pp. 183–240). Washington, DC: American Psychological Association.

Goleman, D. (2004). What makes a leader? *Harvard Business Review, 82*(1), 82–91.

Lussier, R., & Achua, C. (2007). Leadership: Theory, application, & skill development. Mason, OH: Thomson South-Western.

Nohria, N., & Khurana, R. (Eds.). (2010). Handbook of leadership theory and practice: An HBS Centennial Colloquium on Advancing Leadership. Boston, MA: *Harvard Business Review.*

Policies Commission for Business and Economic Education (PCBEE). (2008). *This we believe about the transformation and future of business education* (Statement No. 83). Retrieved from http://nbea.org/newsite/curriculum/policy/no_83.pdf

Simic, I. (1998). Transformational leadership: The key to successful management of transformation organizational changes. *Facta Universitatis, 1*(6), 49–55.

Leadership for Advancing Research in Business Education

Carol Blaszczynski
California State University
Los Angeles, CA

Business education leaders conduct rigorous, relevant, and timely research communicated through both disciplinary and interdisciplinary publications. This chapter addresses the roles of leadership in promoting research in business education by conducting quality research and disseminating research results. In addition, it also presents suggestions for developing a research agenda at institutional levels ranging from elementary through postsecondary, succeeding in research endeavors, and participating in grantsmanship.

SPECIFYING THE ROLES OF RESEARCH IN BUSINESS EDUCATION

Research has been defined "as a search for the truth or new knowledge" (Blaszczynski, 1998, p. 202). Two Policies Commission for Business and Economic Education (PCBEE, 1967, 1987) statements, *The Role of Research in Business and Office Education* and *This We Believe About Research in Business Education*, emphasized the importance of research to the business education profession. The 2006 PCBEE statement *This We Believe About the Value of Professional Associations* asserted that "quality publications support dynamic communities of practice" (p. 1). In 2010 the PCBEE issued a policy statement entitled *This We Believe About Generativity in Business Education,* which identified conducting research as a generative activity, that is, one that helps to "preserve a rich legacy of shared experiences" (p. 1). This 2010 statement introduced the term generativity to many business educators. The role that research, business educators, and professional associations play in generativity has been examined and showcased in business education publications and presentations ever since.

Research plays a central role in the business education profession, serving to advance the profession and create the profession's agenda.

Advancing the Profession

Research is instrumental in building a body of knowledge for business educators. This body of knowledge serves to enhance the profession, assisting in keeping the profession current so that it is both dynamic and relevant rather than static and outdated. All business educators are consumers of research (Wunsch, 1991) and assist in leading the profession through change. Furthermore, research enables practitioners to identify effective strategies for practice. Policy Statement 83 (PCBEE, 2008), *This We Believe About the Transformation and Future of Business Education,* emphasized the role of research in transforming business education: "We believe that business teacher educators must conduct relevant and rigorous research that informs practice [and] incorporate[s] sound research results into content knowledge and pedagogy" (p. 2).

Creating the Profession's Agenda

Research provides the impetus for the business education profession's agenda. One excellent example of this professional agenda is the annual creation of the PCBEE statements. To date, 91 PCBEE statements have been produced by a collaborative body of prominent business educators from secondary through university levels of academia plus state supervisors of business education. These PCBEE statements not only supply guidance for classroom business educators but also provide the basis for seeking support for particular courses of action such as curricular changes and the adoption of innovative technologies. For example, the 2012 statement *This We Believe About Social Media in Education* focused on using social media in education. The recommendations provided by the august PCBEE could provide evidence on the efficacy of using social media to teach about social media to administrators at all institutional levels (PCBEE, 2012). Furthermore, the statements "serve as yardsticks against which the effectiveness of the components of business education and the total discipline can be measured" (National Business Education Association, n.d., para. 3).

Leading and promoting strong research activity by business educators stimulates the profession by increasing its stature.

CONDUCTING QUALITY RESEARCH

The process of conducting high-quality research includes the following steps: identify an issue facing members of the profession and select a researchable problem, locate and review the relevant literature, plan ethically responsible research, consult with knowledgeable colleagues, implement the research method(s), analyze and interpret the data judiciously, write up the research results, and prepare the research results for dissemination.

Identify an Issue and Select a Researchable Problem

The first step in the process of conducting quality research is identifying a relevant professional issue and selecting a problem that is capable of being researched. One important component of framing an appropriate research question is selecting a question to answer or problem to solve ensuring that the research project has an appropriate scope. Business educators may consult *Needed Research in Business Education* (Delta Pi Epsilon, 2008) for potential research projects.

Locate and Review the Relevant Literature

Conducting a thorough review of the relevant literature is a critical step in the planning process before research begins (Wilhelm & Kaunelis, 2005). Scott, Blaszczynski, and Green (2008) outlined an eight-step process designed to locate relevant literature. Although the process was designed to find literature to guide instructional practice, with minor adaptations the process may be used for general research purposes. The eight steps follow:

Determine the search terms, search the relevant databases and indices, search the fugitive literature, retrieve the uncovered information, read and evaluate the information, select the relevant information to guide instructional practice, implement the modified instructional practice, and evaluate the effectiveness of the modified instructional practice. (Scott, Blaszczynski, & Green, 2008, p. 1)

Some of the professional business education literature is considered "fugitive" literature, as it may not be accessible in any index or database. Some business educators are striving to increase the accessibility of the literature, which will increase the visibility of the profession. If the literature is not accessible to researchers both inside and outside business education circles, then its value is perceived to be less important. Furthermore, it can be frustrating to researchers to find they have reinvented the wheel in terms of disciplinary research or that they did not cite a current, relevant source because they could not locate the source.

The professional literature may be consulted throughout the research process to solve research dilemmas and to update the literature before submitting the manuscript for publication.

Plan Ethically Responsible Research

Once a literature review has been conducted, researchers should plan ethically responsible research. Blaszczynski (1998) defined ethical research as "research that does not harm others. It protects the privacy of those who are research subjects and is conducted in an objective, professional manner" (p. 202). The *Publication Manual of the American Psychological Association* (APA, 2010) identified the following three goals underlying the principles that support ethical research and its dissemination:

- Ensure the accuracy of scientific knowledge
- Protect the rights and welfare of research participants
- Protect intellectual property rights

The American Educational Research Association (2011) developed a code of ethics to guide researchers. This code is based on five overarching principles: professional competence; integrity; professional, scientific, and scholarly responsibility; respect for people's rights, dignity, and diversity; and social responsibility (American Educational Research Association, 2011, p. 147). As stipulated by the APA ethical and legal standards (APA, 2010), duplicate publication of data is prohibited. Furthermore, Blaszczynski (1998) asserted that "since research is considered to be an attempt to add new knowledge to a field of study through original work, the quality of that work must be safeguarded" (p. 202). In addition, ethical researchers contribute original work and refrain from plagiarism and self-plagiarism. Self-plagiarism occurs when researchers "present their own previously published work as new scholarship" (APA, 2010, p. 16). To that end, many academic journals require prospective authors of manuscripts submitted for publication consideration to indicate that the manuscript is original, is not under review by another journal, and has not been published elsewhere.

Additional ethical research practices include protecting research participants through maintaining confidentiality, providing for informed consent, and completing the publication's institutional review board's application.

Both new (including undergraduate, graduate, and doctoral students) and experienced researchers may use the Responsible Authorship Quick Guide tutorial created by the Office of Research Integrity in the U.S. Department of Health and Human Services (2006). Tutorial users select a common research mistake from more than 25 topics, read the scenario and excerpt from a paper, specify the error, and receive feedback about their response.

Consult with Knowledgeable Colleagues

New and experienced researchers confer with respected colleagues about the research problem they are attempting to solve. This consultation may include determining the scope of the research problem so that the project is manageable, selecting the research method(s) for the investigation, gathering appropriate types of data, using appropriate data analysis tools, and identifying potential publication outlets. Consulting with knowledgeable colleagues is encouraged throughout the research project, from ideation through publication.

Implement the Research Method(s)

After a review of the literature and consultation with colleagues, researchers implement the appropriate research method(s). The research method should have been approved by the appropriate campus institutional review board. Simply put, research may be quantitative, qualitative, mixed method, or the scholarship of teaching and learning. Quantitative research includes data analysis stemming from experimental or survey research. Qualitative research includes interview, focus group, content analysis, and text responses to open-ended survey items. Qualitative research is perceived by some to be "less rigorous than quantitative research" (Gaytan, 2007, p. 110). However, skilled researchers employ rigorous research methods when conducting qualitative research. Mixed method studies include elements of both quantitative and qualitative methods.

The scholarship of teaching and learning refers to "a growing movement in higher education in which faculty members study and report on teaching and learning in their own classrooms using empirical methods commensurate with traditional knowledge-making research" (Pope-Ruark, 2012, p. 358). Communicating the results of scholarship of teaching and learning studies aids in enhancing practice and provides the impetus for additional research (Kanuka, 2011).

An important consideration in implementing the research method(s) is to select the appropriate research participants. Although it may seem prudent to select research participants easily accessible to researchers, such a selection process results in a convenience sample that is not necessarily generalizable to the population at large. Researchers should use care in selecting the appropriate participants, following the principles of scientific research. For example, researchers should protect the identity of research subjects. Furthermore, if researchers want to conduct research with participants who are minors, stringent rules and procedures must be followed to protect the participants.

O'Connor (2007) identified innovative research strategies from the perspective of those outside of business education circles and those strategies inside business education circles. Outside research strategies include future search, the Delphi technique, and trend analysis. Inside research strategies include case studies, historical research, action research, and biographies.

Analyze and Interpret the Data Judiciously

Data literacy is the "ability to understand and use data effectively to inform decisions" (Mandinach & Gummer, 2013, p. 30). Data literacy is increasing in importance. To advance the profession, researchers must analyze and report data truthfully. To that end, appropriate statistical tests should be carefully selected for data analysis. "It is important to place its use within the context of the research questions that are being asked and the type of data being collected to answer these questions" (Lambrecht, 1999, p. 128).

Blaszczynski (2003) identified the following as essential aspects of credible data reporting and presentation: reporting and acknowledging missing data, conducting and reporting a follow-up of survey research, implementing the appropriate steps to ensure against nonresponse bias, ensuring data integrity, presenting accurate tabular displays, matching tabular and textual presentations, reporting percentages and statistics, formulating sound conclusions, and avoiding faulty recommendations. Lambrecht (1999) emphasized the importance of "having a sound conceptual base to understand or explain why any differences or relationships were observed. By understanding why relationships or differences exist, a researcher is in a better position to offer advice" (p. 139). Lambrecht's advice assists researchers in developing sound conclusions and promoting relevant, substantive recommendations.

Write Up the Research Results

A good practice to follow is to keep a log of research steps that were followed from the first day of the study so that writing up the research results is easier. When the research results are written, it is important to consult the *Publication Manual of the American Psychological Association* (APA, 2010) and its Web site (http://www.apa.org). When collaborating with colleagues, all manuscript authors should read the entire manuscript and provide comments for clarification, as well as make additions and deletions. Research results should be written using academic style.

Scott (2001) advocated using the process approach to scholarly writing. This process comprises three steps: "thinking and planning, composing, and editing and writing" (p. 58). Strategies for writing both quantitative and qualitative articles are contained in an article by Blaszczynski and Green (1999) including commonalities such as manuscript suitability, abstract contents, writing style, and documentation standards. For each type of research, sections are presented about the introduction, review of the literature, study design, research findings, discussion, conclusions, and recommendations.

Prepare the Research Results for Dissemination

Manuscript authors should consult the author's guidelines of the prospective journal they are targeting for publication. After reading the journal guidelines, authors may communicate with journal editors should they have questions about manuscript preparation. In addition, the *Publication Manual of the American Psychological Association* (APA, 2010) may be consulted for scholarly authoring guidelines.

Authors frequently invite colleagues to review an article draft before submitting a manuscript to a journal. The feedback received strengthens the article as colleagues provide a fresh eye and are able to pinpoint errors in logic, unclear passages, and gaps in the manuscript content. Gray (2010) recommended that authors seek two reviewers: one nonexpert and one expert. Early manuscript drafts should be read by nonexperts, whereas later drafts should be reviewed by experts.

Following the steps presented in this section will enable business educators to conduct quality research that is worthy of dissemination to both business educators and those outside the profession.

DISSEMINATING THE RESEARCH RESULTS

Disseminating research results is a major component for leading the business education profession. Research dissemination aids in maintaining and advancing the stature of the profession. Research results are commonly presented at research or other professional conferences and published in targeted publication outlets.

Present the research at conferences. By presenting research results at professional conferences, speakers assist other business educators in staying current and developing professionally. Delivering presentations at local and state conferences is a means to building one's presentation skills and developing a positive professional reputation. Examples of these conference opportunities include local and state business education associations, as well as regional business education associations such as the Mountain Plains Business Education Association, North Central Business Education Association, Southern Business Education Association, and Western Business Education Association. At the national level, opportunities for presentations abound, including the National Business Education Association annual meeting, during which sessions may be presented to affiliated associations, including the Association for Research–Delta Pi Epsilon National Research Conference, which becomes part of the NBEA convention in 2014, and the National Association for Business Teacher Education. Internationally, business educators may deliver presentations at the annual International Society for Business Education conference.

Those business educators specializing in career education have opportunities to present at the Business Education Division of the Association for Career and Technical Education conference or at education conferences such as the American Educational Research Association and Lilly conferences, which focus on the scholarship of teaching and learning.

Interdisciplinary research may be presented at both business education–focused conferences and at conferences outside business education circles. For example, innovative teaching strategies may be presented at NBEA or Association for Research in Business Education–Delta Pi Epsilon, as well as the Lilly conferences on teaching, which are sponsored by the International Alliance of Teacher Scholars.

Presenting the results of research investigations to an audience allows the researcher to refine ideas and perhaps build on comments from session attendees. In some cases, presenters may be encouraged to submit their research results to a particular journal by either editorial review board members or by a journal editor who attended the session.

Publish the Research in Targeted Outlets

The next step in disseminating research results is to publish the research in targeted outlets. Three purposes for publishing research are to

- preserve and document the past;

- disseminate critical information from current scholars; and

- aid the development of the profession's knowledge base.

Lambrecht (2003) asserted, "Business education has a distinguished history of its own research to support the teaching of content about business and for business employment. This is the legacy of the field" (p. 1). The prudent researcher identifies three journals to which research may be submitted before launching the research project. Gray (2010) recommended that researchers use a different approach when considering outlets for their manuscripts. "Instead of starting with the leading journals, start with the appropriate journal" (p. 70). A good practice is to read both current and back issues of the prospective targeted journal as well as the guidelines for authors to determine the scope of the journal. Some journals primarily seek quantitative research articles, whereas others focus on teaching. Gaining familiarity with the focus of the journal increases one's likelihood of successful publication.

Select the Appropriate Publication Outlet

Authors may publish research results in either refereed or nonrefereed journals. Refereed journals are commonly referred to as peer-reviewed or scholarly journals; their reviewers use rubrics to rigorously review the submitted manuscript based on journal guidelines. A listing of refereed journals for both business and education may be found in *Cabell's Directory*, which is accessible online through subscription (Cabells, 2013). *Cabell's Directory* for business includes accounting, economics and finance, management, and marketing. Three education directories are available: educational curriculum and methods, educational psychology and administration, and educational technology and library science. Another directory from Cabell's focuses on computer science and business information systems.

The following lists specific journals of interest to the business educator wishing to publish their research:

- *Journal of Business Education Research.* This is the most highly regarded journal in business education, formerly the *Delta Pi Epsilon Journal* (Scott, Blaszczynski, Green, & Fagerheim, 2008), a publication of the Association for Research in Business Education–Delta Pi Epsilon.

- *Business Teacher Education Journal.* Published by the National Association for Business Teacher Education, this is the second-ranked journal in the profession and focuses on research that advances business teacher education.

- *Journal of Education for Business.* This well-regarded publication "features basic and applied research-based articles in accounting, communications, economics, finance, information systems, management, marketing, and other business disciplines, trends, and professional information" (Taylor & Francis, n.d., p. 1) and provides "a forum for authors reporting on new successful teaching methods and curricula or proposing new theories and analyses of controversial issues" (Taylor & Francis, n.d., p. 1).

- *Journal for Applied Research in Business Instruction.* This journal publishes articles with a focus on business education instruction.

- *Journal for Global Business Education* and *International Business Education Journal.* Although global business educators may publish in almost any outlet, these two publications specialize in the international business arena.

- Those business educators whose specialty is business communication may publish theoretical articles in *The Journal for Business Communication* and pedagogical articles in the *Business Communication Quarterly.*

- Business educators who specialize in career education may choose to submit their research results to publications such as *Career and Technical Education Research* and the *Journal of Career and Technical Education Research.*

- The journals *Issues in Accounting Education, Journal of Economic Education, Journal of Management Education*, and *Journal of Marketing Education* are appropriate publication outlets for business educators with these particular functional specialties.

- Practitioner publications include refereed publications, such as the NBEA Yearbook and the research section of NBEA's journal *Business Education Forum.* Among the nonrefereed publications for practitioners are NBEA's *Business Education Forum* and newsletter *Keying In.*

At many institutions, particularly at the university level, interdisciplinary research is encouraged and valued in the retention, tenure, and promotion process. Interdisciplinary research efforts may be reported in both business education–focused outlets and outlets outside of business education circles.

By disseminating research results at business education conferences and in publications sponsored by business education professional associations, the profession and its members remain vital. Developing a research agenda for both individual researchers and the business education profession strengthens research contributions and may assist in targeting a wider audience for research dissemination.

DEVELOPING A RESEARCH AGENDA

Evans (2012) defined researcher development "as the process whereby people's capacity and willingness to carry out the research components of their work or studies may be considered to be enhanced, with a degree of permanence that exceeds transitoriness" (p. 425). Furthermore, researcher development may be emerging as a field of study distinct from higher education (Evans, 2012). Anderson (2012) asserted, "it behooves researchers to further develop their research capacity" (p. 202). Business educators at all levels are involved with researcher development for themselves, their colleagues, and their students.

University Level

At the university level, faculty should strive to build a sustainable program of research (Scott, 2003). Faculty need to determine whether they wish to use a deep-dive approach (related work on the same or similar subject to demonstrate expertise in the discipline) or a scattered approach, which is less focused. Many faculty wait until earning tenure to use a scattered approach as it has historically been less productive than the deep dive strategy.

Graduate students, frequently in concert with faculty advisors, engage in research by investigating topics of interest related to coursework. Often, they build on those same topics during the graduate program or even continue the program of research at the doctoral level. Traditionally, faculty mentor doctoral students in the scholarly research process. Graduate students may publish their results with or without faculty advisors, who are often second authors.

Encouraging undergraduate students to participate in research, either individually or through collaboration with faculty members, is a high-impact educational practice that promotes student success (Kuh, 2008). Additionally, participating in undergraduate research contributes to three essential learning outcomes: fostering broad knowledge of human cultures, strengthening intellectual and practical skills, and practicing integrated and applied learning. The purpose of undergraduate research is to "involve students with actively contested questions, empirical observation, cutting-edge technologies, and the sense of excitement that comes from working to answer important questions" (Kuh, 2008, p. 20).

Community College Level

Instructors at the community college level often research teaching practices. They engage in action research (Wright, 2013) with the goal of improving student learning. Project results may be published in outlets such as NBEA's *Business Education Forum* or in journals devoted to the scholarship of teaching and learning, such as the *Journal for Excellence in College Teaching*.

Secondary Level

Business educators at the secondary level frequently select research agendas based on technologies and pedagogies. In essence, they conduct research formally or informally, to determine the efficacy of particular instructional methods. For example, they could investigate using an inverted classroom approach to teaching and publish the results of their innovative instructional methods in NBEA's *Business Education Forum* or state business education association journals.

Middle School and Elementary Levels

Those business educators teaching at the middle and elementary school levels may also choose to study the effects of instructional methods on student learning outcomes. Additionally, they may compare and contrast how using different technologies results in higher or lower student performance. Depending on the sophistication of the study, results may be published in state business education association journals or in the *Business Education Forum.*

Business educators at all levels may engage in research by developing an agenda of relevance and interest to themselves and to other practitioners.

SUCCEEDING IN RESEARCH ENDEAVORS

This section reinforces the applicability of research for all business educators, the importance of following rigorous research principles, and development of researchers.

Everyone Has the Potential to Contribute to Research

All business educators may contribute to research:

- First, business educators may conduct research by themselves or with colleagues. Many times collaborating with colleagues produces better research as each person has different perspectives and strengths. Good researcher synergy elevates project quality. When initiating the first research project with a new collaborator, researchers should consider beginning with a low-stakes project. This approach allows testing of the waters during this collaboration. The researchers should determine each person's responsibilities before the inception of the project. Collaborators should be clear about the work division and expectations. This work division clarity would include setting firm deadlines to promote the success of the research endeavor. For those business educators teaching at the university level, it is important to be knowledgeable about the particular criteria for earning tenure and promotion and the expectations for sole authoring and coauthoring.

- Second, business educators may offer a class of students as subjects for research conducted by others, being careful to protect the welfare and privacy of study participants.

- Third, business educators may serve as participants in the research studies of others by completing surveys and agreeing to be interviewed by researchers or for publications such as the *Business Education Forum* and *Keying In.*

Follow Rigorous Research Principles

Adhering to the principles of the scientific approach to research promotes rigor in the investigative process. For research to advance or lead the profession in the appropriate direction, the research findings should be generalizable. That is, the findings should be useful to other audiences. If research is conducted in a sloppy, unscientific fashion, the contribution to the profession will be negligible or, worse, negative.

Rigorous research requires the researcher to select an appropriate sample size. Business education researchers are encouraged to use tables to determine the appropriate sample size needed. When a researcher engages in survey research that produces a small return rate, the researcher follows up with reminders to encourage additional responses. Furthermore, to avoid nonrespondent bias, good researchers follow up with a small number of nonrespondents to ensure that the answers of nonrespondents are similar to the answers of those who responded.

Reliability and validity are two characteristics of rigorous research. Reliability refers to the repeatability of the results. If a respondent indicates an age of 25 and is surveyed the next day, the response should be the same (unless the respondent has celebrated another birthday). Validity refers to the accuracy of the response; in other words, was the response truthful? The response could be reliable (an age of 25 each time) yet not be valid if the respondent is actually 31 years of age.

Grow Your Research Acumen

To become a better researcher, a business educator may read articles about the research process and new research methodologies in publications such as the *Journal of Business Education Research*. O'Connor (2007) described innovative research strategies that may be employed by business educators. Research acumen can also be increased by attending sessions at conferences, such as those offered by the Association for Research in Business Education–Delta Pi Epsilon. In addition, researchers can attend sessions about publishing such as "NBEA Publications—Your Turn" offered at the 2013 NBEA annual conference. Furthermore, research knowledge can be increased by taking pertinent courses related to different types of research methodology. Another way in which to become more research savvy is to work with a more experienced researcher on a project.

Research acumen may also be expanded by engaging in interdisciplinary research. Furthermore, business educators may present interdisciplinary research results at conferences and write to audiences not only inside but also outside business education circles. Research acumen may be developed by daring to experiment with a variety of qualitative and quantitative research methods. Perhaps the leading business education journals could allow for debates about appropriate frames for the business education profession.

All business educators can succeed in research endeavors through their involvement in varying roles: as researchers, as research study participants, and by volunteering their students as research study participants. Following the scientific approach to research and engaging in researcher development helps increase the level of generativity and vitality of business educators.

PARTICIPATING IN GRANTSMANSHIP

Business educators at all levels are encouraged to pursue grants by locating appropriate grant opportunities and writing grant proposals.

Locating Grant Opportunities

Appropriate grant opportunities may be located online at http://www.grant.gov or by using Pivot from ProQuest, which provides information about funding opportunities that are estimated to equal $33 billion through its database, which draws from profiles generated by the Community of Science and Community of Scholars. In addition, Pivot identifies other researchers with the same research interests with whom business educators may collaborate (Pivot, 2013). Grant opportunities are also published in the *Chronicle of Higher Education* as well as by the U.S. Department of Education and field-specific agencies.

Writing Grant Proposals

University-level business educators may learn about writing grant proposals and seek assistance from the research office of their institution. Those business educators wishing to obtain funding from the Association for Research in Business Education–Delta Pi Epsilon (2013) may consult the guidelines and complete the grant proposal available at http://www.dpe.org. Over the years, business educators have obtained more than $165,000 in funding from this organization. Further information about writing a DPE Research Foundation grant application may be found in an article by Scott, Blaszczynski, and Green (2004).

In these challenging economic times, the critical skill of grant writing may result in obtaining funding for complex research endeavors that may not be available from other sources.

SUMMARY

Leadership for advancing research in business education comes from active researchers, business education program faculty, business teachers, and professional business education organizations. Leaders in business education research should move beyond the expected to embrace research that spans disciplinary boundaries and hence enhances the visibility of the business education profession. Investigating complex, even controversial, problems, issues, and trends contributes to the profession's vitality. It is not enough to simply conduct research; the research conducted must be rigorous and relevant and disseminated at conferences and in prominent, accessible publications with wide readership to provide substantive leadership for advancing research in business education.

REFERENCES

American Educational Research Association. (2011, April). *Code of ethics, 40*(3), 145–156. doi:10.3102/0013189X11410403

American Psychological Association (APA). (2010). *Publication manual of the American Psychological Association* (6th ed.). Washington, DC: Author.

Anderson, M. A. (2012). Research in business education: Increasing capacity and application in practice. In W. L. Stitt-Gohdes (Ed.), *Trends and issues in business education* (pp. 188–204). Reston, VA: National Business Education Association.

Association of Research for Business Education–Delta Pi Epsilon. (2013). *Research Foundation.* Retrieved from http://www.dpe.org/researchfoundation.htm

Blaszczynski, C. (1998). Conducting ethical business education research. *The Delta Pi Epsilon Journal, 40*(4), 202–213.

Blaszczynski, C. (2003). Strategies for credible data reporting and presentation. *The Delta Pi Epsilon Journal, 45*(2), 77–86.

Blaszczynski, C., & Green, D. J. (1999). Strategies for writing quantitative and qualitative research articles. *The Delta Pi Epsilon Journal, 41*(4), 205–211.

Cabells. (2013). *Cabells directories of publishing opportunities.* Retrieved from http://www.cabells.com/index.aspx

Delta Pi Epsilon. (2008). *Needed research in business education.* Little Rock, AR: Author.

Evans, L. (2012). Leadership for researcher development: What research leaders need to know and understand. *Educational Management Administration & Leadership, 40*(4), 423–435. Retrieved from http://ema.sagepub.com/content/40/4/423

Gaytan, J. (2007). Qualitative research: Emerging opportunity in business education. *The Delta Pi Epsilon Journal, 49*(2), 109–127.

Gray, T. (2010). *Publish & flourish: Become a prolific scholar.* Las Cruces, NM: Teaching Academy, New Mexico State University.

Kanuka, H. (2011). Keeping the scholarship in the scholarship of teaching and learning. *International Journal for the Scholarship of Teaching and Learning, 5*(1), 1–12. Retrieved from http://digitalcommons.georgiasouthern.edu/ij-sotl/vol5/iss1/3

Kuh, G. D. (2008). *High-impact educational practices: What they are, who has access to them, and why they matter.* Washington, DC: Association of American Colleges and Universities. Retrieved from http://www.neasc.org/downloads/aacu_high_impact_2008_final.pdf

Lambrecht, J. J. (1999). Selecting appropriate statistical tests. *The Delta Pi Epsilon Journal, 41*(3), 128–140.

Lambrecht, J. J. (2003). Guest editorial. *The Delta Pi Epsilon Journal, 45*(1), 1–2.

Mandinach, E. B., & Gummer, E. S. (2013). A systemic view of implementing data literacy in educator preparation. *Educational Researcher, 42*(1), 30–37.

National Business Education Association (NBEA). (n.d.). *NBEA curriculum forum.* Retrieved from http://www.nbea.org/newsite/curriculum/index.html

O'Connor, B. N. (2007). Innovative research strategies for business education. *The Delta Pi Epsilon Journal, 49*(3), 50–55.

Pivot. (2013). *COS introduces Pivot.* Retrieved from http://pivot.cos.com/about

Policies Commission for Business and Economic Education (PCBEE). (1967). *The role of research in business and office education* (Statement No. 8). In *Policy statements: 1959–1996.* Cincinnati, OH: South-Western Educational Publishing.

Policies Commission for Business and Economic Education. (1987). *This we believe about research in business education* (Statement No. 43). In *Policy statements: 1959–1996.* Cincinnati, OH: South-Western Educational Publishing.

Policies Commission for Business and Economic Education. (2006). *This we believe about the value of professional associations* (Statement No. 79). Retrieved from http://www.nbea.org/newsite/curriculum/ documents/PCBEEStatement79_000.pdf

Policies Commission for Business and Economic Education. (2008). *This we believe about the transformation and future of business education* (Statement No. 83). Retrieved from http://www.nbea.org/newsite/curriculum/documents/PCBEE Statement83_000.pdf

Policies Commission for Business and Economic Education. (2010). *This we believe about generativity in business education* (Statement No. 86). Retrieved from http://www.nbea.org/newsite/curriculum/documents/PCBEEStatement86_000.pdf

Policies Commission for Business and Economic Education. (2012). *This we believe about social media in education* (Statement No. 91). Retrieved from http://www.nbea.org/newsite/curriculum/documents/PCBEEStatement91_000.pdf

Pope-Ruark, R. (2012). Exploring scholarship of teaching and learning approaches to business communication research. *Business Communication Quarterly, 75*(3), 237–251.

Scott, J. C. (2001). Using the process approach to improve scholarly writing. *The Delta Pi Epsilon Journal, 43*(2), 57–66.

Scott, J. C. (2003). Conceiving and building a sustainable research program. *The Delta Pi Epsilon Journal, 45*(1), 3–16.

Scott, J. C., Blaszczynski, C., & Green, D. J. (2004). Strategies for writing a Delta Pi Epsilon Research Foundation, Inc., grant application. *Delta Pi Epsilon Book of Readings 2010,* Delta Pi Epsilon National Conference, Little Rock, AR. (pp. 199–202).

Scott, J. C., Blaszczynski, C., & Green, D. J. (2008). Finding relevant literature to guide instructional practices. *Journal of Applied Research for Business Instruction, 5*(3), 1–6.

Scott, J. C., Blaszczynski, C., Green, D. J., & Fagerheim, B. A. (2008). Vital business educators' perceptions about the usefulness of business education periodicals: Making the relevant literature more accessible. *The Delta Pi Epsilon Journal, 50*(1), 4–17.

Taylor & Francis Online. (n.d.). *Journal of Education for Business:* Aims & scope. Retrieved from http://www.tandfonline.com/action/aboutThisJournal?show= aimsScope&journalCode=VJEB&#.U16bF_ldViM

U.S. Department of Health and Human Services, Office of Research Integrity. (2006). *Responsible authorship quick guide: Detecting common mistakes & considering dilemmas in responsible authorship.* Retrieved from http://ori.hhs.gov/education/products/ niu_authorship/mistakes/index.htm

Wilhelm, W. J., & Kaunelis, D. (2005). Literature reviews: Analysis, planning, and query techniques. *The Delta Pi Epsilon Journal, 47*(2), 91–106.

Wright, C. (2013). Using action research to improve teaching and learning. *Business Education Forum, 67*(3), 45–47.

Wunsch, D. R. (1991). How to evaluate research as a research consumer. *Instructional Strategies: An Applied Research Series, 7*(3), 1–6.

Leadership in Professional Associations for Business Education

Tamra Davis-Maxwell and Glenn Bailey
Illinois State University
Normal, IL

Leaders of business education professional associations acknowledge that business educators who join professional associations "with others who share similar work-related interests and goals" receive many advantages (Scott, 2008, p. 285); however, challenges exist within the professional associations that leadership needs to address. According to the Policies Commission for Business and Economic Education (PCBEE, 2006), professional associations "exist to help members value and promote their profession as well as nurture their individual careers" (p. 1). Professional associations provide professional growth and leadership development opportunities for business education professionals. The PCBEE continues to place importance on professional organizations as evidenced in its program of work for 2012–2013. The PCBEE addressed professional organizations with Policy Statement #92, *This we believe about the role of professional organizations in the future of business education,* published in 2013 (Hagler, 2012).

Educators who become involved in their professional associations have access to up-to-date publications, professional networks, an avenue to build leadership skills, and other membership benefits (Shumack & Forde, 2012). According to the National Business Education Association (NBEA, n.d., p. 3), "Leadership in business education is critical if the profession is to move forward in our fast-paced global society." Without innovative leaders, the professional associations may struggle for relevancy, resulting in a struggle for membership numbers. Haynes and Samuel (2006) discussed the responsibility of association leaders by stating, "It is *leadership* that will determine the sustainability of an organization" (p. 2). To meet this obligation to the professional association, leaders should be aware of the current environment of the profession, provide a vision for the organization, and create meaning and value for members.

Leadership sets the stage for the success or failure of organizations. According to Bennis (1999b), leaders are responsible for four roles within a group:

- They provide direction and meaning to the group. Leaders "remind people of what's important and why their work makes a difference" (p. 320).

- They generate and sustain trust that allows the members of an organization to move through periods of dissent and challenge that are a normal part of the group process.

- They are action-oriented risk takers who are curious in order to achieve results.

- They are purveyors of hope because they "find both tangible and symbolic ways to demonstrate that the group can overcome the odds" (p. 321). One way that business education leaders provide direction and meaning is through the history of the profession and its associations to provide future directions for the profession (PCBEE, 2006).

This chapter discusses the contributions of professional associations, responsibility of professional organizations to ensure quality professional preparation and practice, current trends in professional associations, and challenges faced by the leadership of business education professional associations.

CONTRIBUTIONS OF PROFESSIONAL ASSOCIATIONS IN BUSINESS EDUCATION

Multiple and related associations support the business education profession. These associations vary by mission and areas of support for the profession. Many business education professionals are members of multiple associations, and even the leadership within the organizations often overlaps. The parent association for the profession is the National Business Education Association (NBEA).

National Business Education Association (NBEA). "The National Business Education Association (NBEA) is the nation's leading professional organization devoted exclusively to serving individuals and groups engaged in instruction, administration, research, and dissemination of information for and about business" (NBEA, 2013a, para. 1). NBEA provides opportunities for professionals to stay current in the field of business education, advocates for legislation in the field of business education, and serves as a unifying organization for professional organizations in business education. Publications made available by NBEA for sharing information on business education include *Business Education Forum*, NBEA Yearbook, and *Keying In*. NBEA also offers webinars on current issues in business education and multiple social media networking opportunities.

NBEA creates an annual program of work that contains an extensive section on leadership development. Many leadership opportunities are outlined for NBEA members and facilitated through the Leadership Development Task Force. NBEA is currently revising its program of work and incorporating implementation of leadership development materials into the documents governing NBEA and its regions. New ways to introduce members to leadership opportunities are being developed (NBEA, 2012). Additionally, NBEA offers a leadership development program each year during its annual convention using the *Leadership in Business Education* handbook (NBEA, n.d.). This handbook contains a section (pp. 20–21) on membership and identifies the following association membership benefits and services:

- Enhance career growth and development

- Expand influence with linkages among national, regional, and state, territorial, and provincial associations

- Expand professional networks

- Strengthen the image of business education

- Receive the following membership benefits and services:
  o Publications
  o Conferences/conventions
  o Unified voice
  o Awards program
  o Exhibits of instructional resources
  o Group travel
  o Financial planning
  o Group insurance
  o Tax-sheltered annuity programs

NBEA is also the parent organization for five regional business education associations. NBEA automatically assigns a regional membership based on where the member lives. Any NBEA member may participate in a regional activity, and many of the membership benefits are available to all NBEA members, regardless of region. The five regions include Eastern, Mountain-Plains, North Central, Southern, and Western regions of the United States and Canada, as well as American Samoa, Bermuda, Guam, Northern Mariana Islands, Puerto Rico, and the Virgin Islands (NBEA, 2013b).

The Eastern region includes Bermuda, Connecticut, Delaware, District of Columbia, Maine, Maryland, Massachusetts, New Brunswick, New Hampshire, New Jersey, New York, Newfoundland, Nova Scotia, Ontario, Pennsylvania, Prince Edward Island, Puerto Rico, Quebec, Rhode Island, Vermont, and the Virgin Islands. The Eastern region no longer has an active association.

The Mountain-Plains region (Mountain-Plains Business Education Association or MPBEA) includes Colorado, Kansas, Manitoba, Nebraska, New Mexico, North Dakota, Oklahoma, Saskatchewan, South Dakota, Texas, and Wyoming. MPBEA holds its annual conference in June each year. The region's leadership has determined that important membership benefits include a peer-reviewed journal that is published in even-numbered years. It rewards innovative teaching ideas through a program called Share-an-Idea and the winning submission is available on the region's Web site. Each year during the annual conference, the association's past president at the time facilitates a Leadership Development Institute in an effort to prepare future leaders for business education (Mountain-Plains Business Education Association, 2013).

The North Central region (North Central Business Education Association or NCBEA) includes Illinois, Indiana, Iowa, Michigan, Minnesota, Missouri, Ohio, and Wisconsin. NCBEA holds its annual convention in conjunction with a state conference. The host state determines the timing of the convention each year. NCBEA offers summer workshops, a listserv, and conference presentations as a few membership benefits (North Central Business Education Association, 2013).

The Southern region (Southern Business Education Association or SBEA) includes Alabama, Arkansas, Florida, Georgia, Kentucky, Louisiana, Mississippi, North Carolina, South Carolina, Tennessee, Virginia, and West Virginia. According to the SBEA Web site (2013), the region represents more than 3,000 business education professionals. SBEA typically holds its annual conference in October each year. To reach members, the region hosts a group on Facebook. The region also offers a variety of teaching resources through their Web site.

The Western region (Western Business Education Association or WBEA) includes Alaska, Alberta, American Samoa, Arizona, British Columbia, California, Guam, Hawaii, Idaho, Montana, Nevada, Northern Mariana Islands, Northwest Territories, Oregon, Utah, Yukon, and Washington. WBEA provides professional and leadership development through the annual Professional Development Institute and a workshop for the presidents-elect of business education associations in the states, territories, and provinces at the regional conference held annually in February (Western Business Education Association, 2012).

Throughout the regions, most individual states, territories, and provinces also have active business education associations that offer conferences and networking opportunities with other business educators within their boundaries. Several of the states also offer peer-reviewed journals in an effort to improve the knowledge base of the profession. Guidance for locating opportunities and services with specific state, territorial, or provincial business education organizations is available at http://nbea.org/newsite/about/states.html.

Several divisional associations fall under the NBEA umbrella. Each of these divisional associations provides a unique service to its members. Joining a divisional association requires membership in NBEA.

The International Society for Business Education (SIEC-ISBE).[1] The mission of SIEC-ISBE is "to enhance the international perspective of business and business education professionals" (International Society for Business Education, 2013, para. 3). Publications made available by SIEC-ISBE for sharing information on business education include the *International Journal for Business Education* from SIEC-ISBE International and *Journal for Global Education* from the United States Chapter of the International Society for Business Education. Any business education professional who is interested in global business education can benefit from SIEC-ISBE and ISBE activities. Networking activities with professionals from chapters on four continents provide opportunities in international business through improved international educational exchanges; cooperative efforts among individuals, institutions, and businesses; and unification of the goals of business education professionals on a global scale.

Association for Research in Business Education–Delta Pi Epsilon (ARBE-DPE). ARBE-DPE is a national graduate honorary society for professionals who support and promote scholarship, leadership, and cooperation toward the advancement of education for and about business. ARBE-DPE was founded on a shared mission to improve the teaching of business through the engagement of scientific research, development of leadership skills, and advancement of the profession, providing members with team-building and networking opportunities (Association for Research in Business Education–Delta Pi Epsilon, 2013). ARBE-DPE offers opportunities to share research findings through presentations at the annual NBEA convention and through two peer-juried publications: *Journal for Research in Business Education* and *Journal of Applied Research for Business Instruction.*

National Association for Business Teacher Education (NABTE). The primary purpose of NABTE is to promote business teacher education by providing national leadership and services to its member institutions and business teacher educators. Institutional membership is open to colleges and universities offering a business teacher education curriculum approved by state departments of education for the certification of business teachers (National Association for Business Teacher Education, 2013). Associate memberships are also open to any individual business education professional interested in the preparation of business education teachers. Opportunities to share research and best practices in business teacher education are available through presentations at the annual NBEA convention and through a peer-juried publication. NABTE publishes *Business Teacher Education Journal* for sharing information on the preparation of business education teachers.

---

[1]SIEC-ISBE stands for La Société Internationale pour l'Enseignement Commercial–The International Society for Business Education.

Professional Associations Ensure Quality of the Profession

Professional associations contribute to the quality of professional preparation and practice through membership benefits. Benefits of professional associations typically include publications, professional development, networking opportunities, leadership opportunities, and discounted costs on professional materials. However, these benefits are provided as membership benefits for those who join and participate in professional activities as stated by the profession's policy-making body, "Members should take an active role by participating in association activities" (PCBEE, 2006, p. 1).

One of the most valuable benefits members of a profession can derive from their professional associations is access to up-to-date publications. Written by contributors from the field of business education, the information in the professional journals provides a vehicle for sharing the best practices of successful educators with other members (Shumack & Forde, 2012).

According to the PCBEE (1997), "business educators must pursue activities that promote their individual growth and that bring them together with other educators for reflection and planning" (p. 1). Therefore, professional development opportunities are important to the associations and to their members. Through active participation in professional associations, business educators have access to multiple professional development opportunities such as participation in formal instruction, research of best practices, and collaboration at conferences.

Professional associations offer a variety of networking opportunities. According to Shumack and Forde (2012), "peer relationships strengthen morale, encourage the novice teacher, and play a part in success when ideas are brought back to the classroom" (p. 178). Building a professional learning network can lead to professional growth (Davis, 2013). Such a network is collaborative and "may include educators, learners, parents, administrators, employers, community members, governmental representatives, and professional association members" (PCBEE, 2001, p. 1). Professional conferences and trade shows provide ways to build professional relationships. At conventions and conferences, business and education leaders provide keynote addresses, members offer professional development sessions, and vendors/publishers demonstrate their latest products and resources available to educators. Each business education professional association provides conferences throughout the year. Conference dates may be accessed at Web sites for sponsoring organizations.

Professional associations also provide an avenue for leadership development. Shumack and Forde (2012) stated, "successful professionals realize that positive reputations are built over time by forming and maintaining a strong professional network" (p. 178). Most states have state associations in which professionals may begin their leadership careers by serving on committees while developing the skills needed and the reputation required to move into leadership positions at the state, regional, national, and international levels. However, members "must be open and willing to contribute when invited, and professional associations must always be aware of immediately providing opportunities for new members to grow and to be involved" (Shumack & Forde, 2012, p. 178). As professionals, business educators must be willing to strengthen the profession through participation in the associations.

Professional discounts offered by professional associations may be significant. For example, NBEA membership currently provides members with $250,000 in professional liability insurance, discounts on professional publications, and other discounts. Many professional associations offer substantial discounts for students planning to enter the profession. These discounts apply to most costs, including membership and conferences. Additionally, many of the professional associations offer scholarships and/or stipends to students and new teachers to encourage participation in association activities.

TRENDS IN PROFESSIONAL ASSOCIATIONS IN BUSINESS EDUCATION

A Delphi study conducted by Davis and Bailey (2013) found that business education leaders identify multiple trends for professional associations. The panel of business educators interviewed, who serve as association leaders in professional associations, indicated that professional associations are experiencing several positive trends. Many business education associations at all levels are producing quality publications, staying current with technologies, leading change within the profession, providing professional development, and unifying individual organizations under the umbrella of the National Business Education Association. The various professional associations under the umbrella of one parent organization should lead to increased collaboration among the affiliated associations, regions, and state, territorial, and provincial associations allowing for greater coordination of activities. This collaboration and coordination should result in increased services of greater quality at reasonable costs; a study by O'Neil and Forde (2007) indicated that organizations providing valuable and meaningful resources will survive. Providing valuable and meaningful resources is an important issue to be addressed by leadership because "many of the services traditionally provided by professional organizations can now be found in public places and accessed readily through electronic channels—free of charge" (O'Neil & Forde, 2007, p. 47).

Shumack and Forde (2012) summarized the status of current professional associations as follows:

Today, educators weigh carefully membership costs vs. benefits while professional associations are challenged to (a) provide abundant membership services that cost more and more to provide, (b) understand how best to use technology in providing membership services, and (c) fulfill the needs of the profession. (p. 177)

Based on this study, leadership needs to address how to provide valuable benefits while maintaining costs as an important issue for the survival of business education professional associations.

CHALLENGES FACING PROFESSIONAL ASSOCIATIONS IN BUSINESS EDUCATION

Davis and Bailey (2013) found that professional association leaders observed a decline in the number of members and member involvement at all professional association levels: local, state, regional, national, and international. Declining membership numbers appear to be the primary challenge for professional organizations (Davis & Bailey, 2013; O'Neil & Willis, 2005). The association leaders surveyed stated that one reason for this decline may be that professional associations are struggling to earn the respect of their constituencies.

Additionally, the declining numbers of programs to license business education teachers and the challenges facing business education programs in K–12 settings create a challenge for professional association membership numbers and member involvement. With challenges of maintaining viable business education programs, the emphasis on technology and technology instruction is oftentimes offered at the expense of discipline-based knowledge and soft skill development (Davis & Bailey, 2013). This challenge provides opportunities for professional associations to enhance knowledge through conferences and publications.

In 2007 O'Neil and Forde addressed the challenge of maintaining professional association membership levels by stating, "Membership must have value" (p. 46). Current professional association leaders confirmed the need for value. Many new as well as more experienced teachers do not see the relevance of the professional association (Davis & Bailey, 2013). O'Neil and Forde also indicated that professional associations need to be aware of the needs of their current and potential members; failure to understand and anticipate the needs of members would be detrimental to the association.

A related membership challenge for professional associations is the aging of members and leaders. Attracting new members is an important key to maintaining successful professional associations. New association members must replace those who have been members and leaders in organizations if the organizations are able to evolve and reflect the changing needs of the profession (Davis & Bailey, 2013).

Lower attendance at professional conferences and conventions is another challenge to professional associations. O'Neil and Forde (2007) stressed the need for conferences to provide valuable professional growth opportunities because many attendees must personally pay the cost of attendance. Members will not attend conferences if immediate value is not apparent for potential attendees. One way to provide professional growth is through networking, as "technology still falls short of human interaction" (O'Neil & Forde, 2007, p. 49). According to the Davis and Bailey (2013) study, members appreciate and value technological methods for disseminating information; however, the personal interactions that occur at conferences and meetings cannot be replaced by the technological means currently available.

In summary, the challenges that must be addressed by the leaders of the business education professional associations are many. Bennis (1999a) shared that "The global challenges and changes of the emergent millennium…compel the creation of both new forms of organizations and new forms of leadership" (p. 215). A professional association provides a competitive edge to its members by providing professional development for those involved in the association.

ADDRESSING THESE CHALLENGES

Leadership of professional associations has multiple avenues to address the challenges presented in this chapter. Davis and Bailey (2013) offered the following tactics for addressing the challenges facing professional associations in business education:

- Using one-on-one recruitment strategies that involve individual association members in recruitment

- Searching for new cohorts, such as recent college graduates, to include in recruitment activities

- Adapting services such as conference and publication topics to the changing demographics of current and future members

- Surveying stakeholder groups, such as employers, teacher preparation institutions, state teacher licensure agencies, and teachers, on ways to involve additional professionals in the associations

- Using social media to interact with fellow professionals

- Providing recruitment training for membership directors at the state and regional levels

Although these strategies may have been used in the past with some efficacy, membership issues continue to plague the professional associations. The panel of business education association leaders in the Davis and Bailey (2013) research offered the following suggestions for professional association leaders. Professional association leaders may want to consider ways to be more relevant to new teachers in the profession by seeking to learn what these teachers need from a professional association. It is also imperative to determine what current members need to retain their membership in the associations. Understanding that costs may prohibit innovative teachers new to the profession from attending large regional or national conferences, association leaders should consider ways to deliberately include newer teachers in professional development activities. For example, leaders might invite innovative teachers to prepare and present webinars that can be offered through the Internet or open-source avenues. Offering live videoconferencing opportunities for opening keynote speakers at conferences or for designated professional development workshops is another possibility. Innovative teachers who cannot attend the conference might be asked to virtually present to the attendees at a conference. Additionally, videoing some professional development workshops to be modified into podcasts would be a valuable benefit for members unable to attend conferences. All activities of the associations need to strive to showcase the services and programs that reflect credibility within the overall education community. Offering a variety of services throughout the year and between conferences is one way to achieve this goal.

Leaders surveyed by Davis and Bailey (2013) indicated a need to work more closely with teaching universities to determine what new teachers require for becoming active in the professional organizations. Finding ways to recruit and involve students in business education programs into the professional associations and providing them with the tools and resources needed to be successful as novice teachers will benefit the associations. One final suggestion offered was to target publications, workshops, and conferences to K–12 teachers and teachers at community colleges. Involving these teachers in action research to determine best practices for instructional methodologies and other activities related to the business education classroom may provide another avenue of membership for the professional associations.

The PCBEE (2008) also suggested the following actions in order to transform business education. Professional associations must do the following:

- Explore and understand the changes in learners, social context, and business educators to transform their marketing, publications, workshops, and conferences.

- Provide the incentive and a forum for business educators to engage in this transformation.

- Support the development of excellent teachers by providing opportunities to be skillful, innovative, and entrepreneurial in their teaching, given their changing environments.

- Use the new "tools" to enable business educators to network, to engage in professional and leadership development, and to share ideas and best practices collaboratively.

- Ensure that all business education literature is available and indexed electronically so that it can be retrieved not only by business educators but also by other professionals.

- Strengthen existing and implement new partnerships among the varied professional associations to collaborate in promoting and sustaining the transformation of the business education profession. (p. 2)

SUMMARY

This chapter discussed leadership contributions and considerations of professional associations by summarizing the contributions of NBEA, the five regions of NBEA, divisional affiliations, and state, territorial, and provincial associations. The foundation to ensure quality professional preparation and practice is in place and available to any member willing to take advantage and participate within the associations. Current leaders should mentor others who are willing to become leaders within the associations. "The underlying purpose of professional organizations—that of helping members develop professionally—remains the same regardless of the century and the technology available" (Shumack & Forde, 2012, p. 186).

Positive trends within the associations include quality publications, staying current through the use of technology, professional development, and collaboration between NBEA and affiliated divisions. Professional associations also face challenges, primarily in the form of declining membership numbers and decreased participation at conferences and conventions leading to decreased revenues, which can lead to a need to decrease services. Additional challenges can be seen within business education programs whose emphasis is shifting away from discipline-based knowledge and soft skill development. Leaders of professional associations must find ways to provide value to their members and to make prospective members aware of that value. Value could be provided through membership benefits such as publications, networking, professional development, leadership development opportunities, and membership discounts. The value of membership must be visible throughout the year, not just via annual conferences or conventions.

"Viable professional associations are essential to the life of the business education profession" (PCBEE, 2006, p. 2). Addressing the challenges and incorporating suggestions from association leadership into the activities of professional organizations may provide additional revenue-generating streams, help retain current members, entice new members to join, and provide valuable benefits to all members and to the professional community. Incorporating ways for members unable to attend conferences should provide additional value. "Strong, effective leadership must be cultivated and exercised so that the business education profession is able to accomplish this transformation" (PCBEE, 2008, p. 3).

In conclusion, "the organizations that will succeed...are those that take seriously, and sustain through action, their belief that their competitive advantage is their people and their development" (Bennis, 1999a, p. 79). Leaders have the responsibility to find the key in order to sustain professional associations for future generations of business education professionals.

REFERENCES

Association for Research in Business Education–Delta Pi Epsilon (ARBE-DPE). (2013). About us. Retrieved from http://www.dpe.org

Bennis, W. (1999a). *Managing people is like herding cats*. Provo, UT: Executive Excellence Publishing.

Bennis, W. (1999b). The secrets of great groups. In F. Hesselbein and P. M. Cohen (Eds.), *Leader to leader*. San Francisco, CA: Jossey-Bass.

Davis, T. S. (2013, Spring/Summer). Building and using a personal/professional learning network with social media. *The Journal of Research in Business Education, LV*(1), 1–13.

Davis, T. S., & Bailey, G. A. (2013). Perceptions of business education leaders concerning issues and trends facing business education and business education professional organizations: A Delphi study. Manuscript in progress.

Hagler, B. (2012). Policies Commission for Business and Economic Education program of work. Unpublished manuscript.

Haynes, W., & Samuel, A. A. (2006). *Value of membership in professional associations— American Society for Public Administration: A stellar case in point.* International Center for Civic Engagement: Park University. Retrieved from http://unpan1.un.org/intradoc/groups/public/documents/icce/unpan022719.pdf

International Society for Business Education (SIEC-ISBE). (2013). About SIEC-ISBE. Retrieved from http://www.siec-isbe.org/index.html

Mountain-Plains Business Education Association (MPBEA). (2013). About M-PBEA. Retrieved from http://www.mpbea.org/about.htm

National Association for Business Teacher Education (NABTE). (2013). The National Association for Business Teacher Education. Retrieved from http://www.nabte.org

National Business Education Association (NBEA). (2012, June 1). *Professional development and leadership, NBEA Program of Work 2012–2013.* Retrieved from http://nbea.org/newsite/about/documents/ProgramofWork_2012-2013.pdf

National Business Education Association. (2013a). About NBEA: Mission and purpose. Retrieved from http://nbea.org/newsite/about/index.html

National Business Education Association. (2013b). NBEA regional associations. Retrieved from http://nbea.org/newsite/about/regional.html

National Business Education Association. (n.d.) *Leadership in business education.* Retrieved from http://www.nbea.org/newsite/opportunities/pdf/Leadership%20in%20Business%20Education.pdf

North Central Business Education Association (NCBEA). (2013). *NCBEA: North Central Business Education Association.* Retrieved from http://www.ncbea.com

O'Neil, S. L., & Forde, C. M. (2007). The survival of professional organizations: A new thrust. *The Delta Pi Epsilon Journal, 49*(1), 43–49.

O'Neil, S. L., & Willis, C. L. (2005). Challenges for professional organizations: Lessons from the past. *The Delta Pi Epsilon Journal, 47*(3), 143–153.

Policies Commission for Business and Economic Education (PCBEE). (1997). *This we believe about the professional development of business educators* (Statement No. 60). Retrieved from http://www.nbea.org/newsite/curriculum/policy/no_60.pdf

Policies Commission for Business and Economic Education. (2001). *This we believe about the emerging roles of the business educator* (Statement No. 68). Retrieved from http://www.nbea.org/newsite/curriculum/policy/no_68.pdf

Policies Commission for Business and Economic Education. (2006). *This we believe about the value of professional associations* (Statement No. 79). Retrieved from http://www.nbea.org/newsite/curriculum/policy/no_79.pdf

Policies Commission for Business and Economic Education. (2008). *This we believe about the transformation and the future of business education* (Statement No. 83). Retrieved from http://www.nbea.org/newsite/curriculum/policy/no_83.pdf

Scott, J. C. (2008). Lifelong professional development. In M. H. Rader, G. A. Bailey, and L. A. Kurth (Eds.), *Effective methods of teaching business education: NBEA yearbook* (No. 46, pp. 278–291). Reston, VA: National Business Education Association.

Shumack, K., & Forde, C. (2012). Professional association membership: Extending the community of practice. In W. L. Stitt-Gohdes (Ed.), *Trends and issues in business education: NBEA 2012 yearbook* (No. 50, pp. 174–187). Reston, VA: National Business Education Association.

Southern Business Education Association (SBEA). (2013). Southern Business Education Association. Retrieved from http://www.sbea.us

Western Business Education Association (WBEA). (2012). Western Business Education Association. Retrieved from http://www.wbite.org

Business Teacher Education Program Leadership

Robert B. Blair and Martha Balachandran

Middle Tennessee State University

Murfreesboro, TN

Business teacher certification/licensure across the United States is an evolving process. Changes are necessary in order to ensure that business educators prepare students to meet the demands of a dynamic business environment. Technological advancements also play a major role in updating what a business teacher needs to know and be able to do. As "…business historically has been one of the most popular elective areas at the secondary level and frequently the largest major field of study for students at the collegiate level" (Lambrecht & Kesten, 2012, p. 1), it is important that collegiate business teacher educators serve as leaders in updating certification/licensure requirements.

The Policies Commission for Business and Economic Education (PCBEE) further substantiated this need in Policy Statement 83 (2008). The commission stated that collegiate business teacher education programs must prepare future teachers to be skillful, innovative, and highly effective instructors with diverse groups and within a global, virtual, and changing environment.

This chapter provides information about business teacher education programs in various states as well as the alternative routes provided for business education certification/licensure. The first part of the chapter includes an examination of leadership in traditional teacher education programs relating to recruitment, collaboration, standards, licensure structures, accreditation, curriculum development, student assessment, clinical placement, online program delivery, faculty qualifications, and professional involvement. The second part of the chapter discusses alternative teacher education certification opportunities by examining business experience, education, certification timeline, and mentoring elements. The concluding discussion focuses on the requirements for business teacher certification/licensure renewal.

TRADITIONAL COLLEGIATE TEACHER EDUCATION PROGRAMS

The two traditional avenues for obtaining business teacher certification/licensure are through undergraduate and graduate business teacher certification programs. These programs typically prepare candidates to teach business in middle and high schools but may extend to the elementary and postsecondary school levels as well. The structure of the coursework depends largely upon whether the program is housed in the institution's college of education or college of business. If the degree is housed in the college of education, candidates earn an education degree with a minor or emphasis in business. However, when the degree program is housed in the college of business, teacher candidates earn a business major with a minor or emphasis in education.

Traditional programs involve a variety of coursework delivery systems, including any combination of face-to-face, hybrid, and/or online courses. In addition to completing general education and major-specific coursework, teacher candidates must also meet the institution's teacher education admission requirements. These admission requirements typically include a minimum cumulative grade point average (e.g., 2.50 to 3.00), basic skills competency assessment (Praxis I or equivalent), and background check. Teacher education admission requirements must be met before a teacher candidate participates in a clinical experience.

Most teacher education institutions also offer a post-baccalaureate certification/licensure program for those teacher candidates who already hold a degree in a related field (accounting, management, marketing, entrepreneurship, etc.) and decide to change career paths. The post-baccalaureate certification normally requires additional coursework that might include business and professional education prerequisites, methods of teaching business course(s), and clinical experience. The post-baccalaureate certification program is custom designed based upon the credentials that the candidate brings to the situation. Post-baccalaureate candidates must also meet the teacher education admission standards. The post-baccalaureate program leads to certification only, not an additional degree.

Another traditional path to business teacher certification/licensure is through graduate business teacher education programs or master of arts in teaching programs. These programs are attractive to individuals who have an undergraduate degree and business experience and who have decided they want to teach. Candidates study methodology, learning theories, issues, trends, research, and problems in business education. According to Fisher and Hagler (2012), graduate business education programs help enhance the skills, knowledge, and dispositions needed to be effective business teachers.

Recruitment for the Profession

The decline in business teacher preparation programs necessitates that traditional program leaders take a proactive approach to recruiting new business teacher candidates into the profession. The mission of the National Association for Business Teacher Education (NABTE) is to provide leadership for business teacher education.

One of NABTE's leadership initiatives is to assist with the recruitment of new teachers into the profession. On its Web site (http://www.nabte.org/publications.html), NABTE provides several tools for business educators at all levels to use in their recruitment efforts:

Under the subhead "The Business of Teaching: Educating for Success in Business and Life" are links with seven user-friendly, single-page PDF flyers that address the following topics:

- *The Business of Teaching: Educating for Success in Business and Life* (Introduction)

- *Portrait of a Profession: Business Education*

- *Reasons to Major in Business Education*

- *Your "Typical Day" as a Business Education Teacher: Real World, Real Relevance*

- *Employment Forecast: Business Teacher*

- *Is Business Education Right for You?*

- *Inventing Possibilities through Education and Experience*

Business educators can share these flyers with elementary, middle, and high school teachers and counselors; community college and university faculty; academic advisors; and campus career centers to help disseminate information about potential careers for business teachers.

Under the subhead "NABTE Kiosk" at the same NABTE Web page is another useful recruitment tool: a 19-slide looping presentation intended for use at career fairs, recruiting sessions, parent-teacher organization meetings, and other events.

Additionally, NABTE institutional representatives and associate members as well as business education faculty can be instrumental in recruiting. They should take every opportunity to share the news about business education as a career choice through discussions, departmental newsletters, scholarships, awards ceremonies, recruitment fairs, freshmen orientations, student organization events, advisory boards, Web sites, and social media.

Many of the recruitment challenges currently faced by programs, such as budget cuts, program consolidations, and perception of low salaries, will continue to be issues well into the next decade (Gaytan, 2008). However, the trend of demand surpassing supply of new business teachers may not be as prevalent in the future (Hagler, 2009). To address reductions in funding, many school systems are opting to increase class sizes and hire alternatively licensed teachers. For example, several states will hire individuals who hold a baccalaureate degree; through a state-mandated accelerated training program, these individuals will be able to teach for up to three years while they complete certification requirements. Additionally, in several states, individuals who hold a valid teacher's license need only pass the Praxis business education specialty area exam to obtain an endorsement in business.

Collaboration with Institution's Teacher Education Leadership

Regardless of whether a business teacher education program resides in the college of education or college of business, it is important that the teacher education faculty in each area collaborate on program development and delivery, course content, standards alignment, assessment, and all issues related to teacher preparation. All business teacher educators should be knowledgeable about state licensure/certification requirements. To ensure that business teacher education faculty who reside in colleges of business receive appropriate training to stay up-to-date on curriculum, licensure standards, evaluation models, and other related training, they need to work closely with teacher education faculty in the college of education.

Standards and Assessment

The PCBEE's 2005 "This We Believe…" policy statement said, "Learning for and about business is inherently academic. Business education provides a rigorous and relevant contextual learning opportunity for core content (English, math, science, and social studies)" (p. 1). In the same statement, the PCBEE further noted, "Research supports that academic achievement is improved for many students when core content is taught in an authentic context" (p. 1). The business education curriculum provides a framework for contextual application of core content. This curriculum is guided and measured by standards designed to identify what students should know and be able to do upon successful completion of a program of study. Numerous sets of standards that impact business teacher certification/licensure are available at both the national and state levels.

National. The two leading sets of national standards related to business teacher certification have been those developed by NABTE and the National Council for Accreditation of Teacher Education (NCATE). However, as of July 2013, NCATE was replaced by the Council for the Accreditation of Educator Preparation (CAEP) programs.[1] CAEP is now the sole accrediting body for teacher preparation in the United States. The organization plans to release its standards early in 2014 (CAEP, 2013).

---

[1]NCATE and Teacher Education Accreditation Council (TEAC) merged to form the Council for Accreditation of Educator Preparation (CAEP).

The NABTE *Business Teacher Education Curriculum Guide and Program Standards* (2010) provides business teacher education institutions an outline for what should be included in the teacher preparation curriculum as well as guidance for program administration. Even though NABTE is not an accrediting agency, it is the leading organization specifically related to business education teacher preparation. The NABTE business teacher education curriculum achievement standards address the following elements: professionalism, curriculum development, instruction, assessment, classroom environment, student organizations, communication, stakeholders, career development, and subject competencies. Each achievement standard includes a rationale and list of performance expectations.

The NABTE program standards (preparatory and advanced) are well rounded and incorporate best practices from NCATE, National Association of State Directors of Teacher Education and Certification (NASDTEC), Association to Advance Collegiate Schools of Business (AACSB), and Accreditation Council for Business Schools and Programs (ACBSP) (NABTE, 2010). These standards take into consideration the following program elements: purpose, governance, general studies, business studies, professional studies, research, faculty, admission to business teacher education, student retention, student support services, institutional facilities, community resources, cooperation and articulation among schools, assessment and program development, and strategic planning. The program standards are useful in thorough program evaluation and continuous improvement.

Other leading standards for business teacher education were established by NCATE, which until July 2013 was the accrediting body for teacher education. When the new accrediting agency—CAEP—releases its program standards, business teacher education faculty members must know and include these standards in their program, especially when the program is not located in a college of education. Current NCATE unit standards examine the following areas of teacher preparation: "candidate knowledge, skills, and professional dispositions; assessment system and unit evaluation; field experiences and clinical practices; diversity; faculty qualifications, performance, and development; and unit governance and resources" (NCATE, 2008, pp. 12–13).

Although NABTE and NCATE/CAEP are considered the two most important entities that provide standards related to business education teacher preparation, the Common Core State Standards (http://corestandards.org), National Institute for Excellence in Teaching (http://niet.org), and National Board for Professional Teacher Standards (http://www.nbpts.org) should also be considered.

State. State business teacher education standards for certification/licensure should always be based upon the national standards for the discipline. State licensure standards are often driven by curriculum changes. However, in many instances, legislators, higher education commissions, and other politically motivated entities influence the development of the state-level certification standards. Thus, business teacher educators should demonstrate leadership by working collaboratively with state department of education decision makers to ensure that the state standards for business teacher education programs truly reflect the needs of the profession.

It is also important that business teacher educators are actively involved in other areas of teacher preparation. They should assist with the state's teacher licensure structures and the program's accreditation requirements. Additionally, they should assume leadership and/or mentoring roles in curriculum development, online education, student assessment, clinical placement, faculty qualifications, and professional involvement.

Licensure Structures and Renewal

Most states have at least two levels of licensure; some have more with variations in the certification types, requirements, and names. New York, for example, has at least six levels: initial, conditional initial (reciprocity), internship, professional, and two types of transitional. Tennessee has two levels: apprentice and professional.

New teachers in Tennessee receive an apprentice license and are required to undergo evaluation six times during their first year using the Tennessee Educator Acceleration Model (TEAM). The TEAM teaching skills, knowledge, and professionalism performance standards are divided into four domains: instruction, planning, environment, and professionalism (National Institute for Excellence in Teaching, 2012). Three of the first-year apprentice teacher observations are informal and address planning and/or the environment. The other three observations are formal and address all 12 indicators on the instruction rubric. Once teachers have attained their professional license, they are evaluated four times each year.

Teachers are generally required to renew their licenses within a specified period; they may also seek a different type of license or add another teaching area. To qualify for renewal, some states require that teachers meet minimum evaluation standards, complete professional development activities, and perhaps work with a mentor.

Faculty Development and Mentoring

Faculty development and mentoring relationships are important parts of any teacher licensure program. Yohon and Kesten (2009) determined that "new teachers need and want professional development and mentoring opportunities" (p. 23). And most states now require new teachers to participate in an induction program specifically designed to enhance the first-year teaching experience. Induction programs (which include faculty development, mentoring, and/or other types of activities) typically provide support, guidance, and encouragement to beginning teachers. Topics may include classroom management, student and teacher assessment, teacher-related administrative duties, new legislation affecting education, and other pertinent concerns.

According to Unruh and Holt (2010), new teachers who participated in strong support programs improved their sense of value or efficacy as teachers and their sense of satisfaction with their work. Fox and Peters (2013) further noted that teachers from traditional and alternative licensure programs identified mentoring as being a crucial element in their self-efficacy. Unruh and Holt said that efficacy as a teacher and satisfaction with work are essential elements in retaining good teachers, and teacher retention is important to local school systems (2010).

Accreditation

Institutions considered leaders in business education teacher preparation are held to a high level of accountability through several different accrediting agencies. Most institutions maintain regional accreditation (e.g., Middle States Commission on Higher Education and Southern Association of Colleges and Schools Commission on Colleges) in addition to adhering to the advanced standards unique to the field of teacher education.

Teacher education programs will now seek accreditation from the CAEP. In past years, NCATE has required that an accredited institution provide evidence to ensure that graduates have requisite "content, pedagogical, and professional knowledge" (NCATE, 2008, p. 3) and be able to work well with other teachers. NCATE used multiple assessments (basic skills, content, professional skills, portfolio, supervisor observations, cooperating teacher observations, etc.) with appropriate feedback to determine whether candidates were classroom ready. Diversity, integration of technology, reflective practice for continuous improvement, and professional development have also been hallmarks of an NCATE accredited program.

Because about half of the business teacher education programs are housed within colleges of business, often one of two business program accreditations is involved. The AACSB expects evidence to be provided on continuous quality improvement through innovation, impact, and engagement. The 2012 business accreditation standards comprise 15 standards related to the following areas: Strategic Management and Innovation Standards (1–3), Participants Standards (4–7), Learning and Teaching Standards (8–12), Academic and Professional Engagement Standards (13–15). "AACSB accreditation is a voluntary, non-governmental process that includes an external review of a school's ability to provide quality programs...assurances of learning—self-evaluations, peer-reviews, committee-reviews, and the development of in-depth strategic plans" (Association to Advance Collegiate Schools of Business, n.d., para. 1). This accrediting process entails reviews of a school's mission, faculty qualifications, and curriculum.

The other business school accrediting agency is the ACBSP, which strives to be a leader in business education by "supporting, celebrating, and rewarding teaching excellence" (Accreditation Council for Business Schools and Programs, 2013, p. 1). This accrediting agency also focuses on continuous improvement. The ACBSP standards consider leadership, strategic planning, student and stakeholder focus, measurement and analysis of student learning and performance, faculty and staff focus, and educational and business program management.

Regardless of how many accreditations a business teacher education program may boast, the ultimate goal is to assure that teacher candidates are prepared and adequately qualified to facilitate and manage the learning process of those students they are ultimately privileged to teach. Therefore, the business education curriculum is a critical part of business teacher education licensure.

Curriculum Development

Curriculum development for traditional business teacher education programs should be guided by two major resources, the National Business Education Association's *National Standards for Business Education* (NBEA, 2013) and *Business Teacher Education Curriculum Guide* (National Association for Business Teacher Education, 2010). General education requirements as well as the specific needs of the profession in a particular geographic region must also be considered. For the past two decades, much of the focus has been on developing a curriculum that focuses primarily on technology. The current trend, however, focuses on a return to basic business (accounting, business law, economics, personal finance, etc.) in which technology is only a tool, not the platform for the entire course. There is a growing emphasis on soft skills (attitude, interpersonal communication, civility, manners, etc.), which have become more important for prospective employees entering a very competitive job market.

The business teacher education curriculum should require a specialized business methods course. The course should include methodology related to teaching business courses and skills, integrating student organizations, and managing cooperative and internship programs (Lambrecht & Kesten, 2012). Typically, a generic methods course does not prepare business teachers for all the intricacies of a traditional business education program and, as a result, may not adequately prepare them for outcomes assessment or the pursuit of excellence in the field.

Online Delivery

A growing trend in education is the provision of at least some online courses to complete a degree program. According to program information, 26 of the 54 institutions who are members of NABTE offer some type of online delivery for their business education degree program and/or licensure coursework ("Institutions Offering Degrees," 2012).

Completing online courses and understanding their development are important for business teacher education candidates as they may be required to develop and/or deliver online courses at the secondary and middle school levels. The International Association for K–12 Online Learning has established "quality guidelines for online course content, instructional design, technology, student assessment and course management" for increasingly popular online course offerings (Tonks, Weston, Wiley, & Barbour, 2013).

Student Assessment

Whether the business teacher education curriculum is delivered onsite or online, it is important to assess teacher candidates as they progress through their programs of study. Teacher candidates are subjected to multiple levels of assessment to ensure the acquisition of content knowledge, pedagogy, and professional dispositions necessary to be an effective classroom teacher. Before being admitted to a teacher education program at many institutions, a teacher candidate must successfully complete coursework and basic skills assessment. Some states have developed their own basic skills assessments (e.g., California, Colorado, and Georgia) or use components of other standardized instruments (ACT, GRE, and SAT) to document basic skills attainment. The majority of programs, however, use the Educational Testing Service Praxis I (Pre-Professional Skills Test: Reading, Writing, and Mathematics).

Two additional standardized assessments are typically required for business education teacher candidates after acceptance into the teacher education program: the PRAXIS II Principles of Learning and Teaching Grades 7–12 (which measures pedagogical knowledge) and the Praxis II Specialty Area Test for Business Education.

States that have add-on endorsements in related fields such as marketing, economics, and government may also use the Praxis II Specialty Area Tests as requirements for licensure. Specific information about each state's testing requirements can be located on the Educational Testing Service Web site (http://www.ets.org/praxis).

Tennessee's First to the Top initiative partnered with the National Institute for Excellence in Teaching (2012) to develop TEAM as an evaluation tool for classroom teachers. This model is also being used in the teacher education programs across the state to ensure that preservice teachers are aware of how they will be evaluated and expected to grow as professionals upon securing a teaching position. University supervisors of teacher candidates' clinical experiences engage in a four-day training session to prepare to use this tool effectively when evaluating candidates. This model is also being used in many other states.

Another innovative assessment model being used by 28 states and the District of Columbia is the edTPA (formerly the Teacher Performance Assessment). The edTPA model was designed by Stanford University through a partnership with the American Association of Colleges for Teacher Education (AACTE). This assessment model provides teacher preparation programs with multiple measures aligned with national standards, including Common Core State Standards (AACTE, 2013). For business education, teacher candidates must complete three major tasks. These include planning for instruction and assessment, instructing and engaging students in learning, and assessing student learning (AACTE, 2013). These tasks have multiple levels and require teacher candidates to upload artifacts into the edTPA management system during their clinical experience.

Clinical Placement

All traditional business teacher education programs require some form of clinical placement for initial licensure. Clinical placements are labeled in different ways and last for varying lengths of time (one semester to a full year) but serve the same practice teaching purpose. Student teaching, field experience, and teaching internship or externship are perhaps the most common names of these placements.

An example of one state's attempt to redefine teacher education is Tennessee's Ready2Teach program (Tennessee Board of Regents, 2010). This program requires students to demonstrate competency, mastery of content, learning by experience, guidance by experts, teaching by example, and development of strong partnerships with pre-K–12 schools. During their final year, candidates complete residency requirements.

The Residency I component allows teacher candidates to gradually increase their days per week in a school setting until they are spending about 50% of their time at their school assignment. While there, they work with a cooperating teacher performing various teacher duties and informally assisting with instruction; the other half of their time is spent finishing coursework. During the Residency II experience, teacher candidates devote 100% of their time in the school gradually working toward managing the cooperating teacher's full load of classes and duties; their cooperating teacher and university supervisor assesses the candidates' performance.

Instructional Faculty Qualifications

Regional, education, and business accrediting agencies and some professional organizations seek compliance in recruiting, retaining, and developing qualified faculty members to deliver the business teacher education curriculum. Qualifications for business teacher education faculty often include a terminal degree in business education or closely related field, a graduate or undergraduate degree from a teacher education program, teacher licensure, and middle and/or high school teaching experience.

The "Standard P–7: Faculty Section" of the Business Teacher Education Program Standards (NABTE, 2010) recommends that 75% of faculty members be full time, hold doctoral degrees, and be assigned to courses aligned with their educational preparation, teaching experience, and scholarship. There is an expectation that teacher education faculty be held to a high standard of professional and scholarly engagement beyond the teaching load, which includes professional development for continuous improvement. Performance appraisals are also required for documenting the maintenance of these standards.

Institutions accredited by NCATE expect qualified teacher education faculty to have earned doctorates or have exceptional expertise, level-appropriate school experience, and related scholarship. Faculty members are expected to model best practices in the areas of teaching, scholarship, service, and professional development. NCATE requires that faculty performance be evaluated annually. Both the AACSB and ABCSP accrediting bodies have similar standards relating to faculty qualifications.

Professional Involvement

Traditional and alternative business teacher education certification programs should encourage professional involvement of all teacher candidates. Business teacher education faculty members should model the desired professional involvement. One way to engage teacher candidates is through membership in the discipline's professional association. The NBEA's (n.d.) student membership provides business teacher candidates with a myriad of benefits, including liability insurance, journals, publications, webinars, conventions, and leadership and scholarship opportunities. Student membership should be required of every student enrolled in a business teacher education program as part of the business methods course.

Several NABTE institutions require teacher candidates to be members of the NBEA and the respective state business education association. Involvement in professional organizations may greatly benefit candidates, especially when they are evaluated during the first few years of teaching. In addition to providing educator resources, networking opportunities, up-to-date information, and teaching and research strategies and opportunities, professional organizations also provide the foundation for a new teacher to engage in what will hopefully become lifelong learning.

The PCBEE in its 2010 policy statement supported the notion of required student membership by stating that "...business teacher education programs can facilitate generativity by requiring students to join professional associations and instilling in them the desire and responsibility to continue membership throughout their careers" (p. 2). The commission further advocated that "non-traditional teacher education programs... be identified, contacted, and encouraged to promote professional association membership both by the teacher educators themselves and prospective business educators" (p. 2). In 2006 the PCBEE stressed that "the vitality and credibility of the profession is sustained through association activities, programs, and research" (p. 2).

In addition to professional organization membership at all levels, teacher education programs should emphasize the notion that it is a teacher's obligation to find ways to contribute to the profession on local, state, and national levels. Writing for professional publications about best instructional practices, developing professional peer relationships, mentoring, delivering in-service training, and assuming leadership roles in professional organizations are just a few of the many ways that a teacher can contribute to the profession.

ALTERNATIVE TEACHER EDUCATION CERTIFICATION OPPORTUNITIES

The number of individuals attaining teacher licensure through alternative methods has grown significantly in the past decade. The National Center for Education Information indicated that one-third of first-year public school teachers hired since 2005 have entered the profession through an alternative program rather than through a traditional college-based teacher education program. Figure 1 shows data in five-year intervals beginning with the 1985–1986 academic year. During that year, 275 teachers obtained alternative licensure. During the 2008–2009 academic year, 59,000 teachers received alternative licensure. Since then, around 60,000 individuals per year have been licensed through alternative programs (Feistritzer, 2011).

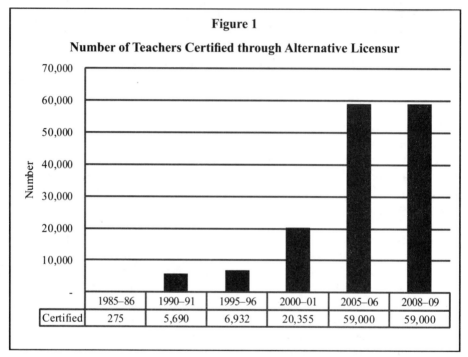

Figure 1

Number of Teachers Certified through Alternative Licensur

	1985–86	1990–91	1995–96	2000–01	2005–06	2008–09
Certified	275	5,690	6,932	20,355	59,000	59,000

The number of alternatively licensed business education teachers has increased as well. In a research study regarding traditionally versus nontraditionally licensed business education teachers, Gaytan (2009) determined that 69% of the study's respondents completed an alternative teacher certification program, whereas 31% completed a traditional program. Most nontraditionally certified teachers in the study "entered the teaching profession because of job dissatisfaction, retirement, change in marital status, or company reorganization" (p. 15). Other reasons individuals might pursue alternative teacher certification include layoffs from previous jobs, need for financial security, "empty nest" boredom, and a desire to work with young people.

Currently, almost all states offer at least one alternative route to teacher licensure; some offer a number of paths. State Web sites provide information about each state's programs; additionally, organizations such as Teach-Now (http://www.teach-now.org) and Teach for America (http://www.teachforamerica.org) provide alternative

Table 1. Web Sites of Post-Baccalaureate Alternative Teacher Licensure Programs by State*

States & Name(s) of Alternative Programs	Web Sites and/or Notes
Alabama Alternate Baccalaureate Level Certificate Career & Technical Alternative Level Certification	https://tcert.alsde.edu/Portal/Public/Pages/ Services/Certification.aspx
Alaska Alaska Transition to Teaching	http://education.alaska.gov/AKT2 http://education.alaska.gov/TeacherCertification
Arizona Arizona Teacher Prep Classroom Qualifier and Internship Programs	http://www.azed.gov/highly-qualified-professionals/ alternative-pathways-teacher-certification
Arkansas Professional Pathway to Education Licensure Master of Arts in Teaching Master of Education Troops to Teachers	http://www.teacharkansas.org http://www.arkansased.org/divisions/human- resources-educator-effectiveness-and-licensure/ educator-licensure-unit/routes-to-educator- licensure
California University Intern Credential Teach California	http://www.ctc.ca.gov/credentials/teach.html
Colorado Alternative Teacher Program Teacher in Residence	http://www.cde.state.co.us http://www.cde.state.co.us/cdeprof/Licensure_alt1_ info.asp
Connecticut Alternate Routes to Certification I and II	http://www.ctohe.org/ARC/pdfs/ARCICatalog.pdf
Delaware Alternative Routes to Certification Program Delaware Transition to Teaching	http://www.artc.udel.edu http://www.dt3p.udel.edu/description
Florida Alternative Certification Program	https://www.altcertflorida.org http://www.fldoe.org/edcert/pathways.asp
Georgia Teaching Academy for Preparation & Pedagogy Intern Certificate Master of Arts in Teaching Troops to Teachers	http://www.destinationteaching.org/how_to_ teach/ pathways/college.phtml http://www.gapsc.com/Certification/ RoutesToCert/AlternativeRoutes.aspx
Hawaii Alternative Program for Shortage Area Alternative Post-Baccalaureate Program Troops to Teachers	http://www.htsb.org/licensing-permits/ preparation-programs
Idaho Content Specialist and Computer-Based Alternative Route Teacher to New Certificate/Endorsement Post-Baccalaureate Alternative Route	https://www.sde.idaho.gov/site/teacher_ certification/alt_routes.htm
Illinois Alternative Route to Teacher Certification Alternative Teacher Certification	http://www.isbe.net/profprep/PDFs/alternate.pdf
Indiana Transition to Teaching Master of Arts in Career & Technical Education	http://www.doe.in.gov/student-services/licensing/ alternative-licensure

Table 1. Web Sites of Post-Baccalaureate Alternative Teacher Licensure...State* (cont.)

Iowa Teacher Intern	http://www.boee.iowa.gov/tilal.html
Kansas Restricted Teaching License Pathway	http://www.ksde.org/Agency/DivisionofLearning Services/TeacherLicensureandAccreditation/ Postsecondary/EducatorPreparation/Restricted TeachingLicenseAlternativePathway.aspx
Kentucky Exceptional Work Experience Certification Local District Training Program Certification University-Based Alternative Route Teach for America	http://kyepsb.net/certification/certaltroutes.asp
Louisiana Practitioner Teacher Program Master's Degree Program Certification-Only Program	https://www.teachlouisiana.net https://www.teachlouisiana.net/Prospect. aspx?PageID=605
Maine	Only mentioned on university Web sites; business education not mentioned as alternative program

Maryland
Resident Teacher Certificate Program
College of Notre Dame & Baltimore County
   Public Schools MAAPP
Tri-County Program for Early Childhood,
   Elementary, or Secondary Education
	http://www.marylandpublicschools.org/MSDE/
	divisions/certification/certification_branch

Massachusetts Preliminary and Professional Licenses Vocational Certification	http://www.doe.mass.edu/educators/directory.html
Michigan Alternate Program Leading to Interim Teaching Certificate Occupational Certificate	http://www.michigan.gov/documents/mde/Final_ MARITC_402558_7.pdf
Minnesota New programs to be established	http://education.state.mn.us/MDE/EdExc/Licen/ TrainTeachMN/050820
Mississippi MS Alternate Path to Quality Teachers Master of Art in Teaching Teach Mississippi Institute	http://www.mde.k12.ms.us/educator-licensure/ alternate-route-programs
Missouri Alternative or Innovative Route Temporary Authorization Teach for America	http://dese.mo.gov/eq/cert/routes-to-certification. htm
Montana Northern Plains Transition to Teaching	http://opi.mt.gov/Cert/index.html?tpm=1_1 http://opi.mt.gov/GetAnswers/questions/174/ Changing+careers http://www.montana.edu/nptt
Nebraska Transition to Teaching, Option I or II Master of Arts in Teaching	http://www.education.ne.gov/EducatorPrep/ TopPages/TTT.html http://www.unk.edu/coe.aspx?id=463

Table 1. Web Sites of Post-Baccalaureate Alternative Teacher Licensure...State* (cont.)

Nevada Secondary Career and Technical Certification (Alternate program name unavailable)	http://teachers.nv.gov
New Hampshire Alternative 3 or Alternative 4 Licensure	http://www.education.nh.gov/certification/ documents/alt3memo.pdf
New Jersey Certificate of Eligibility Alternate Route Certificate of Eligibility with Advanced Standing Alternate Route	http://www.state.nj.us/education/educators/license/ overview
New Mexico Alternative Licensure Program Online Portfolio Alternative Licensure Post-Secondary Vocational-Technical Alternate Program	http://teachnm.org/new-teachers/alternative- licensure-options.html
New York Alternative Teacher Preparation Program: Transitional B	http://www.highered.nysed.gov/ocue/spr/ AlternativeTeacherCertificationProgram.htm
North Carolina Lateral-Entry Program North Carolina Teacher Corps Master of Arts in Teaching	http://www.ncpublicschools.org/licensure http://www.ncpublicschools.org/licensure/lateral
North Dakota Transition to Teaching/Clinical Practice (CTE) Post-Baccalaureate Teacher Preparation Program	http://www.nd.gov/cte/teacher-cert http://www.nd.gov/espb/licensure/types.html
Ohio Alternative Resident Educator Program	http://education.ohio.gov/Topics/Teaching/ Educator-Licensure
Oklahoma Alternative Placement Program	http://ok.gov/sde/faqs/oklahoma-alternative- placement-program
Oregon Alternative Teacher Certification Programs Restricted Transitional License Three-Year Professional Technical License	http://www.ous.edu/programs/teached/files/ AdvisingGuide2005v6.pdf http://tspc.oregon.gov/support/News_Item_ Supplemental.asp?id=%20267&vid= %20 1&sid=4 http://www.ode.state.or.us/search/page/?id=3169 http://www.oregon.gov/tspc/Pages/Foreign- Degree-no-J1.aspx
Pennsylvania Teacher Intern Certification Program	http://www.portal.state.pa.us/portal/server.pt/ community/other_routes_to_certification/8818/ intern_certification/506789
Rhode Island Rhode Island Teacher Intern Program Alternate Route Preliminary Certification	http://www.ride.ri.gov/Portals/0/Uploads/ Documents/Teachers-and-Administrators- Excellent-Educators/Educator-Certification/ Becoming-an-Educator/Standards-for-Alternate- Route-to-Certification-Programs-FINAL-BoR- Adopted.pdf

Table 1. Web Sites of Post-Baccalaureate Alternative Teacher Licensure...State* (cont.)

South Carolina Program of Alternative Certification	http://www.teachercertificationdegrees.com/ certification/south-carolina-alternative http://ed.sc.gov/agency/se/Educator-Services/ Alt-Licensure http://ed.sc.gov/agency/se/Educator-Services/ Alt-Licensure/pace/PACEFAQ.cfm
South Dakota Alternative Teacher Certification Program	http://doe.sd.gov/oatq/altcert.aspx
Tennessee Transitional Teacher Licensure Program	http://www.state.tn.us/education/lic/new.shtml
Texas Alternative Certification Program	http://www.tea.state.tx.us/index2.aspx?id=7073
Utah Alternative Routes to Licensure Program CTE Alternative Preparation Program Transition to Teaching	http://www.schools.utah.gov/cte/business_ licensingapp.html http://www.schools.utah.gov/cte/documents/ business/licensing/ARLFAQ.pdf
Vermont Alternative Licensure Program: Peer Review	http://education.vermont.gov/new/html/licensing/ alternate.html http://education.vermont.gov/documents/EDU- Peer_Review_Overview_Fact_Sheet.pdf
Virginia Alternative Licensure Program Alternative Route for Career Professions	http://www.doe.virginia.gov/teaching/licensure/ multiple_licensure_routes.pdf http://www.doe.virginia.gov/teaching/licensure/ licensure_regs.pdf
Washington Post-Baccalaureate Routes 1, 2, 3 Master's in Teaching	http://pathway.pesb.wa.gov http://pathway.pesb.wa.gov/alternative_routes http://www.wsipp.wa.gov/rptfiles/altcertinterim.pdf
West Virginia Alternative Route to Certification Career & Technical Education Route Transition to Teaching Troops to Teaching	http://wvde.state.wv.us/teachwv/altroute_ certpgm.html http://wvde.state.wv.us/teachwv
Wisconsin Post-Baccalaureate Pathway to Certification Proficiency-Based Licensure Program Teach Development Center Alternative Licensure Program	http://tepdl.dpi.wi.gov/licensing/post- baccalaureate-pathway http://tepdl.dpi.wi.gov/files/tepdl/pdf/ AltRouteProgApprHandbook.pdf http://tepdl.dpi.wi.gov/files/tepdl/smarttaltroute programs.pdf
Wyoming Northern Plains Transition to Teaching	http://ptsb.state.wy.us/EducationResources/ AlternativeLicensingPrograms/tabid/87/ Default.aspx

* Based on information retrieved from state departments of education (and related) Web sites, April–July 2013. Information from state sites included throughout chapter.

certification programs. Table 1 lists state Web site addresses, type(s) of alternative certification, and initial teaching requirements.

Although alternative licensure programs vary from state to state, many of them have similar initial requirements. To enter a post-baccalaureate alternative program, candidates must have completed a bachelor's degree with a major or a specified number of hours of coursework in their chosen teaching field. Several states require a minimum grade point average of 2.5 (e.g., Alabama, Alaska, Iowa, Kansas, and North Dakota) or higher (e.g., Colorado, Connecticut, and Delaware). A few states require individuals to have a teaching position and to be officially recommended by the school superintendent or another designated school official (e.g., Connecticut and Kansas) before beginning an alternative program.

Once accepted into a program, participants typically receive a temporary, initial, or provisional teaching license that is valid for a specific period (licensure names and definitions vary from state to state). Table 2 shows information about teacher certification and program length.

Business Experience

Many alternative routes to teacher licensure, especially in career and technical education (CTE) fields, require industry experience; however, the amount varies among states and among types of CTE programs within states. Additionally, alternative teacher education programs require business experience more than traditional programs (Zirkle, Martin, & McCaslin, 2007). The number of hours and/or years required varies based on the CTE area, the type of diploma (high school, associate's, or bachelor's degree), and the certification plan.

Education and Training

Alternative licensure programs, like traditional teacher preparation programs, have similarities in their education and training requirements and in the methods used to deliver program content. Delivery channels may include workshops, mentoring relationships, face-to-face courses, online modules, and/or other methods. Activities may include portfolio development, teacher observations, and student teaching, among others. Programs require candidates to demonstrate content mastery in their field of study by passing either the Praxis content test or a state-approved content test (Yohon & Kesten, 2009). Additionally, teaching performance is routinely assessed.

Coursework. Most states require alternative licensure candidates to complete courses at specific regionally accredited colleges and universities or other designated state agencies. An individual program of study is assigned based on a candidate's transcript. Requirements usually include a specific number of hours in the candidate's field of study, methods courses related to the field of study, and coursework related to pedagogy. Some states have other requirements included on their state Web sites as

Table 2. Alternative Programs, Requirements, and Completion Time by State*

State	Undergraduate GPA required for alternative program	Basic skills test requirement	Subject area test requirement	No. of years to complete alternative program	Mentor/protégé requirement	Other requirements
Alabama	2.5	√	√	≤3	2.5	Teach only in subject area; teach in no more than two school systems during program
Alaska	2.5	√	√	2–3	√	Invitation to interview; recommendation of district official; cultural workshops; summer field experience
Arizona		√	√	2	√	English immersion training; three years of full-time teaching
Arkansas	2.5	√	√	2–3	√	Request from employing school system official
California		√	√	2+	√	Offer of employment and approval of local teacher union
Colorado	2.6		√	1–2		Statement of eligibility; completion of program through designated agency
Connecticut	3.0	√	√	<1	√	Teaching position; either summer (90 days) or weekend (8 weeks) program plus student teaching
Delaware	2.75	√	√	2		Request from district official to enroll; three seminars and four courses
Florida		√	√	3	√	CD-ROM and online training with online tutor, building-level administrator, and outside educator
Georgia		√	√	1–3	√	Job offer; request from employing school; GPA of 2.5 for some districts and routes
Hawaii		√	√	1–3		Teaching position; program based on teacher shortages in field
Idaho		√	√	2–3	√	School district request
Illinois		√	√		√	Five years industry work experience
Indiana	3.0	√	√	1	√	Evening courses two nights a week for one year; field experience; suicide prevention and CPR/Heimlich certification
Iowa	2.5				√	Three years post-baccalaureate work experience; 50 hours of field experience with students
Kansas	2.75	√	√	≤2	√	Verification that school system will hire and provide supervised practical teaching experience; written certification plan
Kentucky	2.5		√			Offer of employment

Table 2. Alternative Programs, Requirements, and Completion Time by State* (cont.)

State	Undergraduate GPA required for alternative program	Basic skills test requirement	Subject area test requirement	No. of years to complete alternative program	Mentor/protégé requirement	Other requirements
Louisiana	2.2	√	√	1–3		GPA of 2.5 after program completion
Maine		√				
Maryland		√	√	2.5	√	
Massachusetts		√	√	≤5	√	Four years business experience within the past seven years
Michigan	3.0	√	√	3–5	√	Coursework in reading, child development/psychology, family/community relations, diverse learners, and instructional strategies; CPR and first-aid course; field-based experience in classroom setting
Minnesota	3.0	√	√		√	New law regarding alternative licensure; no programs available currently but requirements listed
Mississippi	2.0+	√	√	≤5	√	Overall GPA of 2.5, or GPA of 2.75 in major if graduated in past seven years; practicum consisting of nine Saturdays
Missouri	2.5		√	≤2		Employment with school district
Montana	2.75		√	2–3		The Alternative Certification Program is completed online; proven career track record; teaching practicum; professional portfolio
Nebraska		√				Request from employing school district; completion of 75% of course requirements in field; human relations training; pre-teaching seminars; GPA of 2.75 in prescribed courses
Nevada		√	√	3		One year of paid or unpaid occupational experience
New Hampshire		√	√			Teaching and/or occupational experience; may require portfolio, oral exam, and/or letter confirming enrollment in CTE Certificate Program
New Jersey	2.5–2.75		√			Student teaching experience; for CTE, two to four years of occupational experience; examination in physiology, hygiene, and substance abuse
New Mexico		√	√	≤2		Course in teaching reading; portfolio preparation or student teaching based on alternative program

Table 2. Alternative Programs, Requirements, and Completion Time by State* (cont.)

State	Undergraduate GPA required for alternative program	Basic skills test requirement	Subject area test requirement	No. of years to complete alternative program	Mentor/protégé requirement	Other requirements
New York	3.0	√	√	3	√	Pre-employment component including 200 clock hours and 40 field hours
North Carolina	2.5–3.0		√	3		Program acceptance based on GPA and/or Praxis score conditions. For lateral program, official request from employing school; for Teacher Corps, pre-employment training segment
North Dakota	2.5	√	√		√	Verification of teaching position; history and philosophy of CTE course and coordinating techniques; 2,000 hours of occupational work experience; passing one industry computer proficiency (e.g., Microsoft Word) test; Native American Studies course
Ohio	2.5		√	4	√	Two years of related work experience (CTE); self-paced; enrollment in Intensive Pedagogical Training Institute
Oklahoma	2.5	√	√	≤3	√	Two years of work experience or completion of post-baccalaureate coursework in area; completion of resident teacher program
Oregon		√	√	3	√	Co-application with school district; for CTE, occupational experience; passing district appraisal committee exam; work experience
Pennsylvania	3.0	√	√	3		Pre-program requirements of six hours of college-level math and six of English; continuous program enrollment
Rhode Island	3.0		√	1		Summer pre-service training; teaching position; completion of The New Teacher Project Academy; successful first year may lead to three-year initial certificate
South Carolina		√	√	3	√	Teaching position; induction program; content-area methods course; for CTE, two years of work experience
South Dakota	2.5	√	√	3	√	Coursework in Indian studies and human relations; teaching position
Tennessee	2.75		√	1–3	√	Request to enter program from employing school district; orientation and professional development
Texas				1–2	√	Teaching position; screening requirements vary depending on alternative program and provider

Table 2. Alternative Programs, Requirements, and Completion Time by State* (cont.)

State	Undergraduate GPA required for alternative program	Basic skills test requirement	Subject area test requirement	No. of years to complete alternative program	Mentor/protégé requirement	Other requirements
Utah			√	≤3	√	Letter of eligibility; two to six years of work experience based on educational status; completion of New Teacher Academy; working portfolio; content methods course; professional growth plan
Vermont		√	√			Peer review; portfolio
Virginia		√	√	3		Recommendation of employing school district; five years of work experience or equivalent; field experience
Washington		√	√	2–3	√	
West Virginia	2.5	√	√			Teaching position; for CTE, related work experience
Wisconsin		√	√	3–5	√	Employment verification; portfolio; student teaching; possible GPA requirement
Wyoming	2.75		√	2–3		School district employment; U.S. and Wyoming Constitution courses; teaching practicum; portfolio

* Information retrieved October–November 2012 and May–July 2013. Programs may have additional requirements. Information may not apply to all alternative teacher licensure programs within a state.

well. For example, California requires language courses and a U.S. Constitution course, and Alaska requires computer and cultural courses.

Workshops. Preservice workshops usually take place in the summer before participants begin their first year of teaching and serve as part of the induction process into teaching. These workshops provide information that participants will need when beginning their first year of teaching (e.g., classroom management and assessment). State alternative programs generally require participants to complete workshops throughout the year as well. The workshops may or may not be counted as professional development.

Online training. Online courses and training modules provide a convenient method for delivering alternative teacher education program content to participants. States that offer preservice summer workshops often provide online training during participants' first year of teaching as well. As "teachers of record," alternative participants continue progressing through their programs of study while learning things they will use during their first year of teaching.

Professional development. A wide variety of professional development requirements exists for candidates pursuing alternative licensure. Some states exclude workshops and training related to the alternative licensure program as professional development; others refer to alternative workshops as professional development. Regardless of how professional development is defined within a state, candidates must typically complete a prescribed number of contact hours to obtain licensure.

Assessment

Alternative licensure candidates also take part in preprogram, program, and postprogram assessments. Assessments occur routinely, and outcomes are based on performance in the classroom and on other teacher-related responsibilities. Administrators, mentors, and others may assess candidates. Assessment, along with provided feedback, plays an important role in alternative programs.

Timeline

The length of time to complete most business education alternative certification programs is two to three years. This permits candidates adequate time to complete all the coursework, mentoring experiences, training, evaluation, and assessments required for certification while teaching full-time. The timeframe varies from state to state and program to program.

Certification Renewal

Initial alternative licensure can usually be extended for one to two years allowing time for a candidate to complete all requirements for a standard teacher license. Once a standard license is obtained, the renewal cycle would be the same for all teachers. The renewal cycle usually ranges from 5 to 10 years depending on the state requirements.

SUMMARY

Business teacher education leadership for traditional university programs is multifaceted. One area of program leadership involves recruiting teacher candidates into the profession. To assist in recruiting, NABTE has several resources that business education teachers can download and share with counselors, advisors, students, and others. Program leaders need to collaborate with stakeholders, including decision makers at the state board of education, business and education faculty in institutions of higher education, administrators and other teachers, businesspeople, students, parents, and the community.

Program leadership also involves ensuring that business teacher education programs adhere to national and state standards and that these standards drive student assessment, curriculum development, accreditation, and licensure.

Alternative business teacher education programs, which vary from state to state, have emerged to meet the growing demand for teachers. These alternative programs lead to initial and ultimately standard licensure through business experience, prescribed coursework, and assessment. Regulations and information regarding alternative licensure are typically provided on each state's department of education Web site. Regardless of the certification method, the goal of business teacher education programs is to prepare individuals to be effective teachers and leaders in the profession.

REFERENCES

Accreditation Council for Business Schools and Programs (ACBSP). (2013). About ACBSP. Retrieved from http://www.acbsp.org/?page=about_us

American Association of Colleges for Teacher Education (AACTE). (2013). edTPA: FAQ—General information. Retrieved from http://edtpa.aacte.org/faq#17

Association to Advance Collegiate Schools of Business (AACSB). (n.d.). Accreditation. Retrieved from http://www.aacsb.edu/accreditation/overview.asp

Council for the Accreditation of Educator Preparation (CAEP). (2013). Commission on standards. Retrieved from http://caepnet.org/commission

Feistritzer, C. E. (2011). *Profile of teachers in the U.S. 2011.* Washington, DC: National Center for Educational Information. Retrieved from http://ncei.com/Profile_Teachers_US_2011.pdf

Fisher, D. J., & Hagler, B. (2012). Business teacher education: Preparation and certification. In W. L. Stitt-Gohdes (Ed.), *Trends and issues in business education: NBEA 2012 yearbook* (No. 50, pp. 205–217). Reston, VA: National Business Education Association.

Fox, A. G., & Peters, M. L. (2013). First year teachers: Certification program and assigned subject on their self-efficacy. *Current Issues in Education, 16*(1), 1–16.

Gaytan, J. (2008). Teacher recruitment and retention: An essential step in the development of a system of quality teaching. *Career & Technical Education Research, 33*(2), 117–132.

Gaytan, J. (2009). Traditionally certified vs. non-traditionally certified business education teachers: Do both routes lead to high-quality teacher preparation? *NABTE Review, 36,* 10–16.

Hagler, B. (2009). Business education in the United States: 2006–2007 NABTE survey results. Unpublished manuscript.

Institutions offering degrees or licensure in business education. (2012, October). *Business Education Forum, 67*(1), 62–63.

Lambrecht, J., & Kesten, C. (2012). Major trends and issues affecting business education curriculum development. In W. L. Stitt-Gohdes (Ed.), *Trends and issues in business education: NBEA 2012 yearbook* (No. 50, pp. 1–15). Reston, VA: National Business Education Association.

National Association for Business Teacher Education (NABTE). (2010). *Business teacher education curriculum guide and program standards* (3rd ed.). Reston, VA: National Business Education Association.

National Business Education Association (NBEA). (2013). *National standards for business education: What America's students should know and be able to do in business* (4th ed.). Reston, VA: Author.

National Business Education Association. (n.d.). Member information: Member benefits. Retrieved from http://nbea.org/newsite/member/index.html

National Council for Accreditation of Teacher Education (NCATE). (2008). Unit standards in effect 2008. Retrieved from http://www.ncate.org/Standards/UnitStandards/UnitStandardsinEffect2008/tabid/476/Default.aspx

National Institute for Excellence in Teaching. (2012). *Tennessee Educator Acceleration Model (TEAM) evaluation system handbook.* Santa Monica, CA: Author.

Policies Commission for Business and Economic Education (PCBEE). (2005). *This we believe about business education as core academic content* (Statement No. 76). Retrieved from http://www.nbea.org/newsite/curriculum/policy/no_76.pdf

Policies Commission for Business and Economic Education. (2006). *This we believe about the value of professional associations* (Statement No. 79). Retrieved from http://www.nbea.org/newsite/curriculum/policy/no_79.pdf

Policies Commission for Business and Economic Education. (2008). *This we believe about the transformation and future of business education* (Statement No. 83). Retrieved from http://www.nbea.org/newsite/curriculum/policy/no_83.pdf

Policies Commission for Business and Economic Education. (2010). *This we believe about generativity in business education* (Statement No. 86). Retrieved from http://www.nbea.org/newsite/curriculum/policy/no_86.pdf

Tennessee Board of Regents. (2010). Ready2Teach: A program of the Tennessee Board of Regents. Retrieved from http://www.ready2teach.org

Tonks, D., Weston, S., Wiley, D., & Barbour, M. K. (2013). "Opening" a new kind of high school: The story of the open high school of Utah. *International Review of Research in Open and Distance Learning, 14*(1), 255–271.

Unruh, L., & Holt, J. (2010). First-year teaching experiences: Are they different for traditionally versus alternatively certified teachers? *Action in Teacher Education, 32*(3), 3–14.

Yohon, T., & Kesten, C. (2009). The effect of teaching license certification on challenges and needs of new business and marketing teachers. *NABTE Review, 36*, 17–23.

Zirkle, C. J., Martin, L., & McCaslin, N. L. (2007). *Study of state certification/licensure requirements for secondary career and technical education teachers.* University of Minnesota: National Research Center for Career and Technical Education. Retrieved from http://www.nccte.com/resources/publications/study-state-certificationlicensure-requirements-secondary-career-and

Leadership for Legislative Impact and Business Education Partnerships

Marlene Todd Stout
Indiana University Purdue University
Indianapolis, IN

Strong leadership, legislative advocacy, and business partnerships are essential to the continued prosperity of business education courses and programs. Business education teacher leadership and involvement at the local, state, and federal levels help to inform, support, and promote business education. This chapter addresses leadership and advocacy for business education, the National Business Education Association's (NBEA's) leadership in legislative advocacy activities and initiatives, strategies for states and regions to gain support for business education, and suggestions for forming business education partnerships.

LEADERSHIP IN ADVOCATING BUSINESS EDUCATION

Advocacy begins with a strong belief that business education is one of the most important disciplines in the school curriculum. A passion for the discipline is the first step.

Successful Advocacy for Business Education

Leadership is an essential component in securing support for business education. In addition to a viable curriculum and qualified teachers, business education programs need teachers to become leaders in promoting and advocating for business education. Leadership in business education includes being visionary and "is critical if the profession is to move forward in our fast-paced global society" (NBEA, n.d., p. 3).

Successful business education advocacy contributes to the promotion and security of business education programs. Advocates for business education are leaders who have a strong belief in the value and benefits of business courses for students and who are willing to speak up and speak out for business programs.

Ideas for Advocating Business Education

Taking the initiative to contact policy makers to explain business education and the ways in which it contributes to the policy maker's agenda is fundamental. For example, if the state or a legislator is promoting financial literacy, teacher leaders should meet with them to explain the ways in which business courses such as personal finance help to accomplish this initiative. Documentation that explains course content as well as the advantage of financial literacy as an existing course taught by qualified business teachers should be supplied. This dialogue is also an excellent opportunity for business partner support. Examples of business education leaders advocating for the profession include the following:

- During the revamping of teacher licensing in Indiana in 1989, it was proposed that business education as a teacher license be eliminated by the Indiana State Board of Education. Through the support of Indiana Business Education Partners and the work of business educators, business education remained as a teacher license.

- As a result of business educators' communication and contact with U.S. Department of Education (ED) personnel, staff members from ED's national office are now speakers at national and regional business education conferences and conventions.

- Because conversation with ED staff has increased, the connection between the department's financial literacy goals and the business education curriculum has been strengthened, resulting in conference calls, sharing of materials, and personal visits.

Advocating for business education means contacting policy makers and sharing information that documents the contribution business education courses and programs make to current national, state, and local education issues. The NBEA recognizes the importance of keeping members informed and engaged through the work of its Legislative Advocacy Committee.

NATIONAL BUSINESS EDUCATION LEGISLATIVE ADVOCACY COMMITTEE

The NBEA Legislative Advocacy Committee is dedicated to the development, support, and promotion of a grassroots approach to legislative initiatives, activities, and involvement and to the review of state and national legislation that impacts business education. Under the leadership of Patricia Moody, a former NBEA Legislative Advocacy Committee chairperson, the "One Big Voice," slogan was created. In addition, using her focus on national involvement and grassroots efforts, NBEA legislative activities and commitment were strengthened.

Legislative Advocacy Committee Structure

The NBEA Legislative Advocacy Committee consists of a chairperson (three-year term), a representative from each NBEA geographic region (three-year term), one at-large member (three-year term), the current NBEA president, and the NBEA executive director as an ex officio member (NBEA, 2013).

Duties of the chair. The legislative chair is responsible for the legislative seminar and legislative workshop at the annual NBEA national convention. The legislative chair also conducts committee meetings, disseminates information on current education initiatives and sets the direction for legislative activities with regional NBEA legislative representatives, establishes communications with federal officials, and shares education and legislative initiatives and activities that impact business education with NBEA members. As a legislative leader, the NBEA Legislative Advocacy Committee chair guides and directs legislative activities for NBEA members and works to influence policy makers regarding business education.

Duties of Legislative Advocacy Committee members. Committee members represent the committee throughout their regions. Committee members must exhibit strong leadership skills as they direct and guide legislative activities. They are responsible for arranging a legislative session at the regional convention and for disseminating legislative information to the regional and state business education association boards and legislative representatives. Committee members also promote state legislative grassroots initiatives and encourage a legislative session at state conferences. Through contact with state business education association presidents and state legislative representatives, committee members share information, generate interest, and promote legislative activities that impact business education at K–12, community college, and four-year institutions.

Legislative Process and Agency Contact

Knowledge of the legislative process benefits anyone working with legislative bills or activities impacting business education. Understanding the political process helps teachers know what steps must take place for a legislative bill to become a law. When engaged in legislative advocacy, business educators must be cognizant of whom to contact when supporting a legislative bill or trying to prevent it from being passed and signed into law (Pawlowski & Meeder, 2012).

Legislative law process. The U.S. House of Representatives Web site explains how laws are made, stating that "laws begin as ideas" and lists the following steps (condensed):

1. A representative sponsors a bill.

2. The bill is then assigned to a committee for study. If released by the committee, the bill is put on a calendar to be voted on, debated, or amended.

3. If the bill passes by simple majority (218 of 435), the bill moves to the U.S. Senate where it is assigned to another committee; if released, it is debated and voted on. Again, a simple majority (51 of 100) passes the bill. A bill can also originate in the Senate.

4. A conference committee made of House and Senate members then works out any differences between the House and Senate versions of the bill. The resulting bill returns to both the House and Senate for final approval.

5. The Government Printing Office prints the revised bill in a process called enrolling.

6. The President has 10 days to sign or veto the enrolled bill (U.S. House of Representatives, n.d.).

Departments of education. In addition to the federal and state process for a bill to become law, an awareness of federal and state departments of education and their structures is often the most critical when it pertains to actions that directly impact specific disciplines or programs.

U.S. Department of Education. The Office of Vocational and Adult Education within ED administers and coordinates programs related to adult education and literacy, career and technical education, Carl D. Perkins legislation and reauthorization, financial literacy initiatives, and community colleges (ED, 2013a). At the grassroots level, state departments of education may also propose, administer, and coordinate programs and initiatives that impact business education.

State departments of education. State boards of education often reside within the state departments of education. These departments and boards are often responsible for areas such as learning standards (and Common Core Standards if the state has adopted them); course titles; teacher licensing and certification; promotion of skills and knowledge such as financial literacy and technology for all students; and authorization for subjects to be taught by various disciplines, that is, economics and entrepreneurship in social studies and/or business. State business education supervisors are most often housed within departments of education if the state maintains a business education state supervisor.

Legislative Advocacy Program of Work Activities and Initiatives

The NBEA Legislative Advocacy program of work has the following goals: "(a) develop and implement a plan that will advance the importance of business education in strengthening the country's economy, and (b) advocate the importance of business education to the membership and external stakeholders" (NBEA, 2013, p. 4). These goals set the agenda and activities for the NBEA Legislative Advocacy Committee chairperson and committee members. Activities include arranging and/or conducting a legislative seminar and a lobbying workshop at the NBEA Convention and dissemination of information through the committee's legislative network.

Grassroots activities include training NBEA Legislative Advocacy Committee members to arrange and/or conduct a legislative session at regional conferences and to contact state business education association leaders to encourage them to include a legislative session at state conferences. In addition, the committee chairperson remains current on education and national budget items impacting business education; activities include attending the Association for Career and Technical Education (ACTE) National Policy Seminar, visiting with national legislators, and contacting and meeting with ED staff. Box 1 lists several flyers and information sheets developed by the NBEA and its Legislative Advocacy Committee for use in promoting business education when lobbying for business education.

Box 1. Useful NBEA Materials for Promoting Business Education	
College and Career Readiness	http://www.nbea.org/newsite/member/documents/ NBEACollegeandCareerReadinessFlyer.pdf
Business Education Prepares Students to Be College and Career Ready	http://www.nbea.org/newsite/member/documents/ NBEACollegeandCareerReadiness_PositionPaper.pdf
Our Business Is Your Business	http://www.nbea.org/newsite/member/documents/ BusinessPartnerFlyer_Final.pdf
FACTS Every Legislator Should Know about Business Education	http://www.nbea.org/newsite/member/documents/ Legislator.pdf

NBEA supports national-, state-, and local-level efforts to ensure that business education is understood and valued by legislators, policy makers, business people, parents, and other critical audiences. NBEA's Legislative Advocacy Committee represents association members through ongoing liaisons with U.S. Congressional staff members, federal officials, Congressional committees, state legislatures, and other professional associations. Materials promoting business education are available to assist conversations with legislators, business people, parents, students, counselors, and administrators (see NBEA's Web site at http://nbea.org/newsite/member/index.html).

Legislative Seminars, Sessions, and Workshops

During the NBEA's annual convention, its Legislative Advocacy Committee conducts a workshop designed to provide lobbying techniques and strategies and a legislative seminar to present national education updates to attendees (NBEA, 2012). The following illustrate these two activities:

Legislative workshop example. Marty Corry of Corry Associates of Boston and Charlie Stefanini presented lobbying strategies and suggestions for working with policy makers when advocating for business education at the 2012 NBEA Convention Legislative Workshop in Boston.

Legislative seminar example. At the legislative seminar during the 2012 NBEA convention in Boston, Julie Ewart, ED Region V director of communications and outreach, Great Lakes, discussed current department initiatives, including the Carl D. Perkins Vocational and Technical Education Act, Common Core State Standards, and personal finance. In addition to Julie Ewart's presentation, an ED teaching ambassador fellow talked with teachers about business education and the teaching profession. The Teaching Ambassador Fellowship Program is designed to improve education for students by involving teachers in the development and implementation of national education policy (ED, 2013b).

Legislative Advocacy Challenges and Results

For business education, as with many curricular areas or disciplines, advocacy depends on volunteers. Most NBEA business education professionals are employed, so finding time to actively engage in legislative activities is often difficult or impossible due to school restraints. In addition, state course mandates, college admissions requirements, and local school decisions about elective courses contribute to constraints in advocating for business education.

In spite of these challenges, business professionals continue to work with policy makers at local, state, and national levels. Strides are being made as NBEA connects with education personnel about the business education curriculum. Communication has been established between the NBEA and ED Communications and Outreach, the ACTE Division of Academic and Technical Education, and the Office of Vocational and Adult Education to discuss business education and financial education common goals.

STRATEGIES FOR LEGISLATIVE ADVOCACY AT REGIONAL AND STATE CONFERENCES

Inclusion of a legislative session at regional and state conferences is essential to providing the education and legislative updates business teachers need as they work to promote business education programs within local schools. These legislative sessions provide the opportunity to inform business teachers of national education initiatives, state government activity, and past, present, and future proposals from state departments of education. Such sessions address issues impacting business programs including curriculum, course titles, teacher licensing, Perkins funding, Common Core State Standards, college and career readiness, and increased graduation requirements.

Keys to Successful Legislative Sessions

Two key elements to a successful legislative session include (a) selecting topics that are relevant and (b) actively promoting the session. Scheduling the session at a time that does not conflict with key conference sessions or does not compete with many other sessions are also important strategies. Examples of legislative sessions conducted at NBEA regional conferences include the following:

- **Western Business Education Association.** The 2011 conference featured education updates by Heather Dye, Nevada Department of Education, Office of the Superintendent, arranged by Helen Humbert, member of both the NBEA and WBEA Legislative Committees.

- **Mountain-Plains Business Education Association.** The 2011 conference included a presentation by Sheryl Penning-Keller, Mountain-Plains Legislative Committee member on Common Core State Standards and President Obama's Blueprint for Reform.

- **Southern Business Education Association.** The 2010 conference held a legislative workshop. Packets were available for distribution for each state that included (a) a list of each state's legislative Web site with comments on locating legislators, (b) the new NBEA *Facts Every Legislator Should Know about Business Education* for each chair, and (c) *Our Business Is Your Business* button.

- **North Central Business Education Association** (NCBEA). The 2011 conference included a session on important strategies, tips, and techniques for working with legislators and policy makers presented by Cathy Carruthers and Gary Hutchinson. *Ideas for Legislative Advocacy* packets were also distributed (NCBEA, 2010). At the 2012 NCBEA conference, Julie Ewart, ED Region V director of communications and outreach, Great Lakes, provided national education updates (NBEA, 2012).

Examples of legislative activities conducted by various state business education association conferences include the following:

- **Virginia.** The Virginia association posted a legislative information Web page that includes links to legislative information and U.S. Congressional representatives' e-mail addresses.

- **Pennsylvania.** The Pennsylvania association held a discussion on and distributed the NBEA business education standards. (NBEA, 2012).

- **Indiana.** The Indiana association held a legislative session at its November 2010 state conference at which Marlene Todd Stout shared her experience testifying before the Indiana Senate Education Committee on financial literacy. Attendees also received financial literacy materials to use when advocating for business education.

- **Missouri.** The Missouri association featured a state legislative session at its state conference with presenter Thresia Brinkly, its legislative director, entitled "How to Lobby from Your Laptop / Can You Influence Your Legislators?" This session included a discussion on current education issues that impact all educators now and in the future, with information needed to make a difference in the state capital, Jefferson City, Missouri, and in Washington, DC, and on upcoming education legislation, including copies of pending bills, new books on educational practices, and a copy of the national educational agenda (Missouri Business Education Association, 2012).

State legislative sessions are most successful when they inform and engage teachers. Examples of legislative/advocacy sessions include teacher licensing updates, new course titles or course offerings, Perkins legislation funding updates, legislative strategies and techniques (how-to sessions), career pathways, Common Core State Standards, college and career readiness, college requirements, and teacher evaluation systems and updates.

Engaging Business Teachers in Legislative Sessions and Activities

Involving business teachers in legislative activities and state and regional legislative/advocacy sessions is an important way to disseminate information and generate interest in legislative/advocacy activities. Legislative action takes place at all levels. Working with policy makers such as principals, superintendents, deans, and presidents at the local school or college level often determines the support for business courses, programs, and departments. Including activities that bring policy makers into the classroom or school can generate awareness and support of business courses and programs. Hosting a "state legislator day" when state legislators are invited to visit schools and business classes provides local grassroots communications. A legislative session detailing how to conduct a "state legislator day" with the preparation, activities, pictures, and end results or benefits of the activity would help and encourage other teachers.

When one business teacher takes the initiative to become involved and works to gain support for business classes, other teachers often follow. It cannot be "business as usual." Business teachers must recognize the importance of speaking out and working with policy makers to gain recognition and support for business education and the importance of mentoring fellow teachers. A beginning is to invite fellow teachers to attend or participate in legislative/advocacy sessions. So often, lack of participation is based on not knowing how to work with policy makers and/or not being asked. Conducting legislative sessions that engage business teachers and provide current national, regional, and state education information and updates provides a valuable service to members as they work to promote and secure business programs within their schools and state.

Being proactive in promoting business education is one of the most important aspects of legislative and advocacy endeavors. As state and local governments or policy makers establish regulations and engage in new initiatives about such topics as graduation requirements, course titles, teacher licensing, use of various courses for financial literacy, college and career readiness, Common Core State Standards, or inclusion of courses that generate additional federal or Carl D. Perkins legislation funding, business educators must demonstrate strong leadership in communicating the reasons for including business education. Proactive involvement also includes development of business education partnerships that help promote and support business education.

PROGRAM ADVOCACY THROUGH BUSINESS EDUCATION PARTNERSHIPS

One way to strengthen support for business education and to also demonstrate strong leadership is through the establishment of partnerships. The Policies Commission for Business and Economic Education (2002) stated, "Establishing partnerships is an integral part of any business program. Partnerships must be formed to provide an awareness of and visibility for business education in meeting the needs of a dynamic global environment" (p. 1).

Purpose of Business Education Partnerships

School business partnerships exist to promote and sustain quality partnerships between the academic and business/professional community (Anchorage School District, 2013). One purpose of Perkins IV legislation is supporting partnerships among secondary schools, postsecondary institutions, bachelor's degree–granting institutions, career/technical education schools, local workforce investment boards, business and industry, and intermediaries (Southern Regional Education Board, 2007).

Mutual Benefits of State Partnerships

State government officials and businesses within the state are concerned about economic development, a skilled workforce, a strong education system, and job opportunities. Working with business partners to garner support for business education programs will, in turn, help provide business and industry with a qualified workforce and a stronger economic base; as mutual goals are met, both business and business education programs are strengthened (Richmond Public Schools, n.d.). Sharing the joint benefits of the partnership will generate increased interest and willingness for business people to engage in the partnership.

Types of Partnerships

The development of partnerships is driven by the purpose or need. School business partnerships exist to promote and sustain quality relationships between the academic and business/professional community (Anchorage School District, 2013). Career and technical education partnerships exist with businesses and industries. In Missouri, more than 31,000 employers serve on career and technical education advisory committees each year. These committees provide valuable input concerning the relevancy of career and technical education curricula, equipment, and local job opportunities (Missouri Association for Career and Technical Education, 2002).

The type and nature of business education partnerships vary depending on the need for which the partnership is created. Types of partnerships include the following:

One-to-one institutional partnership. The needs of one school and/or one business drive the agreement. Traditionally, business is the benefactor and the school is the beneficiary. With this arrangement, schools benefit from the generosity of their business partners by receiving up-to-date equipment, incentives for student attendance and scholarship, and opportunities for students to learn about the real-world application of knowledge and skill. Businesses' involvement in such traditional partnerships is typically philanthropically inspired, but it can also be attached to long-term goals that reflect self-interest—a better prepared entry-level workforce that would reduce training costs, increase productivity, and improve products and services (Lankard, 1995). The partnerships share resources while focusing program decisions on improved student learning (Watts & Levine, 2010).

Advisory board partnerships. Advisory board partnerships are designed to assist departments with review of a curriculum, recommendations on equipment needs, student organization assistance, and possibly support from local administrators. In the right hands and with the right structure and formulation, an advisory board can become the lifeblood of an energized program and a school that is well connected and well supported by its community (Pawlowski & Meeder, 2012).

School business partnership program. This type of partnership offers opportunities for students, teachers, businesses, and community agencies to build partnerships that will enhance students' experiences, provide more knowledgeable future employees and consumers, and build bridges of understanding and positive working relationships between the business and education community (Anchorage School District, 2013). The "It's in the Bank" partnership between a bank and high school business education department in Connecticut exemplifies a successful school and business partnership that benefited students through increased financial literacy, rigor, internships, and career pathways and benefited the business partner with greater presence in the school, the opportunity to provide support, and an increased pool of potential employees (Deasy, 2011).

State association partnerships. State association partnerships between business educators and the business community can provide invaluable assistance on statewide issues or situations that impact business education. Although local school partnerships benefit an individual school and program, the state partnership exists to support the business education discipline within the state.

Starting a state partnership. The creation of the partnership begins with the association determining the goals and the mission; establishing the framework; deciding who will assume responsibility for this partnership, such as the president, executive director, or legislative board member; identifying the desired outcomes; and establishing the meeting mechanics (when, where, and how often the meetings take place). An example of a mission statement might be "The mission of the [state] association partners is to provide leadership as an advocacy group to strengthen, support, and promote business education to meet the needs of students and employers" (Indiana Business Education Association, 1995).

Securing partners. The second step is to secure partners that can be of benefit in advocating business education. It is important to seek influential and diverse people within the state from different regions or areas. Members should represent various types of businesses and occupations. Examples of possible partners include legislators, chairs of house/senate education committees, representatives from political parties (both parties), business association lobbyists, and experienced education lobbyists for the teacher, principal, superintendent, independent college and university, collegiate, and admissions officer associations. It is also important to include partners from industries or associations such as manufacturing, banking, Fortune 500 companies, state chambers of commerce presidents or education officers, entrepreneurs, and other state associations, such as state CPA associations.

Business partnerships provide support for local schools and business departments, state business education associations, and national programs (Walker, 2012). Developing a relationship with people from business and industry, lobbyists, other state business associations, and policy makers helps to promote business education and provides mutual support for the benefit of students and businesses.

LEGISLATIVE AND PARTNERSHIP MATERIALS

Materials explaining business education are essential when working with policy makers. These materials help to communicate what business education is and how business education can support a specific bill, program, requirement, or issue that is being sponsored or promoted, and these materials can be left behind for further review. Legislative or advocacy materials provide critical talking points when meeting with legislators, lobbyists, business partners, principals, or other key officials. The NBEA has a range of materials available to help advocate and promote business education.

Examples of Legislative/Advocacy Materials

Sample materials available or produced by NBEA or NBEA members are available on NBEA's Web site (http://nbea.org/newsite/member/index.html) under "Business Education Advocacy" and in the NBEA Bookstore (http://www.mcssl.com/store/nbea-onlinebookstore). Materials include the following:

- *Person to Person: Working with Policy Makers to Support Business Education*

- *FACTS*

  o *Facts Every Business Should Know About Business Education*

  o *Facts Every Legislator Should Know About Business Education*

  o *Facts Every Parent Should Know About Business Education*

  o *Facts Every Student Should Know About Business Education*

  o *Facts Every Counselor Should Know About Business Education*

  o *Facts Every Administrator Should Know About Business Education*

- *College and Career Readiness*

- *Our Business Is Your Business*

- *Talking Points for Financial Literacy*

Partnership Materials

Providing professional documents to business partners helps to convey the quality and professionalism of business education and business educators.

Support documents. Business partners are busy people. Determining when, where, and how often to meet is critical for a successful partnership. Electronic communications such as conference calls, social networking, and e-mail are communication options when traditional meetings are not an option for some business partners. Being open to alternative meeting arrangements may help in recruiting partners that do not have time for face-to-face meetings. Using documents that help support the state association's goals will provide the information the partners need to support the business education issue. Documents provided by the NBEA help to explain business education to partners; a business partner document that explains the mission, purpose, members, and relations with business education shows that business education has the support of people from business and industry.

The following advocacy materials are available in ACTE's Advocacy Toolkit (https://www.acteonline.org/advocacy/#.Ut16X_Qo5wl):

- *Building Relationships with Policy Makers*

- *Visiting Policy Makers*

- *Corresponding with Policy Makers*

- *Hosting Site Visits for Policy Makers*

- *Testifying before Policy Makers*

- *Using Social Media for Advocacy*

The use of advocacy materials and the development of documents for school or a specific state situation is important. Documented facts and information help to "tell the story" and provide talking points when working with policy makers.

SUMMARY

This chapter discusses the importance of leadership in directing and influencing policy, the NBEA Legislative Advocacy Committee, the legislative process, and legislative and advocacy activities and materials. Strong business educator leadership and advocacy is vital to the future of business education. The creation of business education partnerships that support business programs and courses is a fundamental advocacy component that helps defend, maintain, and support business programs.

As national and state education agendas continue to change and course requirements that meet college and career readiness and common core standards increase, business education professionals must expand communications and association with policy makers at the national, state, and local levels. Advocating for business education will continue to be an integral part of being a business educator and leader.

REFERENCES

Anchorage School District. (2013). School business partnerships. Retrieved from http://www.asdk12.org/depts/sbp

Deasy, K. (2011). It's in the bank: A successful school banking partnership. *Business Education Forum, 65*(4), 20–21.

Indiana Business Education Association. (1995). Indiana partners. Unpublished manuscript.

Lankard, B. A. (1995). *Business/education partnerships. ERIC Digest No. 156.* Retrieved from ERIC database at http://www.ericdigests.org/1996-1/business.htm (ED383856).

Missouri Association for Career and Technical Education. (2002). Business partnerships. *Missouri ACTE Newsletter 702.* Retrieved from http://www.mo-acte.org/ mentor-a-legislator/missouri_acte_newletter_702.pdf

Missouri Business Education Association. (2012, July). Preconference sessions & conference agenda. Retrieved from http://www.mo-acte.org/conferences/division programarchive/2012/mbea

National Business Education Association (NBEA). (2012, March 1). *Legislative Advocacy Committee report.* Reston, VA: Author.

National Business Education Association. (2013, June 1). *Program of work (POW).* Reston, VA: Author.

National Business Education Association. (n.d.). *Leadership in business education.* Reston, VA: Author.

North Central Business Education Association (NCBEA). (2010, Fall). Ideas for legislative advocacy. NCBEA Legislative Committee. Retrieved from http://www.ibea.org/ our-organization/advocacy-items

Pawlowski, B., & Meeder, H. (2012, February 28). Advisory boards that matter [Webinar]. Retrieved from http://eo2.commpartners.com/users/acte/session.php?id=8458

Policies Commission for Business and Economic Education (PCBEE). (2002). *This we believe about the need for partnerships in business education* (Statement No. 70). Retrieved from http://nbea.org/newsite/curriculum/policy/no_70.pdf

Richmond Public Schools. (n.d.). What are the benefits of a school-business partnership? Retrieved from http://web.richmond.k12.va.us/Departments/School CommunityPartnerships/About/WhatarethebenefitsofaSchoolBusinessPartner.aspx

Southern Regional Education Board. (2007, January). *Using the new Perkins Legislation to advance high school reform.* Retrieved from http://www.isbe.net/career/pdf/new_ perkins_legislation21.pdf

U.S. Department of Education (ED). (2013a). OVAE Office of Vocational and Adult Education. Retrieved from http://www2.ed.gov/about/offices/list/ovae/index. html?src=oc

U.S. Department of Education (ED). (2013b). Teaching Ambassador Fellowship. Retrieved from http://www2.ed.gov/programs/teacherfellowship/index.html

U.S. House of Representatives. (n.d.). The legislative process. Retrieved from http:// www.house.gov/content/learn/legislative_process

Walker, D. L. (2012, November/December). Building robust community partnerships. *Techniques, 87*(8), 36–38. Association for Career & Technical Education.

Watts, E., & Levine, M. (2010). Examples of partnerships, practices, and policies to support clinically based teacher preparation: Selected examples. Retrieved from http://www.ncate.org/LinkClick.aspx?fileticket=rMrsfjZ2vZY%3d&tabid=715

Leadership in State-Level Business and Career and Technical Education Divisions

Jean M. Kyle

Minnesota Department of Education

Roseville, MN

"A defining challenge of leadership is whether you can answer a question that is as simple as it is powerful: Are you learning as fast as the world is changing?" (Taylor, 2012, para. 2).

Many changes have occurred in society, education, and business since the topic of state-level supervision of business education was addressed in yearbooks published by the National Business Education Association (Briggaman, 1993; Lloyd, 1978). However, many of the guiding principles and concepts that affect the work of the state-level business education supervisor have remained constant.

According to Lloyd (1978), the increase of state-level supervisory positions for business education correlates with the passage of the Vocational Education Act of 1963. As states implemented provisions of the law, they were permitted to use federal funds for state supervisory positions and were able to construct the duties and responsibilities in accordance with individual state vocational education structure and need. Likewise, Briggaman (1993) stated that "constant social, economic, political, and technological changes continue to make achieving the goals of business education increasingly difficult" (p. 154) and stressed that "strong, dynamic, innovative state-level leadership" (p. 154) is a must if business education is to continue its strong educational impact.

Today, the challenges for state supervisors are many; the speed of change in the business world is rapid, and technology is evolving in ways that were only dreamed about in years past. State supervisors are constantly striving to keep pace with a learning curve that appears ever steeper. The aim of this chapter is to assist business education state supervisors in learning and leading, so that they are well prepared to meet and master the formidable challenges they face.

STATE SUPERVISOR COMPETENCIES AND PERSONAL TRAITS

The state supervisor of today is in a multifaceted role that is filled with an astonishing array of responsibilities, duties, and expectations. This role and its incumbent responsibilities vary widely from state to state; the duties are carried out in reference to a constantly changing business, legislative, educational, and societal climate. In this critical leadership role, the state supervisor is often the link between these influential factors and classroom teachers and is the one who communicates much of the "big picture" change to teachers. Although it may be daunting and difficult to manage such a large span, it is a key responsibility of the state supervisor to be current on many topics. These may include but are not limited to education legislation, education funding, state education plans, teacher preparation and licensure, standards and assessment, technology, career and technical student organizations, program development and evaluation, professional development, and all curricular areas of business.

In addition to the necessary professional knowledge, technical skills, and various responsibilities of the state supervisor's role, there is also the more intangible leadership aspect to consider, and that leadership element is quite difficult to quantify. In preparation for this article, the author informally surveyed several current and former state supervisors, business teachers, and business teacher educators regarding their perspectives on state supervision of business education. One of the key questions asked was, "What are the most important leadership characteristics/traits for a state business education supervisor to possess?" The responses were surprisingly similar and offered a robust list of competencies and personal traits, as shown in Table 1.

Competencies and traits that survey respondents identified appear to reflect those articulated as the 12 qualities of leadership by Bethel (1986):

- Be courageous
- Be a big thinker
- Be a change master
- Be ethical
- Be persistent and realistic
- Have a sense of humor
- Be a risk taker
- Be positive and filled with hope
- Be morally strong
- Be a decision maker
- Accept and use power wisely
- Be committed

Table 1. Business Education State Supervisor Leadership Characteristics/Traits

Competencies	Personal Traits
Technology proficiency	"Good listener"
Communication	Energetic
Public speaking	Enthusiastic
Business and industry connections	Honest
Classroom experience; skilled, veteran teacher	Ethical
Standards knowledge	Integrity
Assessment expertise	Style
Professional development experience	Diplomatic
Presentation skills	"Quick study"
Student organization experience	Sense of humor
Professional organization memberships	Consensus builder
Curriculum development experience	Empathic
Organized	Motivated and motivating
Legislative issues understanding	Fair
Research skills/ability	Ability to coach
Knowledge of current business methods	Caring
Accuracy in tasks	Visionary
Handling complex situations	Confident
Ability to balance many complex tasks	Confidence in others
Understanding process and protocol	Supportive
Highly skilled group facilitator	Courage
	Outgoing and friendly
	"Leads by example"

State Supervisor Perspective

The value of prior classroom teaching experience appears to be one of the most important and unchanged elements for success as a state supervisor (Lloyd, 1978). All state supervisors surveyed mentioned prior classroom teaching experience, and many listed it as the most important element for success in the role of state-level leader for business education. Most shared that classroom teaching experience gives a context, background, and depth to the supervisor's job performance that would be difficult to obtain and master in any other preparation for or pathway to the position.

State supervisors in the survey group suggested that it is the skillful application of these identified competencies and personal traits that enables the supervisor to perform well in such a complex role. Furthermore, these state supervisors indicated that the more advanced the supervisor was in employing these competencies and traits, the more likely the position duties and tasks were achieved and state-level goals for business education reached.

A typical response about the span and varied elements of the duties of a state supervisor were stated by Connecticut State Supervisor Lee Marcoux:

> I am responsible for planning and executing programs for the improvement of Business Education in local school districts to benefit students, as well as assuring that these programs are responsive to societal and business needs. I provide assistance to school districts and teachers in the implementation and expansion of Business Education programs. Other responsibilities include: National Board Teacher Certification, Connecticut Future Business Leaders of America, and personal finance curriculum. (personal communication, April 26, 2013)

As business education state supervisor in Nebraska, Bonnie Sibert aptly stated that "Supervisors need to have been a teacher and 'walked in their shoes' to be able to truly support local teachers, postsecondary educators, and administrators" (personal communication, April 24, 2013).

Another perspective on state supervisor characteristics comes from Eric Swenson, Montana state supervisor:

> Perhaps the most important characteristic of a state supervisor is to have experience within the classroom and to have been a local career and technical student organization chapter advisor. This experience really helps the state supervisor [to] be able to identify with the expansive business education curriculum being taught, as well to understand the relationships [among] the curriculum, the business education program, and the career and technical student organizations. (personal communication, April 29, 2013)

Classroom Business Teacher Perspective

When classroom teachers were asked to comment on responsibilities and desired characteristics of state supervisors for business education positions, David Braaten (personal communication, April 22, 2013) from Hopkins High School in Minnesota shared the following:

- **Support:** A state supervisor is a support system to classroom teachers. To me, the state supervisor is the person who knows and understands policy and law as it relates to programs under the federal and state guidelines. This person helps school districts and teachers understand and be in compliance with these structures.

- **Advocate:** The state supervisor is a person who supports and advocates for teachers! He or she stimulates teachers to be creative and innovative in their programming and helps teachers to think outside the box while still adhering to state standards and benchmarks. In addition, this person helps educators find ways to implement new and innovative ideas that will stimulate learning.

- **Resource:** The state supervisor is a wealth of knowledge with resources for the various curricular areas. This person attends the national, state, and local level professional development opportunities to help gather and understand what is trending in the related curricular areas as well as encourages and supports classroom teachers to participate in these opportunities. This person looks for real opportunities for teachers and programs to expand their curriculums, i.e.: personal finance becoming a required subject.

- **Networking:** The state supervisor helps schools and teachers to network and connect with each other. He or she helps connect K–12 and postsecondary education teachers together as well as helps bridge the education community with business and industry partnership opportunities.

Business Teacher Educator Perspective

Another dimension of successful state-level supervision of business education is a strong, positive relationship with faculty in teacher education institutions who prepare future business teachers and provide teacher in-service activities. Preservice teachers are often introduced to a state supervisor through this channel. This relationship building by a state supervisor helps assure there will be well-prepared business teachers to fill classroom openings as veteran business teachers retire.

When several faculty members from teacher education programs were asked to comment on the state supervisor position responsibilities and characteristics, Dr. Jeannette Karjala (personal communication, April 22, 2013), professor emerita, Winona State University in Minnesota and long-time teacher educator responded:

- From a retired university-level business education professor's perspective, a business education content specialist at the state department of education level is designated to work with K–12 business educators. Overseeing the business education content at the state-wide level is important. In addition, the specialist's position involves maintaining business education content standards, evaluating business education programs, helping to ensure quality, and aiding in outreach and communication among the range of educational in-state institutions—elementary, secondary, and postsecondary.

- Basically, the content specialist serves as the "face" of the state's business education program and maintains the right professional tone by reaching out to educators at the K–12 and postsecondary levels to maintain curriculum that is effective, meaningful, and engaging at all levels. The business education content specialist ensures the maintenance of business education as a part of the career and technical education (CTE) family. Business education programs at all levels need to be inclusive, comprehensive, and accessible. Through encouragement of coordination, cooperation, and collaboration among business educators at all levels, the business education specialist ensures that these three C's are incorporated within the business education programs and plans.

RESPONSIBILITY FOR IMPLEMENTING EDUCATION LEGISLATION

A major expectation for business education state supervisors is to be the authority for leading teachers in implementing various legislative enactments relating to education.

The Carl D. Perkins Career and Technical Education Improvement Act of 2006 (P.L. 109-270), commonly referred to as Perkins IV, supports the development of academic and career and technical skills among secondary education students and postsecondary education students who enroll in career and technical education (CTE) programs. Perkins IV was authorized through fiscal year 2012, and the authorization was extended through fiscal year 2013 under the General Education Provisions Act (Carl D. Perkins Act, 2006).

Perkins IV

A notable change from Perkins III to Perkins IV was stronger accountability measures and the move toward a program of study model. Under Perkins IV, two key requirements for receiving funds under the Basic State Grants program are (a) offering CTE programs of study and (b) compliance with accountability requirements. Under the Perkins IV law, secondary and postsecondary education providers must adopt the appropriate elements of at least one state-approved CTE program of study. A working definition of a program of study is that the model incorporate secondary and postsecondary education elements into a coordinated, nonduplicative progression of courses leading to an industry-recognized credential, certificate, or degree. Perkins IV (2006) requires that states and secondary and postsecondary education providers meet targets on statutorily defined performance measures or face sanctions, which is a stronger accountability measure than the law previously provided.

State supervisors usually have a role in their states for implementing Perkins IV, and many have been instrumental in developing their state model for a program of study and technical skill attainment measures. Although the role of the supervisor is not directly addressed in the Perkins Act, the duties that state supervisors carry out under Perkins are allowable and may be funded in part under either administration or leadership sections of the Perkins Act. The Perkins Act clearly defined permissible activities by states in administration and leadership areas, but the states decide on the role and responsibility of a state supervisor in relationship to their state plan for implementation of the Perkins Act (Association for Career and Technical Education & Brustein, 2006).

Perkins V

A plan for Perkins V entitled *Investing in America's Future: A Blueprint for Transforming Career and Technical Education* (U.S. Department of Education, 2012) outlines the reauthorization of Perkins IV). If enacted by the U.S. Congress, this plan shows an effort to create more high-quality CTE programs under Perkins V. This blueprint advances the policy goals for all high school graduates being prepared to be college and career ready and for the United States to have the highest proportion of college graduates in the world. The blueprint calls for rigorous, relevant, and results-driven CTE shaped by four core principles:

- More effective alignment of CTE programs with labor-market needs and high-growth industry sectors, in particular

- Stronger collaboration among secondary and postsecondary institutions, employers, and industry partners in an effort to improve the quality of CTE programs

- A meaningful accountability system based upon common definitions and clear metrics for performance

- Increased innovation supported through systemic reform of state policies and practices

Considerable differences exist between Perkins IV and the proposed Perkins V. State supervisors will need to be fully aware of how these changes will impact their work and the implications of these changes for business programs and teachers.

Many states provide additional funding for CTE through a variety of state and/or local levy (tax) systems. This funding provides additional support for programs and is typically calculated through a funding formula that is set by either a state legislature or, in some states, a local governing body. Some state supervisors have responsibilities connected with the administration of these funding sources.

Developing and/or implementing policies relating to education is another important area of responsibility for state supervisors.

RESPONSIBILITY FOR POLICY DEVELOPMENT

The state supervisor is often called on by teachers, school administrators, professional organizations, or other stakeholders for assistance in developing and/or implementing education policy, specifically those policies relating to CTE and business education. This responsibility requires that supervisors are current in their knowledge of education policy.

A valuable resource for supervisors is the work of the Policies Commission for Business and Economic Education, which "exists to identify and define both existing and emerging issues in business and economic education" (National Business Education Association, n.d., para.12). Commission members annually research, write, and publish two policy statements on what business education professionals believe about current issues facing the profession. The commission's work builds understanding of key issues and focuses response on those issues. By providing a better understanding of what constitutes business and economic education, the commission provides statements that may be used to communicate policy related to business education.

RESPONSIBILITY FOR CURRICULUM AND INSTRUCTION

The major area of state supervisor responsibility relates specifically to assisting business education teachers in their curriculum development and instruction. In addition to the traditional areas for curriculum and instruction, state supervisors provide leadership for newer areas relating to standards and the career clusters initiative.

Program Development / Standards Implementation

State-level supervisors will deal with a wide variety of standards, which may include academic, career and technical, program, accreditation, business, and industry. It is critical that a supervisor understand the purpose for and the use of each set of standards as applied to business education curriculum.

Some states have state curriculum guidelines that may (a) be so specific that they address program- and course-level detail and (b) include state-approved course syllabi and statewide textbook adoption. Other states in which curriculum is a "local control" issue may have state standards, but the curricular pathway to achieving those state standards is determined locally. Supervisors need to understand how their state approaches standards implementation and must be aware of the impact of standards on business education programs in the state. The Policies Commission for Business and Economic Education (1998) stated the following:

Standards provide a framework for curriculum and program improvement in business education. In meeting standards, business teachers may participate in a variety of activities that include collaborating with the business community, implementing school-to-work concepts, incorporating technology, and reflecting on effective work practices for continuous improvement of their teaching. (p. 1)

Standards are an important vehicle for directing program improvement. National, state, and local standards provide the framework for developing the curriculum, establishing program requirements, and evaluating the professional growth of teachers.

National Business Education Standards

The National Business Education Association (NBEA) describes the National Standards for Business Education (4th ed.) as follows:

This collection of national standards is a forward-looking synthesis of what students should know and be able to do in business. As such, the achievement standards and performance expectations outlined in this document can be used to guide the business curriculum in the United States at all levels: national as well as state and local. (NBEA, 2013, p. ix)

These national standards address 10 curricular areas of business: accounting, business law, career development, communication, economics and personal finance, entrepreneurship, information technology, international business, management, and marketing. The NBEA standards incorporate three areas of emphasis into each business education discipline: (a) acknowledgment and deeper understanding of the interrelatedness of the basic business content areas, (b) elevation of the performance expectations for the technical skills needed to succeed in the workplace and recognition of their function as tools for achieving business solutions, and (c) recognition that the world is today's workplace and that critical-thinking skills are crucial to performing the more sophisticated decision making that is required of workers who wish to participate fully in the global economy (NBEA, 2013).

State-level supervisors are often involved in curriculum work with teachers and schools. The NBEA standards provide solid program-level guidance for development of courses that reflect current knowledge about business but incorporate academic content and industry connections as well.

Common Core State Standards

The National Governors Association and the Council of Chief State School Officers led the development of the Common Core State Standards (commonly referred to as Common Core or Common Academic Core Standards and available at http://www.corestandards.org/the-standards). This was an effort to establish a single set of common educational standards for kindergarten through grade 12 for English language arts and mathematics. These standards are voluntarily adopted by each state; currently 45 states have adopted Common Core Standards for English language arts and mathematics (National Governors Association Center for Best Practices, Council of Chief State School Officers, 2010). These standards are designed to prepare students to be college and career ready.

The state supervisor must understand how the Common Core Standards, National Business Education Standards, Common CTE Core (discussed below), and any state and/or local standards interrelate and how various standards align and connect with program- and course-level work.

Common Career Technical Core

The Common Career Technical Core is a state-led initiative coordinated by the National Association of State Directors of Career Technical Education Consortium (NASDCTEc) to establish a set of rigorous, high-quality standards for CTE that states may voluntarily adopt. "The standards have been informed by state and industry standards and developed by a diverse group of teachers, business and industry experts, administrators and researchers" (NASDCTEc, 2013b, para. 1).

In 2001 the U.S. Department of Education Office of Vocational and Adult Education, through its Career Clusters Initiative, identified 16 clusters of careers representing 21st century skills. The career cluster framework is an organizing tool for 16 broad groupings of occupations that include 81 pathways comprising knowledge and skills validated by business and industry.

The vision of the Career Clusters Initiative is to enable learners to transition successfully from education to careers by providing a framework connecting secondary with postsecondary education; connecting academic with career and technical education; and connecting education with business, workforce development, and economic development communities. (Policies Commission for Business and Economic Education, 2008, p. 1)

The Common Career Technical Core includes a set of standards for each of the 16 career clusters, a comprehensive collection of industry-validated expectations of what students should know and be able to do after completing instruction in a program of study. The Common Career Technical Core also includes an overarching set of career-ready practices that apply to all 16 career clusters. The career-ready practices include 12 statements that address the knowledge, skills, and dispositions that are important in order for students to become career ready (NASDCTEc, 2013a).

The Policies Commission for Business and Economic Education (2008) further proclaimed: We believe that career clusters, career pathways, and foundation knowledge and skills provide a framework for business education. Of the 16 career clusters, 5 clusters are an integral part of business education: Business Management and Administration, Finance, Hospitality and Tourism, Information Technology, and Marketing. We believe that business education programs that have embraced the Career Clusters Initiative build a connection among secondary and postsecondary education and the business community. Articulated, dual-enrollment, and dual-credit courses provide a road map for students when planning and completing future coursework for career and technical education content areas. Other avenues for students may include advanced placement and honors courses. (p. 2)

Since 2008 the career clusters have been updated with current titles and pathway configurations (NASDCTEc, 2013a).

RESPONSIBILITY FOR STUDENT ORGANIZATIONS AND PARTNERSHIPS

Another major area of responsibility and effort for many state-level supervisors is a connection with student and professional organizations.

Career and Technical Student Organizations

In many states, the supervisor has direct responsibility for one or more career and technical student organizations (CTSOs). In states where CTSO coordination is not the direct responsibility of the supervisor, it is usually either covered as an expectation under the supervisor's position description or is informally defined and shaped by the supervisor and the executive director of the CTSOs in that state. In business education, the most common CTSOs are Future Business Leaders of America (FBLA), Business Professionals of America, and DECA, all of which offer excellent leadership and growth opportunities for students, teachers, and supervisors.

Bonnie Sibert, Nebraska business education state supervisor, confirmed that successful state supervisors take the role of

being supportive and involved in the career student organizations. In Nebraska our FBLA statewide competitions help us implement changes in curriculum. Many of our very best business teachers are FBLA and DECA advisors. Watching students be successful because of a strong CTSO chapter and chapter advisor is very rewarding (personal communication, April 2013).

Wisconsin Business Education State Supervisor Dave Thomas shared that

I am very fortunate in my state supervision role to also serve as the FBLA State Adviser. The opportunity to showcase over 6,800 FBLA members in leadership opportunities at both the middle level and high school level is a great reminder of the impact that our teachers have upon students on a daily basis. Although FBLA touches on a fraction of the larger population of students who are in Business Education classrooms across the state, seeing students attain what for many may be the biggest academic accomplishment in their high school experience helps to support my statement that I am very honored to be in this role. (personal communication, April 2013)

State Business Education Association and Career and Technical Professional Organizations

Supervisors will often have a liaison role with state professional organizations for business and/or career and technical education. In some instances, this liaison role is a formal part of the position description of a state supervisor but may be optional or less defined. Many supervisors find this role helpful in building relationships with teachers and administrators. Often, through conferences or meetings, there is an opportunity for the supervisor to present information on current topics or policy and procedures of interest and concern to teachers and administrators. As these professional organizations provide professional development for teachers, partnering with these organizations allows supervisors to achieve more with fewer resources. These connections also provide a forum for important issue discussion and a network where collegial relationships are able to develop and grow. These efforts strengthen the profession and advance the field.

National Association of Supervisors of Business Education

The National Association of Supervisors of Business Education (NASBE) is an affiliate of the Business Education Division of the Association for Career and Technical Education (ACTE, 2013). The NASBE (2013–2014) handbook states that it is "an organization of Business Education supervisors who are direct employees of a state, region, or local education agency and has as its purpose furthering the cause of Business Education and the welfare of the field and professional members" (p. 2). Specifically, the organization supports the profession in the following ways:

- To develop and increase the effectiveness of educational opportunities in the area of Business Education commensurate to the needs and abilities of all individuals in the American society.

- To encourage supervision of Business Education at all levels.

- To encourage additional services to Business Education at the national level.

- To stimulate research in Business and Economic Education.

- To promote and develop sound educational practices and policies in the field of Business Education.

- To maintain close cooperation and working relationships with all career and technical education services and organizations.

- To develop, maintain, promote, and coordinate cooperation among the states, regions, and local education agencies for Business Education through the interchange of ideas, materials, problems, and accomplishments.

- To promote the development of a total articulated program of education for and about business.

- To support Career and Technical Student Organizations servicing Business Education programs.

- To provide active leadership for the management of change for business. (NASBE, 2013–14, p. 2)

The NASBE professional organization is the vehicle through which supervisors meet and discuss relevant issues in business education. NASBE members formally meet at the NBEA and ACTE conventions and hold regular Web-based meetings throughout the year. At NASBE convention sessions, supervisors connect with peers, find professional support and collegiality, and learn current trends in business education.

One state supervisor said "Join NASBE! It is the one organization that has provided me with the most support through the years to actually do the job that I do. I grew up in NASBE and followed the lead provided by other veterans." Another said "NASBE supported me and helped me grow and develop into a leader that was ready to take on the tough issues as well as the easy wins."

SUMMARY

"A leader is best when people barely know he exists, when his work is done, his aim fulfilled, they will say: we did it ourselves" (Lao-tzu, as cited by Manz & Sims, 1991, p. 35).

The role of the state-level business education supervisor is one that continues to evolve and develop as the world of business and education changes. If one views the trends and issues affecting business education curriculum, it becomes clear that business education is an important part of the preparation of students who will compete in an increasingly global environment (Lambrecht & Kesten, 2012). There is much to be done—legislatively and in policy arenas—to keep business education a viable option for students.

In conclusion, Jeannette Rankin, first woman elected to the United States Congress, perhaps stated a way to view leadership when she said, "You take people as far as they will go, not as far as you would like them to go" (Maggio, 1992, p. 184). Leaders who are mindful know that despite enormous efforts to lead, progress is not guaranteed. As a classroom teacher, Mary Flesberg (personal communication, April 2013) said the following:

Business education is an area that is in constant flux as the business world changes, a state supervisor position requires a leader who is forward thinking. Classroom teachers depend upon the state supervisor to communicate the path in which business education is moving.

Progress in business education depends on incremental movement through the efforts of many along a continuum of advancement that state supervisors envision and work toward for the continued welfare of the business education profession.

REFERENCES

Association for Career and Technical Education (ACTE). (2013). Business Education Division. Retrieved from https://acteonline.org/business

Association for Career and Technical Education (ACTE), & Brustein, M. (2006). *ACTE Perkins Act of 2006: The official guide*. Alexandria, VA: Author.

Bethel, S. M. (1986, September). 12 qualities of leadership. *Tomorrow's Business Leader*, pp. 9–10.

Briggaman, J. S. (1993). State program leadership perspectives. In M. Bush & H. P. Taylor (Eds.), *Developing leadership in business education* (NBEA yearbook, No. 31, pp. 145–155). Reston, VA: National Business Education Association.

Carl D. Perkins Career and Technical Education Improvement Act of 2006. S250, 109th Cong. 20 U.S.C. 2301 (2006) (enacted).

Lambrecht, J. J., & Kesten, C.A. (2012). Major trends and issues affecting business education curriculum development. In W. L. Stitt-Gohdes (Ed.), *Trends and issues in business education: NBEA yearbook* (No. 50, pp. 1–15). Reston, VA: National Business Education Association.

Lloyd, G. M. (1978). Responsibilities of a state supervisor/administrator of business education. In H. H. Conover (Ed.), *Administration and supervision in business education* (pp. 209–215). Reston, VA: National Business Education Association.

Maggio, R. (1992) *The Beacon book of quotations by women.* Boston, MA: Beacon Press.

Manz, C. C., & Sims, H. P., Jr. (1991). Super leadership: Beyond the myth of heroic leadership. *Organizational Dynamics, 19*(4), 18–35.

National Association of State Directors of Career and Technical Education Consortium (NASDCTEc). (2013a). Career clusters at-a-glance. Retrieved from http://www.careertech.org/career-clusters/glance/clusters-occupations.html

National Association of State Directors of Career and Technical Education Consortium (NASDCTEc). (2013b). Common career technical core. Retrieved from http://www.careertech.org/career-technical-education/cctc/info.html

National Association of Supervisors of Business Education (NASBE). (2013–2014). *NASBE handbook.* Retrieved from http://www.nasbe.us/web_documents/nasbe_handbook_13-14lform.pdf

National Business Education Association (NBEA). (2013). *National standards for business education: What America's students should know and be able to do in business* (4th ed.). Reston, VA: Author.

National Business Education Association. (n.d.). About NBEA: Related organizations (Policies Commission for Business and Economic Education). Retrieved from http://nbea.org/newsite/about/related_orgs.html

National Governors Association Center for Best Practices, Council of Chief State School Officers. (2010). *In the states.* Washington, DC: Author. Retrieved from http://www.corestandards.org/in-the-states

Policies Commission for Business and Economic Education (PCBEE). (1998). *This we believe about the role of standards for business education* (Statement No. 62). Reston, VA: National Business Education Association. Retrieved from http://nbea.org/newsite/curriculum/policy/no_62.pdf

Policies Commission for Business and Economic Education. (2008). *This we believe about the role of career clusters in business education* (Statement No. 82). Reston, VA: National Business Education Association. Retrieved from http://nbea.org/newsite/curriculum/policy/no_82.pdf

Taylor, B. (2012, January 26). Are you learning as fast as the world is changing? *Harvard Business Review: HBR Blog Network.* Retrieved from http://blogs.hbr.org/taylor/2012/01/are_you_learning_as_fast_as_th.html

United States Department of Education. (2012, April). *Investing in America's future: A blueprint for transforming career and technical education.* Office of Vocational and Adult Education. Washington, DC: Author. Retrieved from http://www2.ed.gov/about/offices/list/ovae/pi/cte/transforming-career-technical-education.pdf

Leadership for the Elementary/ Middle School Business Education Curriculum

Keith Hannah
Columbia Junior High School
Fife, WA

According to noted American educator, author, and businessman Stephen Covey, "effective leadership is putting first things first" (Covey, 2004). This simple principle captures the essence of this chapter. Although business education is commonly associated with secondary and postsecondary education, this is often *not* the case when considering elementary and middle school levels. Yet, an education system that introduces business education skills and competencies at an early age *is* quite literally putting first things first. It provides timely, foundational career and life skill–building opportunities and supports, as well as enhances core academic coursework. This chapter describes the need for business education at the elementary and middle school levels, guidelines for curriculum and instruction, and best practices for using research and professional development for continuous elementary and middle school program improvement.

NEED FOR ELEMENTARY AND MIDDLE SCHOOL BUSINESS EDUCATION

Business education is an integral component at all educational levels because of the knowledge and skills it provides across the educational spectrum. Teacher leaders need to understand how each education level provides a cogent scope and sequence in business education, in that one level provides a platform for the next:

- **Elementary level.** The foundation is laid at the elementary level, when business educators serve as resource persons and teach career awareness and technological literacy, according to the Policies Commission for Business and Economic Education (PCBEE, 1999). Keyboarding instruction, if it is to be at all effective, must begin at this level if a student is to gain true keyboard automaticity.

- **Middle level.** At this level, business educators continue to teach learners to use technology effectively in the learning process for all content areas; however, this is also the age when students should start receiving business-specific content. Deeper career exploration opportunities occur via coursework integration, school-based enterprises, job shadowing, and job mentoring activities. This is the age at which it becomes frighteningly apparent if students have not previously had proper keyboarding instruction. If not delivered by this age, the likelihood that a student develops proper keyboard habits is practically nil.

- **Secondary level.** As students move to the secondary level, business education provides learning for and about business, including ways to become effective consumers, citizens, workers, and business leaders. Future business leaders continue with focused career exploration and participate in work experience opportunities and student organizations.

- **Postsecondary level.** Business education at this level primarily prepares individuals for specific careers in business, expands employability options or upgrades technological skills, and prepares future business education teachers (National Career Development Association, 2011).

By examining the recommended focuses of each level, the teacher leader can more clearly articulate to colleagues and administrators the need for business education to begin at the elementary level and continue throughout a lifelong learning path. No one would deny that, if students are not taught math concepts at an early age, they will be ill prepared for more challenging math concepts later on. Business education is no different. Opening students who are early in the educational path to career exploration, as well as technological and financial literacy allows for introduction of deeper concepts and increased rigor overall in a student's education.

CURRICULUM AND INSTRUCTION

Elementary- and middle-school teacher leaders frequently offer instruction in the areas of *keyboarding, computer applications,* and *career exploration.* However, the recent emphasis by the Obama Administration on increased financial awareness and knowledge among students has opened a new curricular topic to these age levels: *financial literacy.* This effort comes in the wake of a disturbing survey from the Financial Industry Regulatory Authority and the Investor Education Foundation showing that young adults display much lower financial literacy than older generations ("Obama Administration Aims," 2009). Although much of this effort's focus has been concentrated on the high school level, elementary- and middle-school teacher leaders have opportunities to support this endeavor.

Career Exploration and Guidance Activities

Career exploration serves different purposes as students move from the elementary through secondary levels. The National Career Development Association's mission is to inspire and empower the achievement of career and life goals by providing professional development, resources, standards, scientific research, and advocacy. This association provides a comprehensive, research-based framework for career exploration to assist educators in delivering age-appropriate career education activities. Although the primary kinds of career development emphasis in grades 10–12 should center on helping youth make quality decisions regarding their educational/career plans at the postsecondary level, the elementary- and middle-school levels have a different focus, which is outlined below (National Career Development Association, 2011).

Career development in grades K–6. At this level, teacher leaders strive to make classrooms reflect the workplace by teaching and reinforcing productive work habits, including arriving at school on time, doing one's best on assignments, finishing assigned tasks on time, cooperating in team efforts, participating in problem solving, and following supervisors' (teachers') directions. Career exploration activities are used to open students' eyes and minds to the wide array of careers. Particularly at the elementary level, students' interests in careers are often based on gender bias. For example, many elementary students still believe police and firefighters are career options for boys and nursing is a career for girls, in spite of the increasing gender diversity in these occupations. This is a fortuitous age to introduce the idea of nontraditional occupations. If gender-based career stereotypes are dispelled early, students are more likely to consider a wider range of career opportunities as they perform career exploration at all education levels.

Career development in grades 7–9. Most of the career development activities that are recommended for grades K–6 should be continued in grades 7–9. The teacher leader provides students opportunities for increased self-understanding, but students should not be encouraged to make specific occupational choices. It is through students' continued development of self-knowledge that they become better equipped to consider tentative occupational choices for serious consideration during the remainder of their secondary years. During this age span, students become aware of career interests, career aptitudes, and work values as applicable to various occupations and themselves.

The teacher leader promotes community volunteer work experience for all youth beginning as early as grade 7. Such work experience is intended primarily to help youth (a) better understand the value of work, (b) increase understanding of their own occupational interests, aptitudes, and values, and (c) make tentative occupational choices that are acknowledged as susceptible to change as self-awareness evolves and environmental influences enact change.

Compared with the secondary-level curriculum, the teacher leader may notice a dearth of formal text-based curricula for elementary- and early middle-school career exploration and, as a result, should prepare to explore the wealth of online resources, guest speakers, and demonstrations available. The career cluster framework, developed in 2001 by the U.S. Department of Education's Office of Vocational and Adult Education, is an organizing tool for 16 broad groups of occupations for students to consider (PCBEE, 2008). Because the focus at these age levels is on exploration, exposing students to the 16 career clusters helps students make sense of the incredible array of occupations.

Many online resources that provide students with exposure to career clusters exist for teacher leaders to access. Some states have compiled comprehensive lists of career resources spanning the elementary- and middle-school levels; see, for example, Missouri (http://tinyurl.com/pryqeq9) and North Dakota (http://tinyurl.com/lhtmhpt). Other types of resources include the following:

- **Workbooks:** *Careers Are Everywhere Activity Workbooks* (http://tinyurl.com/n8f2nen)

- **Board games:** *Career Bingo* (http://tinyurl.com/nzhw9lk) and *Career Jeopardy* (http://tinyurl.com/75nkzqp)

- **Interactive career programs:** *Busy Bees* and *Paws in Jobland*

Furthermore, the teacher leader incorporates guest speakers into career exploration units. Using parents and community members as resources provides affiliation (see the 10 design qualities listed above) for students. Speakers may be invited into individual classrooms for presentations and/or demonstrations related to different careers, or a career fair may be organized allowing students to select areas of interest to explore. Although this may seem daunting, the career clusters provide a framework for organizing speakers. A representative speaker for each career cluster may be invited, or if planning a career fair, several presenters for each career cluster could describe tangible, interactive career learning experiences. As a final consideration when recruiting speakers for a class presentation or career fair, the teacher leaders may challenge themselves to recruit members who are nontraditional in their career areas in order to expand students' perceptions regarding career choices.

Keyboarding and Software Skill Development and Sequencing

Perhaps no aspect of the business education curriculum has brought as much debate in the past decade than keyboarding and software instruction. When should it be taught? Who is best qualified to teach it? At the beginning of the 21st century, many were predicting that the need for keyboarding skills would disappear altogether by 2010, as voice recognition would eradicate the need for keyboarding skill development. Of course, time has proved this to be a fallacy. Although voice recognition is included in the mix of input technologies that students learn to maximize efficiency and performance (National Business Education Association, 2013), the keyboard is still the primary, foundational means of information input. This reality, coupled with the perception of many administrators that students no longer need to be taught how to type, requires the teacher leader to be a more vocal advocate than ever before for this skill. Parents, concerned about the lack of skills they see among students, should be used as advocates for keyboarding instruction. Most districts across the United States have career and technical education (CTE) advisory committees comprising community business members who are possible allies in establishing or maintaining a keyboarding/computer literacy program.

Sadly, there are administrators who believe that elementary students' spending 20–30 minutes a week for a school quarter (or less) in the computer lab using a keyboarding software package will result in touch-typing proficiency. Classroom teachers who are witnessing the deplorable lack of keyboarding skills in today's students know this could not be further from the truth. Although many districts have moved word processing, spreadsheet, database, and presentation software instruction to elementary- and middle-school grades, it seems inadequate not to instruct students at the same time in the proper use of the keyboard.

The ideal keyboarding sequence. The ideal age group for effective keyboarding instruction and learning, according to various research studies, is the upper elementary school level (ages 10–12) (Erickson, 1993, p. 2). Middle elementary students can learn keyboarding, but because of their developmental skills, they have a greater tendency than do upper elementary students to look at the keyboard as they operate it. Lower elementary students (ages 6–7) can learn basic keyboarding skill under the guidance of a skilled keyboarding instructor, but a fundamental question to be asked is whether this instruction is cost-effective and the most productive use of student/teacher time.

Given these parameters, the ideal keyboarding program would give kindergarten through second-grade students a "keyboarding awareness" sequence (Crews, North, & Erthal, 2006, p. 29). Here, instruction would focus on starting and reinforcing proper body position, identifying a left- and right-side keyboarding layout, and becoming aware of which finger to use in making certain keystrokes. When keyboarding instruction begins in grades 3–5, it would focus on basic skill mastery to develop good technique and move toward appropriate speed and accuracy using the touch method while learning the keys. Instruction would not emphasize document formatting but be limited to those documents needed for class assignments. Introductory middle-school keyboarding courses tend to focus on basic skill mastery, but by this age, improper habits are becoming so firmly entrenched (as many students at this point have been using the keyboard for five years or more) that the likelihood of developing touch typing skills is greatly diminished. The teacher leader must be willing to step forward and advocate that formal keyboard instruction begin in middle elementary school and be taught by an appropriately licensed instructor trained in the pedagogy of keyboarding skill development.

How many class periods are necessary to develop application-level keyboarding skill? Research indicates that at least 40 class periods or about 25 hours of keyboarding instruction are necessary to develop application-level keyboarding skill. Application level means the student is able to keyboard without having to hesitate in locating a key (Erickson, 1993). Once students have achieved application-level skill, it is crucial that students continue to be given opportunities for practice and reinforcement. If instruction is started in middle elementary school, such as fourth grade, students should be given keyboard reinforcement time in grades 5–7; it is in these grades that the focus shifts from skill learning to skill improvement with increased emphasis on document production and use of other software applications (Crews, North, & Erthal, 2006).

Computer applications integration. At the elementary school level, learning the writing process and completing a variety of language arts, social studies, and other writing assignments provide students ideal opportunities to practice keyboarding skills, whether through a word processing application, creating a simple spreadsheet, or using presentation software to create visuals. The teacher leader must articulate to other teachers and administrators when it is appropriate to have students use word processing, spreadsheet, database, and presentation software features for class assignments. An in-depth discussion of which features should be introduced is beyond the scope of this chapter; however, a comprehensive K–8 computer literacy scope and sequence based on the National Education Technology Standards developed by Thomson/South-Western (2011) may serve as a guide for teacher leaders as they design course sequencing or work with fellow teachers in other disciplines (Crews, North, & Erthal, 2006). This scope and sequence may be accessed online (http://tinyurl.com/mcvc7ln). What the teacher leader will notice in this scope and sequence is how early many software applications concepts are introduced: students navigating and entering information in cells of a spreadsheet program at an introductory level in first grade! Although many districts may find it challenging to incorporate all of the recommendations in this scope and sequence, it does serve as a powerful, tangible piece of evidence for offering rich keyboarding and computer applications concepts at the early elementary-school level.

The benefit of exposing students to these concepts early allows for more rigorous application at upper elementary, middle, and high school levels. When concepts are introduced, the teacher leader needs to make the curriculum relevant to the particular age group being taught for engagement to occur. Here is an example: anyone who teaches adolescents knows that the role of celebrities in a young person's life is huge. Teachers may capitalize on teaching a letter-formatting lesson to seventh graders by assigning them to write to a celebrity of their choosing in the format taught in class. A variety of online resources are available for finding celebrity fan-mail addresses. For additional motivation, students create envelopes using word processing software and mail these letters (if the budget allows). A "Wall of Fame" that has copies of responses that students have received may be created in the classroom. Once students know the assignment to which the "Wall of Fame" is attached, the teacher leader will be amazed how often students will ask, "When do *we* get to write a celebrity letter?"

In addition to the standard mix of word processing, spreadsheet, database, and presentation software, one might consider what other software applications are suitable to offer at the middle school level. For one, voice recognition software provides students with an efficient alternative to keyboard input and may be included among the input technologies to which students are exposed (PCBEE, 2003). In truth, it can be a life-saver in terms of productivity for students who have not developed keyboard proficiency, because within two weeks, students can be voice writing at 150 words per minute. Having this skill decreases the chance of students' developing a repetitive strain injury, for example, carpal tunnel syndrome, because the time spent at the computer is divided between voice and hands (PCBEE, 2003).

Personal Financial Literacy Development

Although financial literacy instruction frequently occurs at the secondary level, this is not yet the case at the elementary and middle school levels. The question may arise on when it is appropriate to introduce financial literacy instruction. The teacher leader recognizes that this instruction must begin in elementary school and continue throughout middle and high school. Assuming a student who takes one course in personal finance during high school is adequately prepared for the financial decisions that life will present is a fallacy at best. The official stand on this issue by the PCBEE (2011) is that personal financial literacy is essential, beginning in early elementary and continuing throughout life. But, what should be included and how does one decide? The *National Standards for Business Education* (NBEA, 2013) and the *National Standards in K–12 Personal Education* (Jump$tart Coalition for Personal Financial Literacy, 2007) provide a comprehensive framework for what students should know and do in the area of personal financial literacy. The *National Standards for Business Education* (NBEA, 2013) contain eight standards subdivided into personal finance levels 1–4. Level 1 standards are designed for grades K–6 and level 2 standards for grades 6–9. The *National Standards in K–12 Personal Education* (Jump$tart Coalition for Personal Financial Literacy, 2007) include 29 standards in six broad financial literacy areas. Each standard provides benchmarks for grades 4, 8, and 12. In both standards publications, it is easy for the teacher leader to determine which curricular areas should be covered at various grade levels.

Because not all school systems have embraced this philosophy, the teacher leader must be willing to advocate for inclusion of financial literacy instruction beginning in the elementary school grades with elementary and middle school teachers, administrators, and school board members. As the likelihood of a stand-alone financial literacy course is small in the elementary- and middle-school levels, the teacher leader should be prepared to integrate financial literacy instruction within existing curricular offerings. As an example, budgeting basics—such as creating a pie chart to illustrate percentages for major expense categories—may be integrated into an Excel unit in a commonly offered computer applications class. Curriculum materials that integrate personal finance into a core academic class such as math are available. The Actuarial Foundation (2013) has developed a three-lesson mini-unit called "Plan, Save, Succeed" for grades 6–8 math classes. Aligned with the Jump$tart Coalition's national standards as well as the Common Core State Standards for Mathematical Practice (Common Core State Standards Initiative, 2012b), this is just one example of how business teachers may continue to integrate academic and technical instruction.

Junior Achievement (n.d.) also offers a unique, engaging four-week personal finance curriculum, called the Finance Park, designed to fit into a number of business, math, or social studies courses in grades 7–9. From the business education perspective, this unit may be integrated easily with an Excel unit in a stand-alone computer applications course at the middle school level. Teachers serving as resource persons in their districts ought to consider approaching math or social studies teachers about team teaching this valuable unit. The Junior Achievement Finance Park experience begins in the classroom where students learn about financial institutions, debit versus credit, taxes, and budgeting. In areas of the country with a Junior Achievement World facility (e.g., the states of Washington, Florida, and Maryland), this unit culminates with a day at the Junior Achievement Finance Park, where students are immersed in a reality-based decision-making simulation addressing aspects of individual and family budgeting (Junior Achievement, n.d.). Parents are recruited to serve as small group facilitators during the experience. The benefit of parent participation is that these parents see this powerful learning experience firsthand; come out of the experience energized that their students are learning such a valuable, real-world skill; and will frequently talk to administrators and school board members about the value of the program.

The teacher leader should *never* assume that the great things happening in their classroom are common knowledge. After a successful trip to the Finance Park, for example, the teacher leader may arrange to appear before the school board with parents and students who participated in the program to talk about its benefits. No one captures the ear of administrators and board members better than parents and students! If a teacher leader gives a financial literacy certification test to students yielding positive results, the same holds true. That teacher should then consider appearing at a local school board meeting to present the results and invite students to tell about the curricular benefits. Including parents willing to speak about the benefits for their children may have an enormous impact. Parents may be powerful allies and stakeholders for promoting educational initiatives.

Role of Middle-School Student Organizations

Career and technical student organizations (CTSOs) play a vital role in allowing students to showcase their career and technical skills and develop valuable leadership skills. CTSOs such as Future Business Leaders of America and Business Professionals of America integrate with classroom learning, facilitate learning applications, promote goal setting, support competition at the state and even national levels, and encourage business partnership formation and community service activities (ACTE, n.d.). Although many may associate CTSOs with high school and postsecondary levels, these organizations also provide the same opportunities for middle-school students. If a CTSO does not currently exist in one's school building, starting a chapter is a rewarding and powerful professional opportunity for the teacher leader.

Membership in the Future Business Leaders of America is open to all students starting in grade 7 and, in Business Professionals of America, can begin as early as grade 6.

Although starting a chapter may seem daunting in the face of other day-to-day duties of a classroom teacher, one can take several steps to make the initial year relatively stress free and ultimately very rewarding for both the teacher and students:

- First, the teacher leader may contact the state director for the CTSO s/he plans to start. These individuals possess a wealth of information and can dramatically reduce the time needed to locate important resources and required chapter documents that are usually accessible online.

- Second, it is important to remember the teacher leader does *not* have to reinvent the wheel. S/he should locate a local, experienced adviser willing to serve as a mentor or guide. For the teacher leader who *is* experienced in advising a successful CTSO chapter, s/he should actively reach out to local schools that currently do not have a CTSO for their students and offer to be a mentor through the first-year process.

- Third, to minimize apprehension about the first-year process, s/he should consider hand selecting a small group of students for the first-year process. Five to 10 student members are manageable. Ultimately, it will be a year of tremendous learning for *both* the teacher leader and his/her students; however, the more manageable the group size, the greater the likelihood of success in the chapter's inaugural year. Middle-school students are extremely enthusiastic; rest assured, once a chapter is started and experiences some initial success, it will grow into an important and extremely rewarding part of the school's culture.

Common Core State Standards

The final curricular component to be addressed is Common Core State Standards. This initiative, designed through a joint venture of the National Governor's Association and the Council of Chief State School Officers, resulted in a standards-based platform of clear and consistent goals for learning that would prepare America's children for success in *both* college and work (Reese, 2011). The keen observer may note the potential opportunity for CTE in the wording "college *and* work." As of this writing, these standards have been adopted in 45 states, the District of Columbia, four territories, and by the Department of Defense Education Activity (Common Core State Standards Initiative, 2012a). From this statistic alone, it is apparent that these standards are imbedded in the U.S. education system; it is the teacher leader's responsibility to learn about these standards *now* and begin the process of implementing them. It is more important now than ever in the current system of standards-based education to demonstrate how core academic content is supported and delivered through CTE programs at the elementary- and middle-school levels.

Standards overview. Currently, the Common Core includes achievement standards in three areas: English Language Arts; Literacy in History/Social Studies, Science, and Technical Subjects; and Mathematics. The English Language Arts Standards in grades K–5 include expectations for reading, writing, speaking, listening, and language applicable to a range of subjects, *not just English language arts.* The teacher leader must note that this is an opportunity for incorporating these standards into elementary- and middle-school business offerings. It is important to note that the 6–12 Literacy Standards in History/Social Studies, Science, and Technical Subjects are not meant to replace content standards in those areas but rather to supplement them.

The National Assessment of Educational Progress (2009) standards include a high and increasing proportion of informational text (rather than literary text) as students advance through the grades. Because business education content typically involves informational text, this underscores another opportunity for standards inclusion.

Implementation guidelines. Implementation of any new standards systems requires a degree of study by the teacher leader to determine which standards "fit" into their curriculum. The purpose of this section is not meant to tell the teacher leader which standards should be incorporated. Based on his/her curricular offerings, the teacher leader makes an individual decision. The purpose of this section is to give advice on how to approach this new standard set.

The first step for the teacher leader is to access the Common Core Standards and begin the process of familiarization. The entire standards document is available for download at http://www.corestandards.org/the-standards. Viewing the standards components online can be a bit unwieldy as they are subdivided online. The teacher leader might consider printing the standards and creating a three-ring binder organized into sections for each standard. Although the Common Core Standards document is large, experience has shown that this makes it much easier to study the standards.

Once accessed or printed, the teacher leader has the challenge of looking through the standards, one by one, and deciding which standards are *fully addressed* within his/her curriculum. All too often, business teachers believe that they must retrieve any and all standards that even remotely "handshake" with their curriculum as if to indicate, "Look at how valuable my content area is." The truth is that the content *is* valuable, and it *is* important to show that elementary- and middle-school business education supports the state-assessed core academic areas. However, the approach the teacher leader needs to take is one of quality over quantity. S/he should select only those standards that completely fit *and* are assessed. One may find that there are only a handful of English language arts and mathematics standards that are appropriate for a semester-long class. When selecting standards, the teacher leader should follow the principle, "when in doubt, leave it out." What will result is a standards-based curriculum that leaves no debate over the validity of the teacher leader's choices yet clearly supports the state-assessed core academic content areas.

This section outlines curricular areas within business education suitable for inclusion at the elementary- and middle-school levels. Career exploration, keyboarding, computer applications, and financial literacy offered at these levels provide a strong foundation for high school and beyond. Providing CTSO opportunities for middle-school students provides unmatched relevance to instruction and early leadership development opportunities. In this time of standards-based education, the teacher leader must begin implementation of the Common Core State Standards and continue to incorporate the standards mentioned under the sections for career exploration, keyboarding, computer applications, and financial literacy.

BEST PRACTICES AND PROFESSIONAL DEVELOPMENT

Regardless of the level taught, business education is a curricular area requiring constant change. In order to stay current and continue to provide relevant, timely instruction, it is imperative that the elementary- and middle-school teacher leader design a curriculum, practice research-based methodology, and participate in professional associations and personal learning communities.

Using Research to Practice Methodology

Teacher leaders are well versed in instructional methodologies. However, true educational leadership requires a teacher to assess critically the transformation movements in education and be open to incorporating those movements that increase student engagement and ultimately improve their schools. Schlechty (2011) developed a powerful transformation movement entitled "Working on the Work" shown to dramatically improve student engagement and transform the school system.

Working on the Work. According to Schlechty (2011), student responses to a learning task fall somewhere on a five-point continuum: rebellion, retreatism, ritual compliance, strategic compliance, and engagement. The "Working on the Work" framework outlines 10 design qualities for teacher leaders to incorporate into the lesson design process for moving students on the continuum toward true engagement. The beauty of these design qualities is that they are applicable to any curricular area, so they support not only business education content but also the cross-curricular instructional teaming that is found among business teachers at the elementary level.

When designing a curriculum, the teacher leader is not required to include all 10 design qualities in a particular project or lesson; however, the more that can be incorporated, the higher the likelihood that true student engagement occurs. These 10 design qualities and a brief description of each follow (Schlechty, 2002).

- **Content and substance.** Teachers and administrators have a clear, consistent, and shared understanding of what students are expected to know and do at various grade levels.

- **Product focus.** The tasks students are assigned and the activities they are encouraged to undertake are clearly linked in the minds of the teacher leader *and* the students to performances, products, and exhibitions about which the students care and on which students place value.

- **Clear product standards.** When products, performances, or exhibitions are part of the instructional design, students understand the standards by which these products, performances, or exhibitions will be evaluated.

- **Protection from adverse consequences for initial failures.** The teacher leader expects success and recognizes that failure is sometimes part of the learning process. Opportunities are then provided for the student to become successful even when an initial failure occurs.

- **Affirmation.** People who are significant in the lives of students, including parents, siblings, peers, public audiences, and younger students, are positioned to observe, participate in, and benefit from student performances, and the products of those performances, and to affirm the significance and importance of the activities.

- **Affiliation.** Students are provided opportunities to work with others—peers, parents, other adults, teachers, and students from other schools or classrooms—on products, group performances, and exhibitions that they and others judge to be significant.

- **Choice.** What students are to learn is usually not negotiable, but they have considerable choice and numerous options in what they will do and how they will do it in order to learn.

- **Organization of knowledge.** Teacher leaders and support personnel ensure that the materials and media used to present concepts and lessons to students are organized in order to appeal to the personal interests and aesthetic sensibilities of the largest number of students.

- **Novelty and variety.** The range of tasks, products, and exhibitions is wide and varied, as are the technologies that students are encouraged to employ, moving from the simplest and well understood—a pen and paper—to the most complex: sophisticated computer applications.

- **Authenticity.** The tasks students are assigned and the work they are encouraged to do have significance in their lives *now* and are related to consequences that are important to them.

Again, not all 10 design qualities presented above need to be present in every lesson or project. These design qualities provide a research-based framework for teacher leaders to incorporate into their lesson designs to enhance student achievement in any business education curriculum area. "Working on the Work" provides a sound framework on which to build engaging lessons. Throughout the lesson design process, however, the teacher leader continues to access relevant educational research for shaping lesson design and continuous program improvement. Research resources of value to the elementary- and middle-school teacher leader include the following:

- **Association for Research in Business Education–Delta Pi Epsilon.** This association is the official research arm of NBEA, providing timely, relevant research in all aspects of the business education curriculum. Because its research is targeted specifically for business teachers, it is imperative that the elementary- and middle-school teacher leader be a member of this professional association (http://www.dpe.org/membership.htm). As this association's research does not target any one age level or aspect of the business education curriculum, the elementary- and middle-school teacher leader will find relevant research germane to his/her curriculum in the association's publications, the *Journal of Applied Research for Business Instruction* and the *Journal for Research in Business Education*.

- **What Works Clearinghouse.** The What Works Clearinghouse (http://ies.ed.gov/ncee/wwc) is a powerful companion research resource to the Association for Research in Business Education–Delta Pi Epsilon. Where the association focuses specifically on business education, the clearinghouse's research is broader in nature and encompasses the other curricular areas (such as language arts and mathematics) with which the elementary- and middle-school business teacher should partner. The clearinghouse is an initiative of the Institute for Educational Sciences at the U.S. Department of Education. With more than 700 publications available and more than 6,000 reviewed studies, the clearinghouse is intended to inform researchers, educators, and policymakers as they work to improve education for students (Institute of Education Sciences, n.d.). The elementary- and middle-school teacher leader is strongly encouraged to access this resource and canvass the wealth of research available on reading, writing, literacy, mathematics, teacher and leader effectiveness, and educational technology.

Professional Development for the Elementary- and Middle-School Teacher Leader

The teacher leader clearly sees the value and importance of participation in his/her profession as well as continually seeking ways to increase effectiveness in the classroom. National, regional, and state association membership is both a cost- and time-effective means of keeping abreast of developments in business education. In addition to a wealth of publications, these associations provide quality conference opportunities for continuous business education program improvement. As teaching responsibilities increase, however, many have less time to attend conferences. Although there is no substitute for the face-to-face networking and learning opportunities these conferences provide, more virtual professional development opportunities are available for teacher leaders.

Virtual professional development. Virtual learning environments are the way of the future. The cost- and time-effective benefits of face-to-face interaction are achievable through virtual learning. Virtual learning environments offer flexibility, mobility, connectivity, and interactivity (PCBEE, 2009). Without having to leave the classroom, the teacher leader can access and participate in professional development specifically selected and targeted for his or her educational purpose. NBEA has embraced virtual professional development through NBEAconnect (http://nbeaconnect.ning.com), NBEA's ning community. Here, the elementary- and middle-school teacher leader will find discussion groups, blogs, forums, videos, and even archived webcasts, all accessible on demand (NBEA, 2010).

Because the teacher leader seeks ways to give back to his/her profession, s/he may consider proposing and offering a webcast on a topic relevant to elementary- and middle-school business teachers. A discussion may be started on the NBEA ning. Curriculum ideas may then be shared in the forum. It is through the mutual sharing of expertise that business education is strengthened.

Professional learning communities. The idea of improving schools through professional learning communities (PLCs) is currently in vogue. This term has been used so ubiquitously, however, that it is in danger of losing all meaning. Because at the elementary- and middle-school level, business teachers frequently support core academic content, it is important that teacher leaders form a professional learning community with the teachers whose curriculum they are supporting and enhancing.

In order for the PLC to be successful, the teacher leader must ensure that several "big ideas" remain in place throughout the learning community's life cycle (DuFour, 2004). First, the PLC must ensure that students learn. This sounds simple, but in truth, it means that the focus of this partnership must be centered on what students should *learn* rather than what they are to be *taught*. Second, a culture of collaboration needs to exist. Open, two-way dialogue and collaboration are important for the PLC to be successful. Third, a focus on results should exist. PLCs should judge their effectiveness on the basis of student achievement. Every teacher team participates in an ongoing process of identifying current levels of student achievement, establishing a goal to move students to the next level, working together to achieve that goal, and providing periodic evidence of progress. By establishing and facilitating this collaborative process, the business teacher leader will be recognized as the valuable asset to the staff they *should* be seen as.

SUMMARY

Business education at the elementary- and middle-school levels provides a strong platform for building increasingly rigorous career and life skills and supports core academic content. Providing learning opportunities for students in the areas of career exploration, keyboarding, computer literacy, and financial literacy sets students on a powerful trajectory toward success. In this time of standards-based education, it is important to deliver content based on standards related to business education and the new Common Core State Standards. Incorporating these standards in curriculum design provides tangible relevance to outside stakeholders and ensures that what is being taught is truly what *should* be taught. Elementary- and middle-school business teachers who stay abreast of business education and core academic research and are involved in professional associations and learning communities help guarantee that today's elementary and middle school students are prepared for tomorrow's challenges.

REFERENCES

Association for Career and Technical Education (ACTE). (n.d.) Career and technical student organizations. Retrieved from https://www.acteonline.org/general. aspx?id=762#.UlMI76yA6vU

Common Core State Standards Initiative. (2012a). In the states. Retrieved from http://www.corestandards.org/in-the-states

Common Core State Standards Initiative. (2012b). Standards for mathematical practice. Retrieved from http://www.corestandards.org/Math/Practice

Covey, S. R. (2004). *The 7 habits of highly effective people.* New York, NY: Free Press.

Crews, T. B., North, A. B., & Erthal, M. J. (2006). *Elementary/middle school keyboarding strategies guide* (3rd ed.). Reston, VA: National Business Education Association.

DuFour, R. (2004). What is a professional learning community? *Educational Leadership, 61*(8), 6–11. Retrieved from http://www.ascd.org/publications/educational-leadership/may04/vol61/num08/What-Is-a-Professional-Learning-Community%C2%A2.aspx

Erickson, L. W. (1993). *Basic keyboarding guide for teachers.* Cincinnati, OH: South-Western.

Institute of Education Sciences. (n.d.). About us. Retrieved from http://ies.ed.gov/ncee/wwc/aboutus.aspx

Jump$tart Coalition for Personal Financial Literacy. (2007). *National standards in k–12 personal finance education* (3rd ed.). Washington, DC: Author.

Junior Achievement. (n.d.). Junior Achievement finance park. Retrieved from http://www.myja.org/financepark

National Assessment of Educational Practice. (2009). Overview. Retrieved from http://nces.ed.gov/nationsreportcard

National Business Education Association (NBEA). (2010). NBEA community. Retrieved from http://www.nbea.org/newsite/community/index.html

National Business Education Association. (2013). *National standards for business education* (4th ed.). Reston, VA: Author.

National Career Development Association. (2011). Career development: A policy statement of the National Career Development Association. Retrieved from http://ncda.org/aws/NCDA/pt/fli/4728/false

Obama Administration aims for high school financial literacy. (2009, December 15). Retrieved from http://www.reuters.com/article/2009/12/15/us-usa-treasury-education-idUSTRE5BE3GG20091215

Policies Commission for Business and Economic Education (PCBEE). (1999). *This we believe about the role of business education at all educational levels* (Statement No. 64). Retrieved from http://www.nbea.org/newsite/curriculum/policy/no_64.pdf

Policies Commission for Business and Economic Education. (2003). *This we believe about computer-input technologies* (Statement No. 73). Retrieved from http://nbea.org/newsite/curriculum/policy/no_73.pdf

Policies Commission for Business and Economic Education. (2008). *This we believe about the value of career clusters in business education* (Statement No. 82). Retrieved from http://nbea.org/newsite/curriculum/policy/no_82.pdf

Policies Commission for Business and Economic Education. (2009). *This we believe about virtual learning environments* (Statement No. 85). Retrieved from http://nbea.org/newsite/curriculum/policy/no_85.pdf

Policies Commission for Business and Economic Education. (2011). *This we believe about personal financial literacy* (Statement No. 88). Retrieved from http://nbea.org/newsite/curriculum/documents/PolicyStatement88_2011.pdf

Reese, S. (2011). CTE and the Common Core State Standards. *Techniques, 86*(7), 16–20.

Schlechty, P. C. (2002). *Working on the work.* San Francisco, CA: Jossey-Bass.

Schlechty, P. C. (2011). *Engage students: The next level of working on the work.* San Francisco, CA: Jossey-Bass.

The Actuarial Foundation. (2013). Plan, save, succeed. Retrieved from http://www.actuarialfoundation.org/programs/youth/FinancialLiteracy.shtml

Thomson/South-Western. (2011). *Learning with computers levels k–8.* Retrieved from http://facstaff.uww.edu/rogersh/scopseq/Scope%20%20Sequence%20final.pdf

Leadership in Secondary Education Business Programs

DeLayne Havlovic
Omaha Public Schools
Omaha, NE

Business education programs are a vital part of the curriculum for high schools. According to the Policies Commission for Business and Economic Education (PCBEE, 2002), business education programs enable individuals to participate in a global economic system, function in a global environment, develop information technology skills, and integrate business concepts into academic knowledge. The *National Standards for Business Education* by the National Business Education Association (NBEA, 2013) identifies knowledge and skills essential for success outside of high school for both college and career readiness. Teachers, department leaders, and administrators in business education are responsible for assuring that students have the skills necessary for and about business.

This chapter provides insight for secondary curriculum leaders on trends and issues most relevant for business education. It also provides insight on keeping business education programs more relevant and responsive to the needs of the professional community in preparing secondary students to be college and career ready.

STUDENT RECRUITMENT FOR BUSINESS EDUCATION PROGRAMS

A successful business education program's top asset is students. With the educational focus often leaning toward the Common Core State Standards (Common Core) and core assessment, business educators frequently struggle to maintain program enrollments and to ensure programs are viable in the eyes of those making decisions regarding curriculum.

Enrollment Statistics and Changing Student Audiences in Business Education

In Nebraska, business education enrollment numbers for 2009–2010 to 2010–2011 decreased by 7%. Although courses such as Accounting and Business Law showed decreases, other areas noted substantial increases. The areas experiencing increases included personal finance, information technology applications, and dual-credit high school courses offered in conjunction with a college or university, for example, college accounting and entrepreneurship (Nebraska Department of Education, 2013). To continue to be viable, high school business programs must demonstrate necessary college, career, and life preparedness and/or provide a basis for the college preparatory mentality, such as when students earn a weighted grade (when a higher GPA value is placed on courses of higher rigor) or college credit.

In 2010 the Omaha Public School District in Nebraska proposed an economic and financial literacy course as a high school graduation requirement. The Omaha Public Schools Board of Education demanded that this requirement be implemented immediately because of pressure within the community to offer such a course. Other school districts throughout the United States follow a similar trend and are adding or have required an information technology applications course either for graduation or as a requirement during students' freshman year so they can be better prepared to function in high school and meet demands for technology applications by educators in all high school departments.

Effective Strategies and Tools for Student Recruitment

In 2005 the Foundation for the Future of Business Education identified marketing concepts for successful business education enrollments. For current students, the needs may vary depending on career explorations or pathways of student interest. If a school can target students based on identification of a career pathway of interest, students and school counselors (when enrolling students) can have a better awareness of the business education programs available to them. High school students may also be enticed by the opportunity for jobs and internships in their area of interest and the opportunity to gain experiences in a field of interest.

Parents should also be targeted in business department marketing plans. Communication with parents needs to take place so they are aware of how business education programs benefit in savings at the postsecondary level. Parents need to understand how skills learned in a business education course translate into college and career readiness after high school. Parents may also be interested in the financial savings for college through dual enrollment and college-articulated high school business courses (Foundation for the Future of Business Education, 2005).

High school business education departments may see the benefits of a strategically aligned recruitment week or series of recruitment activities that promote their programs within their own schools. Some activities could include the following:

- Plan schoolwide business trivia questions during homeroom

- Set up information tables at lunch, open houses, or during parent-teacher conferences

- Organize teacher visits to potential feeder classes (e.g., accounting teacher visits a required economics class or digital media teacher visits an information technology applications class)

- Use assessment data to target specific students (e.g., send a personalized letter to the highest-achieving students on a math exam to encourage enrollment in accounting)

- Send special "reminder" items to homerooms of students who are eligible to enroll in the next level of a course (e.g., Payday candy bar with a note stating "Marketing II Pays!")

- Encourage business student organization or National Business Honor Society students to continue in the program or provide students an incentive for getting a friend to enroll in a course

- Plan middle school recruitment and transition activities (e.g., open house activities, brochures or postcards mailed to homes, and/or automated phone calls)

Successful secondary business education programs use a variety of techniques to build and retain student enrollment. Program leaders should determine what strategies bring the most benefit and enrollment to the program.

Community Involvement

Often, linking schools to local business communities brings great benefit to students. This, in turn, can bring more visibility to a business department and provide tangible benefits for students. For example, at Hoover High School, Alabama, students gain career experience through high school internships. Those same students carry their excitement about their experience back to their schools and classrooms, which can create a stronger market for those same courses and experiences when their peers register for classes (Meggison, 2012).

According to Melinda Rangel with Newton High School, Kansas, (personal communication, February 2013), her community embraced the concept of a National Business Honor Society. After introducing their business pathway advisory board members to the concept of starting a chapter, the business group was so supportive that they helped with the funding of the charter fee and were special guests at the installation ceremony. Adding a National Business Honor Society built bridges between the school and community, and now advisory board members look forward to meetings to learn about the continued successes of Newton students who have become members.

BUSINESS EDUCATION PROGRAM PLANNING

According to Westerberg (2009), research from the Marzanno Institute indicated that "with clear learning goals in place, high schools can go from good to great." Curriculum standards should be a guide to how deeply a student can master a topic. Curriculum content standards need to be focused on specific and necessary content so that mastery of the most relevant topics can be made.

National Standards for Business Education (NBEA, 2013) provides curriculum leaders with a solid framework for implementing courses. The framework, provided by the NBEA, the nation's largest professional organization devoted exclusively to business education, recognizes that competencies attained through business education are essential to all individuals in today's fast-changing society. Numerous business educators and business professionals work to review and revise the standards when they are regularly updated.

Navigating the National Standards Resource

National Standards for Business Education is designed for those working in curriculum development to better understand the progression of business content knowledge and skills. Each standard has a set of more specific performance indicators noted as level one (elementary), level two (middle), level three (secondary), and level four (postsecondary and collegiate). Although it is not common for business education courses to be found at the elementary level, it should be understood that some of those foundation-level skills are infused within other areas. For example, economic concepts should be covered through elementary mathematics and social studies content areas. When a secondary business education teacher or program specialist plans his/her business curriculum standards, students should be ready for level-three content (NBEA, 2013).

In addition to using the *National Standards for Business Education*, it is also important to have local input on standards and curriculum. Advisory boards exist for many career and technical education (CTE) programs as a requirement of federal Perkins funding legislation (Carl D. Perkins Career and Technical Education Improvement Act, 2006). Carol Andringa, business education curriculum specialist and supervisor from Lincoln (Nebraska) Public Schools took advantage of statewide business education "visioning" sessions to enhance local standards. These sessions brought business and industry professionals and business education teachers together to discuss critical components that should be covered in courses. Business and industry representatives shared content that was most critical for their emerging workforce needs. The visioning session data were then used by business teachers during a standards revision process. The outcome provided Lincoln Public Schools and other school districts in the state with a strong foundation for the business curriculum. Andringa's colleagues matched the state work with input from their own advisory board members. Local input from advisory boards tailored the needs of the community to the standards and content needed in the school district's business program courses.

Business Education Course Pathways

Many states and local school districts have adopted career cluster models. According to the Virginia Department of Education's Office of Career and Technical Education Services (2013), career clusters help students investigate careers and design their study around career goals.

The National Association of State Directors of Career Technical Education Consortium (NASDCTEc, 2012) presented results of the States' Career Cluster Initiative. This model has representation from 16 unique career clusters designed to represent all possible career areas. Areas unique to business education and represented as a course in the *National Standards for Business Education* (NBEA, 2013) include the following:

- Arts, audiovisual technology, and communications

- Business management and administration

- Finance

- Hospitality and tourism

- Information technology

- Marketing

Within these clusters, pathways exist that identify a program of study or series of courses that tie directly to individual clusters (Table 1).

Schools in Baltimore (Maryland) County Public Schools follow state-approved programs of study in business education. According to Kara Lynch, supervisor of business education, this school district offers students business education pathways in the business, management, and finance clusters. In addition, the district offers programming in business education through the National Academy Foundation and specialty magnet programs.

Business Career Academies

Another increasingly popular model for delivering business programs is through business career academies. States and school districts are trying to fill demand for schools with career-focused education through career academies, which typically follow a small learning-community model. This type of learning community creates a cadre of students focused on a similar topic (such as finance or computer networking), taught by a coordinated team of teachers from multiple subject areas. The curriculum is typically college preparatory with "relationships between academic subjects and career fields" (Association for Career and Technical Education, 2009, p. 3). Career academies are also most successful when they have employer partnerships that bring resources from outside the school to the students to "increase motivation and achievement"

Table 1. Business Education Career Clusters and Their Associated Pathways within Clusters

Arts, Audiovisual Technology, & Communications	Business Management & Administration	Finance	Hospitality & Tourism	Information Technology	Marketing
• Audiovisual technology & film • Printing technology • Visual arts • Performing arts • Journalism & broadcasting • Telecommu-nications	• General management • Business information management • Human resources management • Operations management • Administra-tive support	• Securities & invest-ments • Business finance • Accounting • Insurance • Banking services	• Restaurants & food/ beverage services • Lodging • Travel & tourism • Recreation, amusements & attractions	• Network systems • Information support & services • Web and digital com-munications • Program-ming and software development	• Marketing manage-ment • Profes-sional sales • Merchan-dising • Marketing communi-cations • Marketing research

(p. 4). Regardless of the type of business program model used at the secondary educa-tion level, funding for such programs remains critical as they are complex in staff and content and are often more expensive to maintain.

Career Clusters, Pathways, and Funding

At the secondary level, many local districts rely on funding from the Perkins Act (2006) to support and expand business education, as well as other CTE program areas. Although individual state departments of education implement and monitor their respective individual school districts' Perkins grant, they must ensure that program guidelines are followed according to federal guidelines.

In most states, Perkins funds cannot be used to support a course that does not fit into a career cluster and pathway model. With this model, there are also no specific business education courses. All courses are aligned with three or more semesters of content specializing in a certain area. One such example would be Nebraska's Career and Technical Education standards and approved program of studies (Nebraska De-partment of Education, 2013).

BUSINESS EDUCATION AND COMMON CORE STATE STANDARDS

A recent development impacting business education and other CTE programs is the Common Core State Standards Initiative. This is a state-led effort coordinated by the National Governors Association Center for Best Practices and the Council of Chief State School Officers.

Common Core Background

Forty-five states in the United States have formally adopted the Common Core State Standards. According to the National Governors Association Center and the Council of Chief State School Officers, Common Core State Standards provide a consistent, clear understanding of what students are expected to learn. These standards will provide teachers, students, and parents a framework for future success in college and careers. Common Core State Standards currently exist for all grade levels between kindergarten and high school graduation in the subject areas of mathematics and English language arts (Common Core State Standards Initiative, 2012).

Leaders in Common Core

Whether a state is designated as a Common Core state is determined by high-level decision makers in the state. The nation's governors and education commissioners lead the Common Core State Standards Initiative. These standards are important because they provide guidance to students, parents, and educators on expectations for college and career. The standards are to be equivalent from state to state across the United States. As textbooks and educational media are developed, Common Core language is a key and consistent component within the latest educational materials.

College and Career Ready

High schools are being charged with assuring that students are ready for a higher level of thinking. These students deserve to be ready for a well-paying job after high school graduation or to be ready for college upon graduation from high school.

According to the NASDCTEc (2012), career-ready practices are defined as "experiences that can be practiced using many different approaches in a variety of settings" (p. 1). Students should be tasked with accomplishing such standards, better preparing them for a career in business. This preparation can and should take place both in and outside of the business education classroom.

Integrating the Four Cs of the Common Core

The four Cs of the Common Core are communication, critical thinking, creativity, and collaboration. The statements and standards found within the Common Core State Standards in math and English language arts lead to these four skills. Students need to be able to communicate and work in an environment requiring these skills, and also to be able to apply these four skills to day-to-day educational situations (Erkens, 2013).

State Standards and the Common Core

Before standards-based education, the curriculum was defined by the textbook. As standards were formed, educators moved to a criterion-based method of describing student outcomes. State-developed standards have come with their faults. Drawbacks of state standards include inconsistencies among states, too many standards with too little direction in a material best practices curriculum, and too little time to effectively present all of this information to students. Under the Common Core, a consortium of states share an agreement of what these most critical elements are (specifically regarding language arts and mathematics). The Common Core State Standards have been developed in a way that lends them to being taught across the curriculum (Kendall, 2011).

Integrating the Common Core into Business Programs

Middle- and secondary-level business educators should know that the skills addressed in the Common Core State Standards are already being addressed in business classrooms. For example, many of the *National Standards for Business Education* (NBEA, 2013) "crosswalk"[1] with the English language arts standards identified for the Common Core. See, for example, Table 2.

Table 2. Crosswalking the Common Core to NBEA Standards

Common Core State Standards (English Language Arts, Speaking, and Listening)	National Standards for Business Education (Information Technology Section)
CCSS.ELA-Literacy.SL.11-12.5 Make strategic use of digital media (e.g., textual, graphical, audio, visual, and interactive elements) in presentations to enhance understanding of findings, reasoning, and evidence and to add interest.	NBEA National Standards for Business Education: Information Technology, Interactive Media, Level 3 Performance Expectations: • Identify and select appropriate multimedia file formats and properties • Create multimedia content and prepare it for delivery • Configure multimedia delivery tools

Crosswalking the *National Standards for Business Education* (NBEA, 2013) with Common Core State Standards can create buy-in and respect for noncore areas on both sides of the table. According to Sarah Heath, district career and technical education coordinator for Jefferson County Public Schools in Golden, Colorado, buy-in was quite challenging. Jefferson County business teachers started the Common Core process with a great deal of professional development. As a beginning, middle school business education teachers were asked to partner with a mathematics teacher from their

---

[1]Crosswalking is a method of matching content from one set of educational standards to a different set of standards for a different curricular area. For example, a Business Education standard on Internet research could be correlated to a standard in Language Arts related to summarizing information for writing text. This method demonstrates relevancy between content areas and allows for collaboration between curricular areas.

school. The groups worked together as a team to crosswalk standards. Following the crosswalk activity, content team groups formed to build curricular materials for teacher and classroom use.

In addition, according to Heath, support for collaboration was challenging. Monetary compensation for time and classroom resources had to be earmarked and provided to make this process happen. For many school districts, finding such resources can be very difficult. Follow-up to ensure teachers are meeting all of the standards for their own curriculum and for Common Core requirements can also be a challenge. In some states (e.g., Colorado and Nevada), a standards portal is used during the lesson planning process, and standard materials and notations are strategically placed by teachers into lesson planning documents.

A critical component for satisfying business educators' classroom and curriculum demands is accomplished through their professional development.

LEADERSHIP THROUGH PROFESSIONAL LEARNING COMMUNITIES

Most effective professional development today is active, not something given or presented to teachers. Often, the best professional development involves dialogue and participation. Educators frequently report that they need more opportunities to talk and reflect with their colleagues; but according to an educational report, only 46% of teachers reported that their professional development led to collaboration with colleagues. Teachers and administrators can develop professional learning communities. These communities should be considered teams or small groups that support each other professionally through their common goals. Common goals could include but are not limited to departmental support and literacy improvement across the curriculum (Gregory & Kuzmich, 2007).

Teachers have different learning needs than those of their students. Adults have more years of life experience to bring into a situation and to use in solving career-driven problems. According to research analyzed by Gregory and Kuzmich (2007), four types of learning apply to both students and adults. It must also be understood that different life events can create differences in how learning information is perceived.

- **Experimental:** Adults connect new ideas or actions.

- **Self-directed:** Adults need choice and opportunities.

- **Life applicable:** Adults need learning that has life applications.

- **Performance centered:** Adults appreciate hands-on learning that is engaging and provides an opportunity for reflection.

As secondary education curriculum leaders develop professional development models, these four components should be considered. Professional learning communities, when done well, can provide educators with great power in shaping their professional development and responding to the needs of their students (Gregory & Kuzmich, 2007).

BUILDING QUALITY SECONDARY BUSINESS EDUCATION PROGRAMS

No program in a secondary school can be of high quality without quality instructors and leadership. Strong teachers are the frontline defense that ensures a program will remain viable and strong. According to Gaytan (2009), teachers state a wide range of reasons why they entered the education profession. Those reasons can range from a lifelong desire to teach and work with students and a passion for business education (or other content area) to prior job dissatisfaction, the economic stability of the education profession, or the need for a career change due to corporate restructuring.

Business teachers now have multiple paths for entering the profession. Gaytan (2009) indicated that differences existed between business education teachers who went through traditional versus nontraditional business education preparation programs in terms of their plans to remain in teaching. Teachers completing nontraditional preparation programs were statistically more likely to leave the teaching profession once the circumstances that caused them to enter the teaching field had changed. This decision would likely be made by changes in the same external factors that previously put them into education as a career. however, no clear connection or evidence suggests whether traditional or nontraditional methods of teacher preparation are more effective. It should be understood that leading business education programs currently see and will see departments that need a wide range of skill sets within business education.

Support for New Teachers

New teachers require added professional development to strengthen their teaching career. School districts have many different approaches to doing this. Such programs and opportunities can include mentoring, induction programs, and more specialized support based on curriculum training needs.

Yohon and Kesten (2009) cited the following support strategies for new and emerging teachers:

- Giving new teachers the opportunity to observe other teachers

- Assigning new teachers to smaller classes

- Assigning mentors to new teachers

- Providing new teachers with shared planning time with their colleagues

- Providing new teachers with frequent and relevant feedback on their classroom instructional practices

In many situations, business teachers do not have the mentoring opportunities that exist in other school departmental areas (e.g., math, science, and language arts).

Even business education colleagues in the same school often teach widely different curriculum topics. This situation enhances the critical need for state-, regional-, and national-level professional development for business education teachers.

Supporting Teachers as Leaders in Secondary Business Education

Whether in a large or small school, business education leaders often take on the role of mentoring and building strong and professional colleagues. Larger schools frequently see the need for instructional coaches or curriculum supervisors who are able to work with large groups of teachers. The duties of instructional coaches or supervisors can range from staff development and training to classroom observations, appraisals, and classroom mentoring. Although smaller schools may not have nearly the same number of colleagues teaching business courses, they still need departmental training and mentorship.

In some cases, the business education teacher becomes the leader for teachers outside of business areas. The role of this person often includes supervision of specific areas in the CTE field, for example, family and consumer sciences, industrial technology, agricultural education, or health sciences. In addition, the scope of business education classes and the support needed can vary extremely from teacher to teacher. For example, a high school's accounting or personal finance teacher will have much different support and professional development needs than those of the computer applications and programming teacher.

Instructional Coaching

Regardless of the business content being delivered, teachers benefit from instructional coaching throughout their careers. According to Kennedy (2011), the professional development that teachers need fall into multiple categories. The lowest-quality category includes teachers who might be considered weaker teachers due to temporary conditions such as being new to the field or experiencing a temporary life issue. Middle categories represent the largest percentage of teachers who can be moved to be even more effective in the classroom with good administrative coaching. Kennedy referred to best teachers as "peak performers" who are often the teachers who lead professional development and school-based initiatives.

Thirty-second feedback sessions. A teacher is observed by an instructional leader for a short time (typically less than 15 minutes). Immediately after the session, either a verbal feedback session or a written note is provided to that teacher describing the positive aspects of what the instructional leader observed—an introduction, specific facts of what was observed, how the students were impacted by the teacher's work—and a praising or appreciative statement.

These short bursts of professional interaction and feedback are intended to lead to a higher level of trust and comfort for both the teacher and instructional leader. They also often lead to more productive discussions on what a teacher can do to improve in the classroom (Kennedy, 2011).

Five-minute feedback. Supporting colleagues as a curriculum leader often needs greater interaction and feedback than 30-second feedback can provide. More advanced five-minute feedback sessions in which the teacher is asked more questions about what he or she did in the lesson and how the lesson was prepared can be held. In addition, the coach may quote a research statement or provide a statistic demonstrating that the feedback is connected to educational best practices.

Formal Observation and Feedback Methods

In many school situations, formal teacher observations and evaluations are conducted by the principal or assistant principal. Depending on the structure of the school and school district, that role may be delegated to department heads, curriculum specialists, or instructional supervisors. Danielson (1996) identified the following four domains used in evaluating instruction:

Planning and preparation. The core ideals of instructional planning are emphasized in the first domain. In a business education classroom, the teacher should demonstrate thorough knowledge of business content. The teacher must also display understanding of district, state, and national content standards relating to the specific instructional situation.

Classroom environment. Business education teachers should demonstrate classroom respect and rapport and manage their classroom with appropriate procedures. Not only should student learning be well managed, but the classroom should exhibit a strong culture for learning.

Instruction. A teacher with strong instructional ideals communicates with students clearly and accurately. Students are provided feedback for and about learning; the classroom is an engaged environment where the teacher uses a variety of questioning/discussion techniques.

Professional and leadership responsibilities. The educator is a professional who maintains student records/reports with accuracy and confidentiality conveying results to both students and parents. Outside the classroom, the teacher demonstrates professionalism by working with other colleagues and by involvement in organizations such as the NBEA. The professional educator contributes positively to the school and community.

Danielson (1996) indicated that curriculum leaders must follow consistent evaluative techniques, language, and criteria that incorporate these four domains. Criteria for each domain lead to a determination on whether the teacher is performing at an exemplary, distinguished, proficient, basic, or below-basic professional level.

CAREER GUIDANCE AND SCHOOL COUNSELING

Effective secondary-level business educators should have a partnership with career guidance and school counseling staff in providing comprehensive student services expected of professionals. Counselors are dedicated to serving as system leaders in the school and advocate for students' educational needs. As schools are constantly striving to be better, administrators seek methods of change that bring greater student success. School counselors often have access to the data needed for such school improvement.

Business educators should consider the school counselor an ally in student success and should work as partners with them. Business educators should be willing and open to accepting and infusing guidance activities into their classrooms. They should request having open conversations with counselors about what the content of a business education course includes and how those courses can better prepare students for college and career.

Business educators should use available data to both improve the entire school and their individual departments. For example, a business teacher could work with the school counselor to determine what students would be best suited for a particular class based on assessment results or career interest inventories aligned with classroom guidance activities (American School Counselor Association, 2003).

Structured career guidance activities are crucial in preparing students for successful education and career transitions. Business educators and school counselors need partnerships both in and outside of the classroom to best prepare students for college and career (Association for Career and Technical Education, 2008).

COMMUNITY RESOURCES AND ADVISORY BOARDS

Another focus for secondary-level business educators is using community resources and gaining input from advisory groups. Business educators need to rely on their local business community and should form partnerships with local business leaders for input on what should be the most critical components of their course sequence to prepare students for college and careers. Business leaders can give educators the right focus on outcomes that best meet the needs of a local community and economy, and those same leaders can bring training and real-life professional development to classroom teachers.

Requirements of the federal Carl D. Perkins Career and Technical Education Improvement Act (2006) require an active advisory board for each entity receiving funding. An advisory board can be a single board that covers and represents multiple career fields encompassed in a school district's CTE program or it can be a very specific and focused group for a specialty group such as a business education program academy of finance or academy of information technology. Most important, an advisory board should connect and meet the needs of the local community and region (Pawlowski & Meeder, 2012).

LEADERS IN TECHNOLOGY

Business educators frequently are the leaders of technology in their schools because they possess the technology expertise colleagues and administrators need to manage their schools, classrooms, and offices. Business educators work with students in preparing them for technology use in high school, college, and careers; they also often naturally lead technology innovation and movements in education.

Why technology? Technology can improve student achievement across the curriculum when used and implemented properly. Research indicates that "technology's use in the classroom can have an additional positive influence on student learning goals that are clearly articulated prior to the technology's use" (Pitler, Hubbell, Kuhn, & Malenoski, 2007, pp. 2–3). Business teachers frequently see how student use of technology stimulates learning and increased engagement and enjoyment of a particular class. The same can be true across the curriculum. Technology can enhance development of critical thinking and problem-solving skills.

Planning Effective Instructional Strategies Incorporating Technology

Technology added to a classroom as a curriculum enhancement with no professional development or plan for implementation will not achieve the desired goal of higher student achievement. Educators need to consider several questions when planning the implementation of technology.

What will the students learn? Educators and administrators must consider evidence of student learning when using technology. Students can often demonstrate a technology application, but it is equally important for that student to apply the purpose and reason behind that same application. For example, when a business teacher demonstrates how and when to use a pivot table in Microsoft Excel, the expected outcome would be for that student to apply a pivot table to a real-life situation in the future. A critical question across the curriculum is whether the technology should be learned or whether the learning of another topic is enhanced with a technology application.

Teaching with new technologies. The cycle of technology will expand and change many times during the career of a business educator. Many curriculum standards in business education and information technology refer to the concept of "emerging technologies." Teaching with a new technology should be a gradual process. According to Wiske, Rennenbohm Franz, and Breit (2005, p. 115), the process can begin with "minor changes and evolve over time through trial and error." As teachers adopt a new technology, they should integrate these components "gradually" and "reflect on results" (Wiske, Rennenbohm Franz, & Breit, 2005, p. 115).

Technology and Professional Development

Professional development is a key component of adding technology to a curriculum. Without professional development, teachers will not be comfortable with the new technology in a way that leads them to use it in the classroom. Professional development should focus on "explicit understanding" around the technology and should not be a one-time occurrence. Many training opportunities should be provided and assessment of the technology's use should be reviewed on a regular basis (Wiske, Rennenbohm Franz, & Breit, 2005, p. 117).

SUMMARY

Leadership in business education at the secondary education level takes on many facets. For students, business education plays a vital role in developing students by preparing them for college and career. The business education teacher and curriculum leader is charged with ensuring that the knowledge and skills presented to those students is the most essential and relevant to meeting the demands for college entrance and future business and industry colleagues.

Business education leaders at the secondary level embrace students and learning. Those leaders also need to understand the importance of embracing other teachers in the content area and what they need to further develop as professionals. They must develop partnerships with school counselors and with community business leaders. Their knowledge of technology places them in influential roles in schools.

Secondary-level programs remain the core of business instruction; business educators and curriculum leaders are at the forefront of assuring a strong foundation for that core.

REFERENCES

American School Counselor Association. (2003). *The ASCA national model: A framework for school counseling programs* (2nd ed.). Alexandria, VA: Author.

Association for Career and Technical Education. (2008). *ACTE issue brief: Career and technical education's role in career guidance.* Alexandria, VA: Author.

Association for Career and Technical Education. (2009). *ACTE issue brief: The role of career academies in education improvement.* Alexandria, VA: Author.

Association for Career and Technical Education. (2012). *ACTE issue brief: CTE's role in leadership development.* Alexandria, VA: Author.

Carl D. Perkins Career and Technical Education Improvement Act of 2006. S. 250, 109th Cong. 20 U.S.C. 2301 (2006) (enacted).

Common Core State Standards Initiative. (2012). Implementing the Common Core State Standards. Retrieved from http://www.corestandards.org

Danielson, C. (1996). *Enhancing professional practice: A framework for teaching.* Alexandria, VA: ASCD.

Erkens, C. (2013). Attending to the demands of the Common Core (presentation). Omaha Public Schools Administrative Seminar, January 30, 2013, Omaha, Nebraska, Professional Development Conference. Retrieved from https://docs.google.com/file/d/0BySh6YtfmFIuSnN5UGRhWnBmekE/edit?pli=1

Foundation for the Future of Business Education. (2005). *Effective strategies and tools for marketing business education.* Reston, VA: National Business Education Association.

Gaytan, J. (2009). Traditionally certified vs. non-traditionally certified business education teachers: Do both routes lead to high-quality teacher preparation? *NABTE Review, 36,* 10–16.

Gregory, G. H., & Kuzmich, L. (2007). *Teacher teams that get results: 61 strategies for sustaining and renewing professional learning communities.* Thousand Oaks, CA: Corwin Press.

Kendall, J. (2011). *Understanding Common Core State Standards.* Alexandria, VA: ASCD.

Kennedy, K. (2011). Coaching champions (presentation). Professional Development Conference Presentation, Omaha Public Schools Teaching and Learning Institute, August 2, 2012, Omaha, Nebraska.

Meggison, P. (2012). Model business education programs. In W. L. Stitt-Gohdes (Ed.). *Trends and issues in business education: 2012 yearbook* (No. 50, pp.159–173). Reston, VA: National Business Education Association.

National Business Education Association (NBEA). (2013). *National standards for business education: What America's students should know and be able to do in business education* (4th ed.). Reston, VA: Author.

National Association of State Directors of Career and Technical Education Consortium (NASDCTEc). (2012). *The career ready practices of the common career technical core.* Retrieved from http://www.careertech.org/career-technical-education/cctc/careerreadypractices.html

Nebraska Department of Education, Career Education Division. (2013). Retrieved from http://www.education.ne.gov/BMIT/pdf/enrollments-2010-11_BMM-CIS.pdf

Pawlowski, B., & Meeder, H. (2012). *Building advisory boards that matter: A handbook for engaging your business partners.* Alexandria, VA: Association for Career and Technical Education.

Pitler, H., Hubbell, E. R., Kuhn, M., & Malenoski, K. (2007). *Using technology with classroom instruction that works.* Alexandria, VA: ASCD.

Policies Commission for Business and Economic Education (PCBEE). (2002). *This we believe about the need for business education: Policy Statement 71.* Retrieved from http://nbea.org/newsite/curriculum/policy/no_71.pdf

Virginia Department of Education, Office of Career and Technical Education Services. (2013). Career clusters: Pathways to college and career readiness. Retrieved from http://www.doe.virginia.gov/instruction/career_technical/career_clusters/index.shtml#content

Westerberg, T. R. (2009). *Becoming a great high school: Six strategies and one attitude that make a difference.* Alexandria, VA: ASCD.

Wiske, M. S., Rennenbohm Franz, K. R., & Breit, L. (2005). *Teaching for understanding with technology.* San Francisco, CA: Jossey-Bass.

Yohon, T., & Kesten, C. (2009). The effect of teacher license certification on challenges and needs of new business and marketing teachers. *NABTE Review, 36,* 17–24.

Leadership in Community College Business Programs

Jean Condon, Kathleen McCune, and Cathy Nutt
Mid-Plains Community College
North Platte, NE

What do Walt Disney, Jim Belushi, Billy Crystal, Clint Eastwood, Tom Hanks, Calvin Klein, and Nolan Ryan have in common? All of these successful people began their leadership journey by first attending a community college. Comprehensive community colleges are both a principal provider for academic instruction and a major source of career preparation programs including workforce development through stand-alone adult training programs. No other segment of postsecondary education has been more responsive to its community's education and workforce needs. In fact, at local community colleges, students can learn at any point in their lives while taking advantage of low tuition, convenient campus locations, open admissions, and comprehensive course offerings (Kasper, 2002–2003).

This chapter focuses on the challenges faced by community college leaders, the importance of maintaining a current business program curriculum, faculty qualifications for community college business programs, a professional identity for community college business faculty, and the importance of professional rapport with external stakeholders at all levels of education as well as industry.

ADDRESSING UNIQUE CHALLENGES FACED BY COMMUNITY COLLEGE LEADERS

Roles for community college leaders are ever changing due to the comprehensive range of community college offerings in serving community needs. These ongoing changes keep community college leaders continuously re-examining mission statements, updating technologies and equipment, and locating funds for new programs. It behooves career and business division leaders to provide input to other college leaders regarding relevance of current programs as well as emerging community needs that the community college should address. Likewise, *career and business* division leaders must specifically focus on how programs offered in their division address the overall community college mission.

Career Division Mission Statement

A mission statement directs community college leaders to establish a statement of purpose. This statement should guide the actions of leaders and guide the development of the strategic plan through the decision-making process in determining the relevance of current programs and need for additional offerings.

Purpose of mission statements. A mission statement developed at the division level should align with the community college's mission. Just as the community college's mission statement represents the institution's vision of how it would like to be seen by its community, so should the division mission statement guide the vision of the department. It is important that faculty leaders are aware of the mission statement and can communicate this vision to all stakeholders. Components of a mission statement should be clear.

Components of a mission statement. Mission statements usually include a purpose statement, how-to statement, and value statement. An ideal mission statement should be inspiring to employees. Stakeholders will be reassured when they are exposed to the statement because they will be able to see that the college is committed to their purpose. Effective leaders can promote the mission statement, in whole or in part, in a number of ways: displaying it on business cards for distribution, providing a framed mission statement to new faculty members, printing it on department letterhead, or including it in an e-mail signature line.

"A mission statement is best written in collaboration. It should be a statement that stays relevant no matter the difficulties the college may face and can serve as an instrument that rallies the troops to overcome adversity" (Khatib, 2008, para. 6).

Facilities and Technologies

The mission statement should provide direction for the community college's investment in facilities and technologies, as it is important that community colleges stay on the cutting edge. This need constantly challenges the community college's resources, faculty, time, and programs.

On most college campuses, instructional technology tends to be thought of as the technology tools (e.g., clickers, learning management systems, tablets, handheld devices, touch screen devices, etc.) instead of a process that involves planning, implementing, evaluating, and managing the use of technology to enhance teaching and learning. When planning for instructional technology, it is important to learn how it is perceived by stakeholders in the process to ensure that those involved in planning its use have similar understandings of what it is and how it should be approached. (Mitchell, 2011, p. 47)

It is especially important for leaders of business divisions to conduct a needs assessment to determine a community college's true needs regarding technology. This assessment will avoid costly mistakes in making decisions regarding the purchase and use of facilities and technologies that are vital for preparing students to enter the workforce with skills required by future employers.

Regardless how leaders plan for facilities and technology improvement, it is important to obtain input from all users. Community college leaders must follow Mitchell's (2011) advice—keep learning in mind, make it worthwhile, and try it before you buy it—and look at all possible solutions.

Funding

Leaders at the community college level face funding challenges in maintaining efficient facilities and obtaining quality technologies, similar to other educational institutions.

Local and state funding. In addition to tuition and fees, community colleges rely on local tax funds, usually property taxes, and state legislative appropriation for funding. Legislators in many states continue to consider new strategies for funding community colleges. One strategy that continues to be proposed is to allocate a portion of higher education state funding based on the performance of institutions in areas such as retention and graduation.

Grant funding. Trends in total institutional revenues for community colleges indicate significant shifts toward external revenue sources and away from core state and local funding for basic operations. The fastest-growing revenue categories for community colleges have been government grants and contracts—federal, state, and local programs for training. Grants help support and grow programs and activities. They can also provide extra visibility and credibility both inside and outside of institutions. Because of the need for and variety of grants available, community colleges are employing full-time grant writers to tap this funding source. Locating the appropriate grant that fits the division, community college, and community can be challenging, but rewarding.

Federal funding. Recently, a federal focus on community college funding has emerged:

President Obama's budget proposal for the 2013 fiscal year re-affirms his commitment to community colleges by directing scarce federal resources to job-training and student-aid programs (Field, 2012, para. 1)

The proposed $8-billion community college to career fund would support states that form partnerships with businesses to train an estimated two million workers in high-growth and in-demand areas (Field, 2012, para. 5)

According to a fact sheet released by the White House, the proposed new fund would train workers for unfilled jobs through apprenticeships, on-the-job training, and internships. It would also support industry efforts to develop skills consortia, standardize industry certifications, develop new training technologies, and offer grants to state and local governments that encourage companies to locate in the United States. (Field, 2012, para. 21)

Regardless of the funding source, it is important to remember that funding should align with the division budget, the needs of students, and the needs of potential employers. Leaders must involve faculty to set budget priorities, so that appropriate and necessary business programs are maintained and enhanced.

MAINTAINING A CURRENT BUSINESS PROGRAM CURRICULUM

Because of community colleges' key role in postsecondary education in responding to workforce needs, maintaining a current business program curriculum is critical for the community college in order to sustain a competitive edge in the education provided. Community college business division programs must continue to provide the skills necessary for student success in business/industry. Leaders of community college business divisions must assure that the curriculum-monitoring process focuses on areas of standards, business/industry needs and job placement, technology integration, and student organizations.

Standards

Leaders at the community college must continually re-evaluate the standards that guide the program curriculum. These standards should be consistent with the *National Standards for Business Education* (National Business Education Association, 2013).

Community college leaders and faculty should be encouraged to consider the standards when developing courses or making program changes. The expectation of community college leaders is for faculty to continually revisit standards before making program changes.

Business/Industry Needs and Job Placement

If a business program does not produce the knowledge, skills, and attributes in students that business/industry desires, students will not be hired and the program cannot be considered successful. Community college leaders should encourage and support faculty to engage with local business/industry representatives and use the gained insight to evaluate and change program requirements as needed. This interaction is possible through a variety of valuable contacts, such as program advisory boards, business partnerships, internship contacts, industry tours, and guest speakers.

Business/industry trends must also be monitored and community college programs and courses adjusted to satisfy business/industry needs and growth. The business sector will add close to 3.8 million jobs in the next few years; some of the best business-related jobs are predicted to be accountants, bookkeeping clerks, compliance officers, executive assistants, insurance agents, and financial advisors ("Best Business Jobs," 2013). Community college leaders should assure that these trends are included in the current business program curriculum.

Technology Integration

In order for community college leaders to maintain a current business program curriculum, they must also focus on the technology necessary for the workplace. "The first wave of the modern era in the use of technology in business education occurred when calculators replaced the ubiquitous slide rule in the 1970s" (Cauley, Aiken, & Whitney, 2009, para. 3). Technology integration in business education since then has been in a constant state of change.

It is critical that students are provided with learning experiences using current technology so they are workplace ready. Schlenker and Mendelson (2008) stated, "By teaching students to use workplace technologies most effectively, we can better prepare them to work, communicate, and interact in the 21st century workplace" (p. 22). Furthermore, this technology competence may be what gives the community college a competitive edge. "In today's competitive market, the school that deploys the best technology may be the school that attracts the best students" (McKenzie, 2007, p. 62).

To accomplish this competitive edge, community college leaders need to begin looking at the prevailing technology in industry today. "Enabling this far-flung modern workplace is a whole host of technologies, from e-mail to cell phones to Web conferencing to process management software. To be successful in business today, every executive must be comfortable with many of these new technologies" (Schlenker & Mendelson, 2008, p. 22). Technologies that businesses currently use include e-books, Wi-Fi, smart phones, apps, video conferences, podcasts, webinars, wikis, blogs, cloud computing, tablets, and social media—just to name a few. "Corporate portals and online collaboration tools are becoming standard in the business world. Not only will these tools support online learning but they will practically be part of the woodwork when students enter their professional environments" (Schlenker & Mendelson, 2008, p. 24). Ultimately, faculty must be encouraged by community college leaders to make these technologies available and used in a way that complements the work environment. Schlenker and Mendelson stated that "technology should not be used to make the classroom more virtual but to make the classroom more corporate" (p. 24).

Business Student Organizations

To maintain a current business program curriculum, community college leaders must also reflect on the value of business student organizations, such as Phi Beta

Lambda and Skills USA, in enriching the business curriculum. Community college business division leaders must understand the role that student organizations play in enhancing the educational experience of the student. Involvement in student organizations is an important part of the life of community college students. This involvement allows students the opportunity to meet peers with similar interests; to deal honestly and fairly with one another; to develop leadership abilities through participation in educational, professional, community and social activities; to promote high standards in career ethics, workmanship, scholarship and safety; to enhance the ability of students to plan together, to organize and carry out worthy activities and projects through the use of the democratic process; and to build a resume and network for employment after graduation. Community college business division leaders must support student organizations, and business faculty must assure that the student organization's work and activities align with the program's curriculum. Chapter 16 of this Yearbook provides more information about student organization leadership.

FACULTY QUALIFICATIONS FOR AND PROFESSIONAL IDENTITY IN COMMUNITY COLLEGE BUSINESS PROGRAMS

Qualified faculty are essential for community college business programs. Faculty with necessary qualifications must be recruited and then community college leaders need to help faculty build a professional identity that will allow them to best serve students.

Faculty Recruitment

"Community college leaders recognize that to deliver high-quality academic programs, colleges must attract capable faculty to carry out the educational mission. It is the faculty who provide the credibility and leadership necessary to build educational programs" (Winter & Kjorlien, 2001, para. 1). With higher salaries in the business sector and the retirement of current full-time faculty, it is sometimes difficult to recruit faculty with appropriate business academic and experiential backgrounds to teach full time at the community college level. It is important for business program leaders to have clear and well-defined recruitment policies and selection criteria in order to employ the highest quality faculty. Community college faculty should possess the knowledge, skills, and abilities needed to meet the challenges of teaching today's community college students (see below). In addition, faculty transcripts must reflect the specified degree and credit-hour requirements established by the institution. According to Rifkin (2000), some practical procedures adopted by colleges include ensuring that the recruitment process coincides with the academic calendar; producing advertising that reflects the college's mission, goals, and values; implementing a training program for hiring; and establishing an open-meeting process when awarding faculty positions.

Community college business programs rely on faculty with strong leadership skills. These leadership skills include an appreciation and possession of interpersonal intelligence, the ability to foster effective teams, and the ability to collaborate. As in business/industry, leaders in community colleges embrace a synergistic approach to fulfilling the institutional missions they have developed.

Interpersonal intelligence. Community college leaders and faculty must possess a high degree of intellectual intelligence. However, leaders require more than mere knowledge or intellectual intelligence; they also require a great deal of interpersonal intelligence. In business and in the classroom, interpersonal intelligence offers "staying power."

Interpersonal intelligence is often referred to as emotional intelligence (also emotional quotient or EQ). According to O'Neil (1996), it is a different way of being smart. It is the ability to make good decisions, to manage moods, to control impulses, and to maintain empathy. It is those social skills that enable leaders to lead others.

Community college faculty and staff respond to and interact with forces within and outside the classroom, particularly in terms of the diversity of the student body.

America's community colleges have provided access to higher education and an opportunity for a better life to the most diverse student body in history. The famous "open door" has welcomed students of all ages and ethnicities, students with disabilities, students with different learning objectives, and students with a wide difference in level of preparedness and prior educational experience. (Boggs, 2011, p. 3).

The diversity that community colleges and their faculty face extends beyond the student body to interaction with colleagues, four-year institutions, business partnerships, and communities; these interactions demand more than intellect: they require interpersonal skill or emotional intelligence on the part of its leadership—the other "80 to 90 percent of the abilities that distinguish the best leaders" (Goleman, 2001, para. 1).

Team building. Effective teamwork is also important in successfully relating to diversity within and outside community colleges. In today's dynamic, ever-evolving educational environment, it is unrealistic for a single leader to be accountable to everything in an organization. "Many leaders have realized that, in light of the increasing responsibilities placed upon school leadership, it is far more important to create the perfect leadership team than be the perfect leader" (Munby, 2008, p. 33).

A key ingredient to effective team building is a clear commitment to purpose. With a clear purpose, the community college team leader—be it a teacher, administrator, or president—is responsible for selecting the best team members. Each must have a role to play. "The key to creating effective dynamic teams is not to assemble teams with the most popular or most vocal individuals, but [to] do so according to the specific purposes of the team and with the best individuals possible" (Basham & Mathur, 2010,

p. 31). Once team players are selected, it is just as important to ensure that the community college "playground" is safe. Leading causes of team failure are absence of trust, fear of conflict, lack of commitment, avoidance of accountability, and inattention to results ("A Purposeful Approach," 2005).

Community college leaders must be aware that team building takes time. According to one community college academic dean, "You're not going to haul 12 people into a room and by the end of the day build yourself a cohesive team. It takes time to get to know one another and how team members' skills will complement each other" ("A Purposeful Approach," 2005, p. 7).

Faculty collaboration. Faculty collaboration—which may be considered akin to teamwork—is also important in community colleges. After all, through teamwork or collaboration, community colleges are achieving outcomes using a synergistic approach. Although both are necessary, it is important to distinguish between the two and to appreciate the many ways collaboration is used to achieve success among the various stakeholders involved.

According to McLeod (2010), "Teamwork and collaboration are cousins, but they're not twins" (para. 8). Teamwork often requires a team leader to assemble and guide members to a single, common goal that requires structure, deadlines, incentives, and rewards. Collaboration, however, is much more creative and flexible. Rather than a common goal, collaboration depends on shared goals in which the incentives and rewards differ among stakeholders. With teamwork, the task at hand might be clear from the start. In collaboration, members discover over time what is possible: it is an evolutionary process.

Effective leadership within community colleges can encourage and embrace collaboration. Often, departments are small, and course offerings are many. Collaboration creates a larger scope for a department and, in turn, greater results.

For faculty within a community college department, team teaching is an excellent way of collaborating. Team teaching can be as simple as inviting a colleague to a single class session to speak about his/her expertise. Or a course can be organized as a series of rotating units, taught in sequence (Moffat, 2010). Team teaching can even extend outside the business division to include work with faculty from other areas such as agriculture to teach a course such as agricultural business, or with English to teach business English.

Effective community college leadership can also encourage collaboration among departments, thus creating benefits for both the institution and the student. These leaders can encourage alliances with faculty in various disciplines. They can guide faculty to create courses for various programs, not just for business programs, and can consider offering electives for the benefit of all students.

Effective leaders should encourage collaboration between full-time and adjunct faculty. This collaboration is often quite common and necessary, especially among departments within small community colleges where there are not enough faculty to deliver the wide variety of courses that degrees require. Moffat (2010) related this scenario, "One department chair at a community college was the only full-time faculty member in her department, though she hired, supervised, and assessed the work of more than twenty adjunct faculty" (p. 284).

Collaboration at the community college does not have to be complicated. However, it does require effective leadership to encourage and embrace it. Benefits of collaboration in a community college can be great. "At its best, collaboration is deeply creative. A good collaboration can represent a huge investment of time and energy, yet yields far more than the sum of its constituent parts. It can transform the scholarly lives of faculty and students; it can reshape the curriculum; it opens new avenues in teaching" (Moffat, 2010, p. 294).

Professional Identity for Faculty

In addition to assuring that community colleges recruit college faculty with appropriate qualifications, it is also important for community college business division leaders to establish an environment that supports faculty in developing an appropriate professional identity.

To best serve students, leaders must maintain a collective environmental focus: the bigger picture. Within that bigger picture, community college leadership must also encourage the professional identity of faculty. Community college faculty are the mainstay of their institutions. Their leadership plays multiple roles in developing, sustaining, and driving the mission of community colleges. Their hard work, dedication, and passion for college education have allowed community colleges to thrive in the past century. Supporting faculty members in developing a professional leadership identity includes establishing professional goals, supporting professional development, and motivating colleagues.

Professional goals. Goals and visions for professional development should be clear, focused, and align with college priorities and goals. The professional community college faculty is organized around instruction, delivery methods, and the education of students for the work force. Faculty members are engaged in modifying courses to fit the needs of students, using teaching technologies in the classroom, and incorporating a variety of applied activities centered on knowledge and technical skills. A professional identity that supports its members in these activities is ideal. Cohen (2003) supported this belief: "Teaching has always been the hallmark of the community college; a corps of professionalized instructors could do nothing but enhance it. A professionalized faculty might well direct much of its attention to designing a curriculum to fit an institution that shifts priorities rapidly" (p. 97).

Professional development. To fulfill the professional goals of faculty, community college leaders must provide the means for professional development. This is particularly important as faculty retire and new faculty members are appointed. According to Rifkin (2000):

> In order to sustain the new existing faculty, recruitment efforts need to be coupled with retention and renewal efforts…Because a substantial proportion of the community college faculty are part-time (approximately 40 percent), ensuring high-quality instruction and continuity of standards for full-time and part-time faculty is of growing importance…Many colleges have implemented standards for recruiting, training, and providing development opportunities that apply to both full-time and part-time faculty. (para. 12)

Community college faculty leadership development programs allow faculty to improve instructional materials, keep abreast of new technology and methods, and network with colleagues. The goal of many professional development programs is to provide faculty with resources, training, and opportunities that support their professional development using a hands-on approach. In order to make professional development meaningful to faculty, however, it is important not only to show how but also why a professional development activity is valuable to them and to their students; professional development is indeed most effective when it responds to the needs of students. Faculty development must also align with college values, goals, objectives, and mission statement and specifically collegewide performance goals and faculty professional development objectives. Other goals include creating a positive and supportive working environment that recognizes and celebrates achievement and improving institutional effectiveness, which also supports student success.

One professional development activity that has been successful at many colleges is peer coaching or faculty mentoring. Peer coaching is when two faculty members voluntarily work together to improve or develop their teaching approach. Benefits to peer coaching include improved faculty morale, increased collaborations, faculty motivation, and increased pedagogical choices.

Colleague motivation. Community college leaders can also provide the necessary motivation to maintain a strong faculty. Successful leadership requires an understanding of what motivates different types of people. Motivating also employs a specific set of leadership skills: empowering, delegating, briefing, and reinforcing the value that each brings to the institution. Faculty personalities differ in terms of what motivates them; this might range from recognition and honors to autonomy, career development, and teamwork.

According to Siddique, Aslam, Khan, and Fatima (2011), whatever methods of motivation are used, faculty members should receive opportunities for personal and professional growth. Faculty motivational methods should be challenging and include unique learning experiences Faculty should be encouraged to do research, read publications, and attend workshops, seminars, and conferences. Leaders should also create a friendly environment for their faculty members in which they feel accepted and valued by everyone.

Bumham (2012) suggested these methods of motivating colleagues:

(1) Maintain a positive disposition. Optimism and friendliness go a long way toward improving the mood of people you're working alongside, and these qualities can enable them to feel more efficient throughout the day. (para. 2)

(2) Avoid always taking the spotlight. Often it's tempting to dominate the conversation or try to steer your peers a certain way—instead, allow yourself to give fair time to opinions and ideas other than your own. (para. 3)

(4) Notice small details. Often when you interact with coworkers, you only notice when something goes wrong—instead, make a considerable effort to appreciate the small details and useful qualities within your coworker's output that might be overlooked by others. (para. 5)

These methods lead colleagues to feel appreciated and respected, while allowing them to exercise their own choices and ideas.

Interpersonal connections, teamwork, and collaboration make better institutions better. Leaders in a community college can do wonderful things on their own, but leaders can do much better with a collective environmental focus. With the idea of "we are all in this together," the collective efforts are more rewarding.

PROFESSIONAL RAPPORT WITH EXTERNAL STAKEHOLDERS

The collective environmental focus should extend beyond the community college. Community colleges and all that they have to offer have a significant impact on the world around them. Considering that community colleges are affordable, collectively they are significant. They "serve 44 percent of all U.S. undergraduates" (Snyder, 2012a, p. 34). Additionally, "community colleges are a launching point for first-time students and a place adult students return to get new skills, providing millions of Americans with an "on-ramp" to the middle class" (Snyder, 2012a, p. 34). According to Snyder, "Community colleges need to get better at telling our story. Community colleges also must accept—even embrace—the reality that we can't do it alone" (2012b, p. 4).

Rather than looking inward, community college leaders must continue to widen the visual field and embrace the environment beyond the walls of their individual institutions. Business division community college programs should be designed with the idea of preparing students for business jobs or for four-year degrees. The needs of businesses must be regularly assessed and articulation agreements with secondary and four-year institutions should be sought.

We need to collaborate with employers to better understand their needs and respond with career-relevant programs that allow them to remain globally competitive. We must work with four-year institutions to provide a higher education continuum that anticipates market conditions and respond accordingly. And we must listen to our students, understanding that they are the best source of innovation and inspiration we have. Most importantly, community colleges need each other. Throughout the nation, great things are happening that deserve to be celebrated and championed as best practices. (Snyder, 2012a, p. 35)

Secondary Education Colleagues

A part of the community college leadership role is to develop relationships with other colleges and universities, as well as with K–12 schools. Community colleges serve as an intermediary between these different levels of educational institutions. "Community colleges are often acclaimed for their agility, dedication to mission, and passion in supporting local needs" (Sutin, 2012, para. 1). The collaborative relationship between K–12 schools and community colleges include such programs as dual credit, career academies, classroom visitations, and career exploration events. By strengthening the community college's relationship with K–12 schools, leaders encourage students to view community college education as their first enrollment option.

It is important that leaders at both the high schools and community colleges connect career education with business and industry. Students' career paths should begin in high school and seamlessly continue through any postsecondary education. As Bortolussi (2006) stated, "The most important aspect should be the student's career path and not that the student is in high school or in college. It should be the focus because it is upon this "seamless" career path that the student travels" (p. 34). Career academies and dual credit courses are starting points to this career journey for high school students. The role of the community college leadership in this process is to offer quality course offerings—no matter the venue or the age of the student—that meet the needs of the workforce.

Collegiate Colleagues

It is also important for community college leadership to foster rapport with all collegiate colleagues. "As enrollment at community colleges has grown, and as universities look to tap into other pipelines of qualified students, articulation agreements have become more common" (Fain, Blumenstyk, & Sander, 2009, para. 5). Students served by community colleges often choose to further their education. To serve these students, community college leaders should work to establish articulation agreements and transfer programs.

O'Meara, Hall, and Carmichael (2007) defined an articulation agreement as "a formal collaborative agreement between education institutions that enables a student to complete a program of study at one institution and, using accumulated credits, attain a degree at another institution in a shorter period of time" (p. 10). The authors further defined transfer programs as more informal and that "acknowledge credits taken at one institution, not necessarily as part of a completed program or degree, that are subsequently accepted by another institution" (p. 10).

Advisory Boards and Partnerships with the Business Community

Beyond the educational partners at the secondary and collegiate levels, community college leaders must foster rapport with advisory boards and partnerships within the business community. Because of the resources that community colleges possess and training opportunities they can provide, community college leaders should work closely and often in partnership with the private sector. "Community colleges provide access to training that help residents attain jobs, but perhaps more importantly, they also provide 'upskill' training that allows workers to retain their jobs and for their employers to stay competitive" ("Colleges Are Part," 2013, para. 1).

Working closely with industry, community college leaders are improving communities, as well as the lives of those individuals within them. Western Nebraska Community College, for example, was crucial in keeping international retailer Cabela's headquartered in Sidney, Nebraska. In addition, a program at Columbus State Community College in Ohio provides professional development for incumbent workers to become supervisors. ("Colleges Are Part," 2013). Considering the resources of community colleges and the needs of industry, it is vital that leaders develop partnerships between the two. According to Marklein (2010):

> Over the next decade, nearly eight in 10 new jobs will require higher education and workforce training, economists project. As part of his goal for the USA to have the highest proportion of college graduates in the world by 2020, Obama last year challenged the nation's 1,200 community colleges to produce an additional 5 million graduates. (para. 3)

In order to match community college resources to the needs of the private sector, leaders must emphasize the need for advisory boards. Common types include the following: "community advisory board, composed of influential political and community leaders; the alumni board, made up of distinguished graduates; the professional board (often a specialized kind of alumni board); the emeritus faculty board; and the development board, which assists in fund raising" (Olson, 2008, para. 6).

Advisory boards can provide the necessary information for community college leaders to develop appropriate programs for industry to thrive, giving value to both. "Partners participate for diverse reasons. Among these are opportunities to make a difference, to network, to be recognized, to influence curricular activities, and to contribute to society. Effective and ongoing partnerships are characterized by mutual benefits gained from these experiences" (Policies Commission for Business and Economic Education, 2002, para. 1).

An effective advisory board provides benefits for the community college and its leaders. "The benefits of well-managed boards are many, but the key one is that they get people actively involved in the department or the college. Once board members are fully invested in the institution, they are more likely to support it financially and in other material ways" (Olson, 2008, para. 7).

The community college is no longer just a slice of higher education. With active and selective advisory boards representing the private sector and communities, community colleges are affecting lives and growing industries. Colleges are indeed "part of communities' economic DNA" ("Colleges Are Part," 2013).

SUMMARY

Community colleges are the mainstay of all aspects of education and industry. As an educational bridge, community colleges provide the necessary link among high school, higher education, and a career. Leadership within community colleges is imperative for fulfillment of each institution's mission. To remain current with industry needs and to deliver the prerequisites for students to become skilled and work ready, community colleges require a continued re-evaluation of standards and curriculum. Community colleges also require ongoing teacher and staff professional development to improve interpersonal intelligence, team building, and collaboration. In addition, community colleges must continue to network and develop rapport with those outside the institutional walls: secondary education colleagues, collegiate colleagues, industry advisory boards, and business partnerships. Leadership in community college business programs will affect individuals, education, and industry for years to come.

REFERENCES

A purposeful approach to team work. (2005). *Academic Leader, 21*(6), 1–7.

Basham, M. J., & Mathur, R. P. (2010). Dynamic leadership development in community college administration: Theories, applications, and implications. *New Directions for Community Colleges, 2010*(149), 25–32.

Best business jobs. (2013). *U.S. News money—careers—best jobs—business 2013*. Retrieved from http://money.usnews.com/careers/best-jobs/rankings/best-business-jobs

Boggs, G. R. (2011). Community colleges in the spotlight and under the microscope. *New Directions for Community Colleges, 2011*(156), 3–22.

Bortolussi, V. (2006). Seamlessly connecting high school to college to career. *Techniques: Connecting Education & Careers, 81*(3), 34–35.

Bumham, J. (2012). How to motivate coworkers. Retrieved from http://www.ehow.com/how_8694710_motivate-coworkers.html

Cauley, F. G., Aiken, K., & Whitney, L. (2009). Technologies across our curriculum: A study of technology integration in the classroom. *Journal of Education for Business, 85*(2), 114–118.

Cohen, A. M. (2003). *The American community college* (4th ed.). San Francisco, CA: John Wiley.

Colleges are part of communities' economic DNA. (2013, January 30). *Community College Times—American Association of Community Colleges.* Retrieved from http://www.communitycollegetimes.com/Pages/Workforce-Development/Colleges-are-part-of-communities-economic-DNA.aspx

Fain, P., Blumenstyk, G., & Sander, L. (2009). Sharing ideas: Tough times encourage colleges to collaborate. *Chronicle of Higher Education, 55*(23), A20–A22.

Field, K. (2012). Federal budget's details offer grist for debates. *Chronicle of Higher Education, 58*(25), A1–A4.

Goleman, D. (2001). Nothing new under the sun. *People Management, 7*(3), 51.

Kasper, H. T. (2002–2003, Winter). The changing role of community college. *Occupational Outlook Quarterly,* 14–21.

Khatib, M. (2008, November 21). The importance of a mission statement. Retrieved from http://EzineArticles.com/1726214

Marklein, M. (2010, October 5). Obama seeks to partner businesses, 2-year colleges. Retrieved from http://usatoday30.usatoday.com/news/education/2010-10-05-communitycolleges05_ST_N.htm

McKenzie, R. B. (2007). Faculty: Embrace the tech-supported classroom. *Bized, 6*(2), 62–63.

McLeod, L. E. (2010, November 8). Teamwork v. collaboration (and why I'm finally lifting my ban on sports analogies). Retrieved from http://www.huffingtonpost.com/lisa-earle-mcleod/teamwork-v-collaboration_b_780213.html

Mitchell, R. L. (2011, Summer). Planning for instructional technology in the classroom. *New Directions for Community Colleges, 2011*(154), 45–52.

Moffat, W. (2010). Creativity and collaboration in the small college department. *Pedagogy, 10*(2), 283–294.

Munby, S. (2008). Building the perfect team: Leadership in the twenty-first century. *Education Review, 21*(1), 31–38.

National Business Education Association (NBEA). (2013). *National standards for business education: What America's students should know and be able to do in business.* Reston, VA: Author.

Olson, G. A. (2008). The importance of external advisory boards. *Chronicle of Higher Education, 54*(24), C3.

O'Meara, R., Hall, T., & Carmichael, M. (2007). A discussion of past, present, and future articulation models at postsecondary institutions. *Journal of Technology Studies, 33*(1), 9–16.

O'Neil, J. (1996, September). On emotional intelligence: A conversation with Daniel Goleman. Retrieved from http://www.ascd.org/publications/educational-leadership/sept96/vol54/num01/On-Emotional-Intelligence@-A-Conversation-with-Daniel-Goleman.aspx

Policies Commission for Business and Economic Education (PCBEE). (2002). *This we believe about the need for partnerships in business education: Policy statement 70.* Retrieved from http://www.nbea.org/newsite/curriculum/policy/no_70.pdf

Rifkin, T. (2000). Public community college faculty. *American Association of Community Colleges.* Retrieved from http://www.aacc.nche.edu/Resources/aaccprograms/pastprojects/Pages/publicccfaculty.aspx

Schlenker, L., & Mendelson, A. (2008). Technology at work. *Bized, 7*(1), 22–26.

Siddique, A., Aslam, H. D., Khan, M., & Fatima, U. (2011). Impact of academic leadership on faculty's motivation and organizational effectiveness in higher education system. *International Journal of Academic Research, 3*(3), 730–737.

Snyder, T. J. (2012a). Big ideas needed: Urgency, innovation, collaboration. *University Business, 15*(2), 34–35.

Snyder, T. J. (2012b). White House roundtable reinforces need for urgency, innovation, collaboration. *Community College Week, 24*(11), 4.

Sutin, S. E. (2012, November 19). Essay on leading community colleges during time of transition. Retrieved from http://www.insidehighered.com/advice/2012/11/19/essay-leading-community-colleges-during-times-transition

Winter, P. A., & Kjorlien, C. L. (2001). Business faculty recruitment: The effects of full-time versus part-time employment. *Community College Review, 29*(1), 18.

Leadership in College and University Business Programs

Beryl C. McEwen

North Carolina A&T State University

Greensboro, NC

Business education programs exist at all educational levels: elementary, middle school, high school, and postsecondary, including the doctoral level. Not surprisingly, the nature and scope of the discipline varies depending on the educational level. Business education at the college and university levels is primarily responsible for preparing students to become business educators and providing foundation courses to prepare students for roles in modern businesses and other types of organizations (Webber & Englehart, 2011).

Furthermore, leadership of business education also varies based on the educational level at which it is offered. The purpose of this chapter is to discuss business education leadership at the college and university levels. This includes the nature of college-level business programs; the role of business education at the college and university levels; and leadership perspectives related to academic programming, students, and quality assurance. The chapter concludes with a discussion of best practices for leadership of business education programs.

NATURE OF COLLEGE/UNIVERSITY-LEVEL BUSINESS EDUCATION

At the college and university levels, the terms "business programs" and "business education" are not synonymous, as they tend to be at the middle and secondary levels where a group of business discipline courses is often referred to as a "business program." At the college and university levels, business programs are divided into several groups or majors, including accounting, business information technology, business teacher education, entrepreneurship, finance, general business, human resource management, management, marketing, operations management, organizational behavior, strategic management, and supply chain management, among other subdisciplines. Except in the case of business teacher education and sometimes business information technology, all business programs are offered through colleges or schools of business. As such, this chapter will focus on leadership of business programs, sometimes called "business education" or "management education," solely from the perspective of colleges and schools of business.

The nature of college- and university-level business education is characterized by groupings of business courses offered as associate degrees, bachelor's degrees, master's degrees, doctoral degrees, and certificates designed to prepare students for varying levels of employment in for-profit and not-for-profit organizations. At the college and university levels, business programs are almost always designed for career preparation. Although an occasional elective course might focus on personal use skills, for example, *personal finance*, business courses are taught from the perspective of corporate or entrepreneurial organizations. Business programs provide professional training, and the business college or school is classified among the institution's "professional" colleges and schools.

ROLE OF BUSINESS EDUCATION PROGRAMS AT COLLEGE AND UNIVERSITY LEVELS

To clarify the role of business education at the college and university levels, it is first important to distinguish between "college" and "university." College is the term used to describe the level of the education system that offers associate degrees (two-year programs) and bachelor's degrees (four-year programs) as their primary mission. Universities typically do not offer associate degrees; they offer bachelor's, master's, and doctoral degrees as their primary mission. Although bachelor's degrees are offered at both the college and university levels, for the purposes of this chapter, the bachelor's degree will be discussed as part of university-level programs, and the discussion of college-level programs will be limited to associate degrees.

Considering the distinction made in the previous paragraph, the role of college-level business programs is to provide students with entry-level business skills that allow them to assume fairly technical, nonsupervisory roles in business and industry as well as provide personal business skills (Rader & Meggison, 2007). At the university level, business programs are designed to prepare leaders and managers in business and industry, small business, governmental, and other not-for-profit organizations. University-level business programs are also designed to ensure "generativity"[1] in business and management education by preparing the next generation of business teachers for roles in public schools and business professors for colleges and universities.

---

[1] "A concern for people besides self and family that usually develops during middle age; especially: a need to nurture and guide younger people and contribute to the next generation—used in the psychology of Erik Erikson" (Generativity, n.d.). Also see Policies Commission for Business and Economic Education (2010).

LEADERSHIP OF BUSINESS PROGRAMS

Leadership of academic programs in higher education involves responsibility for ensuring effectiveness in teaching and learning. This basic description also includes responsibilities for coaching and developing instructional staff, managing student issues, monitoring program outcomes, and designing curriculum content and instructional design (Vilkinas & Ladyshewsky, 2011). Leadership of business programs, while not vastly different, also requires a broad understanding of the vast array of business programs (majors and minors); appreciation of the value that each adds to the workforce, civic understanding, and professional growth, as well as to new business development; and the synergies that should and do exist among all business programs.

At the college and university levels, leadership for business programs is provided by department heads, sometimes called department chairs, and by academic deans. The size of the programs usually determines the organization of the program and the number of associate/assistant deans supporting each program. Simply defined, academic leadership is the process of persuading others to pursue the objectives of the leader or the leadership team. As Wilcox and Ebbs (1992) noted, leadership is "distinguished by vision that creates focus, by the ability to help others grasp the 'big picture' and communicate meaning to develop commitment…" (p. 27). Leadership should not be confused with management, which means the functional operation of the academic units that offer the business programs (Kotter, 2013). This chapter focuses on leadership, not management of business programs.

Leadership of business programs, among other things, must focus on the development and maintenance of academic programs, recruiting and supporting students, and assuring the high quality of programs and graduates. As such, this chapter continues by discussing leadership from the perspectives of academic programming, student services, and quality assurance.

LEADERSHIP PERSPECTIVE: ACADEMIC PROGRAMMING

Developing and maintaining "in demand" business programs is at the very foundation of business education at the college and university levels. Determining the programs that should be offered depends on a clear and accurate understanding of the needs of the marketplace, mostly local for college-level programs. However, regional, national, and global needs influence business program offerings at the university level. The changing demands of the marketplace are reflected in college- and university-level business programs.

The Business Curricula

Although professional organizations, such as the National Business Education Association, and many states present standards for secondary-level business curricula, the same is not true for college- and university-level business programs. Most curricula are designed by faculty groups with input from professional organizations, advisory boards, textbooks, each other's programs, and their accrediting agencies. Other determinants of academic programs are faculty expertise for program delivery, facilities and technology, instructional materials, and extramural funding. Quality control is assured through the curriculum review process, which usually begins with the departmental committee proposing the curriculum, progresses through departmental and school or college-level approvals, and ends with approval by the university-level curriculum committee or the faculty senate.

Faculty Qualifications and Recruitment

Academic programs and curricula must be supported by a talented and diverse faculty. Identifying, recruiting, hiring, and retaining talented faculty is an important part of leading business education programs. The process of identifying and recruiting talented faculty usually begins with department chairs who design and disseminate position announcements and scout for talent at professional meetings. In some cases, the department chair simply appoints a search and screen committee, which then begins the recruitment process. Most business positions are posted with professional organizations, accreditation agencies, and support agencies, such as The PhD Project. Recruiting through these organizations is very important for attracting credible and talented faculty and helps to carefully screen out unsuitable candidates. In addition, it is also important to work closely with the institution's human resources division to ensure that employment laws and regulations are carefully observed.

Most tenure track positions require a doctoral degree (Ph.D., D.B.A., or Ed.D.). College-level programs will sometimes accept a master's degree for adjunct faculty positions. Once hired, faculty must be mentored to successfully complete the tenure and promotion process in their institutions and to find their places as leaders in their profession. Mentoring programs can be formal or informal but are usually encouraged and supported (Inzer & Crawford, 2005).

Department chairs contribute greatly to the mentoring of new faculty, assisted by other senior faculty. Where formal mentoring programs exist, department chairs are largely responsible for supervising them.

Facilities and Equipment

Facilities and equipment are very important to the quality of business programs that an institution offers. They help to set the tone and image of the programs, and they offer students a learning environment that will help them to transform from students to employees or entrepreneurs (Thille, 2010). Classrooms, laboratories, libraries, case rooms, financial trading rooms, course management systems, and similar traditional and virtual spaces equipped with appropriate technology help to provide the dynamic environment in which college and university business programs thrive. Establishing and maintaining these spaces require that deans and department chairs understand the value that they add to business programs and also requires them to be very skilled in managing budgets, as facilities and equipment are "big ticket items" that greatly challenge limited departmental funds.

Instructional Materials

Instructional materials for business programs include textbooks, workbooks, cases, simulations, formative assessments, software, clickers, and other hand-held devices. A wide variety of instructional materials is available commercially, including many textbooks that now come with lecture slides and cases, and a range of learning assessments. Materials are also available free online, for example, at the Multimedia Educational Resource for Learning and Online Teaching (MERLOT) Web page.[2] Leaders in business education are often required to build consensus around the materials that will be adopted for use, so that students have similar experiences in all sections of multisection courses. Deans and department chairs or those to whom they delegate management of the unit's library budget should ensure that faculty input guides the purchase decisions, ensuring that the materials selected will be widely used to support teaching and learning.

Budget and Program Funding

"Colleges and universities have never had sufficient resources to meet all the objectives of their faculties and administrators..." (McCorkle & Archibald, 1982, p. 6).

What was true in 1982 is still true today. Funding for business programs is usually derived from student tuition and fees, state appropriations (except in the case of private institutions), corporate and foundation support, alumni support, and federal funding (also called funded research). Leadership of business programs will include both raising funds and managing budgets. Responsibilities for fund-raising are usually shared among the department chair, the dean, and the university's development office, now often called "University Advancement." Most funds do come with "strings attached" and must be used only to support specific line items, for example, undergraduate scholarships, graduate scholarships and assistantships, faculty professional development, merit increases, and instructional technology. Budgeting and program funding require collaborative decision making, including faculty input, as limited resources must be used to support the most important programs and initiatives each academic year.

LEADERSHIP PERSPECTIVE: STUDENTS

Students are, by far, the most important part of business programs; without students, the programs will cease to exist. Effective leadership of business programs include recruiting, retaining, and graduating students who are prepared for the global workforce. This demands attention to students' many and varied needs.

Student Recruitment, Retention, and Graduation

Leaders can gauge local, regional, and national standards and trends for student recruitment, retention, and graduation by referring to a variety of state and national reports, for example, the *National Collegiate Retention and Persistence to Degree Rates* (ACT, 2012). Information garnered can help in strategic planning and short-term goal

---

[2]Available at http://www.merlot.org/merlot/materials.htm;jsessionid=C599E2D9ABCF0409ED3 6298CE2EBBC38?category=2202&sort.property=overallRating.

setting. For example, realistic goals should be set for recruitment, first-year retention (from freshman to sophomore year), as well as four- and six-year graduation rates. Once the goals have been established, support programs and services must be provided to ensure that targets are met. The chair might work with the library to provide supplemental or remedial materials and with the office of career services to provide internships, cooperative education opportunities, and job placements.

Business program leaders should be aware of factors impacting student progression to timely graduation, including course scheduling. Required courses must be available when students need them; multiple required courses should not be scheduled in the same time slot; and prerequisite courses should be available with the frequency that will allow students to enroll as needed. Well-trained and easily accessible academic advisors should be available to guide students and help them find the information they need to make well-informed decisions. Academic support, such as tutoring and supplemental instruction, should be provided, and learning communities might be established and supported. More information about the services that students value, especially in their undergraduate education, might be drawn from the National Survey of Student Engagement data and a variety of similar sources (Moore & Shulock, 2009).

Business Student Professional Organizations

Student professional organizations are vital as they help students become part of a community that will help them to develop as leaders and to find friendship and academic support. A variety of honor societies, such as Beta Gamma Sigma and Pi Omega Pi, and professional student organizations such as the American Marketing Association, Collegiate Entrepreneurs Organization, and Society for the Advancement of Management are available to serve students. Department chairs and deans should encourage students to actively participate in professional organizations and begin to learn through involvement with fellow students, faculty, and industry professionals.

Career Guidance

Because the goal of most students entering a business program is to begin a career, career guidance must be provided through the business programs or through an office of career services. Through close collaboration with corporate partners, many business programs offer a variety of internship or cooperative education opportunities, including some international opportunities. At the college and university levels, career guidance focuses more on resume writing and electronic posting than on aptitude testing and career exploration. Leaders of business programs should encourage students to attend mixers and campus interviews sponsored by career services and recruiters and to build an appropriate wardrobe to help them project the right image. Students should also avail themselves of interviewing and etiquette workshops.

Graduate Programs

Graduate programs usually receive more funding, especially in state appropriations, than do undergraduate programs. Graduate programs are also more likely to attract corporate and other funded research projects because graduate students can support their research by serving as research assistants. As such, department chairs and deans are considered successful if they are able to establish strong, successful graduate programs. Effective leadership in graduate-level business programs also includes mentoring graduate students, providing them with appropriate experiential learning opportunities, and preparing doctoral students to become effective professors and practitioners who can be promoted to senior leadership positions in their organizations. Successful graduate students are even more critical to the image of business programs than are graduates of bachelor's degree programs.

LEADERSHIP PERSPECTIVE: QUALITY ASSURANCE

Quality assurance is important in brand development and sustainability. A good quality control / quality assurance program is essential to both the substance and the image of college-level business programs, especially graduate programs. Many factors contribute to quality, and several are discussed below, beginning with faculty professional development, evaluation, and promotion.

Faculty Professional Development, Evaluation, and Promotion

Faculty development can occur through a variety of methods, although many programs sponsor on-site seminars and workshops to help faculty develop their professional knowledge and skills. Professional development can help faculty to maintain currency in the discipline, but it is also often necessary to acquire new skills such as those related to curriculum development and effective assessment. Department chairs and senior faculty should also be responsible for guiding the program by developing course and program evaluations as well as broad evaluations of student learning outcomes. Often, the institution will have systems in place, and the leaders of business programs must ensure that all faculty learn to appreciate and even value assessment and data-driven decision making. Leadership must also build a strong mentoring and peer evaluation system that will perpetuate excellence among the faculty.

Formal annual faculty evaluation is the responsibility of deans and department chairs. But faculty can and should be included in the processes that determine the reward system, for example, the criteria for promotion and tenure and even the design of the assessment rubric. Honest and objective peer evaluation should be encouraged and rewarded. It certainly has the potential of strengthening the professional skills of the faculty, ultimately leading to high-quality business programs.

Deans and department chairs have many leadership roles, but probably none is more important to the morale of the department than promotion and tenure review and recommendations. Personal and professional validation of faculty is linked with promotion and tenure, as are the quality of programs and the focus and well-being of the academic department (University of Virginia, 2011). Effective leadership is required to ensure that all new faculty hires are aware of the tenure and promotion criteria and the progress they must make each year to achieve that all important goal. Those who attain tenure and initial promotion, usually from assistant to associate professor, must be encouraged to continue working and striving to be successful in each post-tenure review assessment and ultimately to earn promotion to full professor rank.

Community Resources

The community is an excellent source of speakers, job shadowing, internships, cooperative education opportunities, job placements, and case studies. The community can also provide undergraduate and graduate research opportunities, funding for programs, and advocacy. As leaders of business programs, deans and department chairs have to form collaborative relationships with the community to ensure that the business programs are relevant and well supported; for example, effective advisory boards can be an excellent asset in maintaining relevant curricula.

Advisory Committees

Business, industry, and labor representatives are often very willing to share their wealth of expertise and to offer advice and often make strong advisory committee members. Business program advisory committees play an important role in guiding, strengthening, and improving existing business programs. Once the advisory committee is selected, it can be expected to provide financial and technical support, advocate for the program as needed, vet new programs to ensure that they are of the highest quality, and provide suggestions for improvements. An advisory committee's role is not to "rubber stamp" what already exists but rather to be innovative to assist in building the highest possible program quality (Minnesota State Colleges and Universities, n.d.). Advisory committees link business programs with the workforce, and good leaders are likely to establish and sustain excellent advisory committees, which in turn, provide the external oversight needed to maintain high-quality business programs.

Research Responsibility

Leadership in both scholarly and funded research is one of the elements that distinguish business programs at the college and university levels from their counterparts at the secondary level. Research productivity is a requirement for faculty promotion and tenure and is included in annual evaluations for those in tenure track positions. Deans and department chairs should be both generators and consumers of research so they may lead by example, because it is difficult to motivate others to do what you are not able or willing to do.

Research projects may originate from industry-relevant questions. As noted by Oosthuizen (2010), "The depth and focus differentiates academic research from research conducted by consultants and industry practitioners, which generally focuses on the urgent resolution of current problems in specific organizational settings" (para. 2). Golder and Mitra (2008) conducted a study that found that research has a positive influence on academics' perceptions of a business school and that research also improves recruiters' perceptions. "Recruiters pay higher salaries to students at schools that are increasing their research output" (para 3).

Accreditation

Accreditation is a mark of excellence in academic programs. Most programs that are not accredited work and strive to get accredited, and those who have accreditation cannot afford to lose it. Three agencies offer business program accreditation: (a) Accreditation Council for Business Schools and Programs, (b) International Assembly for Collegiate Business Education, and (c) the very prestigious Association to Advance Collegiate Schools of Business (AACSB) International. Business teacher education programs are also accredited by the Council for the Accreditation of Educator Preparation as part of the institution's education programs.

Accreditation helps stakeholders to distinguish business program quality and is a useful tool for prospective students when they select a reputable business program (International Educational Development Program, n.d.). Accreditation is so highly valued in the very competitive arena in which business programs exist that a dean who loses program accreditation is likely to also lose his or her job in the institution. Business programs display accreditation as a badge of honor, and those with AACSB International accreditation typically place the seal of the organization and a statement such as "…is among the less than 5 percent of the world's business programs that have achieved AACSB accreditation" on their Web sites and in their printed literature. John Fernandes, president and CEO for AACSB International (2012), stated the following about achieving and maintaining accreditation:

Schools must not only meet specific standards of excellence, but their deans, heads of business units, and academic and non-academic staff must make a commitment to ongoing improvement to ensure that the institution will continue to deliver the highest quality of education to students. (para. 6)

From the discussion in this chapter, it should be clear that leading business programs is a formidable task that demands not only professional expertise but also strong commitment to the discipline and to higher education. Most important, it requires a passion for contributing to the learning and development of the next generation of business leaders. This chapter concludes with a brief presentation of some of the best practices for leading business programs at the college and university levels.

BEST PRACTICES IN LEADING BUSINESS PROGRAMS

A best practice is defined as a "working method or set of working methods, which is officially accepted as being the best to use in a particular business or industry…" ("Best Practice," 2013, para 1). Learning from the successes of others is a good way for those who are beginning leadership roles in business programs to experience some early successes.

Curriculum Development

AACSB International (2003) noted that business curricula must assure that graduates are prepared to begin business and management careers consistent with the learning goals of the program. When developing a new curriculum, leaders of business programs should do the following:

- Avail themselves of high-quality resources, such as those available from the National Center of Excellence for Computing and Information Technologies (http://www. coeforict.org/resources); the Business Teacher Education Curriculum Guide and Program Standards, especially helpful for business teacher education programs (more information available at http://www.nbea.org); and material and webinars from organizations such as ASCD.

- Draw from both content-specific sources, such as AACSB International, and from process-relevant sources, such as the Association of American Colleges and Universities, to provide effective leadership in curriculum development.

- Invest the time and effort needed to complete a thorough curriculum mapping. Mapping allows faculty and business program leaders to engage in a purposeful alignment of learning goals with program goals and priorities, ensuring that each course adds value to the business programs and that students are well prepared to begin their careers. Curriculum mapping helps to assure program accountability.

Technology Integration

Kolowich (2012) and other researchers have found that, although colleges and universities are making considerable investments in instructional technologies, many faculty were simply not using technology in their courses. Among the reasons for this seeming disinterest in instructional technology is lack of expertise among faculty coupled with lack of support. This suggests that deans and department chairs have an opportunity to encourage and effect greater faculty use of instructional technology by providing the faculty with the professional development and continuing support they need. Best practices for encouraging faculty use of instructional technology include the following, adapted from the "Attention, Relevance, Confidence, Satisfaction (better known as ARCS) Model of Motivation" (Surry & Land, 2000):

- Showcase practical uses of technology, preferably using very credible faculty members who are well respected by their peers

- Build the use of technology into the reward system, for example, the annual evaluation of faculty and student evaluation of each course

- Provide basic and continuing professional development and encourage faculty to form a support group of peers who learn and use the new and emerging technologies

- Invest in the purchase and maintenance of the technology, making it convenient and comfortable for faculty to integrate it into their courses once they have learned how to do so

Policy Adoption

Above all else, it is important that the business education department chair be inclusive when developing policies—get input from all stakeholders—and keep the policy development process as transparent as possible. Even the most apathetic faculty, staff, and students prefer to have an opportunity to participate, although they may not take advantage of it. Policies that are designed and handed down are more likely to be met with resistance. Best practices in policy adoption include the following, adapted from Kezar and Eckel (2004):

- Value shared governance, and seek opportunities to include stakeholders in the policy-making process. Make the decision-making process as broadly based as possible and proceed at a pace that allows for broad involvement. Allow for multiple rounds of review and revision, followed by a formal vote to adopt the policy.

- Educate stakeholders about the newly adopted policy, and post all policies where stakeholders would intuitively try to find them.

- Educate stakeholders about the process for periodically updating the policy.

- If breach of the policy will lead to sanctions, be clear about the sanctions and any process for filing appeals.

Continuous Improvement

College- and university-level business programs must function in a constant state of growth and change and continuously improve. To become complacent is to lose ground. One reason for continuous improvement in business programs is maintenance of accreditation. The need to demonstrate every five years that high standards are being maintained motivates accredited business programs to engage in continuous improvements. The best practices shared by Bailey, Chow, and Haddad (1999) are still very relevant today. Their suggestions include the following:

- Establish a committee structure that will ensure that groups of faculty are continuously monitoring such things as excellence in curriculum development; student recruitment, retention, and graduation rates; diversity among students, faculty and staff; and technology and other infrastructure that support learning and work.

- Develop and regularly update the unit's strategic plan, and have a clear action plan to support it. End each academic year with a very honest and thorough scorecard.

- Develop a clear financial plan, budget well, and be a good steward of all funds, regardless of the sources.

- Engage in continuous self-assessment, including assessment of student learning, job placements, and accomplishments of graduates.

SUMMARY

Meeting the leadership challenge in business education demands commitment and hard work, but it offers a wonderful opportunity to help build the discipline. Department chairs and deans, who are at the forefront of leadership in business programs, must be prepared to invest in themselves and in those whom they lead. They must be prepared to build strong teams and to empower others to actively participate in building strong business programs that prepare highly marketable graduates and maintain competitive programs that will continue to attract talented undergraduate and graduate students.

Effective leadership by deans and department chairs will encourage faculty to help build and maintain excellent business programs. Leaders will use the resources available to them to build their programs. The challenges that come with leading in a very dynamic academic environment must be met by leaders' strong commitment to serve and to invest in educating future business leaders and educators. Although the tasks are very demanding, many opportunities exist to learn from the best practices developed over many years of research and practice.

REFERENCES

AACSB International. (2003). 2003 business accreditation standards: Curriculum management and content. Retrieved from http://www.aacsb.edu/accreditation/business/standards/aol/curriculum_management.asp

AACSB International. (2012). Eleven business schools from six countries earn AACSB accreditation [Press release]. Retrieved from http://aacsb.edu/media/releases/2012/Eleven-Business-Schools-from-Six-Countries-Earn-AACSB-Accreditation.asp

ACT. (2012). *National collegiate retention and persistence to degree rates.* Retrieved from http://www.act.org/research/policymakers/pdf/retain_2012.pdf

Bailey, A. R., Chow, C. W., & Haddad, K. M. (1999). Continuous improvement in business education: Insights from the for-profit sector and business school deans. *The Journal of Education for Business, 74*(3), 165–180.

Best practice. (2013). In *Cambridge dictionaries online.* Retrieved from http://dictionary.cambridge.org/dictionary/british/best-practice

Generativity. (n.d.). In *Merriam-Webster* [online dictionary]. Retrieved from http://www.merriam-webster.com/medical/generativity

Golder, P. N., & Mitra, D. (2008, October 16). MBA recruiters value academic research. *Bloomberg Businessweek: Business schools.* Retrieved from http://www.businessweek.com/stories/2008-10-16/mba-recruiters-value-academic-researchbusinessweek-business-news-stock-market-and-financial-advice

International Educational Development Program. (n.d.). Accreditation of management education institutions. Retrieved from http://www.iedp.com/IEDP_Exec-ed-accreditation

Inzer, L. D., & Crawford, C. B. (2005). A review of formal and informal mentoring: Processes, problems, and design. *Journal of Leadership Education, 4*(1), 31–50.

Kezar, A., & Eckel, P. D. (2004). Meeting today's governance challenges: A synthesis of the literature and examination of a future agenda for scholarship. *The Journal of Higher Education, 75*(4), 371–399.

Kolowich, S. (2012, August 24). Digital faculty: Professors and technology, 2012. Retrieved from http://www.insidehighered.com/news/survey/digital-faculty-professors-and-technology-2012

Kotter, J. (2013, January 9). Management is (still) not leadership [HBR Blog Network]. *Harvard Business Review.* Retrieved from http://blogs.hbr.org/kotter/2013/01/management-is-still-not-leadership.html

McCorkle, C. O., & Archibald, S. O. (1982). *Management and leadership in higher education.* San Francisco, CA: Jossey-Bass.

Minnesota State Colleges and Universities. (n.d.). *Program advisory committees: A handbook for faculty in career and technical programs.* Retrieved from http://vfc6.project.mnscu.edu/index.asp?Type=B_BASIC&SEC=%7B3BA72DEF-2CE5-4AD7-9FF7-2B9356B02FDB%7D

Moore, C., & Shulock, N. (2009, September). *Student progress toward degree completion: Lessons from the research literature.* Sacramento, CA: Institute for Higher Education Leadership and Policy, California State University Sacramento. Retrieved from http://www.csus.edu/ihelp/PDFs/R_Student_Progress_Toward_Degree_Completion.pdf

Oosthuizen, C. (2010, October 17). The value of academic research. Retrieved from http://www.bizcommunity.com/Article/196/98/55035.html

Policies Commission for Business and Economic Education (PCBEE). (2010). *Policy statement 86: This we believe about generativity in business education.* Retrieved from http://nbea.org/newsite/curriculum/documents/PCBEEStatement86_000.pdf

Rader, M., & Meggison, P. (2007). The business education curriculum. *The Delta Pi Epsilon Journal, 49*(1), 26–31.

Surry, D. W., & Land, S. M. (2000). Strategies for motivating higher education faculty to use technology. *Innovations in Education and Training International, 37*(2), 1–9.

Thille, C. (2010). *Educational technology as a transformational innovation.* Paper presented at the White House Summit on Community Colleges, Washington, DC, October 5, 2010. Retrieved from http://www2.ed.gov/PDFDocs/college-completion/11-education-technology-as-a-transformational-innovation.pdf

University of Virginia. (2011). Policy: Promotion and tenure. Retrieved from https://policy.itc.virginia.edu/policy/policydisplay?id=PROV-017

Vilkinas, T., & Ladyshewsky, R. K. (2011). Leadership behavior and effectiveness of academic program directors in Australian universities. *Educational Management Administration & Leadership, 40*(1), 109–126. doi:10.1177/1741143211420613

Webber, J. W., & Englehart, S. W. (2011). Enhancing business education through integrated curriculum delivery. *Journal of Management Development, 30*(6), 558–568.

Wilcox, J. R., & Ebbs, S. L. (1992). *The leadership compass: Values and ethics in higher education.* Washington, DC: ERIC Clearing House on Higher Education.

The Business Teacher as Leader

Donna Gavitt
Selinsgrove High School
Selinsgrove, PA

What is a teacher leader? An expectation of becoming a teacher leader begins with first becoming an expert teacher and instructional role model. But there is much more in terms of time and *process* to becoming a teacher leader in terms of leadership options. This chapter examines the following topics relating to the business teacher as leader: the expert teacher, becoming a teacher leader, nourishing teacher leadership, meeting the challenge, building capacity through teacher leadership, implementing teacher leader voice in policymaking, curricular needs, and focusing on the future.

THE EXPERT TEACHER

The definition of a teacher leader can only be examined within the context of education, which is characterized by constant change and transformation. The teaching profession is guarded, guided, and directed by multiple sources, the most powerful of which is politics. Policy directives come from local boards of education, state and federal governments, administrators, and legislators—as the interpreters of these varied policy directives—often analyzing the impact on the student after the fact.

Acknowledging these ever-changing influences outside the business teacher's classroom, how they become experts in education, who defines them as experts, and when, how (or if) they become teacher leaders always is and will be a moving target. Mielke and Frontier (2012) explained what an expert teacher is not, "Becoming an expert teacher is not a gift bestowed on a chosen few but a journey through a challenging, thorny pathway that requires constant pruning" (p. 12).

Ericsson, credited as the world's foremost expert on expertise, stated that expertise is developed through deliberate practice. To be an expert teacher, one must "concentrate on carefully selected, specific aspects of performance and refine them through repetition and response to feedback" (as cited by Mielke & Frontier, 2012, p. 12). The process for developing teaching expertise is what teachers practice with their students for learning to occur: repetition and response to feedback. To become an expert teacher is to consciously practice focusing on one task—for example, asking meaningful questions—then deliberately practicing until the skill is consistently applied and mastered, or becomes a habit of the mind. Expert teachers understand they must work to continually improve and reflect on their practice of teaching, adjusting accordingly with an attitude that they are on a journey of continual development and improvement.

Defining teacher quality unequivocally leads to the goal of "the ability to bring about student achievement" (Hardy, 2009). Through teacher evaluation, teaching practice has been traditionally measured by planning, instruction, professional responsibilities, classroom environment, and community involvement; all of which, if done well, would bring about student achievement.

Student achievement has recently become a substantially measurable data collection element, partially as a result of federal grant initiatives such as Race to the Top and partially because accountability must be measured as a concrete result or consequence. Marzano (2012) pointed out that two purposes of teacher evaluation are to measure teacher effectiveness and to develop and grow effective teachers, with development as the dominant force. Marzano's definition reinforced Mielke and Frontier's idea of a "journey" that requires "constant pruning." Expert teachers must be *effective* teachers with growth and development pivotal to the goal of student achievement. When factoring in teachers' expectations for individual school progress, value-added assessment, school profiles, and a host of other intricately calculated data, the "development" and the "process" are sometimes lost in the "result." When evaluators and legislators begin to focus on teaching practice and what happens in the classroom as a result of student-teacher relationships, only then can an expert teacher truly affect student achievement with growth for both the student and the teacher (Domenech, 2011).

Whitaker (2004) reinforced the notion of self-reflection as a means for continuous growth. He wrote that expert teachers "seldom engage in behaviors that cause harm to students. Yet, though the best teachers seldom need to do any emotional repairing...they are continually working to repair, just in case" (pp. 65–66). This extraordinary sensitivity, trust, and credibility established with students is protected by expert teachers who go to great lengths. One-to-one unconditional respect between teacher and student is the mark of a great teacher with a humble realization of the purpose of education, which is to educate all equally.

It is difficult to recognize expert teachers with a constant barrage of negative information by education critics about the poor quality of education in the United States today. As executive director of the American Association of School Administrators, Domenech (2013) stated that American public schools have done better than most would be led to believe and are the best they have ever been. Graduation rates are at their highest levels, and dropout rates are at their lowest. National Assessment for Education Progress achievement in reading and math is at its highest level, as is the achievement of minority students. However, American education is ranked in comparison to other countries and not by how much progress was made in the past 50 years. The situation becomes even more negative when efforts to improve education quality focus on weeding out bad teachers and implementing flawed evaluation systems. Expert teachers, however, are not dissuaded by faulty statistics.

A quality teacher is a master of learning and able to teach "how" to learn. *Lifelong learning* is a goal of many education institution mission statements, recognizing that knowledge and skills are constantly changing to accommodate changing demand in the workforce. The expert teacher, as learner, "models continual improvement, demonstrates lifelong learning, and uses what they learn to help all students achieve" (Harrison & Killion, 2007, p. 74). An expert business educator embraces changes inherent in the discipline and revises the curriculum accordingly. Teacher leaders—always "pruning"—are "catalysts for change…visionaries who are never content with the status quo but rather looking for a better way" (Harrison & Killion, 2007, p. 76). They communicate and inspire other business educators by sharing new knowledge and best practices in schools and participating in professional organizations on their journey to teacher leadership (Policies Commission for Business and Economic Education [PCBEE], 2010).

According to Reeves (2006), "the myths of the singular heroic leader and teacher are unsatisfying and fundamentally flawed" (p. xviii). The author continued, "You are modest enough to know that you cannot achieve the objectives alone, but you are confident enough to know that one person can serve as a catalyst for the entire organization" (p. xviii). The teacher in a classroom can influence student achievement more than a student's background can. Hard work and innovation requires patience, perseverance, and expertise, requiring a much longer period of time than it takes to simply gather and manipulate numbers. Numbers and scores have little significance for the student whose efforts are given just a number. Of greater significance to future success is the power of meaningful relationships and the ability of a great teacher to unlock the potential of their students by nurturing their self-worth and demonstrating persistence and patience, which are also qualities for learning.

Haycock and Darling-Hammond (as cited by Reeves, 2006) reaffirmed "what all of the studies conclude is the most significant factor in student achievement: the teacher. Teacher quality trumps them all, and by a decisive margin" (p. 18). A teacher leader balances membership in the team and knows the impact one teacher can make.

If federal and state education policy directors and politicians focused solely on building the quality of teachers with as much concentrated effort as they currently give to testing, there would be sizeable increases in student achievement. Moore and Berry (2010) asserted that "today's top-down accountability, driven by narrow, standardized, multiple-choice tests, will never provide a sufficient framework to determine teaching effectiveness" (p. 37). Policy makers seldom ask successful educators for their ideas about creating a modern teaching profession that will give students the education they so deserve. The authors predicted that "teachers who can customize learning experiences and facilitate them in both physical and virtual environments will be highly sought after" (p. 37). The overwhelming glut of information available to students 24/7 presents challenges but also many opportunities. Teacher leaders must be open and ready to accept new strategies and methods for delivering content.

Teachers are held responsible for standardized test scores (in this respect, standardizing students) but are asked to focus and adjust for each student (individualized student learning). These illogical contradictions are not lost on astute, dedicated teachers, but they also understand the lifeline connection of dollars to schools if the districts do not meet the "regressive high-stakes testing benchmarks" (Moore & Berry, 2010). This conundrum continues to play out under the No Child Left Behind Act. As teacher evaluations focus more and more on complicated school data and less and less on how effective the teacher is in each classroom, dedicated and learned teachers must walk a fine line between what they know to be best practice and what they are being told to do to get government funds for their school. Top-down accountability stifles motivation, inspiration, and empowerment; blame snuffs out creative risk taking to achieve new pathways to greater student achievement. According to Moore and Berry (2010), dedicated and astute teachers realize the logical inconsistencies of their conflicted mission as "renegade status and defy certain policies to make a positive difference" (p. 37). Crowther (2009) commented on his research for more than 30 years relating to expert teachers becoming teacher leaders: "It is evident there is a long and distinguished though often understated and even unsung tradition of teacher leadership in our schools" (p. 58). He continued that "teachers know who their leaders are—the ones who teach well, work hard, are prepared to stand up for what they believe, are able to work with and command respect among diverse colleagues, and are in it for the children rather than for themselves" (p. 58).

BECOMING A TEACHER LEADER

Roles of teacher leaders and pathways to becoming a teacher leader are as varied as the teachers themselves. Teacher leaders demonstrate integrity, advocate for students, and work toward success for their students, school, community, and even the future of education practice. Teacher leadership is a vital part of community and culture building in schools. "Teacher leadership thrives in innovative environments and is driven underground by standardized ones, where it may resurface to turn against the system itself, in defense of teacher's dignity and of the students they serve" (Crowther, 2009, p. xi).

Teacher leaders very often assume such leadership roles as mentoring new teachers, serving on school committees, writing parts of a curriculum, or being a department chair (Harrison & Killion, 2007). Becoming a leader requires ongoing knowledge renewal, foresight, and flexibility for meeting the challenges of change and advocating for education through community and professional relationships. Moore and Berry (2010) revealed that "bringing teachers' voices from the margins to the center of policymaking is the goal of the Teacher Leaders Network, a virtual community of expert classroom practitioners established by the Center for Teaching Quality" (p. 36).

Teacher leaders maintain a line of sight on the goal—student achievement—regardless of how blurry the line of sight becomes. Reeves (2006) explored the *why* of leadership effectiveness by exploring several propositions. "Most important, 'messy' leadership—the practice of reviewing data, making midcourse corrections, and focusing decision making on the greatest points of leverage—is superior to 'neat' leadership in which planning, processes, and procedures take precedence over achievement" (p. xi).

Teachers become leaders because they are avid learners and experts in conveying their love of learning but also as a result of their experiences. Never before has the phrase *lifelong learning* been so urgently relevant. Harrison and Killion (2007) produced a list of ways teachers can lead. One of the most important leadership roles identified for teacher leaders to assume is that of *learner*. Learners model continual improvement, demonstrate lifelong learning, and use what they learn to help all students achieve. A teacher leader is not afraid to admit s/he does not know it all, and is eager to learn from his/her colleagues.

A teacher leader is not satisfied unless s/he has explored all avenues of learning in order to customize learning to be more effective with each student. This is exemplified in the willingness to share new information, examine and use new teaching strategies, self-examine and engage continually in reflective practice for teaching effectiveness, modify what works, change what does not, and teach with the realization that one can learn from peers, students, and mistakes every day.

As a curriculum specialist and resource provider, the business teacher leader assists other teachers in defining the ever-changing and expanding business environment. These changes create greater urgency to update course content to inform students of changes for college and career readiness. The future for opportunities in the job market stresses "tectonic shifts" in labor demand and the focus shifting to teaching students *how* to learn. Workers must be prepared to continuously relearn new technology, operations, and perhaps a new job altogether in order to remain marketable and mobile in this new undefined labor force. Through continuous learning and research, teacher leaders prepare themselves and their students for future success.

Another instructional specialist role assumed by the business teacher leader occurs when examining the impact of social media on business processes and incorporating these processes into the curriculum. Introducing social media into the classroom is a challenge, considering restrictions in many schools' acceptable use policies. Teachers must nevertheless learn, teach, and embrace the value of social media in business. Research indicates this phenomenon has truly transformed some businesses and created opportunities where there were none—the essence of entrepreneurship. On reinventing the workforce, Cognizant Technology Solutions warned, "millennials prefer to work in heterarchies[1] instead of hierarchies…a dynamic network of connected nodes, without predefined priorities or ranks" (Frank, 2012, pp. 20–21). Teacher leaders revise curriculum to facilitate student learning and decision making about opportunities, choices, and preparation for the future workforce. As a curriculum specialist, a teacher leader understands content standards and their linkage with new technologies and curriculum content (Harrison & Killion, 2007).

Frank (2012) identified a new enterprise information technology model of the future of work in the context of "social, mobile, analytics, and cloud" or SMAC. "The SMAC stack does not represent the next new technology to be 'bolted onto' your existing business model. Instead, these technologies will transform the business model itself" (Frank, 2012, p. 3). This new way of thinking about business structure and processes is much needed and readily accepted by the next generation of business leaders sitting at their computers in the classroom. The practice of continuous research, relearning, and rewriting becomes a habit of mind for business teacher leaders. "We believe business education has the opportunity and responsibility to take the lead in promoting and integrating appropriate use of social media across the curricula to best prepare students to compete in the global economy" (PCBEE, 2012, p. 3).

Business courses traditionally lie outside the realm of what many administrators, guidance counselors, and policy writers consider *academic*. This fundamental flaw in how business education is perceived negatively impacts the preparation of students for a career in business or for a college business major. Business education teacher leaders "promote an understanding of the vital role business education plays in the success of American business and the world economy" (National Business Education Association, n.d., para. 2).

Secondary education principals influence the curriculum of their institutions as administrators. Their own background major is influential in the curriculum decisions they make. Drage and Anderson (2007) stated that "the finding that principals' responses were influenced by their educational background…indicates a need for business educators to keep their administrators apprised of student accomplishments" (p. 56). Business teachers can track successes of their students by compiling these successes into an annual newsletter sent to administrators, guidance counselors, media outlets, and businesses in the community. As a result of developing this type of resource, the Pennsylvania Business Education Association documented students who went into a business occupation after high school or college. Students credited their *initiation* into business to completing business courses in high school. Many of

---

[1]"A heterarchy is a system of organization where the elements of the organization are unranked (non-hierarchical) or where they possess the potential to be ranked a number of different ways" ("Heterarchy," n.d.).

their mentors were teacher leaders dedicated to teaching quality for the success of their students. These former students believed business education played a vital role in their success. National Board Certified Teacher John Holland said it best: "It is the creativity, passion and commitment of expert teachers who know what and how to teach students at any given moment that makes students successful" (Moore & Berry, 2010, p. 37).

In a standards-driven environment, business educators struggle for clear direction about what standards to use. Clearly, teacher leaders use and promote reading and writing standards and, most recently, the Common Core State Standards. Business content overlaps all core content standards, as exemplified in the *National Standards for Business Education* (National Business Education Association, 2013), which provides the most comprehensive standards for teaching business content. Likewise, the Pennsylvania Department of Education (2013) posted Business Computer Information Technology Standards on the Pennsylvania Department of Education website (http://PDEsas.org), providing guidance for consistent business content. Teacher leaders are cognizant of and share resources to elevate their learning and that of colleagues, thus promoting a community of learners.

NOURISHING TEACHER LEADERSHIP

How do these teacher leaders grow? In an environment of criticism, reduced funding, and diminished priorities, this is the big question. However, a recently released study from The New Teacher Project (TNTP, 2013) revealed insights into this issue regarding teacher leaders. The research involved asking high-performing teachers in high-need schools about their classrooms and careers. Three key results from TNTP research follow:

- They treasure the opportunity to make a difference in student lives but struggle with the burdens of the profession; as a result, 60% plan on leaving teaching within five years.

- They measure their own success as teachers through a variety of indicators, including student grades and scores as well as feedback from colleagues and students.

- They rank their preparation programs and formal professional development programs lowest on a list of factors contributing to their success as teachers (TNTP, 2013).

What factors then actually affect teacher leader growth? Marzano (2012) stated the following:

We need to acknowledge a crucial issue—that measuring teachers and developing teachers are different purposes with different implications. An evaluation system designed primarily for measurement will look quite different from a system designed primarily for development…the vast majority of respondents believe that teacher evaluation should be used for both measurement and development but that development should be the more important purpose. (p. 15)

Marzano clearly differentiated among poor evaluation systems; some have not measured teacher quality (between effective and ineffective teachers) accurately, and others have not helped develop a highly skilled teaching workforce. Getting the process right and training all teachers in that process would be a monumental accomplishment. Marzano's recommendation was not for a certain pattern or framework to use in planning lessons; it was for applying and nurturing the *process of teaching*, the day-to-day work with students one-on-one and collaboration with peers and mentors.

Successful teacher leaders are driven to become better teachers and to be proactive daily in improving their practice. They seek out information directed at achieving these goals, not waiting for a prescribed or canned professional development opportunity. As a teacher for 16 years in public education and teaching in postsecondary education, this author has in fact found few ongoing professional development programs—whether a weekend conference, daylong workshop, webinar, training week in the summer, or even three-credit college course—that truly address sustaining the process for teaching that would be deemed more valuable than day-to-day on-the-job experience. The *practicing process* however, resembles the National Board Professional Teaching Standards program for developing and growing teachers on the path to becoming experts (Allen, 2010). In this process, teachers work together to develop expertise using self-reflective practice. As a result, teacher leadership evolves best in a sustained professional learning community referred to as cohorts: teachers who are helping, guiding, critiquing, and promoting a self-sustaining community of expert teachers.

MEETING THE CHALLENGE
The journey toward teacher leadership is achieved through constant practice and "pruning"—evaluating, revising, and reflecting on what happens each day in the classroom with all students. Teacher leaders seek out and thrive in safe learning communities.

Planning and organizing, classroom management, and teaching strategies are all part of the process. But unless teachers evaluate the quality of student responses and the responses to feedback, all good planning is benign. Without follow-up, teachers are not "pruning" their teaching practice. The process is 24/7 teaching—every minute—consciously and often subconsciously analyzing for effectiveness, which eventually becomes a habit of the mind. A teacher leader engages in active learning practice, which then becomes role modeling for those who follow.

The development of more teacher leaders in schools and communities is the answer to meeting the challenge of higher student achievement. Teacher leaders understand the importance of professional collaborative relationships and must inform policy makers in order to address teacher retention issues in America's schools. The TNTP Project (2013), addressing the issue of irreplaceable teachers, pinpointed policies and processes that undermine a strong teacher workforce and offered common-sense solutions:

Improving our nation's urban schools requires creating policies and working conditions that will attract more outstanding teachers and encourage them to stay in the classroom. We should be building the profession around its finest practitioners. Today, too little is known about the opinions and experiences of top-performing teachers, because researchers rarely focus specifically on them. (p. 24)

This author, as a school board director for a small rural Pennsylvania school district, has watched the progress of a community of teachers supporting one another in their quest to become expert teachers. They have mentored and supported each other in a purely individually self-motivated professional learning community; results in student achievement have been steady and undeniable in the past eight years. They are now teacher leaders in every sense, helping to grow other teacher leaders. This learning community (cohort) continues regardless of administrative changes, providing the greatest advantage to students in terms of continuity of learning and continuity of best practice in a community of dedicated teachers who work with and support one another.

Today, this small school district in the heartland of North Central Pennsylvania has 20 National Board Certified Teachers for a student population of 1,800 in three elementary schools and one junior/senior high school.

Even though completing the application can take teachers up to 300 hours (outside the working day), cost several thousand dollars, and leave them feeling overwhelmed and exhausted, the hardship is worth it, say teachers who have attained what many consider the gold standard of teacher credentials: the National Board for Professional Teaching Standards (NBPTS) certification of National Board Certified Teachers (NBCTs). (Allen, 2010, p. 1)

Federal and state subsidies support the National Board Certified Teachers program by providing partial or total funding, depending on the state. For any business teacher who is motivated to grow and refine their daily practices, the National Board for Professional Teaching Standards is a proven pathway to quality, sustained instructional practice—the path to teacher leadership and role models for teaching expertise.

BUILDING CAPACITY THROUGH TEACHER LEADERSHIP

What is meant by *building capacity*? ASCD defined the teacher-leadership model as one of its "models" of school improvement (Moore & Berry, 2010, p. 37). Emphasis is on local leadership and expertise: local teachers who implement changes for improved growth and student achievement. In other words, improvement depends on the teachers, which requires developing a common language to share experiences for continued improvement. The teacher leader plays a hybrid role requiring him or her to turn to colleagues inside and outside their immediate sphere for support, knowledge, and teacher voice in guiding public policy. As the teacher leader's role expands, compensation models must be congruent with this new role. According to Renee Moore, former Mississippi Teacher of the Year, "Evaluations should be carried out by our most expert teachers, not underprepared and overworked administrators" (Moore & Berry, 2010, p. 39).

According to Simon (2012), the Montgomery County Public Schools (Maryland) has produced "rich evidence of success." The district is in the second generation of a teacher evaluation model crafted by teachers (their union), principals, and administration. Indeed, the union contract stated, "For the union, taking responsibility for the improvement of the quality of teaching and learning represents an expanded role" (p. 59). This contract began a collaborative 18-month process of redesigning the teacher evaluation system, renamed the Professional Growth System. This new philosophy on teacher evaluation—clearly an example of building capacity—viewed teaching as "incredibly complex work" (p. 59). Most important, the focus was on "the nurturing of good teaching—not the sorting and ranking of the teacher workforce" (p. 59). Panels of teachers and principals oversaw about 40 consulting teachers ("the best of the best") who worked with new teachers and veteran teachers needing help. This procedure epitomizes the value and the role of teacher leaders in building capacity for student achievement. Teachers are the evaluators; they hire and oversee the work of teachers. "Montgomery County's evaluation system is rigorous and holds teachers to high standards, but teachers feel they are part of a learning organization and their craft is respected. The teachers' union is a partner with the district in improving schools" (Simon, 2012, p. 63).

Crowther (2009) said it best:

In recent years…teacher leadership has sometimes become so formalized and data-driven that long-term reflection and deep conversation have been replaced by the pressure to meet short-term targets in meetings. In its deeper and most authentic sense, it is time to bring teacher leadership back in as a collective collegial effort through conversation, inquiry, and action to transform curriculum and pedagogy together so that all students' needs can be served effectively. (p. xi)

The role of a teacher in the success of students has not changed. What *has* changed is the misunderstanding and misinterpretation of the role of teachers and public education overall. Teacher leaders must be a voice in policy making and legislation affecting the most underrepresented and vulnerable of all our populations: our students.

IMPLEMENTING TEACHER LEADER VOICE

Teacher leaders have a responsibility in educating other teachers, their communities, and policy makers about the profession of teaching and the critical value of education. Collaboration and sharing with other teachers is highly valued by teachers. In the TNTP (2013) survey of irreplaceable teachers, 96% of respondents said they valued positive feedback from colleagues they respect. The lack of time and opportunity for this type of communication was also a factor for dissatisfaction with teaching that teacher leaders must strive to overcome. The barrier most commonly ranked among the top three by respondents was "insufficient time for planning or collaboration with other teachers" (p. 19), which speaks not only to a lack of time but to the desire these teachers have to engage with their colleagues. "Teacher leadership thrives in innovative environments and is driven underground by standardized ones, where it may resurface to turn against the system itself, in defense of teachers' dignity and of the students they serve" (p. xi). The best of the best must stand up and hold their ground; the fight is worth the struggle.

Teacher leaders can influence parents and community members through participation in community organizations and school-to-community organizations within the district. Teachers in the TNTP (2013) survey identified isolation as a barrier. "Adding to this sense of isolation is the sense that people outside their school don't understand their views on important issues. For example, only 13 percent of our respondents believe elected officials represent their views fairly in making important decisions" (p. 18). Many elected officials demand that educators graduate students who are problem solvers who can analyze situations and act. Yet, many officials follow their leaders, cutting funds and needed support in a system barely staying afloat with increasingly diverse learning issues. Administrators in collaboration with teacher leaders could potentially lead to systemic change when the focus is placed on learning and not on how to pay for everything.

Mistakes are made in developing education policies at the highest levels. But not unlike the classroom, policy makers must also evaluate results and change direction quickly (or one would hope) if policies do not lead to greater student achievement for all. Ravitch (2011), a former U.S. assistant education secretary, did precisely that:

Adult interests were well served by NCLB [No Child Left Behind Act]. The law generated huge revenues for tutoring and testing services, which became a sizable industry. Companies that offered tutoring, tests, and test-prep materials were raking in billions of dollars annually from federal, state, and local governments, but the advantages to the nation's students were not obvious. (p. 101)

The teacher leader voice is critical in communicating what happens to students in classrooms and in schools. A thrust among states today is to assure that students are financially literate when leaving their formal education. This thrust is a challenge to all business teachers to become leaders of reform and promote financial literacy as required content for students to succeed before leaving high school. These business teacher leaders must educate administrators to the value of business education for student success and achievement. Moore and Berry (2010) coined the phrase "teacher-preneurism," indicating a new purpose and professional identity in making decisions about "deliverables." Arial Sacks, a team member of the Teacher Solutions 2030 Team,[2] envisioned these new professional identities as follows:

These roles could include developing curriculum materials, mentoring teachers, creating partnerships between my school and other organizations. I could also participate in policy work outside my school and/or be a freelance writer...the beauty of a hybrid role is that I would always maintain a classroom teaching practice. Teaching is the soul of my work in education. (as cited in Moore & Berry, 2010, p. 39)

In short, teacher leaders stand up for what they believe is best for students.

FOCUS ON THE FUTURE

"Collaborative relationships comprise a recognized key success factor for many businesses," according to Miertschin, Kovach, and O'Neil (2013, p. 40). "Teamwork, collaboration, and relationship building all involve working together toward a common goal, yet teamwork and collaboration are elements that take place in a progression toward building professional relationships" (p. 41).

Collaborative relationships can have this effect in education, as evidenced by the Maryland Public Schools success, "the nurturing of good teaching—not the sorting and ranking of the teacher workforce" (Simon, 2012, p. 59). Business education teacher leaders recognize and develop relationships with other teachers in other disciplines for the academic success of all students. Business is constantly evolving, and business educators adjust to the content change but may get caught up in the outdated structural mind-set concerning business education.

Creating success for students is not accomplished in just one way. Clearly, experts are calling for greater technology training in most fields. The issue today is that jobs are changing; technology is replacing technology at rates not seen before. Schools cannot afford to emphasize four-year degrees when more jobs will exist in technical fields in which those who possess the skills will get the job. Business educators can lead the way. Entrenched beliefs that the best path to success is a four-year degree must be reversed. Carnevale, Strohl, and Melton (n.d.), writing for Georgetown University Center on Education and the Workforce, stated, "Our findings make it clear that while getting a degree matters, there is significant variation depending on which major you pick" (p. 3).

Business teacher leaders must maintain a focus on academic achievement for all students. As iterated by the PCBEE (2005), business teachers must be prepared to accept a role in a standards-based accountability environment and lead "outside the box" to address the need for business education. As an educated society, higher education is increasingly emphasized. But what is meant by "college education?" Does this mean just four-year degrees? What about shorter-term professional certificates and on-the-job programs? Should there be more options offered for non-college-bound students that would help them improve their career prospects? And given their real-life situations, what can be done to make new, alternative paths genuinely viable? (Johnson, 2012). Business teacher leaders have a unique opportunity to fill a void in preparing all students for postsecondary business education and for workforce success.

Research supports the need for more rigorous business education.

Non-technical majors—the arts (11.1%), humanities and liberal arts (9.4%), social sciences (8.9%) and law and public policy (8.1%)—generally have higher unemployment rates. Conversely, health care, business, and the STEM fields

---

[2]"With support from the MetLife Foundation, the Teacher Leaders Network has sponsored The Teacher Solutions 2030 Team: 12 accomplished teacher leaders who have worked together to imagine a brighter future for students and the teaching profession" p. 36.

(science, technology, engineering and math) have been more stable and higher paying for recent college graduates. (Goudreau, 2012, para. 7)

According to the Bureau of Labor Statistics (2013) in the United States Department of Labor, computer network support specialists comprised the largest of 24 newly defined occupations with employment around 168,000 in 2012. "Several newly defined occupations earned high wages relative to the U.S. annual mean of $45,790. Nurse anesthetists had an annual mean wage of $154,390, nurse practitioners, $91,450, and nurse midwives, $91,070. Information security analysts had an annual mean wage of $89,290 and computer network architects, $94,000. The highest-paying major occupational groups were management, legal, computer and mathematical, and architecture and engineering occupations" (Bureau of Labor Statistics, 2013, para. 5). "To lead out of the box, one must learn how to *think* outside of the box. If we possess the ability to envision a desirable future, then we'll be able to lead 'outside of the box'" (Houston, Blankstein, & Cole, 2007, p. 31). Business educators can make a substantial positive difference—business content is necessary and contributes to lifelong success of each and every student. Business teacher leaders are confident in what they teach and possess the expertise to teach it. "It really doesn't matter why the system is the way it is today. What matters most is what a leader will do today and tomorrow to improve the educational experience for each of our students" (Houston, et al., 2007, p. 34). An educational leader recognizes the value in opportunistic education experiences.

Business teacher leaders have a unique opportunity to change the direction of business education in America today. With all the uncertainty and confusion surrounding testing and a lack of true leadership at federal and state levels, business teacher leaders have a chance to demonstrate to local administrators and business communities how valuable business is to public education through a standards-based curriculum. Business teacher leaders can be a catalyst for collaboration among fellow educators in guiding students to greater achievement. Business teacher leaders are avid learners; but most important, teacher leaders speak from the heart and *believe* that students will be more successful in all aspects of their lives if they are given the opportunity to master academic business content skills. Many legislators at state and federal levels believe that public education is failing and needs to function more like business, as evidenced by the drive in many states for vouchers for private charter schools and cyber schools. If education continues to be viewed as a public funding problem, the opportunity to create better organizations and teachers through an analysis of the work culture is lost.

From a business perspective, Gostick and Elton (2012) studied highly successful companies around the globe to determine what managers of these organizations did to achieve such dramatically better financial results than their peers during the terrible market conditions experienced the past few years. The researchers' core finding was that in the highest-performing cultures, leaders not only create high levels of *engagement* (strong employee attachment and a willingness to give extra effort), but they also create environments that support productivity and performance, in which employees feel *enabled*. Additionally, they help employees feel a greater sense of well-being and drive at work: people feel *energized*. Educators would most likely agree that this culture hardly depicts the education reform of today. But teachers can become leaders inside organizations, within workgroups and schools, and then begin to change minds of policy makers. Business education teacher leaders *believe* that what they do is necessary in molding and refining a durable product (their students). The business of business education is "guiding human knowledge and growth in our students, our peers, and our organizations" (Gostick & Elton, 2012, p. 12).

SUMMARY

As true *teacherpreneurs*, business teacher leaders see opportunity where others see challenges:

Out-of-the-box leaders have the choice and the ability to focus on the future and not dwell on the past. When everyone around you is thinking about test scores and accountability, out-of-the-box leaders are reflecting on such things as integrated learning experiences, authentic assessment, performance portfolios, music and the arts, higher order thinking, and organizational cultural values such as caring. (Houston, et al., pp. 34–35)

The world and job markets for students are changing at exponential rates. Business teacher leaders must step outside the box, take a leadership role, and focus on educating students to grow the next generation of business educators and business leaders. Business teacher leaders

believe generativity is a process for ensuring longevity of the discipline and the well-being of the next generation. A positive legacy is established through teaching, mentoring, collaborating, participating in professional associations, and utilizing other creative contributions...Behaviors and actions that exemplify generative activities include learning a new skill, teaching a skill, developing new courses and teaching ideas, serving in a leadership role for a professional business education organization, and conducting research. (PCBEE, 2010, p. 1)

Business teacher leaders continue to publicize their motto: "We *believe* that business education is not an option for some—business education is a mandate for all" (PCBEE, 2002, p. 2).

REFERENCES

Allen, R. (2010, November). National Board Certified Teachers: Putting in the time, energy, and money to improve teaching. *Education Update, 52*(11). Alexandria, VA: ASCD.

Bureau of Labor Statistics, United States Department of Labor. (2013, March 29). Occupational employment and wages news release. Retrieved from http://www.bls.gov/news.release/ocwage.htm

Carnevale, A. P., Strohl, J., & Melton, M. (n.d.). *Select findings from what's it worth? The economic value of college majors*. Washington, DC: Georgetown University Center on Education and the Workforce.

Crowther, F. M. (2009). *Developing teacher leaders: How teacher leadership enhances school success* (2nd ed.). Thousand Oaks, CA: Corwin Press.

Domenech, D. (2011, December 19). U.S. education is still the best in the world—But here's what we can learn from others. Retrieved from http://www.eschoolnews.com/2011/12/19/u-s-education-is-still-the-best-in-the-world%E2%80%94but-heres-what-we-can-learn-from-others

Drage, K., & Anderson, M. (2007). Role of business education in the secondary school curriculum: Views of secondary school principals. *Business Education Forum, 62*(1), 51–56.

Frank, M. (2012, November). *Don't get SMACked: How social, mobile, analytics and cloud technologies are reshaping the enterprise.* Retrieved from http://www.cognizant.com/InsightsWhitepapers/dont-get-smacked.pdf

Gostick, A., & Elton, C. (2012). *All in.* New York, NY: Free Press.

Goudreau, J. (2012, October 11). The 10 worst college majors. Retrieved from http://www.forbes.com/sites/jennagoudreau/2012/10/11/the-10-worst-college-majors

Hardy, L. (2009). The quest for quality. *American School Board Journal, 196*(9), 21–25.

Harrison, C., & Killion, J. (2007). Ten roles for teacher leaders. *Educational Leadership, 65*(1), 74–77.

Heterarchy. (n.d.). In *Wikipedia*. Retrieved from http://en.wikipedia.org/wiki/Heterarchy

Houston, P. B., Blankenstein, A. M., & Cole, R. W. (2007). *Out-of-the-box leadership.* Thousand Oaks, CA: Corwin Press.

Johnson, J. (2012). One degree of separation. *Educational Leadership, 69*(7), 16–21.

Marzano, R. (2012). The two purposes of teacher evaluation. *Educational Leadership, 70*(3), 14–19.

Mielke, P., & Frontier, T. (2012). Keeping improvement in mind. *Educational Leadership, 70*(3), 10–13.

Miertschin, S. L., Kovach, J. V., & Lund O'Neil, S. (2013). Leadership for building collaborative professional relationships. *Business Education Forum, 67*(3), 40–43.

Moore, R., & Berry, B. (2010, May). The teachers of 2030. *Educational Leadership, 67*(8), 36–39.

National Business Education Association (NBEA). (2013). *National standards for business education: What America's students should know and be able to do in business.* Reston, VA: Author.

National Business Education Association. (n.d.). About NBEA: Vision statement. Retrieved from http://nbea.org/newsite/about/vision.html

Pennsylvania Department of Education. (2013). Standards aligned system. Subject area 15: Business, computer and information technology. Retrieved from http://www.pdeas.org/standard/StandardsBrowser/158211/Business%20Computer%20Information%20Technology%20Standards%20t

Policies Commission for Business and Economic Education (PCBEE). (2002). *This we believe about the need for business education: Policy statement 71.* Retrieved from http://www.nbea.org/newsite/curriculum/policy/no_71.pdf

Policies Commission for Business and Economic Education. (2005). *Policy statement 76: This we believe about business as core academic content.* Retrieved from http://

www.nbea.org/newsite/curriculum/policy/no_76.pdf

Policies Commission for Business and Economic Education. (2010). *Policy statement 86: This we believe about generativity in business education.* Retrieved from http://www.nbea.org/newsite/curriculum/documents/PCBEEStatement86_000.pdf

Policies Commission for Business and Economic Education. (2012). *Policy statement 91: This we believe about social media in education.* Retrieved from http://www.nbea.org/newsite/curriculum/documents/PolicyStatement91_2012_000.pdf

Ravitch, D. (2011). *The death and life of the great American school system: How testing and choice are undermining education.* Philadelphia, PA: Perseus.

Reeves, D. B. (2006). *The learning leader.* Alexandria. VA: Association for Supervision and Curriculum Development.

Simon, M. (2012). Tale of two districts. *Educational Leadership, 70*(3), 58–63.

The New Teacher Project (TNTP). (2013, August 13). Ideas and innovations: Overview. Retrieved from http://tntp.org/ideas-and-innovations

Whitaker, T. (2004). *What great teachers do differently.* Larchmont, NY: Eye on Education, Inc.

Developing Business Students' Leadership Characteristics for Workforce Roles

Gary Hutchinson

Hinsdale South High School

Darien, IL

Great leaders are almost always great simplifiers, who can cut through argument, debate, and doubt to offer a solution everybody can understand. —General Colin Powell, borrowed from author Michael Korda (Harari, 2004, p. 260).

Employers are more interested in adolescents who are leaders and who possess different skills (van Linden & Fertman, 1998). According to the National Association of Colleges and Employers (2012), 8 of the top 10 skills that employers desired were related to leadership. Employers are demanding these skills. Instructors of business education at the secondary and postsecondary levels are faced with the challenge of providing students with more opportunities than ever before in leadership and personal development for career and societal success.

Students enroll in business classes to acquire knowledge and skills for various reasons: personal use, preparation for employment, or professional development as required by an employer. Whatever the reason, business education instructors need to provide not only the education required to obtain a degree or certification but also the education desired by employers. J. Willard Marriott, Jr., chairman and CEO of Marriott International stated, "Our nation's long-term ability to succeed in exporting to the growing global marketplace hinges on the abilities of today's students" (Casner-Lotto & Barrington, 2006). Business education is a vital component in developing the leaders of tomorrow. This chapter will identify and discuss the leadership traits and skills needed by future workers as well as the instructional programs and strategies business education instructors need to offer to prepare students for leadership roles in the workforce.

LEADERSHIP KNOWLEDGE AND SKILLS

By leadership we mean the art of getting someone else to do something you want done because he wants to do it. —Dwight D. Eisenhower (1954).

Numerous insights on and definitions of leadership have already been discussed in previous chapters. A general theme among leadership definitions is that leaders in the workforce need different abilities and skills in order to lead. Typically, project-based and career-focused business education programs not only provide multiple opportunities for students to step up and lead but also often require them to do so (Magnuson, 2013). So what leadership knowledge and skills should business educators address? Many discussions about leadership from studies as well as business leaders focus upon the abilities of the individual. Casner-Lotto and Barrington (2006) stated that characteristics of a leader include "the ability to leverage the strengths of others to achieve common goals" (p. 16).

Dee Hock, founder and CEO emeritus of Visa mentioned specific characteristics on how much control a leader needs to possess:

Control is not leadership; management is not leadership; leadership is leadership. If you seek to lead, invest at least 50% of your time in leading yourself—your own purpose, ethics, principles, motivation, conduct. Invest at least 20% leading those with authority over you and 15% leading your peers. (LeadershipNOW, n.d., para. 4)

Results of a study addressing recruiting and skill gaps revealed one leadership skill to be the ability to inspire others (Petrie, 2011). Tim Tassapoulos, chief operating officer of Chik-fil-A, looked at leadership as an intentional influence (Grenny, 2009). According to Dr. Lance Secretan (cited by Moor, 2008), "Leadership is not a formula or a program, it is a human activity that comes from the heart and considers the hearts of others. It is an attitude, not a routine" (p. 1).

With so many different insights regarding leadership, do these general definitions and/or insights regarding leadership apply to students in business education programs? They should. Are business educators developing these characteristics for workforce roles? They should. Are students leaving business education classrooms with the leadership traits businesses expect? They should.

Leadership Traits Businesses Expect

Businesses need and desire leaders. What leadership traits do employers expect in the workplace? Expectations vary; however, the ability to be a leader has consistently been seen by business as one of the most critical skills needed by workers and also often cited as one of the most deficient.

Leadership traits consist of numerous basic skills; reading, writing, and communicating are part of being a leader. In order for students to be workforce ready, they must not only develop leadership traits but also the basic skills that, when put together, give them abilities or traits of a leader. There is more, however. J. William Marriott, Jr., chairman and CEO of Marriott International stated: "To succeed in today's workplace; young people need more than basic reading and math skills. They need substantial content knowledge and information technology skills; advanced thinking skills; flexibility to adapt to change; and interpersonal skills to succeed in multi-cultural, cross-functional teams" (Casner-Lotto & Barrington, 2006, p. 24).

When developing leaders, William Fitzpatrick of Shell Trading and Shipping looks for individuals "who can build relationships, have presence, and have intellectual capacity, people who have been involved in the community, in civic activities, individuals who can engage with people both inside and outside the company" (Casner-Lotto & Barrington, 2006, p. 25).

Businesses consider and expect specific leadership traits for their leaders. Compiled from a variety of studies (Casner-Lotto & Barrington, 2006; Glaser,1984; Hoyle, 2006; Shead, 2013; Weisman, 2013), the following traits are what businesses seek and need to be part of the business education curriculum:

Accountability	Intelligence
Commitment	Knowledge of foreign languages
Competence	Making appropriate choices concerning health
Creativity/innovation	and wellness
Visionary	Motivation
Honesty	Preparation
Humility	Professionalism and a work ethic, teamwork/
Inspirational	collaboration, and oral communications

In their research study, Casner-Lotto and Barrington (2006) provided what they found to be the most important skills for a leader at each educational level (see Table 5):

Table 1: Three Most Important Skills (percentage of graduates shown to possess)

Skill	High School Graduates	Two-Year College Graduates	Four-Year College Graduates
Professionalism and work ethic	80.3	83.4	93.8
Teamwork and collaboration	74.7	82.7	94.4
Oral communications	70.3	82.0	95.4

Source: Casner-Lotto and Barrington (2006).

In addition, their study showed how basic knowledge and applied skills should be combined and why they are considered "most important." Professionalism and a work ethic, teamwork and collaboration, and oral communications are rated as the three "most important" applied skills needed by entrants into today's workforce. More than any basic skill, a knowledge of foreign languages will "increase in importance" in the next five years. Making appropriate choices concerning health and wellness is the number one emerging content area for future graduates entering the U.S. workforce. In addition, the creativity or innovation of future workforce entrants is projected to "increase in importance." These traits when coupled with basic knowledge are considered to be what most businesses expect in their leaders and are what business education instructors have been addressing for years.

Leadership Traits Students Lack

However, there are employers who rate leadership less important than other traits, primarily because of specific skills these employers think graduates lack. The Casner-Lotto and Barrington (2006) research found that improvements are needed in several areas. At the high school level, graduates are "deficient" in the basic knowledge and skills of writing in English (grammar, spelling, etc.), mathematics, reading comprehension, written communications (clear and effective memos, letters, and complex reports), and critical thinking / problem solving. However, these graduates were found to be "adequate" in three "very important" applied skills: information technology application, diversity, and teamwork/collaboration. Two- and four-year college graduates were found to be better prepared than high school graduates for the entry-level jobs they fill; however, they were also "deficient" in writing in English, written communications, and leadership.

Workforce employers are not specifically clear on the traits and skills they desire in their leaders, as it varies from business to business. Generally, businesses need leaders and business educators to help produce these leaders. It is imperative that business education instructors identify the characteristics that need to be taught and which traits businesses expect.

BUSINESS EDUCATORS' ROLE IN DEVELOPING LEADERSHIP TRAITS

Research (Casner-Lotto & Barrington, 2006) has shown several important skills that business education students need to possess but lack when trying to move into leadership roles. Decision making, reasoning, critical thinking, and soft skills are mentioned by employers as the most critical leadership traits students need to possess but often lack. Students who step into a leadership role need to make informed decisions. Leadership skills become even more essential when coupled with students' knowledge and ability to think. For students to be effective future leaders, their basic skills in reasoning and critical thinking in making a decision, coupled with background information or data, are key in leadership development.

The leader's soft skills (sometimes referred to as people skills) are more critical than ever as organizations struggle to find meaningful ways to remain competitive and productive. Because these skills are an essential element for organizational and personal success, developing these skills is critical. Traditionally, people do not receive adequate soft skills training, either during secondary school instruction or as part of on-the-job training ("Why Soft Skills," n.d.).

Employers provide input essential in identifying skills considered vital in the workplace. Therefore, educators and employers must partner to develop the structures and support for students to acquire the skills needed for employment and continuing education. Several educational studies have found that critical thinking, reasoning, decision making, and the soft skills should not be taught as a separate topic but should be incorporated into existing subject matter (Glaser, 1984). Business courses are the ideal subject areas for developing leadership skills, which sets business education apart from other subject areas.

Decision-Making Skills

Decisions are constantly made in all leadership roles. The ability to choose between right and wrong or good and bad is essential and must be practiced at every opportunity. Different decision-making techniques are available, for example:

- Identify the purpose of the decision. What exactly is the problem to be solved? Why should be it solved?

- Gather information. What factors does the problem involve?

- Identify the principles on which to judge the alternatives. What standards and judgment criteria should the solution meet?

- Brainstorm and list different possible choices. Generate ideas for possible solutions.

- Evaluate each choice in terms of its consequences. Use standards and judgment criteria to determine the cons and pros of each alternative.

- Determine the best alternative. This is much easier after going through the above preparation steps.

- Put the decision into action. Transform the decision into a specific plan of action steps and execute the plan.

- Evaluate the outcome of the decision and action steps. What lessons can be learned? This is an important step for further development of one's decision-making skills and judgment ("Decision Making Skills," 2002).

Steps in the decision-making process vary but are similar and should be practiced constantly whether it is a one-time or everyday choice. It may take a few seconds or it may take several hours, days, or even longer when applying a decision-making process.

Business instructors need to teach a decision-making process and allow students to apply it to their leadership development.

Reasoning Skills

Decisions can be reached haphazardly (just because) or by reason. A reason is a basis for some belief, action, fact, or event. Reasoning skills deal with the process of getting from the problem to the solution, using good sense and basing decisions on reasons or logical conclusions rather than just on emotions. In short, when the best way to handle a situation or determine the best solution to a problem is identified, a logical (rather than purely emotional) reason for coming to that conclusion must follow ("Decision Making Skills," 2002). Van Linden and Fertman (1989) felt that exposure to the principles of reasoning would provide adolescents with the ability to make educated leadership decisions.

Critical Thinking Skills

Simply stated, critical thinking is a decision-making process. Specifically, one must carefully consider a problem, obstacle, or situation in order to determine the best solution. When thinking critically, take time to consider all sides of an issue, evaluate evidence, and imagine different scenarios and possible outcomes ("Decision Making Skills," 2002). Much like decision-making skills and reasoning skills, basic critical thinking skills can be applied to all types of situations.

Always part of any decision a leader makes, decision-making, reasoning, and critical thinking skills are together three "basic" skills that a leader must possess. Because these skills should be incorporated into the existing curriculum, it is an easy application for business instructors. These important "basic" leadership traits are fairly concrete concepts that business instructors teach, but there are traits that are not so easily taught or obtained by students. Soft (or people) skills are more critical than ever as organizations struggle to find meaningful ways to remain competitive and be productive. Teamwork, leadership, and communication are underpinned by soft skills development ("Why Soft Skills," n.d.)

Soft Skills

In an increasingly global, technological economy, they [policy and business leaders] say, it isn't enough to be academically strong. Young people must also be able to work comfortably with people from other cultures, solve problems creatively, write and speak well, think in a multidisciplinary way, and evaluate information critically. (Gewertz, 2007, p. 25)

Soft skills refer to a cluster of personal qualities, habits, attitudes, and social graces that make someone a good employee and compatible to work with (Lorenz, 2009). Hard skills are part of the skill set that is required for a job, sometimes referred to as technical expertise (Robles, 2012). Employers typically seek candidates with both soft and hard skills when filling positions. Students entering today's dynamic workplace must possess business-related, nontechnical (soft) skills as well as technical competence (hard skills). Research shows that individuals with excellent soft skills have better career success and contribute far more to their organizations than people with only excellent technical skills (Bush, 2012).

With soft skills increasingly becoming the hard skills of today's work force, it is not enough to be highly trained in technical skills without developing the softer, interpersonal, and relationship-building skills that help people to communicate and collaborate effectively ("Why Soft Skills," n.d.). Students who possess such skills are more adept and academically savvy. They are able to gain a further understanding of tasks and successfully engage with them, enabling them to gain more control over their learning (Hunter, 2013).

Business educators have traditionally been successful in teaching technical skills. Although technical skills are effective tools for accomplishing a task, they must be complemented by soft skills to enhance productivity. By teaching these soft skills, business educators have the opportunity to add significant value to their students' learning (Policies Commission for Business and Economic Education [PCBEE], 2000).

Research shows many different skills that are considered "soft" (Lorenz, 2009; Robles, 2012):

Ability to accept and learn from criticism	Proper dress and grooming
Ability to follow directions	Responsibility
Acting as a team player	Self-confidence
Being polite	Showing initiative
Courtesy	Social skills
Flexibility/adaptability	Strong work ethic
Integrity	Strong written and verbal communication skills
Positive attitude	Time management abilities
Problem-solving skills	Working well under pressure
Professionalism	Working well with others

Employers find students (new employees) deficient in various skills, many of which are the soft skills listed above. Not only are employers finding students lacking in soft skills, employers have different expectations of the skills their employees should possess.

Soft skills "are as important, if not more important, than traditional hard skills to an employer looking to hire—regardless of industry or job type. This could offer a major breakthrough as educators and training providers seek to develop and cluster training courses to fit business and industry needs" (Phani, 2007, para. 11).

INSTRUCTIONAL STRATEGIES FOR DEVELOPING LEADERSHIP TRAITS

So what does it take in order to develop a leader for the workforce? The role of business education in the educational system is crucial. "The business education profession historically has recognized the changing needs of society, students, workers, and business. In the context of the changing needs of these stakeholders, the business education profession has endeavored to provide relevant learning experiences" (PCBEE, 2008, p. 1).

What are specific expectations in preparing the workforce leaders of tomorrow? Characteristics needed to become the leader that businesses desire should be incorporated into every business class taught. Many business education curricula prove successful with leadership training because they teach not only leadership theory but identify the specific actions and qualities that make someone an effective leader. They are also able to put these theories into play through different instructional programs and strategies. These opportunities reinforce high academic standards, while providing authentic contexts where students apply what they have learned (PCBEE, 1998).

Leadership skills are expected by employers in the workplace, and what business educators provide must be much more than employers expect. All leadership traits should be taught with other content skills. "An exemplary standards-based business curriculum addresses these essential skills including problem solving, critical thinking, collaboration, creativity, and communication. Rigorous courses engage students and challenge them to become self-directed, independent learners, as well as collaborative team members" (PCBEE, 2007, p. 1). Business educators are in a unique position to take the lead in establishing these experiences because of their business expertise, educational background, and ties to the business community.

Teaching Leadership Skills

Career and technical education, more specifically business education, is a vital component in the development of tomorrow's leaders (Association for Career and Technical Education, 2012). In the past, learning how to work with and lead others was often learned in the workplace, while moving up the organizational ladder. However, as many experienced employees in today's workforce near retirement and jobs become more complex, as well as simultaneously collaborative and self-directed, it is becoming essential that new workforce entrants come prepared with leadership ability and experience (Magnuson, 2013).

Numerous programs and effective instructional strategies are available for introducing and developing leadership traits in secondary and postsecondary students. These programs and strategies must teach leadership traits as well as the basic skills necessary for students to become leaders ready for the workforce. Education for and about business must assist learners in acquiring the knowledge, skills, abilities, and attitudes necessary to function successfully in the global business and economic environment (PCBEE, 2008). Teaching these traits/skills is critical to the success of the student in the workforce overall and as a leader.

Youth leadership development programs. Youth leadership development programs go beyond the classroom and provide opportunities for business education students to learn from experts the traits and skills necessary to become an effective leader. Programs are being offered by many colleges, universities, and commerce organizations throughout the United States. The goal of these programs is to assist students in the further development of traits and skills learned in the classroom. Instructors in these programs include local business owners, business instructors, and college/university faculty.

Many of these programs link high school students with members of the local business community to help students develop the skills and knowledge they need for success (College of DuPage, 2013). Content of programs of this type include goal setting, leadership skill assessment, time management, proper interviewing skills, resume writing, work attitude, diversity in the workplace, ethics, and Internet site protocol. Sessions are facilitated by professionals from the local business community.

Mentors, apprenticeships, internships, and work programs. Traditional classroom environments are not always the best way to engage students. These isolated settings may help students learn content but do not always contribute to the development of decision-making, problem-solving, and other higher-order thinking skills needed for further education, employer-based learning programs, and lifelong learning (PCBEE, 2005).

Different types of work programs are available to business students. Much like the youth leadership development programs, work programs allow the student to apply what has been learned in the classroom. These programs can offer the student "on-the-job training," often with pay and educational credit. Some programs are tied to a specific class, offering students' credit for both coursework and work outside the school day. Educators use transition-to-work strategies to engage all students in a rigorous and relevant curriculum, to provide them with life and career connections, and to have them explore ever-changing and challenging opportunities in the workplace. Students are motivated and learn best when they understand the relevance of their instruction (PCBEE, 1998).

Career and technical student organizations. Another way that students can receive leadership education and training is through career and technical student organizations (CTSOs). Many leadership traits/skills needed are taught in the classroom but reinforced through participation in a CTSO, as these organizations blend student leadership and academics to assist students in becoming successful leaders. In business education at both the secondary and postsecondary level, CTSOs include but are not limited to the following:

- Business Professionals of America (BPA)

- DECA

- Future Business Leaders of America–Phi Beta Lambda (FBLA-PBL)

- Skills USA

- National Business Honor Society

- Pi Omega Pi

- Junior Achievement

The mission or goals of the top three CTSOs at the secondary level tell the story:

- **BPA:** "The mission of Business Professionals of America is to contribute to the preparation of a world-class workforce through the advancement of leadership, citizenship, academic, and technological skills." (BPA, 2013, para. 5)

- **DECA:** "DECA prepares emerging leaders and entrepreneurs for careers in marketing, finance, hospitality and management in high schools and colleges around the globe." (DECA, 2013, para. 1)

- **FBLA:** "Our mission is to bring business and education together in a positive working relationship through innovative leadership and career development programs." (FBLA, 2013, para. 1)

CTSO conferences and competitions provide unique opportunities to extend classroom learning. Contests that assess decision making, critical thinking, and even soft skills are numerous. Combined with the rigors of the classroom, participating in CTSOs and/or community activities develop secondary and postsecondary students' leadership skills in communications, decision making, getting along with others, learning management of self, understanding self, and working with groups (Wingenbach & Kahler, 1997).

Organizations and initiatives foster future leaders by teaching students to lead through in-class and associated leadership training, by placing students in workplace contexts where they observe leadership in action, and by empowering students in authentic leadership roles. In addition, CTSOs also provide explicit leadership training to students through a variety of approaches—from classroom instruction to workshops and conferences (Magnuson, 2013). Opportunities for CTSO leadership positions exist at the local, state, and national levels.

Other leadership instructional strategies. Previously, little research has explored specific instructional strategies used in student leadership development. With increased emphasis on the need for developing leadership in students preparing to enter the workforce, Jenkins's (2013) research focused on gathering data on instructional strategies used by a national audience of leadership educators, primarily at the postsecondary level; however, these strategies are equally effective at the secondary level. According to research results, instructors showed a preference for instructional strategies that emphasized the following:

- Class discussion (interactive lecture/discussion, and small group discussion).

- Forms of conceptual understanding (group projects/presentations, research projects/presentations, and guest speakers).

- Personal growth (service learning, reflective journals, icebreakers, individual leadership development plans, and in-class short writing).

Instructional strategies seldom used were traditional assessment (e.g., exams and quizzes) or skill building (e.g., games, role play activities, and simulations). Although numerous opportunities exist for incorporating student leadership development into a curriculum, challenges continue to exist.

Challenges in Student Leadership Development

Prospects for developing needed leadership skills for students as they enter the workforce are encouraging; however, several challenges must be considered:

- Providing consistency in the leadership skill development curriculum as content is incorporated into business education courses to assure adequate leadership education and training

- Keeping students active in programs addressing leadership development

- Identifying the crucial leadership skills students will need to be successful and developing those skills to the needed level

- Keeping the programs and strategies formal but real-world or participatory

- Continuing to think outside the box to keep a vision for the future

Youth leadership development programs, mentor/apprenticeship/internship/work programs, and CTSOs separately and combined with coursework provide valuable experiences for future workplace leaders. This "training" saves businesses valuable resources and produces a quality student ready to move into workplace leadership roles.

SUMMARY

No one is born with all the skills necessary to become a leader in the workforce. These skills must be learned, developed, and mastered. Leadership traits are what businesses desire in their employees. Business education instructors can instill these traits in students.

Leadership skills must be fostered throughout time. Business education instructors need to provide future entrants into the workforce the background to assume roles requiring them to make decisions considering the implications of those decisions—in short, to be a leader! Business education students must have the opportunity to develop and practice leadership skills. The knowledge and skills that are demanded in the global workplace of the 21st century must continue to be integrated throughout business education programs (PCBEE, 2007).

Numerous methods exist for business educators to develop student leadership traits—identifying what businesses want and expect; developing decision making, reasoning, and critical thinking skills; developing students' soft skills; and exposing students to numerous programs that can further develop leadership skills. Learning and observing leadership provides essential scaffolding for leadership development. But it is only through authentic leadership opportunities—projects for which teachers step into the background and allow both setbacks and successes to fall completely on students—that students can fully internalize how to successfully lead others (Magnuson, 2013).

Henry Kissinger once said, "The task of the leader is to get his people from where they are to where they have not been" ("Tomorrow's Leaders," 2013). Business educators must get them started.

REFERENCES

Association for Career and Technical Education. (2012, December). CTE's role in leadership development. *ACTE Issue Brief.* Alexandria, VA: Author.

Bush, C. E. (2012, Spring). The case for soft skills training. *Planet elearn.* Retrieved from http://www.monarchmedia.com/enewsletter_2012-2/case-for-soft-skills.html

Business Professionals of America. (2013). About BPA. Retrieved from http://www.bpa.org/about

Casner-Lotto, J., & Barrington, L. (2006). *Are they really ready to work? Employers' perspectives on the basic knowledge and applied skills of new entrants to the 21st century U.S. workforce.* The Conference Board, Partnership for 21st Century Skills, Corporate Voices for Working Families, and Society for Human Resource Management. Washington, DC: Partnership for 21st Century Skills. Retrieved from http://www.p21.org/storage/documents/FINAL_REPORT_PDF09-29-06.pdf

College of DuPage. (2013). Student Leadership Academy. Retrieved from http://www.cod.edu/academics/ohsp/sla/index.aspx

DECA. (2013). About us. Retrieved from http://www.deca.org/about

Decision making skills and techniques. (2002). *Time-management-guide.com.* Retrieved from http://www.time-management-guide.com/decision-making-skills.html

Eisenhower, D. D. (1954, May 12). *The American Presidency Project. 108 – Remarks at the Annual Conference of the Society for Personnel Administration.* Retrieved from http://www.presidency.ucsb.edu/ws/?pid=9884

Future Business Leaders of America. (2013). FBLA-PBL mission. Retrieved from http://fbla-pbl.org/web/page/625/sectionid/614/pagelevel/2/parentid/614/main_interior.asp

Gewertz, C. (2007, June 12). "Soft skills" in big demand. *Education Week, 26*(40), 25–27.

Glaser, R. (1984). Education and thinking: The role of knowledge. *American Psychologist, 39*(2), 93–104.

Grenny, J. (2009, June 5). Leadership: Intentional influence. Retrieved from http://www. businessweek.com/stories/2009-06-05/leadership-intentional-influencebusinessweek-business-news-stock-market-and-financial-advice

Harari, Oren. (2002). *The leadership secrets of Colin Powell.* New York, NY: McGraw-Hill.

Hoyle, J. (2006). *Leadership and futuring: Making visions happen* (2nd ed.). Thousand Oaks, CA: Corwin Press.

Hunter, M. (2013, August 4). Students know why soft skills are important. Retrieved from http://gulfnews.com/life-style/education/students-know-why-soft-skills-are-important-1.1216145

Jenkins, D. M. (2013). Exploring instructional strategies in student leadership development programming. *Journal of Leadership Studies, 6*(4), 48–62.

LeadershipNOW. (n.d.). Leading thoughts: Building a community of leaders. Retrieved from http://www.leadershipnow.com/leadershipquotes.html

Lorenz, K. (2009, January 26). Top 10 soft skills for job hunters. Retrieved from http://jobs.aol.com/articles/2009/01/26/top-10-soft-skills-for-job-hunters

Magnuson, P. (2013, February). CTE delivers leaders. *Techniques: Connecting Education and Careers, 88*(2), 34–35.

Moor, K. (2008, March 30). Leadership: A human activity. Retrieved from http://www.theleadershiphub.com/blogs/leadership-human-activity

National Association of Colleges and Employers. (2012, October 24). The skills and qualities employers want in their class of 2013 recruits. Spotlight for career services professionals. Retrieved from http://www.naceweb.org/s10242012/skills-abilities-qualities-new-hires

Petrie, N. (2011, December). *Future trends in leadership development.* Greensboro, NC: Center for Creative Leadership. Retrieved from http://www.ccl.org/leadership/pdf/research/futureTrends.pdf

Phani, C. (2007, January 8). The top 60 soft skills at work. Retrieved from http://www.rediff.com/getahead/2007/jan/08soft.htm

Policies Commission for Business and Economic Education (PCBEE). (1998). *This we believe about the relationship between business education and students' transition to work: Policy statement 63.* Retrieved from http://www.nbea.org/newsite/curriculum/policy/no_63.pdf

Policies Commission for Business and Economic Education. (2000). *This we believe about teaching soft skills: Human relations, self-management, and workplace enhancement: Policy statement 67.* Retrieved from http://www.nbea.org/newsite/curriculum/policy/no_67.pdf

Policies Commission for Business and Economic Education. (2005). *Policy statement no. 77: This we believe about work-based learning.* Retrieved from http://www.nbea.org/newsite/curriculum/policy/no_77.pdf

Policies Commission for Business and Economic Education. (2007). *Policy statement 80: This we believe about rigor in business education.* Retrieved from http://www.nbea.org/newsite/curriculum/policy/no_80.pdf

Policies Commission for Business and Economic Education. (2008). *Policy statement 83: This we believe about the transformation and future of business education.* Retrieved from http://www.nbea.org/newsite/curriculum/policy/no_83.pdf

Robles, M. M. (2012). Executive perceptions of the top 10 soft skills needed in today's workplace. *Business Communication Quarterly, 75*(4), 453–465.

Shead, M. (2014). Five most important leadership traits. Retrieved from http://www.leadership501.com/five-most-important-leadership-traits/27

Tomorrow's leaders are rebuilding high-performing teams today. (2013, May). Retrieved from http://transearchinternational.blogspot.com/2013/05/tomorrows-leaders-are-rebuilding-high.html

Van Linden, J. A., & Fertman, C. I. (1998). *Youth leadership: A guide to understanding leadership development in adolescents.* San Francisco, CA: Jossey-Bass.

Weisman, S. (2013). The 5 self-leadership traits expected of employees in a high performing, high morale workplace. Retrieved from http://www.workplacecommunicationexpert.com/5-self-leadership-traits-expected-of-employees-in-a-high-performance-high-morale-workforce

Why soft skills matter: Making sure your hard skills shine. (n.d.). Retrieved from http://www.mindtools.com/pages/article/newCDV_34.htm

Wingenbach, G. J., & Kahler, A. A. (1997). Self-perceived youth leadership life skills of Iowa FFA members. *Journal of Agricultural Education, 38*(3), 18–27.

Business Student Organization Leadership

Sandy Mills
Virginia Future Business Leaders
of America–Phi Beta Lambda
Winchester, VA

Anne Rowe
Virginia Department of Education
Richmond, VA

Pose the question, "What is leadership?" to 10 individuals, and they will likely have 10 different answers. Leadership was defined by long-time leadership expert James Burns (1978) as "leaders acting—as well as caring, inspiring, and persuading others to act—for certain shared goals that represent the values—the wants and needs, the aspirations and expectations—of themselves and the people they represent" (p. 12). Every student will eventually be expected to demonstrate leadership as employees and as members of society. More important, the teacher is called upon to model these qualities to ensure that students are college- and career-ready for their role in the success of the country's economic stability.

But how do educators meet these expectations and demonstrate these qualities, all while trying to meet competency requirements and individual needs of student learners, as well as perform all of the other duties assigned by administrators? The answer lies in career and technical student organizations (CTSOs), which have been a critical part of a comprehensive career and technical program philosophy since the Smith-Hughes Act of 1917 (Stanislawski & Haltinner, 2009).

This chapter delves into the role of CTSOs, specifically those for business students, and aspects of successful student organizations in developing leadership potential for students and advisers. To provide current information for this chapter, 12 key state contacts in three national business-related CTSOs, 70 local CTSO chapter advisers, and 102 CTSO student members dispersed throughout the country participated in a survey or were interviewed on their involvement in business student organizations. Their responses are referenced throughout the chapter.

OVERVIEW OF BUSINESS STUDENT ORGANIZATIONS

The three CTSOs whose curricula correlate with the National Business Education Association's (NBEA, 2013) *National Standards for Business Education* and business-related career pathways share commonalities. The mission statements and guiding principles of Business Professionals of America, DECA (formerly known as Distributive Education Clubs of America), and Future Business Leaders of America–Phi Beta Lambda reveal three common themes: leadership, citizenship/service, and academic excellence. CTSOs share the same purpose: the development of the whole student.

CTSO goals are generally articulated as developing leadership skills, creating career awareness, connecting with the community in an effort to create civic awareness and responsibility, and evolving individuals who are socially connected through professional networking (Alfeld, Hansen, Aragon, & Stone, 2007). Other student organizations offer opportunities for student development, including the National Business Honor Society, whose fundamental components are involvement, leadership, and achievement. The National Business Honor Society was created to honor and recognize outstanding business education students and is an official division of the National Business Education Association (National Business Honor Society, n.d.).

ROLE OF STUDENT ORGANIZATIONS IN BUSINESS EDUCATION CURRICULUM

Policy statements published by the Policies Commission for Business and Economic Education (PCBEE) have addressed student organizations throughout the years; the first mention of student organizations was in its policy statement 2:

1. The business teacher should actively participate insofar as possible in the business and professional organizations and activities in the community.

2. Every school should have an organization for business students such as Future Business Leaders of America (FBLA) and Distributive Education Clubs of America (DECA).[1] (PCBEE, 1997, p. 6)

The PCBEE encompassed the entire concept of student organizations' role in business education in a later policy statement when it identified general benefits of student organization activities in policy statement 30:

- "Strengthen the business education program"

- "Enhance the curriculum with practical experiences through projects and activities"

---

[1]"Business Professionals of America had not been chartered at the time of this policy statement.

- "Provide role models through student leaders, alumni, teachers, advisers, and business people"
- "Develop character, citizenship, and patriotism"
- "Facilitate intelligent career choices" (PCBEE, 1997, p. 61)

The fact that business student organizations serve as a vehicle for students' academic excellence is also addressed in the same PCBEE policy statement 30:

- "Provide opportunities for practical application of classroom theory"
- "Improve communication skills—written, oral, nonverbal, and listening"
- "Teach organizational skills"
- "Develop problem-solving and decision-making competencies" (PCBEE, 1997, p. 62)

The personal benefits for students identified in the same policy statement include the following:

- "Develop poise, self-confidence, and personal responsibility"
- "Develop positive work attitudes" (PCBEE, 1997, p. 62)

In developing well-rounded individuals, this policy statement goes on to state that membership and participation in student organizations provide opportunities for students to do the following:

- "Develop positive attitudes toward social responsibility"
- "Engage in services to the community"
- "Instill a sense of business ethics and moral responsibility"
- "Learn to work together as a team"
- "Strengthen student-teacher rapport" (PCBEE, 1997, p. 62)

Additionally, policy statement 30 states that student organization membership and participation develop leadership skills by enabling students to do the following:

- "Direct activities of the office to which elected"
- "Preside at meetings and conferences"
- "Work effectively within committees"
- "Lead and participate in group discussion"
- "Learn when to follow and when to lead as part of a team" (PCBEE, 1997, p. 62)

Student organizations also play a role in leadership development for students who actively participate.

ROLE OF BUSINESS STUDENT ORGANIZATIONS IN DEVELOPING LEADERSHIP

Leadership skill development for all students is a required, integral part of all career and technical education (CTE) instructional programs. Integrating leadership skill development into CTE instructional programs enables students to fully use the subject matter content they receive (State of Washington Office of the Superintendent of Public Instruction, 2011).

Leadership Skills

According to Lekes et al. (2007), CTE students were significantly more likely than their non-CTE counterparts to report that they had developed the following skills during high school: problem solving, project completion, research, math, college application, work-related communication, time management, and critical thinking skills. The workplace readiness skills that Lekes et al. referenced and the leadership development that is included in CTE instructional programs allow students to relate their curriculum competencies to real-world expectations.

From interviews with national CTSO staff and survey responses of key state contacts for all three organizations, leadership was the most heavily emphasized goal for each organization. Lisa Smothers, national Future Business Leaders of America membership director, stated that critical thinking skills, problem solving, moral ethics, time management, project management, and professionalism are vital leadership characteristics in a future leader.

Good communication skills and team building were the two most frequently referenced traits of an effective leader. Chris Young, director of DECA's High School Division, ranked communication as the number one trait of a good leader. Young further stated that "students and advisers should hone their public speaking skills, know how to write a concise correctly formatted letter, and should also be savvy with today's ever-present social media."

According to Alfeld et al. (2007), working on project teams is the primary method of getting work accomplished in today's business world and, as such, is clearly a crucial skill for a business professional. The global nature of business enterprise requires students to be flexible with diversity in all forms (both physical and emotional), defend their point of view, and most important, employ active listening when dealing with their peers. With project-based learning (CTSO chapter management and competitive events), students develop their investigative and research abilities and workplace skills such as understanding diversity, competition, quality management, and teamwork to become life-long learners.

Opportunities for Leadership Training

CTSOs offer training through classes and chapter management activities designed to develop the total leader at local, state, regional, and national conferences. These organizations use motivational speakers, curriculum-related workshops, and webinars to disseminate information to members. The *National Standards for Business Education* (NBEA, 2013) is one source used to develop themes for leadership training. According to the survey of national and state key contacts discussed in this chapter, leadership training topics are also identified from recommendations from advisers, surveys from past conference attendees, state officers, and board of directors members. These leadership training topics generally focus on goal setting, career clusters, event/project management, fund-raising, branding, career preparation, workplace readiness, and best practices of chapter management/chapter advisement.

The state contacts for the three identified business student organizations agreed that leadership training is mostly the responsibility of the local adviser and that a concentration of time and resources is devoted to officers of the organization at the local, state, and national levels. National DECA has a variety of training modules conducted at the national level. "Train-the-Trainer" is the name of a three-day workshop designed to train individuals to present turnkey modules on such topics as chapter development, DECA in the classroom, branding, and "Cool Ideas" for state associations. Key state leaders are trained who subsequently train their key contacts, who in turn train local chapter members and advisers. This "trickle-down" mentality works well within their association.

Future Business Leaders of America offers training to key state contacts via a biannual summit in which association leaders share technology tools, negotiation strategies, and best practices with fellow state specialists/advisers. The annual Institute for Leaders, held in conjunction with the national leadership conference offers track-based training for students and advisers in areas such as leadership, entrepreneurship, and career development.

National and state association activities provide effective theoretical and informational training for students; however, the local level is where students' true leadership skills are developed through experiences in their daily activities. For example, a student might attend a workshop designed to explain their role as a chapter officer. That same student may be enrolled in an accounting course that teaches them how to prepare a financial report. The student organization gives the student the opportunity to apply their academic knowledge in a real-life experience when they stand at their local chapter meeting to present the treasurer's report.

BUSINESS STUDENT CTSO EXPERIENCES AT THE LOCAL LEVEL

Participation in a local-level CTSO chapter includes activities designed to expand students' leadership abilities, contextualize their academic instruction, encourage them to pursue their education, and equip them with job-related skills in their career field of interest (Association for Career and Technical Education, 2011).

Most students participating in the survey of national and state key contacts indicated they participate at the local level. More than half had attended a state conference, and

35% had participated in a national/international conference. Nationally, the student perception/reflection of past experiences identifies communication as the most prevalent leadership skill to which they were introduced at their respective organizational conferences (Figure 1).

Figure 1. Student Survey of Leadership Training

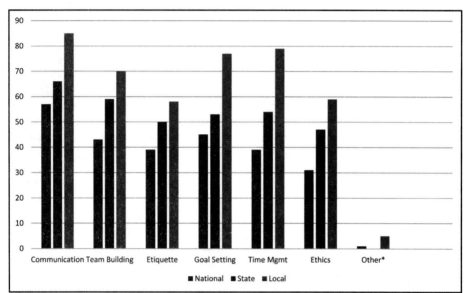

■ National ■ State ■ Local

* Other topics included community service, networking, and career preparation.

Workshop training was by far the most predominant method in which the students were introduced to leadership concepts; however, many of the students commented on the fact that their local chapter involvement was key to their leadership development: "Through our chapter, I have learned how to manage my time well and to set high goals because with a big team of people a lot can get done for our school but more importantly our community. It is fun getting out with my peers and making this a better place for everyone involved, and it's great to see our chapter evolving so rapidly," said one CTSO student respondent.

Many students participating in the survey responded that the skills they learned in their CTSO transferred to their other organizational involvement as well. One CTSO student respondent said, "I have learned community relations with my CTSO chapter, and that has helped me to come up [with] new ideas to help my community in other organizations. Time management and teamwork have been other skills that are easily transferable to other groups I am involved with."

COMPONENTS OF SUCCESSFUL CTSO CHAPTERS

Career and technical student organizations were developed to enhance the vocational student's high school experience. During the early 19th century social-efficiency movement, the comprehensive high school evolved and concurrently sponsored academic and vocational aims for its learners (Barlow, 1976). CTSOs are not "clubs" to which only a few CTE students belong; rather, a CTSO is a powerful instructional tool that works best when integrated into the CTE curriculum and classroom by a CTE instructor who is committed to the development of the total student (Kentucky Department of Education, n.d.). The next four sections address the components of a successful chapter.

Program of Work

Visitors of an effective chapter are more than likely to see a program of work posted throughout the business department. The program of work is a road map outlining the year's chapter activities. Programs of work should be well rounded and should include the core values of the CTSOs: leadership and promotion, business skills and knowledge (competitive events), community service, financial (fund-raising), and social activities. Early in the school year, officers and chapter members should meet and develop their plan of action for the year. Committee chairs should be designated for each activity.

Project-Based Chapter Events and Activities Tied into Competitive Events

Exposing students to project-based management processes is a high-level tool that can be used throughout their life, personally and professionally. A project management process should include goals, action steps, due dates, assignments, and ongoing evaluation/tracking procedures for each project. All activities/projects should tie into a competitive event so that the activities are easily processed to fit into competitive event parameters at the conclusion of the project. A core component of each CTSO is community service, and every CTSO has a community service themed competitive event. If students investigate the specifications of the competitive event before planning the project, they can ensure that all components of the competition are covered in project implementation and the actual program/event.

Student Members

Motivated students who are emotionally and mentally invested in the chapter and its activities are key components of a successful chapter. Student leaders need to initiate programs and activities and encourage their classmates to get involved. The larger the percentage of members involved, the higher the level of organizational success. Older students should mentor younger members to achieve continuity, as turnover is imminent as students graduate. Many teachers indicate that once a strong group of students has graduated, they have to start over by developing officer teams, but a good adviser will ensure that the grade levels of the chapter leaders are diverse. It is imperative that both advisers and upper-class leaders model the enthusiasm for the chapter that is necessary to entice the students to join and get involved as underclassmen.

Advisers

From personal observation and experience, teachers need to provide academic and technical leadership for a strong instructional program that, in turn, produces a strong student organization that prepares students for leadership positions in their careers. Advisers are by far the most important component of a strong CTSO local chapter. What characteristics are prevalent in an adviser of a successful chapter?

Participation. At least one CTE teacher is the adviser of the local chapter. Advisers should be active in the local chapters. The most successful chapters distribute duties among several advisers to encompass five core chapter activities: leadership and promotion, skills and knowledge, community service, financial, and social components. Advisers should assume responsibility for one or more (depending on the number of advisers) of the components and should be the administrator(s) of all the events associated with that area. For example, an accounting teacher should be the lead teacher for the financial and fund-raising components of the entire chapter; that same teacher may head up the competitive events process and prepare the students for their individual and team competitions such as accounting, banking and financial systems, etc.

A cocurricular classroom. Conceptually, every student enrolled in a CTE course is a member of the local CTSO chapter, and CTSO activities should be integrated into the course curriculum and class activities so that every student benefits from the organization. Educators in effective chapters and successful business programs use the CTSO as a tool to bring a level of relevance and rigor to the subject matter taught in the class. Results of the 2012 survey of chapter advisers indicated that 71% of CTE educators integrated their CTSO into their classroom activities, including 48% that integrated CTSOs often, frequently, or daily in their classrooms.

Role model. One of the most important roles a teacher plays in a CTSO is the role of mentor. Advisers who lead by example—dressing professionally, communicating effectively, and demonstrating good team work—will inspire their students to model such behaviors for the rest of their lives. Advisers should also represent professionalism through their membership and involvement in their subject-area professional associations.

"Teachers get the student excited and energized for competition and organization participation. Strong student leadership stems from active and committed teacher leadership," said a CTSO student respondent. Effective business programs produce successful CTSO chapters, and successful chapters enhance enrollment in business programs. Advisers play a crucial role in effective CTSOs.

ROLE OF ADVISERS IN DEVELOPING AND RETAINING A QUALITY CTSO

Advisers can open the doors for young people to share their unique identity with the world and their ability to make a difference. For some people, leadership is a natural character trait. Because of their circumstances, natural attributes, experiences, or relationships, some students will emerge naturally as leaders. But for other young people, the power of leadership potential is dormant; they simply have not had the opportunity for their leadership to emerge (Ambrose & Goar, 2009). These students need a role model from whom they can seek guidance. Oftentimes, teenage students will disregard their parents, but teachers can have a huge impact on their growth and development as leaders because students will model their behavior.

Because teachers are under a tremendous amount of pressure to meet the demands of the profession, it would be very easy for a teacher, especially a new one, to be overwhelmed at the thought of advising a student organization. A key benefit of advising is connectivity to students, which will transcend into a better educational experience for everyone involved (Ambrose & Goar, 2009). The following excerpts from the 2012 survey of CTSO advisers offer beneficial advice on several topics to all CTSO advisers and business educators.

Link between a Quality Business Program and a Quality CTSO

CTSO adviser respondents to the survey discussed throughout this chapter unanimously indicated a connection between a quality business program and a quality CTSO. The following five comments are a sampling:

- "When you have a strong CTE program, you have students who are knowledgeable and excited about participating in the co-curricular organization. In my opinion, you cannot have a strong organization with a weak program. The teachers get the student excited and energized for competition and organization participation. Strong student leadership stems from active and committed teacher leadership."

- "A quality program in which all department teachers participate equates to a quality student organization."

- "A quality business and marketing program infuses the CTSO mission and focus into every lesson possible. The CTSO must be reinforced in every CTE class taught."

- "Students get to exemplify what they are learning in the classroom by participating in student organizations and competitive events. A quality program and student organization go hand in hand, giving the community an opportunity to see how well students are being prepared for the real world as well as to see how they compare to students across the state and country."

Having a quality program is essential to having a quality student organization. A quality program will attract the best-of-the-best students in a school. Students who are dedicated to participating in a quality program will naturally want to be associated with a quality student organization. Having a quality program feeds into your student organization.

One theme resonating in many of the comments was the importance of incorporating CTSO activities into the everyday classroom curriculum. This cocurricular component and value of student organizations is emphasized in PCBEE Policy Statement

29: "Business education curriculum must provide numerous opportunities—through in-class cocurricular, and extracurricular student activities—for students to develop positive interpersonal and leadership skills" (PCBEE, 1997, p. 59–60).

PCBEE Policy Statement 39 relating to the future of business education asserted the belief "that business student organizations must remain an integral part of the business curriculum because these organizations provide opportunities for students to develop leadership skills" (PCBEE, 1997, p. 81).

Advice for Advisers in Developing CTSOS

The first year of teaching can be an overwhelming experience, especially in the field of CTE. Stanislawski and Haltinner (2009) stated that a wide and varied range of teacher education literature focused on teaching strategies; little research or discussion relates to the preparation of future business and marketing teachers for their roles and responsibilities of CTSO advisement. Career switchers who enter the CTE education field face their own set of dilemmas, perhaps never even having heard of CTSOs. Many current CTE teachers relied on peer assistance when they began their role as a CTSO. According to an adviser respondent, "I worked with two experienced advisers who were self-taught and very motivated to have a chapter that excelled. They were wonderful mentors." But what if a veteran teacher is not available? "It is called 'jump in feet first, sink to the bottom, come up for air, dive back under, come up for air again, maybe start bobbing around and finally spending more time on top of the water," said one adviser respondent.

Many advisers must navigate their way to a successful chapter, one step at a time. "Each year, I challenge myself to take on one new component," said one adviser respondent. L. E. Younger, a business and information technology educator in Wythe County, Virginia stated: "Build resources and keep good documentation. Learn from feedback, and repeat and improve what brought success. Most importantly, make [the CTSO] interactive with your classroom activities at every opportunity."

In summary, teachers concur that quality programs require adviser leadership that is developed during a teacher's career. CTSOs have the opportunity to have many varied activities.

Effective Activities for Maintaining a Quality Student Organization

Successful chapter advisers look for innovative ways to increase chapter membership, entice younger members to get involved to promote continuity, and engage their students in meaningful projects. Local chapter advisers who have garnered success in their CTSO activities related the following effective strategies:

- Conduct roundtable discussions on how to improve the chapter

- Recruit, welcome, and actively involve students with a high level of enthusiasm

- Provide incentives for membership recruitment, fund-raising, and event participation

- Have door prizes at every meeting to encourage attendance

- Sponsor curriculum-enhancing fund-raisers such as selling business cards that are designed and printed by student members

- Sponsor an etiquette luncheon for members to learn social and table manners

- Host induction ceremonies to stress the professionalism of the organization

PCBEE (2000) Policy Statement 67 suggests that advisers of quality student organizations conduct activities with a focus on the soft skills necessary to enhance productivity in the high performance workplace by strengthening the link between the school-based and the work-based environment through the *curriculum, student organizations,* and *business partnerships.* The same policy suggests using learning strategies in the school-based environment, including participating in student organizations, because they serve as a natural link between school- and work-based experiences (PCBEE, 2000).

Successful Student Organizations and Success in Competitive Events

Each organization's competitive events program is designed to measure students' academic grasp of curriculum content in their respective business fields. Of the advisers surveyed, 98% indicated a connection between successful student organizations and success with competitive events. According to an adviser respondent, "Success with competitive events comes as a by-product of a successful student organization as well as a successful program. In a well-operated student organization, students are informed as to the criteria for the competitive events in which they participate. They are encouraged to prepare themselves over and above that which is taught through the classroom and general activities of the chapter." Another adviser wrote, "Competition is what drives a capitalistic society; with the competitions, students are allowed to test their attributes against peers, which enables them to sharpen their skills. Competition readies the students for the business world."

However, one adviser respondent did not think a correlation existed between a successful program and competitive events: "Rural high schools are at a distinct disadvantage because we do not have the staff or funding to offer so many of the courses that correlate to the events. It limits our ability to compete in many of the events." Whether or not students compete in a lot of events, the survey comments imply the experience is beneficial to students who do participate.

It is a tremendous confidence builder for a young adolescent to develop a presentation with visual aids and learn to present it to others. Learning how to be a resilient teenager by taking safe risks in a student organization is very valuable. It can pave the way to becoming active citizens, positive role models, and great team players, which are necessary skills for life (Ambrose & Goar, 2009). Overall, successful business marketing programs will generate successful student organizations, and students are going to want to be a part of successful organizations that increase program enrollment. Finding the balance between the two is truly the key to success.

Other Best Practices for Quality Student Organizations

Other relevant tips and techniques from successful chapter advisers include the following:

- Find a mentor, that is, someone who has been successful and is willing to assist.

- Incorporate CTSO activities into daily lessons; involve all students in the class, and membership will increase as their involvement increases.

- Hold regular chapter meetings before, during, or after school. Chapter officers should meet before the general meeting to plan the agenda and ensure everything is ready for the meeting.

- Always serve some type of snack/beverage at chapter meetings to entice students to attend; also give bonus points, gifts, or some type of incentive to those who attend.

- Conduct icebreakers so students get to know their fellow members outside the parameter of the classroom.

- Support students as they plan, implement, and organize activities for the chapter. Act more as a consultant to ensure that students benefit from the experience.

- Attend CTSO meetings outside the local chapter such as regional leadership or state conferences. Students enjoy getting to travel.

- Promote the CTSO in CTE classes and promote the program in your CTSO activities.

- Encourage students to participate in national incentive programs to earn pins and recognition from the national level.

- Conduct a civic project to enlighten members to the needs of the community.

- Praise students often and publicly for their accomplishments.

- Host competitive event parties in which students work with their peers to study and prepare for competition.

- Promote the CTSO chapter by conducting a school service project that helps out the school and/or the administration.

- Include a competition component to fund-raising; this will increase sales.

- Hold a job fair for the entire school and invite the chapter's business partners.

- Have any adviser getting ready to retire train or be available to assist any new adviser.

Former CTSO students offered their perspectives in the following statements. As a former student, state/national officer Khalil Andraos wrote, "The best practices in leadership development that made a lasting impression on me as a business leader include the importance of developing strong relationships with others on a personal and business level, learning to handle both successes and failures/shortcomings, delivering effective public speeches to different types of audiences, and implementing a well-thought-out structure to internal and external meetings, seminars, and team-building activities." Another former CTSO state officer indicated how her CTSO experience made a lasting impression on her as a business professional: "Critical life skills have set me apart from other business leaders. Things such as asking relevant questions in meetings, following through promptly on commitments, writing thank you notes, eliciting other people's viewpoints, arriving early for meetings, treating everyone with professionalism and courtesy, and triple proofing everything for errors before sending them out. These may sound trivial, but I've learned repeatedly that being a diligent, prompt, reliable, professional person first not only makes a positive impression, but also establishes a solid foundation for achieving success in every endeavor."

SUMMARY

Student involvement in CTSOs helps produce academically advanced students who are engaged in the learning process, are connected with the community, and are prepared to transition from high school to their postsecondary education and/or their careers because of their involvement in the student organization. CTE students are not just "taught" leadership, they live it, and the adviser is the most important component to the success of this process. Pose the question "What is leadership?" to 10 individuals familiar with career and technical education, and one should get one answer—participation in career and technical student organizations.

REFERENCES

Alfeld, C., Hansen, D. M., Aragon, S. R., & Stone, R., Jr. III. (2007). *Looking inside the black box: The value added by career and technical student organizations to students' high school experience.* St. Paul, MN: National Research Center for Career and Technical Education.

Ambrose, W. L., & Goar, L. G. (2009). Student organization integration: Initiatives for positive youth development—The ultimate leadership experience. *Journal of Family Consumer Sciences Education, 27* (National Teacher Standards 5), 65–83. Retrieved from http://www.natefacs.org/JFCSE/v27standards5/v27standards5Ambrose.pdf

Association for Career and Technical Education. (2011). *Expanding career readiness through career and technical student organizations.* Alexandria, VA: Author.

Barlow, M. L. (1976, May). 200 years of vocational education, 1776–1976; The vocational education age emerges, 1876–1926. *American Vocational Journal, 51,* 5, 45–58. ERIC No.: EJ139040.

Burns, J. M. (1978). *Leadership.* Cincinnati, OH: Harper Row.

Kentucky Department of Education. (n.d.). Career and technical education, Kentucky. Student organizations. Retrieved from http://cte.ky.gov/organizations.html

Lekes, N., Bragg, D. D., Loeb, J. W., Oleksiw, C. A., Marszalek, J., Brooks-LaRaviere, M., Zhu, R., Kremidas, C. C., Akukwe, G., Lee, H-J., & Hood, L. K. (2007, May). Career and technical education pathway programs, academic performances, and the transition to college and career. Retrieved from ERIC database (ED 497342).

National Business Education Association (NBEA). (2013). *National standards for business education: What America's students should know and be able to do in business.* Reston, VA: Author.

National Business Education Association. (n.d.). National Business Honor Society. Retrieved from http://www.nbea.org/newsite/about/nbhs.html

Policies Commission for Business and Economic Education (PCBEE). (1997). *Policy statements: 1959–1996.* Cincinnati, OH: South-Western Educational Publishing.

Policies Commission for Business and Economic Education. (2000). *This we believe about teaching the soft skills: Human relations, self-management, and workplace enhancement* (Statement No. 67). Retrieved from http://www.nbea.org/newsite/curriculum/policy/no_67.pdf

Stanislawski, D., & Haltinner, U. (2009). Model for preparing marketing and business teachers to meet the challenge of CTSO leadership and advisement. *Delta Pi Epsilon Journal, 51*(3), 166–176.

State of Washington Office of the Superintendent of Public Instruction. (2011). Career and technical education program standards. Retrieved from http://www.k12.wa.us/CareerTechEd/FormsStandards.aspx